Arguing Islam after the Revival
of Arab Politics

ARGUING ISLAM
AFTER THE REVIVAL
OF ARAB POLITICS

Nathan J. Brown

OXFORD
UNIVERSITY PRESS

Oxford University Press is a department of the University of Oxford. It furthers
the University's objective of excellence in research, scholarship, and education
by publishing worldwide. Oxford is a registered trade mark of Oxford University
Press in the UK and certain other countries.

Published in the United States of America by Oxford University Press
198 Madison Avenue, New York, NY 10016, United States of America.

Library of Congress Cataloging-in-Publication Data
Names: Brown, Nathan J., author.
Title: Arguing Islam after the revival of Arab politics / Nathan Brown.
Description: New York, NY : Oxford University Press, 2017. | Includes
    bibliographical references.
Identifiers: LCCN 2016014065 | ISBN 9780190619428 (hardcover)
Subjects: LCSH: Islam and politics—Arab countries. | Arab
    countries—Politics and government—20th century. | Arab
    countries—Politics and government—21st century.
Classification: LCC BP173.7 .B759 2017 | DDC 322/.109174927—dc23
LC record available at https://lccn.loc.gov/2016014065

9 8 7 6 5 4 3 2 1

Printed by Sheridan Books, Inc., United States of America

To Jacob, Evan, Joseph, and Albert.

CONTENTS

ACKNOWLEDGMENTS

This book is my attempt to make sense of what I have heard and seen in Arab politics over the course of a scholarly career that began in the 1980s.

I have worked on researching the topic and drafting this book intermittently over some years. The idea first came to me about a decade and a half ago. But had I written it then, it would have been very different. Its subject matter and the way that I understand it have changed. Only in 2010 did I begin sketching out the project and I did not begin drafting until 2014.

But to say that it took me a while because I was sidetracked on to other projects is not quite correct.

The other research I carried out before focusing on writing this book—on Islamist movements, judiciaries, constitutional politics, and authoritarianism—has overlapped with the current project. Some of that overlap is apparent in places in which the current book discusses those subjects directly.

But far more profoundly, I have spent not merely the past ten years but all of my scholarly career attempting to understand arguments I heard from those whose politics I studied—arguments that intrigued me, whether or not they persuaded me (and they most often did not). What coherence there is in my scholarly work over the past thirty years is an attempt to probe how politics is experienced and why people act and speak as they do in a political world that is somewhat different from my own.

In this book, I attempt to explain what I have heard; I aim not to resolve differences but to help make them comprehensible.

In carrying out the research for this book, I had very able assistance from a series of students, research assistants, and guides of various sorts. In alphabetical order, they are Sarah Abdel Gelil, Rawda Ali, Starling Carter, Fatima Fettar, Sarah Kuhail, Dalia Naguib, Julia Romano, Mariam Serag, Scott Wiener, and Laila Abdelkhaliq Zamora.

A number of colleagues and collaborators on related projects also deserve special mention. Marc Lynch has been a party to many conversations connected with this book that have shaped my thinking very deeply. Jonathan

A. C. Brown, Michaelle Browers, and Andrew March attended a daylong workshop that helped me reshape the manuscript into something like its current form. Anonymous reviewers for Oxford University Press were extraordinarily kind, thoughtful, and helpful. Tarek Masoud gave me valuable substantive and organizational advice. At Oxford, Anne Dellinger worked enthusiastically and swiftly as an editor. Harvey L. Gable prepared the index.

My colleagues at the 2014 research group, Balancing Religious Accommodation and Human Rights in Constitutional Frameworks, at Bielefeld University's Center for Interdisciplinary Studies (ZIF) helped me refine the manuscript. I also shared with them meals, evening conversations, and an ideal contemplative setting. Mokhtar Awad, Katie Bentvoglio, Dina Bishara, Lamis El Muhtaseb, Amr Hamzawy, Abdulwahab Kayyali, Clark Lombardi, Mara Revkin, Oren Samet-Mariam, Emad Eldin Shahin, and Scott Williamson have all coauthored shorter works with me that have helped shape my thinking in this book. Several other colleagues have been very generous with their time, thoughts, reactions, and comments. I owe deep thanks to Michele Dunne, Dörthe Engelcke, and Nadia Oweidat.

The ideas for this manuscript were also developed in a series of informed conversations with friends and colleagues, some of whom may be surprised to know that what I learned from them went into this book. In this regard, I should mention Zaid al-Ali, Abdulwahab Alkebsi, Lina Atallah, Yussuf Auf, Dina Bishara, Judith Kohn Brown, Sarah El-Kazaz, Skip Gnehm, Hafsa Halawa, Mahmoud Hamad, Amy Hawthorne, Hisham Hellyer, Satoshi Ikeuchi, Kirsten Lundeberg, Mirette Mabrouk, Marwan Muasher, Khalid Fathi Neguib, Jacob Olidort, Marina Ottaway, Ann Patterson, David Risley, Bassem Sabri, Mark Schwehn, Annelle Sheline, Charlotta Sparre, and Alanna Van Antwerp. There are many residents of the Arab world who trusted me in very frank conversations; I do not mention them by name here both because there are so many and because most would likely prefer not to be named.

I owe thanks to a number of institutions who supported various aspects of this project: a Guggenheim Fellowship provided very generous help; George Washington University granted me a sabbatical leave; Bielefeld University's Center for Interdisciplinary Studies (ZIF) hosted me for a portion of 2014; the Carnegie Endowment for International Peace supported me as a nonresident senior associate; and the Project for Middle East Political Science supported some supplementary research.

At several points noted in the text, I have included updated passages from some of my previous publications: parts of *The Rule of Law in the Arab World: Courts in Egypt and the Gulf* (Cambridge: Cambridge University Press, 1997); "Shariʿa and State in the Modern Muslim Middle East," *International Journal of Middle East Studies* 29, 3 (1997): 359–376; *Constitutions in a Nonconstitutional World: Arab Basic Laws and the Prospects for Accountable Government* (Albany: SUNY Press, 2001); "Egypt and Islamic Sharia: A Guide for the Perplexed," Carnegie Endowment for International Peace (2012); and "Islam and Constitutionalism in the Arab World: The Puzzling Course of Islamic Inflation," in Asli Bali and Hanna Lerner, eds., *Constitution Writing, Religion and Democracy* (Cambridge: Cambridge University Press, 2016). All are reprinted with permission.

Julie Corwin provided very strong support and commented on the manuscript, helping me restrain some of my rhetorical excesses, slim down some repetitive passages, and clarify the argument.

My nephews Jacob Pastor, Evan Brown, Joseph Lea, and Albert Brown all entered adulthood as I was working on this book. They have yet to share with me their thoughts on the role of religion in public life. But I dedicate this book to them in the hope that they will live in a world where ultimate issues can be argued more fruitfully and respectfully than has sometimes happened in the past.

Introduction

Politics is a way of ruling divided societies without undue violence—and most societies are divided, though some think that is the trouble.

Bernard Crick, *In Defence of Politics*, 33

A rab publics have come to argue vociferously about religion. How do they argue? Does it matter?

I hope to show how these arguments over religion take place, how contentious they are, and the varying degree that they affect policy outcomes. And I will also show that they can aggravate conflict and polarization. But these problems stem less from their religious character than their lack of traction in policy making. There are few mechanisms available to induce those arguing to come to an agreement or affect a decision. It is their ineffectual nature, much more than their content, that makes arguments increasingly divisive.

IDEALISM, CONFUSION, SURPRISE, AND CYNICISM

This book has a title that may make its author seem contentious ("arguing") and optimistic ("revival"). Neither adjective fits. I aim not to take part in any debates but to understand various participants and positions as sympathetically and even as empathetically as I can. And I also seek to understand the effects of those debates. I am not particularly optimistic; indeed, the revival I speak of is real but not particularly cheerful, in part because it is often disagreeable and in part because it is incomplete.

Nor is this book a reaction to events in the Arab world since 2011. I felt some of the hope (heavily tinged with nervousness) shared by so many during the uprisings of 2011. I felt disappointment (tinged with despair) as the Arab world lapsed into what I refer to in the conclusion as the cruel palindrome of choosing between Isis and Sisi.

But I focus on neither the uprisings nor their aftermath; instead it is longer-term trends that draw my attention. My interest is motivated by a curiosity in what I feel have long been underappreciated aspects of Arab politics: the revival of a public sphere in which political arguments move thick and fast.

That curiosity was born a full decade before the upheavals of 2011; it was formed by a sequence of idealism, confusion, surprise, and, finally, cynicism.

My initial idealism sprouted from some gleanings from political philosophy, especially readings in various streams of liberal and democratic thought premised on how we should speak with each other in an egalitarian and respectful manner and, implicitly (perhaps overly so), how we should listen.

But while those writings could be inspiring, I also found them confusing. Those who were most concerned with combining democratic institutions and behaviors with respect for autonomous individuals often seemed to be writing more for each other than for the individuals and populations whose humanity, dignity, and autonomy they so respected. They wrote in prose I found difficult, even inaccessible. Such writings seemed designed to constrain the very passions that motivate the political activity of many people.[1] Some of the writings seemed tinged by an assumption that there are clear, right answers to policy questions but that actual political discourse is so problematic it obscures those answers. Such a notion suggested an assumption of false consciousness, not a very helpful one for a set of approaches based on mutual respect. The egalitarian ethos seemed more than mildly contaminated by elitism.

My suspicion was not boundless. I soon learned that there were those who could use some of the concepts generated by this line of philosophical inquiry in a very grounded, empirical fashion in a Middle Eastern context (the work of my then yet-to-be colleague Marc Lynch influenced my initial thinking deeply in that regard[2]). More than a decade ago, I began to think about writing a book about the politics of public debates in the Arab world. I put aside the idea to work on Islamist movements, but that research only deepened my interest.

Just as I was turning back to the subject came the surprise of the 2011 Arab uprisings. My shock did not come from the fact that members of Arab societies were arguing about politics. For my own part, I had noticed the way in which political discussions had gradually become more detailed, open, and critical in the 1990s. When the first Arab Human Development Report was issued in 2002, I was a bit taken aback, but not by the content of the report. Indeed, the document, while critical of existing realities in the Arab world, seemed tame by the standards set by the arguments I had heard. Instead what surprised me was the surprised reaction in Western journalistic and policy circles, lauding what seemed to many external observers to be an unprecedented introduction of self-criticism.

But of course the authors of the report were not criticizing themselves in any personal way—they were lashing out (as much as any United Nations document would allow them) against their rulers, and they were deeply critical of prevailing social and political practices. And this was hardly something new. In fact, by that year, I could not remember the last time I had heard a citizen of an Arab state say something good about his or her political system in casual conversation.[3]

And not just in casual conversation—older and newer media were awash in political talk, much of it critical. That criticism knew boundaries, but those were unclear and often crossed. In 2005, browsing in an Egyptian bookstore, I was astounded when I saw the title *I Hate Husni Mubarak*.

So, criticism and political talk was something that I had become increasingly aware of. In the 2000s I learned how those arguments were often simply not heard outside the Arab world; as forests of apparently well-rooted truisms were felled in Arab arguments they seemed to make few sounds outside the region. Or, less charitably, arguments among citizens of the Arab world were a surprise to those outside the Arab world only because they had not been listening to them.

But I was also struck by how much the critical talk seemed unconnected to political action. Many argued about the need for fundamental change but fewer tried to do anything about it.

What shocked me profoundly, therefore, was when large numbers of people began to act on their complaints, most dramatically in 2011.[4] In that year, masses of residents in many societies rose up against their political systems, shouting so all could hear the complaints that had gestated over a decade or even a generation. I visited Egypt and Jordan in December 2010 and found a dour and despairing mood indeed; I returned to both places in March 2011 and found a buoyancy and spirit of activism that seemed to have come from nowhere. Of course I had been witnessing (or hearing) some of the wellsprings for years, but I had generally doubted whether words would be translated into action. (When asked in the fall of 2010 whether a mass uprising in Egypt was likely, I remember answering, "It's not impossible," which seemed then to be an unjustifiably daring statement.)

Yet as they began to act, argumentative citizens struck out in some dissonant directions. In the year following the uprising, I was made uneasy by their political choices. Most leading political actors seemed to be very suspicious of each other and in shaky control of the political systems they wished to operate or redesign. I was initially persuaded that a strong consensus on political reform would sustain a more promising process. But that proved a misjudgment; the apparent political consensus broke apart as political systems and processes seemed to either shunt popular pressures aside or set them against each other. I could not resist a bit of cynicism—or at least a grimmer mood—as the mass movements of 2011 metastasized into coup and civil conflict in Egypt, fizzled in Jordan, Kuwait, Morocco, and Palestine, and led to complicated and bloody civil wars in Yemen, Syria, and Libya.

The politics that concerns me in this book is not always pretty; the revival of which I speak has not always been joyful.

OVERCOMING FEAR OF RELIGION

Why do I focus on religion? Not because of my own faith; in my own life, I generally detach questions of justice, morality, and political and social behavior from those of faith and the divine. But in most of the societies I have studied, religion provides an important anchor for such discussions. Indeed, in some ways this book is a story of how thoroughly religious many Arab public discussions have become.

Religion provides one of the main languages of public debate in the Arab world. This book is my contribution to understanding debate over religion in the public sphere in the Arab world and its relationship to public policy.

When I focus on religion in public life, I do not mean to say there are no Arabs who detach (as I do) public behavior from questions involving the divine—I have met many. But they rarely do so explicitly in public—and that is the point. To do so would be to talk in a language that would not make a lot of sense to their audience, perhaps even be self-defeating and alienating. It would be tantamount to claiming that divine guidance and ultimate values have no role in social life. A more commonly voiced attitude is that an individual's beliefs or private behavior is between him and God, but social conduct should be governed by God's merciful and beneficent instructions.

Religion Provides the Language for Such Discussions

But such a close connection between religion and public debate deeply concerns many people, including some of the most influential thinkers about politics.

Many public discussions in Western settings—and many scholarly and philosophical approaches that inform much academic thinking—betray a strong suspicion about the politics of religion. Religious differences can be politically frightening because they seem so deep and so unfriendly to discussion and compromise—necessary ingredients to any attempt to manage differences politically. Behind this nervousness about religion is a worry that ultimate truths are not open to argument, that religion breeds absolute thinking and even intolerance. These associations between religion and intolerance seem reasonable. And they are particularly potent perhaps in the Arab world, where the religion involved is Islam, with its heavy legalistic bent. Public arguments in the Arab world can very easily take on a religious guise.

But on this point, my own experience leads me to inject a note of skepticism about the fear of religion in public discourse. The concerns mooted seem to be the mirror image—or the retort—to the equally reasonable-sounding reciprocal suspicions I have heard from some pious individuals. Religiously inspired thinkers often argue that those who seek to avoid ultimate truths can find no secure grounding for any moral code. Many opponents of secularism fear that exclusion of religion breeds not tolerance and pluralism but anomie or hedonism.

While both these views seem reasonable, I find them unhelpful. It is not merely that they contradict each other. They simply do not fit with my experience.

I have not seen religion as inexorably linked to political intolerance nor have I seen secularism as tied to narcissism, egoism, and social dissolution. In both cases, there are many possible intellectual paths to break the supposed links. For instance, the supposed path from religious faith to rigid intolerance can be diverted by a religiously sponsored humility, appreciation of others' humanity and dignity, or willingness to engage in rational speculation on the most difficult religious issues. At the same time, secularism can and frequently does anchor morality in an insistence on shared humanity.

So I do not share the fear of religion in public in its most sweeping form for empirical reasons: the nervousness is simply counter to how readily I have seen many pious friends and acquaintances show real willingness to engage in give-and-take on religious issues and how many of those with a secular bent can refer with derision and even intolerance to the beliefs of their fellows. My point is not that religion makes people virtuous interlocutors, or that tolerance is a ruse, but only that I have seen no clear link between willingness to engage and secularism within my own circles of colleagues and friends.

I do not dismiss the concerns about religion in public life; I wish to proceed only without the assumption that religion is inherently a danger to political life.

And I also wish to explore religion as more than belief or faith. Indeed, in the Arab world religion can come up in many guises that are distinct from faith even if often connected to it: religion is sometimes structure and bureaucracy, sometimes practice, sometimes campaign fodder, sometimes ritual, and sometimes law. The Western European experience often leads us to privilege religion in two guises only: individual belief ("faith") and authoritative structure ("church" in juxtaposition to "state"). Given the other forms in which religion is expressed in the Arab world, we should not be so restrictive in our understanding of where religion will arise and the guises it will take.

And it should therefore be no surprise that while I describe religion as "anchor" and "language," as I have, I also strive to avoid making discussions seem too fixed and clear—the anchor has a very long chain and language can be a source not only for communication but also for misunderstanding of both the comic and tragic variety.

And it is a sense of tragedy in particular that has characterized many past writings on politics in the sense used here—starting with Jürgen Habermas, who, as we will soon see, lamented the way the public sphere had been corrupted and controlled, and who has been followed by waves of liberal theorists who focus on what politics can be in part by decrying what it has become. Even less explicitly normative scholars often approach such discussions to tie the public arguments immediately to regime type—implicitly claiming that such debates are of interest to the extent they explain the origin or fate of authoritarianism and democracy, less attentive to the ways public discussions might affect more mundane political outcomes.

WHAT POLITICS REALLY IS; WHAT POLITICS REALLY DOES

This book is designed not to provide a sense of drama of any variety but instead to make forays in two directions.

First I seek to describe, providing what might be called an ethnography of current Arab politics as it really is. I am interested, to be sure, in possible trajectories of change but I worry a rush to probe possibilities for democratic opening or authoritarian resurgence may miss the real ways in which Arab political systems are changing.

An emphasis on how politics should be discussed can lead us to overlook how it is actually discussed. In June 2013, as Egypt approached a wave of demonstrations and ultimately a coup against President Muhammad Morsi of the Muslim Brotherhood, I was warned by a religious figure to be careful where I walked because I have a short beard—one that might be taken as a nonverbal political statement. Such a symbol of a kind of religiosity, he feared, might expose me to a kind of nonverbal political response.

Not all political speech is ideal. In fact, not even all rarefied academic discussions are ideal. Shortly after that warning about my beard, I attended a presentation at an academic conference in the United States by a very accomplished and respected colleague who argued that opposition to a specific policy initiative—an opposition apparently grounded in public reason—could in fact be refuted in terms of public reason. I noticed that the most effective way in which he undermined the positions he was attempting to refute in front of an audience predisposed to sympathize with him was by reading sections of his opponents' writings slowly with an arched eyebrow, inserting an occasional sarcastic remark.

Neither harassing people with beards nor repeating an opponent's words with a derisive tone and subtly contemptuous gestures is ideal political speech.

But such forms still deserve our attention because this is how much politics is practiced.

That leads me to my second purpose: to explain the effects of political arguments over religion in the Arab world. I am interested in whether people experience the political world differently as politics revives or whether the vitality of political arguments over religion changes policy. I find that the arguments do indeed deeply affect the way that various groups understand the political order but that the effects on policy outcomes are far more limited. The problem is not that religious disagreements are unmanageable but that political systems and institutions are generally not configured to reflect political arguments of any sort. Arguments about religion are generally not resolved (or managed) politically in the Arab world today, it is true, but the problem, as I will show, has less to do with their religious nature and more to do with the inability of weak structures to translate political talk into political practice.

NOTES

1. I first explored this idea in "Reason, Interest, Rationality, and Passion in Constitution Drafting," *Perspectives on Politics* 6, 4 2 (008): 675–689.
2. My introduction came through his book *State Interests and Public Spheres: The International Politics of Jordan's Identity* (New York: Columbia University Press, 1999) and his article "Taking Arabs Seriously," *Foreign Affairs* 82, 5 (2003): 81–94.
3. My puzzlement at the reaction was unusual but not unique: the *Economist* account of the report noted, "Across dinner tables from Morocco to the Gulf, but above all in Egypt, the Arab world's natural leader, Arab intellectuals endlessly ask one another how and why things came to turn out in this unnecessarily bad way." "Self-Doomed to Failure," *Economist*, July 4, 2002.
4. I explore this distinction between clear political preferences and unclear willingness to act in "Constitutional Revolutions and the Public Sphere," in *The Arab Uprisings Explained: New Contentious Politics in the Middle East*, ed. Marc Lynch (New York: Columbia University Press, 2014).

PART 1

Publicity, Religion, and the Revival of Politics

Of course, I too look at American television. When I see debates between presidential candidates, I get sick.

Jürgen Habermas, "Further Reflections on the Public Sphere,"
in, Craig Calhoun, ed., *Habermas and the Public Sphere*, 467

[That]even this prepolitical authority which ruled the relations between adults and children, teachers and pupils, is no longer secure signifies that all the old time-honored metaphors and models for authoritarian relations have lost their plausibility. Practically as well as theoretically, we are no longer in a position to know what authority really is.

Hannah Arendt, "What is Authority?" in *Between Past and Future:*
Six Exercises in Political Thought, 92

The most striking change about Arab politics in the last few years is that it has now become so alive. Violence and oppression are very real, but so are political arguments. Their liveliness affects how religion and religious authority are understood and practiced. In this book I study how politics operates and what effects it has on how Islam is understood, shapes, and is shaped by public life.

Both my initial claim (about the vivacity of Arab politics) and my project (to study how Arab politics interacts with religion) seem to go beyond brash to preposterous. In chapter 1, I work to return them to the realm of the merely brash. I do so in two steps. First, I explain what I mean by the "revival" of politics. Second, I provide a detailed overview of the questions and the findings.

In chapter 2, I disentangle some useful concepts involving publicity, politics, and religion from some of their normative foundations to make them more amenable for critical analysis. But I also show that a complete divorce from normative concerns will miss why they are so powerful and what they mean to those who deploy them in making public arguments about politics.

CHAPTER 1

Understanding the Revival of Politics

News will come from Rome—but it will be rumor confounded with fact, fact confounded with
self-interest, until self-interest and faction become the source of all we shall know.
John Williams, *Augustus*, 24

W hen I first journeyed to Arab societies in the early 1980s as a doctoral
student of political science, one thing struck me in Egypt (where I
spent the most time) as well as Jordan and Syria (where I briefly visited):
nobody spoke much about politics. What few discussions I heard were
guarded and private. There was politics aplenty in the sense that governments acted in ways that deeply affected people's lives. But there was a
vacuum of politics in terms of public discussion. A combination of deep nervousness and profound lack of interest (seemingly very different but sometimes difficult for me to disentangle) inhibited or even prevented political
conversations, especially as one moved into the public realm. Public spaces
were strangely devoid of political discussions: the largest public squares
in major cities showed no signs of political assemblies (except for those
occasionally arranged by the regime); and all coffeehouses and restaurants
seemed to have televisions that showed only sports. If one picked up a newspaper (and not many people did), one read about the comings and goings of
officials, the arrival of basic commodities (such as meat), and the departure
of prominent citizens from this world. A few journals or newspapers carried
highbrow pieces from a few public intellectuals, but the resulting debates
were fairly circumscribed in content and limited to a small number of participants. Overall, there was precious little about the politics of this world in
many media; if one watched the television news, official comings-and-goings
seemed to dominate much of the broadcast.

Everything is different today. Politics has edged out even sports in personal and coffeehouse conversations. It forges some personal ties and ruptures others. Public squares have filled with demonstrators in some places and witnessed violent clashes over political issues. Newspapers are crowded with (and occasionally even invent) news and an enormous amount of analysis and argument. Engaged members of the public swap rumors and views in personal conversations or by text messages. Boisterous political talk fills the airwaves, often sparking far more discussions than do sitcoms, soap operas, and even sports. That politics is often ugly, and it can be used to dehumanize those who have different views and justify violence against them. Official attempts to control what is said are still very much robust and occasionally quite fierce.

Arab politics—*in the sense of discussion and argument about public affairs*—has been reborn. It is pursued, sustained, and developed in many overlapping institutions and practices. The structures of political argument do not merely overlap. They interact in novel ways that, while they hardly replace older hierarchies and structures of authority, still modify, steer, and even occasionally undermine or limit them. An authority figure who would brook no public dissent a generation ago now finds his words moved into media where they are easily mocked.

In their rich cacophony, the circles in which arguments take place often clash with each other. That rich cacophony will be the object of our attention in the first half of this book.

The sense of politics that I am employing here—as old as the word itself—is used today primarily by normative political theorists concerned with how we should speak to each other. Phrases like "deliberative democracy," "public sphere," and "ideal speech" pepper their writings, many of which presume that politics takes place in a liberal and democratic society. As we will see, these concepts can enlighten and ennoble us but can also obstruct our understanding of empirical realities.

Indeed, this inquiry into arguments among residents of the Arab world would be of less interest if it were not connected to a second, perhaps grittier, meaning of politics—*the struggle over public policy outcomes*. For a long time, politics in the first sense of public argument seemed to be in hibernation in most Arab societies. In the second sense of the word, of course, politics was of course always fully alive. There was public policy and political power to be sure. But politics in that second sense was brutally and ruthlessly predicated on the suppression of politics in the first sense. Sometimes open and even violent contests for political authority occurred (though these seemed to decline in much of the Arab world in the last third of the twentieth century as regimes seemed to settle in). And there were, of course, private conversations and samizdat forums for arguments that rulers could not suppress. So, as regimes entrenched themselves and effectively presented themselves as inevitable, there was little point and sometimes considerable risk to politics in the sense

banned by the Slut

of publicly arguing and discussing (and also organizing peacefully) to affect matters of public interest.

Remarkably, the revival of Arab politics began just as politics seemed most futile—and indeed, the despair caused by futility served as the midwife of the revival.

So of course, struggles over allocation, policy, power, and authority had never disappeared. Powerful actors lined up on different sides of critical economic debates, for instance. Politics according to those meanings never died. In the latter chapters of this book, I will consider how the revival of politics as public argument has affected politics in the second sense, focusing on policy outcomes related to the public role of religion. In the remainder of part 1, I will focus on the revival of politics in the sense of public argumentation.

But politics in the primary sense I am using here requires the existence of a public sphere. Hannah Arendt wrote, "Whenever people come together, the world thrusts itself between them, and it is in this in-between space that all human affairs are conducted."[1] No Arab society ever had that in-between space completely controlled by the state (such domination was the basis for Arendt's image of totalitarianism[2]); Arab authoritarianism, especially as it ground on and on, was based more on the futility than the domination of activity and talk within that space. Arab politics never fully died, but it was nearly lifeless and seemed pointless under prevailing authoritarian conditions. It is that revival of public argument that leads me to use the term "revival" with only a touch of exaggeration.

When Arab authoritarianism gradually gave way to semiauthoritarianism from the 1970s onward, and when semiauthoritarianism in turn faltered in 2011, the space between residents of the Arab world could be pried open even further than it had before. Thus, Arendt's in-between space has come alive in the Arab world in recent decades, increasingly escaping from the harsh constraints imposed by authoritarian political systems. The years since 2011 have been cruel ones in many Arab societies, especially in the political realm. Journalists are imprisoned; commentary on social media is polarized and policed; and few political orders could be described as liberal or permissive. But the arguments continue.

To many external observers, the change suddenly became visible in 2011. But for those living in or closely following the region, it was far from sudden. At a regime level, many authoritarian Arab political systems had, as I say, given way in the last quarter of the twentieth century to semiauthoritarian regimes, where opposition movements could operate, organize, and occasionally agitate but were denied the opportunity to win elections. At the broader social level, newer media (satellite television and internet-based), and—just as important—older ones (such as the daily newspaper) gradually made it easier in many countries to participate in public debates from a variety of ideological perspectives. At a very local level, the state retreat from social welfare commitments opened opportunities for a host of formal and informal groups and organizations to operate in areas once dominated by officially controlled bodies.

UNDERSTANDING POLITICS

These various trends have been noticed by political scientists, sociologists, anthropologists, and scholars in the humanities. But various disciplinary contributions have not covered for each other's blind spots. First, those who focus on the large-scale political changes and their normative implications can edge into a celebratory (or sometimes cynical) tone: the changes are seen as potentially democratizing or as simply entrenching authoritarianism more deeply—as if the only political change that draws interest is democratization. Second, those who take more grass-roots or empirical approaches often overlook the effects of discussions. Third, both groups often (though not always) miss the ways that various spheres of argument interact.

MACRO AND NORMATIVE VIEWS

Some normatively informed political scientists whose focus usually falls outside the Arab world have shown great interest in exploring public discussions about politics. Led by generations of intellectuals from Aristotle to Arendt, much of this interest is motivated by important and sometimes quite lofty normative concerns: how can we reason together; talk and deliberate across our differences in experiences, outlooks, and values; inform and be informed by each other; and come to common decisions about public matters? How can we structure public discussions to encourage such deliberation and realize the public interest rather than engage in mere horse-trading, bargaining, sloganeering, threats, coercion, and appeals to passion and private interests rather than public reason? How can we make sure that all citizens have access to— and the ability to participate in—such discussions?

I do not dismiss such goals, but I fear that when we keep our eye on the horizon of virtuous politics, we may trip on some very hard political realities— ones that we would be better advised to treat as building blocks rather than obstacles. Politics, even in the sense that I use the term here as centering on public discussion, is rarely so lofty as we might hope; it is grounded very much in earthly concerns. Even in the heady year of 2011, Arab political argumentation was hardly ideal; in the years since, official oppression and violence have proven very much alive. But those troubling trends have been woven into political arguments and have not silenced them.

Public discussions take place to be sure, but real ones are emotional, argumentative, manipulative, passionate, and edge into disrespect, prejudice, and even threats. Students of public spheres will immediately notice that we will speak far more about "arguments" and far less about "deliberation" than is the norm for scholarly writings on the subject. Much of what is politically significant hardly seems like deliberation but it certainly can be argumentative.

If we focus only on the critical-rational and the egalitarian and fair deliberations, we will therefore miss most politics. If we instead turn our attention to all forms of actual political discussions, not only will we see that there are certain forms of argumentation privileged over others in the actually existing public spheres, but we will also incorporate the obvious but often underappreciated phenomenon that some participants have privileged entry to public spheres. In a television talk show or on a dais at a public rally, only a few voices speak. Even those who enter small face-to-face gatherings hardly leave hierarchies of wealth and power at the doorstep.

Of course, the normative theorists who have inspired much of our interest have long been forced, however reluctantly, to acknowledge these realities when they confront genuine politics. It is instructive here to turn to Jürgen Habermas, one of the most sophisticated normative theorists of the politics of the public sphere. He presents much of his thought in prose so difficult to penetrate it is never quite clear if it has been translated from the original German: "I think an empirically meaningful approach to our selective and even colonized forms of public communication is to see how they work within certain procedural dimensions of formal inclusion, of the degree of political participation, of the quality of discussion, of the range of issues, and, finally and most important, of how the presuppositions of those public debates are really institutionalized." Immediately after making this comment, Habermas explained himself in the uncharacteristically earthy terms quoted in the epigraph to part 1: "Of course, I too look at American television. When I see debates between presidential candidates, I get sick." Real politics in real public spheres can be nauseating. But, as Habermas hastens to add, "we at least have to explain why we get sick. . . ."[3] And I seek to do more: not merely to live with the sense of unease and explain it but also to embrace and explore its sources.

Micro and Empirical Approaches

Those from a range of other disciplines in the social sciences and humanities (anthropology, communication studies, and sociology, for instance) with a more finely grained focus are very aware of the ways in which new forms of politics and discourse carry within them gradations, affirmations, and subversions of hierarchy, status, and power. But the focus often remains highly localized, often centering on the participants themselves; the broader political implications of the emerging public spheres have attracted less interest. And there is still a strongly hopeful tilt to many such efforts—a sense in which these public spheres empower those who enter them. Overall, there is far more interest in their effect on the participants than on their impact on the society.

And there is a common blind (or at least hazy) spot that can be of enormous significance. Both micro- and macro-level approaches have often led us to miss the interaction among apparently discrete spheres, one that will emerge as critical to our inquiry: the way that a newspaper article is circulated quickly through newer social media technology; that a discussion group relies on a website; that parliamentary debates are fodder for television talk shows; that demonstrators in a public square circulate their slogans among those not attending. Exploring such linkages is critical to understanding who speaks, how they speak, and what effect political debate and discussion has. Indeed, the ways in which various spheres interact drives much of Arab politics today, and the way in which the linkages detach argument from speaker can have significant effects on authority and power (as we will see in parts 2 and 3).

THE QUESTIONS AND THE FINDINGS

This, then, brings us to my project in this book: to understand and map the reborn forms of Arab politics as they really are and the effects they really have. I do so while moving beyond a concern for only good or ill. In particular, I present various sites of Arab public life to understand when various spheres arose, who participates in them, and how. I pay particular attention to how the various forums interact with each other. I develop a more comprehensive sense of the Arab public sphere but also present its effect on policy outcomes: the revival of Arab politics does matter for policy, but only under specific conditions. It has great impact on how people assess their governance structures, however.

And I focus on religion.

The public sphere seems to be terrain friendly to religion in the Arab world. The re-emergence of Arab politics took place at a time when religion in general seemed to be resurging as a public force in Arab societies, so that Arab politics often has taken on a strong religious coloration.

Focusing on religion will raise a set of concerns which I address more fully in chapter 2. Religion in general (and Islam specifically) excites some suspicions and fears, even among those who celebrate public deliberation. Indeed, if Habermas's early writings on the public sphere mourned its corruption by the state and by capitalism and consumerism, his followers often showed more concern about religion. When they turn to the world today—especially given the existence of substantial Muslim communities in Europe, faith-based politics and movements in the United States, and the political force of Islam in the Middle East—it is religion in politics that causes special concern.

I am focusing particular attention on religion and especially on arguments about the Islamic shari'a precisely because there is a strong religious coloration to much public life in the Arab world. Many previous writers have explored the "democratization" of the Islamic shari'a in recent decades: matters that had largely been within the domain of discourse among scholars and specialists have burst out in many different public settings. If the Islamic shari'a is the set of divine instructions that Muslims believe has been given to them, then the number of people exploring what those instructions are and how to interpret and apply them has multiplied greatly as education, a participatory spirit, and a dedication to increasing the role of religious values in public life have spread. Most significantly, as new public spheres have opened and overlapped, discussions and debates have become more inclusive but also more confusing.

While the demos is now forcing its way into religious discourse, it does not speak in a single voice, a single manner, or a single place. Indeed, actual democratic politics should teach us three things critical to any exploration of the intersection of religion and politics: (1) that democratic politics engenders cacophony as much as consensus; (2) that it does not eliminate but reflects and even reproduces gradations of wealth and power (though of course it also can undermine, tame, or redirect their effects); and (3) that it allows expertise and authority to continue to speak powerfully even as participatory institutions operate.

I have much assistance in this exploration of the newly lively nature of the in-between spaces where politics now operates, because most of the initial charting has been done by others. We have learned a lot about actual and emerging public spheres in the Arab world—some have studied the new and constantly shifting technologies; some have focused more on hoarier ones (such as the printing press); and others have probed forms of face-to-face and oral communication. And that extensive work allows me to move forward not simply through my own research but through synthesizing and bringing together much work that others have done. I hope that I am moving our understanding forward, probing not simply what public spheres actually exist and how they operate, but how they interact.

My general questions are thus clear. Who participates in discussions of how the Islamic shari'a should inform these areas of policy and governance? How do they make arguments, and how do arguments evolve? How do the various forums interact? And how do the debates within the public sphere(s) affect policy outcomes?

I focus on debates and discussions about specific issues where I have garnered expertise in conducting various research projects over the years—constitution writing, personal status law, and education curricula. And I explore them in places within the Arab world where I have been led by those projects. I have selected these issues and areas not because I feel I already know them well enough to draw conclusions. In fact, my selections are based on my unwillingness to draw quick conclusions—familiarity can breed an appreciation for complexity and even contradiction as well as reveal how much remains to be learned. I selected these areas only because I felt sufficiently familiar to ask questions in more helpful forms.

I focus on four kinds of public spheres with special interest in how they interact:

- small group discussions that straddle the public/private divide, such as diwaniyyas in Kuwait or piety groups in Egypt;
- public spaces of assembly, such as public squares and mosques;
- media, both new and old; and
- parliaments, an institution etymologically founded in speaking and argument—or, in Arabic, sitting (implicitly socially)—rather than legislation.

I pursue this inquiry largely as a set of reflections, both on what I have found and (perhaps much more) on what I have learned from the explorations of others. (More prosaically, what I mean is that I will rely a bit eclectically on primary and secondary work.) I advance themes, ideas, and arguments more than definitive answers.

But those themes, ideas, and arguments are hardly without content.

First, I show that while religion has distinctive elements, it is hardly as problematic for public life and politics as many fear.

Second, I show not only that politics as argument about public affairs has been revived in the Arab world in many spheres but that those spheres overlap and interact.

Third, while arguments are lively, much of the argumentation that takes place is aimed at sympathizers rather than opponents; the point is often to preach to the choir rather than persuade the doubters.

But fourth, because arguments are made in public, words can be detached from the speaker with great ease. Arguments cross the boundaries among spheres more readily than a speaker's authority does. The effect is that points of view often meet but noisily and contentiously and in a manner that is sometimes polarizing.

Fifth, when we move to the effect of the arguments, we will see how political structures in the Arab world are generally constructed to shut out rather than reflect public voices. There are exceptional cases, however, and paying attention to both the rule and the exceptions will show us that it is the problematic political structures in the Arab world—and not the public nature of religion—that makes religious arguments difficult to resolve. Even when there is a disconnect with policy outcomes, however, the effects of the arguments are real since they help shape overall attitudes to the political order. Likely future trajectories for Arab political systems are better envisioned not as a binary between democracy and authoritarianism but according to the degree to which governance structures are effective and open.

There is a place for far more formal social-scientific inquiry, but that is generally not how I arrive at the conclusions in this book. Such inquiry makes most sense when basic conceptions and ideas are clear and capable of being rendered into subjects of empirical inquiry. I draw on much empirical work here, but I am convinced that our understandings of the basic contours of Arab politics still requires a set of approaches that are a bit more flexible, even jury-rigged; we need to work a little more on erecting the scaffolding even as we proceed with the more detailed work on building our knowledge.

I am not presenting a single, unified research project, only designed to advance a set of causal explanations. I proceed instead in a more opportunistic manner, based on work I have done in the past and what others have discovered. Thus, I do not restrict myself to a single country but draw on the places I know best; I do not attempt to probe regional variation with much depth because my scope is a bit too wide. I seek to understand general regional trends, tilting toward the experience of established and relatively stable states, rather than to give a more specific, country-by-country coverage. Indeed, I do not seek to cover Arab societies in their diversity but to paint with fairly broad strokes, drawing especially from those places I am more familiar with in order to make general observations that are designed to travel rather than pinpoint with their specificity. My notes are often to give guidance to an English-language reader interested in pursuing a topic in more depth rather than provide comprehensive documentation of all contributions to political arguments.

Careful readers might suspect three blind spots in this inquiry. The first is more apparent than real. The second two require some effort to correct.

First, the topic might seem to have been chosen in a moment of blind hope in 2011. But that is a blind spot that I do not suffer from; as I made clear in the foreword, this project was conceived and parts carried out before the political upheavals of 2011. My interest is of longer and more sustained standing.

But the other blind spots are ones that I have to acknowledge, though I will work both to correct and, at least in part, to justify them on the grounds that I wish to focus the causal part of my analysis on policy outcomes.

I do not include jihadist groups as thoroughly as might seem warranted at first glance. They argue with words as well as violent means; they stand outside many structures but still can participate in the debates in question. I do not include them much in this book for two reasons. First, one of the main tools I have used here—careful conversations with participants in the debates—is not available. They use words to be sure, but they also speak in ways that are violent and symbolic and at the same time in ways that are deliberately outrageous.

The issue is not just squeamishness. There is a justifiable reason why jihadist groups stand at the margin of my analysis: they stood at the margin of many of the debates that occupy my attention and they do not aim at changes in public policy. It is not personal status law or educational curricula that draw their ire but the entire political order.

When Islamist groups began organizing in many Arab societies in the 1970s and 1980s, they did so in a pluralist environment in which lines among various orientations were sometimes blurry. But by the late 1980s and certainly the 1990s, jihadist groups were the target of significant state repression and many non-jihadists sought to distinguish themselves as less radical. In that sense, those more inclined to systemic rejection withdrew—and were driven out of—the public sphere. Their influence could be felt, of course—many more mainstream groups defined themselves by their opposition to jihadist interpretations of Islam. Arguments continued, though they were often indirect. In the aftermath of the Arab uprisings, jihadist groups were first easily cast as irrelevant: the change they sought could be achieved through normal politics or popular mobilization, it seemed.

The rise of the Islamic State, the Egyptian coup of 2013 and the subsequent massacres, and the decay of the state in Libya and Iraq made jihadists a far more active presence; not coincidentally, during that period they began to discover ways of making their increased public presence (for they had never totally disappeared) heard. I will work to incorporate that renewed forceful presence into my understanding of Arab politics.

The final blind spot I should acknowledge is that I deal here with societies in which state institutions function, however badly. Those places in the Arab world with weak or decayed states do not fit easily into my inquiry, focused as I am in half of the project on policy outcomes. But I hasten to emphasize that institutional decay is a growing phenomenon in some societies and I try to incorporate that possibility in some of my analysis.

THE STRUCTURE OF THE BOOK

I close by advancing an exposition on the meaning of the title of part 1 of this book: by "a republic of arguments" I mean to suggest that I am interested in understanding what happens when politics is a public concern and people argue about it in public. I refer to this realm of argumentation as a "republic" (perhaps a bit more etymologically punctilious than current usage requires), since it is arguments about things that are public that concern me. And I am particularly focused on arguments about how political authority should be used in religious matters.

Out of this discussion I hope to broaden our understanding of how actually existing public spheres arise and operate in the Arab world by probing a specific set of arguments about Islam. I have a particular interest in such arguments when they do not occur in fully democratic settings but still show signs of vitality and richness.

In this book, I describe a very vital set of public spheres, though not always pretty ones. Some emerge from below but all are policed from above. Coercion and verbal abuse are hardly excluded. Their sometime unattractive nature does not make them unmanageable. The fact that they concern religion makes some of the republic of arguments a bit distinctive but hardly oxymoronic. Instead, we will see how the most problematic aspects of the politics that concern us stem from the nature of existing political structures that make public officials much less likely to hear—or listen for—what is said and increase the likelihood that arguments will be unproductive and unpersuasive.

But before we probe these issues, we first have to probe the terms we use to explore the republic of arguments. I begin with an explanation of critical concepts (what I mean by politics, publicity, and argument) and try to disentangle some empirical questions about publicity and religion from the normative ones which drove many past writings (chapter 2).

I then turn in part 2 to consider the spaces in which politics is carried out in the Arab world, how the various spheres bump against each other, and how Islam is debated. Chapters 3, 4, and 5 comprise my ethnography of the existing public spheres in the Arab world. Referring to the republic of arguments, I seek to show not simply that these spheres exist but also some of their critical properties. I explore the way they cannot be explained merely as constructions of authoritarian regimes (chapter 3) and then the important ways they are linked with each other (chapter 4). In chapter 5, I introduce religion fully into the analysis, showing how the Islamic shari'a is argued in the Arab world today.

In part 3, I move to understand whether the arguments make any difference for policy outcomes. What happens when the republic of arguments meets the realities of Arab regimes? In particular, I trace the effects of the arguments in three areas.

Chapter 6 probes the religious provisions of Arab constitutions showing how the revival of a vital but contentious public sphere has led to considerable argument about religion without preventing some important agreements over textual provisions—but also how those textual provisions are more important for their expressive rather than legal content.

In chapter 7, I move the focus to personal status law and show a strange disconnect between the law as it is experienced and the law as it is debated. While arguments are thus disconnected to a degree from social reality and generally do not have an effect on policy or legal text, there are some important exceptions. Where a state actor seeks to hammer out consensual support for a change, it often can do so, managing (though hardly resolving) sharp differences over principle.

Finally, in chapter 8, I turn my attention from the most dramatic areas (struggles over political and religious identity in foundational texts) and the most sensitive (family life) to a far more mundane one: the content of textbooks. Here normal politics operates in its full exclusionary nature in the Arab world, provoking heated debates but blocking them from having much outcome—and thus sharpening divisions rather than managing them.

In the conclusion (chapter 9), I reflect on the resulting political dynamics in the Arab world, showing that the revival of politics in the sense of strong public debates has been hampered in its effects by problematic political structures; reborn politics offers excitement and engagement but not more just or responsive political orders. Indeed, the republic of arguments founders in its efficacy in part on the unjustness and unaccountable nature of existing political structures.

NOTES

1. Hannah Arendt, *The Promise of Politics* (New York: Schocken, 2005), 106.
2. The account of an Arab political system that comes closest to (and draws on) Arendt's presentation of totalitarianism is Samir al-Khalil, *Republic of Fear: The Politics of Modern Iraq* (Berkeley: University of California Press, 1989). A more ambivalent use of Arendt in an Arab context can be found in Lisa Wedeen's *Ambiguities of Domination: Politics, Rhetoric, and Symbolism in Contemporary Syria* (Chicago: University of Chicago Press, 1999).
3. "Further Reflections on the Public Sphere," in *Habermas and the Public Sphere*, ed. Craig Calhoun (Cambridge: MIT Press, 1992), 467–468.

CHAPTER 2

Religion in Public

Rethinking secularism . . . does mean working through the debates of the public sphere to find common ground for citizenship, rather than trying to mandate the common ground by omitting the kinds of reason citizens can bring to their public discussions with one another.

Craig Calhoun, "Secularism, Citizenship, and the Public Sphere,"
in Craig Calhoun, Mark Juergensmeyer, and Jonathan Van Antwerpen, eds.,
Rethinking Secularism, 88

What does it mean to argue in public? Is religion a safe subject for public arguments? I turn in this chapter to elaborating and modifying some very old concepts that will help us answer these questions.

The details of Arab politics will be mentioned only in passing in this chapter as we instead develop more general ways to approach the politics of arguing religion. I seek to show here that public argumentation in the region does not look much like what normative theorists of deliberation and publicity expect (or hope), and that much of the republic of argument involves discussion of religion and religiously grounded claims. I seek to undermine some suppositions of many normative writings: their suspicion of religion in public; the assumption that publicity largely promotes appeal to public reason; and that doing things in public suggests the existence of "the public" as a unitary thing.

But I do not dismiss the normative concerns at all. First, the primary foils in this chapter—chiefly liberal political philosophers—have begun to grapple with the questionable nature of some of their assumptions. My criticism will often not seem cutting, chiefly because it amounts to a claim that they have not yet gone far enough.

Second, while I will first partially detach important terms from their normative connotations for the purposes of political analysis, I will not stop at developing only a hardheaded skepticism. Because the normative attraction of these ideas is so strong for people who act in politics I will partially reattach them.

The discussion in this chapter is necessary since I am using some old concepts in different ways and in unusual contexts. As we have already seen in in chapter 1, many theorists who write on the public sphere do so in ways that obscure or do not account for the reality of public political discourse, which is often better described as "argument" rather than "deliberation." But even as we look to the reality of political discourse and the languages and tactics deployed by participants, even as we acknowledge the fact that participation is not equally possible for all, we still need to use concepts with heavily normative connotations. In this chapter, I will not avoid all such normative concerns, but I will try to tilt the balance more heavily toward the empirical, and I will try to show that religion is a natural rather than a discordant subject for political discussions in what I call the republic of arguments.

The first two parts of the chapter explore each of two key concepts in turn—publicity and arguing—freeing them of some (though not all) of their fraught normative meanings. In the third section, we harness rather than simply discard some of the aspects of normative writings I am suspicious of (the faith in the unity and power of "the" public; the aversion to religion) in order to understand the politics of publicity and of religion.

DOING THINGS IN PUBLIC

What does it mean to do something in public? The answer seems obvious—and indeed, it is not complicated. When we describe something as taking in place in public we mean that it is accessible to all who choose to have access to it. That definition is simple and we will use it. The problem for our purpose is that while the definition is clear, there are many positive effects that are often consciously and unconsciously associated with publicity. We wish to avoid assuming—or implicitly inserting—those effects into our definition since publicity's effects are far more mixed than its champions hope. We will see how those positive effects are based in part on Habermas's writings on the public sphere and on the writings of those who advocate what they call "deliberative democracy."

In this section, we will try to sort through some of the implications of publicity. We will begin by first exploring some of the insights of normative theorists, starting with Habermas, but the analysis presented might seem cynical by comparison with that of these theorists—this book is not premised on placing much hope in publicity. Second, we will broaden our critique of the normative literature to show how advocates of deliberative democracy hope that public deliberation makes democracy safe for liberalism and republicanism.

But we will see that they often rely on false or exaggerated ideas about a singular, identifiable public and idealize public discourse. Finally, the section will offer a view of publicity that is friendlier toward religion, which many advocates of deliberation and publicity hope to relegate to the private realm to the greatest extent possible. Looking at the way religion is disputed in the public sphere should lead us to question any sharp dichotomy between rationality and religion. Religion is not inherently irrational, and publicity is not inherent liberal.

Starting with Habermas

When discussing publicity, we need to start with a touch of subtlety and care for two reasons.

First, in purely descriptive terms, we must guard against the impulse to regard "public" as characterized only by open, equal, and unlimited access or as always standing in sharp distinction to "private." When something happens in public, we generally mean that it is visible to those who care to look (or audible to those who wish to listen), but we should never forget that participation beyond viewing or listening is sometimes sharply restricted. Discussion might be limited to specific participants, and it might be unidirectional or very limited (a leader addressing followers; reporters asking questions of an official in a televised news conference). A public address does not mean one in which everybody is speaking but only one to which anyone can listen.

Doing something in public can incorporate or overlap with a private dimension. To do something in private means that access is restricted—that not everybody can hear or see. In that sense "private" is quite distinct from "public." But we need to be careful about making too much of this distinction. Some political and social theorists—especially but not exclusively those writing from a feminist perspective—have expressed the concern that the line between public and private serves to mask the degree to which power and hierarchy can operate continuously across the supposed divide. But even if this were not the case, private and public intersect in all kinds of ways; they are hardly mutually exclusive categories under most sets of circumstances. When a group of political leaders discusses an important policy question in a closed room, they are blending public and private: the process of discussion takes place in private but the outcome of that process could be publicly visible if it results in a legal or policy change.

Scholars have spent some time probing the effects of conducting discussions in public and in private knowing that these things can be knit together.[1] When a couple argues on the street about a private matter, they may be transgressing boundaries of what is proper, but they are also showing how private and public are hardly contradictory. When pious people assemble to pray, they may do so as a private act of worship but they can do so in a public place or in a manner that has public ramifications.[2] In chapter 7, for example, we will focus on how public and private become particularly and inextricably intertwined in debates about personal status law in the Arab world.

The second reason for proceeding carefully in our consideration of what is "public" is that it immediately involves us in the tremendous hopes placed in publicity—hopes that can be so inspiring that they sometimes cloud our judgment. Doing things in public has become associated with deliberation and democracy, and indeed, publicity is often offered as an antidote for many of the disappointments that merely procedural aspects of democracy can bring. Publicity's effects are more complicated and uneven than is often realized. Once unleashed as a force, it works in a variety of ways. Those who study publicity have to concern themselves not only with what should happen but also with what does happen.

The starting point for many scholarly explorations of the public sphere—and to this day, one of the most helpful contributions—is Jürgen Habermas's *The Structural Transformation of the Public Sphere*,[3] a foundational book that continues to set the agenda for a vast amount of both normative and empirical work even though Habermas himself has made many subsequent influential contributions, especially in the normative realm. Normatively, the appeal of Habermas's public sphere is as a place—an ideal space to be sure but also one that some real historical locations have approached—that enables critical rational discourse. It is also a place that privileges appeals to the public interest rather than the self-interest of its participants; when we try to persuade others we cannot do so simply by presenting what we want but instead have to persuade them (and make ourselves available for persuasion) about what is for the good of the whole.

Habermas's book is foundational in both its normative and empirical claims. First, it explores how we should speak with each other, or, only slightly more specifically, how we should deliberate about matters of public concern (a line of inquiry subsequently taken up by political theorists and philosophers).[4] Second, the book provides a meticulous early history of the newspaper and the coffee house—two institutions that epitomized the bourgeois public sphere for Habermas, a public sphere that, not coincidentally, hosted critical rational deliberations. The first set of normative contributions are probably more lasting for most intellectuals—and indeed, have been the springboard for much of his subsequent writing—but many historians have followed down the more empirical path.[5]

In fact, Habermas's twin normative and empirical contributions have sent scholars off in two different, not always intersecting, paths—the first devoted to discovering the ways in which public deliberations can make things better; the second instead studying existing or historical public spheres. Habermas's own subsequent writings emphasized the normative dimension but do not ignore the empirical ones; I will not draw on much of the more normative work here since it focuses so heavily on how we should speak to each other in an ideal society, not what we actually do. But I will mention two aspects of his writings that will inform our subsequent inquiry. First, he has struggled to come to terms with departures from purely rational deliberation generally and religion specifically. In the process, he has come to acknowledge that his conception of politics needs to make concessions to real peoples' concerns and what they actually say. Second, he has developed an openness to modern democratic political structures and institutions by exploring how they could interact with the public sphere where much arguing takes place.[6]

One often overlooked dimension of Habermas's focus in his initial book on early modern western Europe is quite relevant to our own inquiry: for all the association of the public sphere with both democracy and liberalism in subsequent writings, the early modern public sphere explored by Habermas was neither fully democratic itself nor did it operate in a broader liberal context. While there were some consultative political structures and some freedom for public discussions, the general political environment was anything but democratic and liberalism was far from hegemonic.

In this book, we are similarly concerned with an Arab world where there is significant political participation and some pluralism even in the absence of fully democratic practices and liberal norms. Unlike Habermas, who asks how the public sphere should interact with political structures, we will probe how they actually do so, freeing ourselves of the assumption that publicity matters only for its association with liberalism and democracy.

Publicity, Deliberation, and Democracy

Yet as much as we might insist on a distinction between publicity and democracy, that distinction can get lost: for many, democracy, liberalism, and even republicanism meet and become one on the hallowed ground of the public sphere through rational, public-interested deliberation. The reasoning is so powerful that we will pause here to consider the sources of its strength. Ultimately, the Arab republic of arguments is not necessarily a democratic place, and we will see ways in which politics as argument and politics as struggles over policy are not well linked. An undemocratic republic of arguments is not always a good thing, but we will see here that it is not an oxymoron. In this section we will probe the normative appeal of deliberative democracy but then turn to consider how it may actually be exclusionary and lead us to miss the distinction between a single public and the reality of multiple separate, overlapping, and sometimes conflicting publics.

To be sure, powerful hopes undergird the elision among liberalism, democracy, republicanism, and publicity. Formal democratic structures without a liberal or republican spirit can provide for a measure of accountability, popular participation in governance, and decision-making mechanisms that reflect the interests and views of the majority. But they can work in a clumsy manner, with elections only periodically held, administered in accordance with rules partly designed by those who seek to win them, involving parties that inspire mainly cynicism, and reducing the public's choices to stark binaries or personality contests. Such procedurally democratic elements can also have pernicious effects. Among those effects identified by liberals and republicans over the years is the fact that procedural democracy can trample minority rights, reward appeals to momentary whims, empower those who cobble together fleeting coalitions of private interests, and promote pandering to public passions. Short terms and private concerns can sway critical decisions and debase public discussions. Such at least is the set of fears that animate some liberal and republican reservations about democracy—reservations that seem to have some empirical foundation.

Publicity and deliberation are embraced by liberals who hope they can offer ways to correct for democracy's flaws. It is even hoped that they allow us to embrace a conception of democracy that goes beyond mechanical electoral and procedural elements to include ethical and public-spirited considerations in our understanding of democracy. Publicity and deliberation can help democracy become safer in the eyes of liberals and republicans. The basic ethos of liberalism centers on individual autonomy and the treatment of other individuals as ends rather than only as means; the basic ethos of republicanism is governance in accordance with the public interest, a public interest that is understood as arising from the community as a whole just as much as from the individual interests of its members.

Democrats, liberals, and republicans use public deliberation as a way of allowing their core values—governance in accordance with the will of the people, the dignity and autonomy of the individual, and the public interest of the entire community—to come together instead of pull in separate directions. It holds the promise of continuous political participation outside of episodic formal electoral channels; it insists that we speak to each other respectfully in order to persuade; it explores ways we can make decisions based on public reason and rational discussion in addition to majority vote or haggling out a compromise. Seen this way, public deliberation is held up as a tool to make democracy safe for liberalism and republicanism. One of the most sophisticated and lucid presentations of the argument for deliberative democracy makes this conception clear:

> Persons should be treated not merely as objects of legislation, as passive subjects to be ruled, but as autonomous agents who take part in the governance of their

own society, directly or through their representatives. In deliberative democracy an important way these agents take part is by presenting and responding to reasons or by demanding that their representatives do so, with the aim of justifying the laws under which they must live together. The reasons are meant both to produce a justifiable decision and to express the value of mutual respect. It is not enough that citizens assert their power through interest group bargaining, or by voting in elections.[7]

Of course, advocates of deliberative democracy and other approaches that seek to combine participation, civility, and the public good do not insist that all public discussion be deliberative and that all decisions be taken only as a result of public deliberation. They do allow for some arguments from self-interest and passion. They also permit some voting, bargaining, and elite decision-making in addition to deliberation. But they insist that critical matters are properly decided by participatory and rational deliberation.[8]

While we have much to learn from scholars of deliberative democracy and similar approaches, there are three problems with relying too extensively on their views in political analysis.

First, they place almost unbearable hopes on the public sphere and at times rush so quickly over what people actually do to what they should say that it seems sometimes that those who care most about the public sphere are those who would keep most real people out of it.

From the beginning of democratic decision-making, critics have noted that the skills necessary for participation in public discussion are hardly equally distributed but are indeed more likely to be cultivated by the wealthier and better educated—as our brief discussion of rhetoric below will make clear. *an elitist character*

Sometimes deliberative democrats seem frustrated most of all by the failure of real people to adopt progressive policy positions, hoping that better political deliberation might induce them to favor more egalitarian or tolerant policies. Indeed for some scholars, it seems the frustration with existing democratic practices is that publics do not embrace the progressive policy options that normative theorists might prefer, leaving those theorists to come close to alleging that publics have been manipulated into a state of false consciousness.[9]

Of course, people might indeed make better choices if public debates followed ideal rules. But the matter is not so simple. Such rules would restrict who can participate. If we are more inclusive and relax the insistence that we speak in specific ways, we might allow real people to barge into the public sphere. Less than pristine entrance requirements—allowing arguments grounded in emotion and identity and short on ideals of rationality and appeals to a common public interest—also allow excluded groups greater visibility. Even television talk shows can be defended on the grounds that they do not disqualify those who speak in less rarefied terms.[10]

And indeed, privileging calls to a single public interest can exclude individuals and groups who perceive their interests as distinct from the broader community, as Harold Mah has noticed when reviewing historians' use of the concept of the public sphere:

> The historians who seek to study social movements in the public sphere avail themselves of that initial aspect of the public sphere as a staging ground for autonomy—for the free expression of persons from any social background. What these historians ignore is that full entry into this space is reserved for those who have fulfilled the public sphere's other conditions, which are given by its particular narrative of rational modernity. Groups that enter the public sphere to express their group identities and interests are frozen in the preliminary condition of the development of the public sphere; and instead of empowering them as effective agents in the public sphere, that frozen condition makes them ultimately appear as the opposite of the public, as the narrow expression of social particularity.[11]

The point is not that trash talk and identity politics are always good but only that barring them may also exclude their speakers. Placing barriers and restrictions on those who are deemed to be talking trash or preaching group interests may be elitist in effect and work very much contrary to any spirit of inclusiveness.

This leads to the second way in which normative writings, with their attempt to privilege the public interest, can lead us astray: the hopes that are placed in the public sphere can make us assume too easily that there is a single public, and, just as implausibly, a single public interest, as Mah notes: "The transformation of social groups into persons who fuse into unity is, of course, a phantasy, and one that is always at odds with an empirical reality of conflicting social identities and interests."[12]

For our inquiry into religious arguments in the Arab world, we will have to come to terms with the existence of multiple, shifting, and sometimes conflicting publics—small communities of the faithful; scholarly communities; a nation-state and its citizenry; voters; readers; viewers; worshippers—that intersect and overlap, sometimes crossing national boundaries and sometimes reinforcing them. And even when publics appear to be more unified—that is, when there is a unified sphere in which various perspectives are presented—the existence of that public should not lead automatically to the assumption that there is a single public interest; as Ian Shapiro has argued, "Gutmann and Thompson's emphasis on deliberation attends too little to the degree to which moral disagreements in politics are shaped by differences of interest and power."[13]

Finally, normative writings on deliberation, democracy, and the public sphere can lead us to look away from, discount, or be suspicious of religion.[14] That is an inclination that might serve us poorly, since there is much argument and even some deliberation about religion in the Arab world. In probing such things, however, we are bucking a trend. In this section we will present liberal suspicions of religion but also show that religious arguments can be rational and public-spirited.

Why are so many suspicious of religion in public? For many, the profanity of the public sphere is a positive end to be achieved. Indeed, the phrase I used earlier, hallowed ground, to describe the intersection of liberalism and democracy is something of a misnomer in this regard. In a very real way, the public sphere as conceived by normative theorists can be ground that is infertile for that which is holy—or more specifically to public discussions and arguments grounded in religion.

With a strong secular bias, much of the focus on critical-rational discourse and deliberation in the public sphere posits religion as something that belongs in the realm of the personal; because members of the public differ in their understanding of religious truths, those truths can become dangerous if overly active in public. In earlier decades, the suspicion of religion—or more broadly, in terms coined by John Rawls, any "comprehensive doctrines" that are shared by only a portion of the political community—in public discourse was more profound. More recent normative writings have relaxed strictures somewhat and bowed to the inevitable entrance of religious arguments in public, seeking now more to police, channel, and regulate rather than disqualify them.[15]

Only in very recent years has the insistence on taking the public nature of religion seriously in both empirical and normative terms begun to gain ground.[16] This is not to say that religion was denigrated—in an ideal public sphere, members would respect each others' religious beliefs but not argue from their own. Religion is welcome as long as one does not speak about it too much. As Gutmann and Thompson put it bluntly, under democratic deliberation, "it would not be acceptable, for instance, to appeal only to the authority of revelation, whether divine or secular in nature."[17] Yet even as they cautiously open the gates to religion, normative theorists of deliberation make surprisingly little effort to understand it. Many writings consider how religion can be integrated in a liberal constitutional order; few of those writings actively engage actual religious writers. Habermas himself, whose attitude to religion has become friendlier (or at least more resigned), might be guilty of this, at least when it comes to Islam. In an essay on Islam in Europe, he requires the religious to "do more than merely conform to the constitutional order in a superficial way. They must appropriate the secular legitimation of constitutional principles under the premises of their own faith." He allows that "it is the religious communities themselves that will decide whether they can recognize their 'true faith' in a reformed faith."[18] But in that essay, his approach seems very much to suggest what Muslims must do before he considers their actual views—he quotes not a single Muslim and shows little interest in Islamic thought beyond references to "fundamentalism." Rawls showed a similar willingness to admit Muslims on liberal terms but very little interest in engaging actual adherents of the religion.

For many of the devout, this is not religious neutrality but hostility to religion. They are welcomed as long as they understand and present their religion in a way that the fairly uncurious, liberally minded will accept. To the religious, secularism can present itself as an intellectual sleight of hand in which universal and divine truths are transformed into particularistic and private opinions and thus disqualified from public deliberation.

Religious arguments often involve faith but they also can partake of rational and public-spirited elements. Indeed, much religious discourse is highly rational in that it deploys critical, logical, and even syllogistic reasoning and analysis in the pursuit of right answers. Most of the Islamic legal tradition is highly rational in that sense. Further, in the hands of many participants, public arguments about Islam and Islamic law also have increasingly incorporated the use of *maslaha* (originally a far more technical term but increasingly used to mean public interest far more generally).[19]

But we should not quickly rush to embrace religious rationality as evidence of the creation of a democratic or liberal public sphere: when it operates in this manner, the Islamic tradition not only brings religious justifications into the public realm (which many writings on public reason would lead us to regard warily indeed); it also can have the paradoxical effect of restricting respectable speech to individuals with a highly specialized training in religious texts and discourse. Allowing some forms of public deliberation over religion can be just as snobbish as liberal deliberation.

Thus, the point is not that religious arguments are democratic or liberal; they often are not. The point is simply that they are made in public and can have a deeply public spirit, that they can be highly rational even as they are faith-based, and that in any empirical inquiry into religion and politics, we therefore need to prepare ourselves for the reality that religion will force us to think about publicity in some unfamiliar ways.

Indeed, even though the Islamic religious tradition can lend itself to rational and public-interested deliberation, it still is emphatically not secular. Much intellectual effort in that tradition has focused on understanding divine instructions for social conduct. There is a limit to how much liberals will be convinced by such reasoning. Andrew March, even while presenting one of the friendliest frameworks for considering religious arguments in public reason, acknowledges that "where one does need to accept particular revelatory claims, or the authority of certain clerical figures . . . the religious arguments are far less compelling, troubling, and enduring."[20] As we shall see in chapter 5, much public argumentation concerning Islam does focus on the Islamic shari'a, encouraging a kind of religious discourse that emphasizes interpretation of revealed texts. And while few Sunni Muslims would explicitly claim that specific figures have unquestioned authority, the nature of this discourse can easily privilege specific individuals and institutions because of their training and prestige (and among many Shi'a, clerics have even stronger claims to authority). Of course, much current shari'a-based discourse has wandered quite far from more established forms of textual exegesis, but at its core, public argumentation about Islam is predicated on the principle that texts and revelation can be reasonably invoked as justifications. That will always likely violate liberal principles, but it does not make the arguments less than public.

We now have some idea of what we mean by talking and doing things in public and how discussions of Islam in public might not be what liberals are used to but still need to be taken seriously as public arguments.

WHY ARGUING? PUBLIC SPHERES, DELIBERATION, AND CONTENTIOUS REALITIES

But why does it matter whether or not something is public? Does the fact that words are uttered or actions are taken in public change their impact or meaning? Our discussion thus far has been of deliberation, but in this book I prefer to speak of arguing. Why?

In this section we will see that when people talk or act, it does indeed matter whether or not they are doing so in public. People talk and act differently in public and their words and deeds have different effects when they are audible or visible to all. But those differences do not necessarily make things more equal, public spirited, or rational. Real public spheres can be less refined than many hope. Thus we now move to incorporate ways of talking (and to a lesser extent acting) into our analysis, seeking to disentangle still further the close association that has grown up between public spheres and deliberation. In the process, I will make clear why I speak of "arguing" rather than "deliberation," as is far more common.

When arguments take place in public, there must be a specific medium or technology of communication (web posting, leaflet, audible discussion) and a space, real, virtual, or metaphoric (public meeting, cyberspace, newspaper) where the argument is accessible. As discussed above, Habermas's use of the term "public sphere" is simultaneously abstract and historically and institutionally concrete. We will use it in this study in the latter, far more concrete sense. But there are two factors that complicate these fairly straightforward concepts.

First, as noted above, there are different publics. Or, rather, different spheres have varying degrees of accessibility and rules of access that make publics manifest and operate in different ways. For instance, only a few can contribute content to newspapers; only the literate can read them. But they are also a place that permits sustained argumentation. Public squares are far more accessible but also places where the broad public can generally participate only through listening to speeches, personal conversations, or slogans. The variation among publics can be partly hidden because of some of the tremendous hopes placed in the public sphere, as we shall see in a moment. And there is also recognition that some forms of public argumentation might overwhelm deliberative mechanisms.[21]

Second, even though we need to keep in mind the variation in technologies, spaces, and publics, we need also to be very aware that various spheres can be linked (as we will explore in far more detail throughout this book). To take the example of newspapers, when a newspaper is read in a public gathering, it can serve as the basis for a discussion in which the illiterate can participate; when journalists follow leads provided by web-based discussions, they are amplifying even as they are transforming the discussion.

Agnosticism about Publicity

Publicity, it is hoped, will not only make things different; it will make both discussions and decisions better.[22] But in this section, we will see that while some have argued that the public nature of discourse will encourage speakers to be more rational and persuasive, "deliberative," in their speech, this hope has a shaky foundation. The ideal of the public sphere as an arena in which interlocutors attempt to transcend personal interest for the sake of cooperation and the public good does not reflect the reality of the public sphere as we know it.

Nobody is naïve about publicity or sees it as a panacea. But there is a strong strain of writing on the public sphere that sees public discussions as a place not simply for argumentation, bargaining, and counting heads but also for deliberation among autonomous and rational individuals who are self-consciously operating in the context of a political community.

This is why there has been such great interest in deliberation—defined different ways, but usually referring precisely to such discussions that are based on rationality and public reason. We began our exploration of deliberation above. Here we will continue by probing its link with publicity.

Of course, not all images of public discussions—even those earning the privileged description of "deliberations"—are pristinely restrictive. Adam Przeworski defines deliberation a bit modestly as "a form of discussion intended to change the preferences on the bases of which people decide how to act."[23] More recently, a group of scholars has allowed some limited use of self-interest in deliberative discussions, reserving their stringency for the insistence that deliberation requires that coercion be completely absent.[24] Cass Sunstein recognizes that deliberation must be carefully structured to avoid polarized politics. He also relaxes requirements for agreement on fundamental principles, allowing "incompletely theorized agreements"— in which "people agree on practices, or outcomes, despite disagreement or uncertainty about fundamental issues"—a "central role in constitution-making."[25] Habermas, whose early work emphasized "critical rational discourse" and demonstrated a consequent discomfort with mass politics, is far less insistent that his later "discourse ethics" be so pure. Martin Shapiro begins his examination of the "giving reasons requirement"—the demand that public officials be able to adduce reasons to explain their actions—by noting that it is essential to the distinction between power and authority.[26] But he then describes an extremely wide range of ways that courts have approached the requirement. The (perhaps unintended) effect is to show that "reason giving" can be less determinative of politics than it initially appears. So deliberation is increasingly defined in broader ways that increasingly bow to reality.

I would like to push the encounter with reality a bit further—and it is this encounter that will lead me to prefer "arguing" to "deliberation"—to refer to public discussions.

Interest in political deliberation centers on its role in authoritative decision-making. And when it comes time for making a decision, publicity—and the deliberation that it enables and even encourages—is hoped to provide a measure of public spiritedness. Those who follow Przeworski's definition of deliberation sometimes counterpoise it to bargaining (in which preferences remain unchanged by persuasion but participants hammer out a compromise) and aggregation (in which preferences also remain unchanged but decisions are taken by simply adding those preferences, as in voting).[27]

The most clearly democratic institution in which the term "deliberation" is regularly used outside of scholarly circles may be in the American jury system: a group of citizens is chosen to hear the evidence in a legal case in which none of them has a personal interest; they then hear the evidence presented to them, discussing among themselves. With no personal stake, there is no room for horse-trading (at least based on personal interest); while they vote, they need unanimity (or something approaching it) in a manner that encourages consensual decision-making rather than majoritarianism.

When many talk of the public sphere, their image of politics is one that might resemble a jury room. When forced to make arguments in public, it is hoped, leaders will come under the pressure of what Jon Elster and others have called "the civilizing force of hypocrisy"; that is, "when discussing under public scrutiny, actors may be forced or induced to pull their punches and refrain from the most blatant expressions of self-interest."[28]

It should therefore make us pause when we note that juries carry out their deliberations in private.

And indeed, when we encounter the work of empirical research on deliberation we find a world far more complicated by the effects of publicity.[29] We find discussions that become more difficult to resolve when they become public; voices acceptable in restricted settings forcibly silenced (or intimidated by public disapproval) when they are heard by the many; complicated arguments reduced to bumper-sticker slogans that are trotted out by participants who primarily listen to themselves; positions growing farther apart through the course of discussion; and prejudices being clothed in apparently reasonable garb. We find that some public discussions are unidirectional (words flow only from speaker to audience); others are limited to official actors, even in apparently liberal and democratic settings.[30] And we also find that much of the research on deliberation focuses on small group discussions, even when it is motivated by a desire to harness the hoped-for virtues of face-to-face interaction to public policy decision-making.[31]

The point is not that publicity is the enemy of public interest, rationality, and deliberation. It is only that these apparently good things are far less tightly linked than many want to believe. Those who speak of the "civilizing force of hypocrisy" may be getting their hopes up far too high. The problem is partly on the "civilizing" side—publicity advocates underestimate political leaders' shamelessness. Leaders do occasionally paint themselves into corners, but they also often escape by explaining that the seemingly principled position they took on yesterday's issue does not apply to today's question. Nor is it clear that "civilizing" private interest in public garb offers very much—a threat that purports to appeal to the public interest may differ little from one that is uncloaked by any higher appeal. A political leader who explains to her interlocutors something like "We share with you the goal of preventing civil conflict, but we are worried that if you do not concede, reasonable people like us may lose control over our less reasonable followers" is likely to be understood by all speakers and listeners as attempting naked intimidation.

But a deeper problem with relying on the "civilizing force of hypocrisy" is that publicity may not deliver the hypocrisy that is expected. Its advocates assume (but rarely demonstrate) that publicity privileges appeals to public reason. This claim may have grown fashionable but it is very much contrary to older prejudices about democracy. It is also dubious empirically. Political leaders speaking in public often seek to appeal to and mobilize their own constituencies far more than they work to persuade their opponents. They may sometimes seek to do so in ways that avoid alienating others, but just as often they may find that alienating others helps mobilize their own constituency. At other times they may appeal to the uncommitted by exciting prejudices and promoting divisions rather than advancing arguments cast only in terms of public reason. Many leaders may calculate that they will gain most by proving their credentials to—or energizing—their supporters.[32] In other words, publicity will often encourage leaders to preach directly to the choir of their own party, ignoring the pews of filled with other citizens.[33]

The Public in Its Own Sphere

How do we understand the public sphere if we pay more attention to the people who are really in it?

Publicity and transparency do not guarantee that actors will attempt to transcend their own private interests; in fact, the relationship between public interests and private interests is not straightforward, and members of the public may be much more interested in or motivated by private interests than public ones. Publicity is not inherently democratic, and its normative value is not always easy to discern.

In many situations, publicity and transparency actually privilege appeals to private interest. Publicity may induce those who actually do think in terms of public reason to cast their language in the terms of private interest. In Iraq, for instance, Kurdish leaders were able to justify their agreement to the country's Transitional Administrative Law in March 2004 only by explaining that it met the specific needs of Kurds. Any reference to Iraqi interests—sincere or not—would have only undermined their case among their own constituency. Indeed, Kurdish leaders were far more willing to concede to genuine national concerns in private than they were in public. Thus, to claim that private interest must masquerade as public reason offers us less than has been claimed.

The confusion between the two may have deeper roots than hypocrisy. Not only might we encounter private interest masquerading as public reason, but we might also meet public reason masquerading as private interest. And sincerity itself may go unrecognized in a cynical political world.

Opening up the doors to the public is not even necessarily democratizing. It is true that some public spheres confront authoritarian regimes with difficulties and offer mobilizing channels to oppositions—a phenomenon that, when it has occurred, has provoked some deep enthusiasm for newer information technologies.[34] But the relationship between democracy and publicity is far from simple. Fundamental to the interest in deliberation is the idea that reasonable arguments are distributed far more equally than the power and resources that one brings to the table for bargaining. As noted above, the critics of deliberative democracy doubt this: they worry that those who are more powerful will be better able than the weak to present their arguments as reasonable or disguise their interests as disinterested arguments. As Tali Mendelburg has observed, "Not everyone is taken with deliberative prescriptions to the ills of democracy. The more one fears that discussion enhances

democracy & publicity

the influence of the powerful at the expense of the disadvantaged, the more inclined one is to turn a skeptical eye on deliberative solutions."[35]

Indeed, those who insist that nobody can bring private interests to the table may only be deepening existing inequalities by rendering unspeakable the way that differentials of power are woven into a deliberative context. Critics of deliberative democracy do not argue against deliberation itself, but they do worry that the emphasis on deliberation can at best ignore the value of inclusiveness and at worst encourage exclusion. As Iris Marion Young has written, "A deliberative forum can abide by the principles of reciprocity, publicity, and accountability without being inclusive. Indeed, it might be easier for a homogenous body of gentlemen to abide by them than for a public differentiated by, for example, class or gender."[36]

None of these sobering observations should come as any surprise. Writings on public discussions that date back to ancient Athens include suggestions that involving more people debases argumentation; that rhetoric (the art of persuasion) is a different field of study than logic; that such an art can be learned and therefore is likely to bias decision-making toward the wealthier and better educated and in any case can easily be deployed for private ends. Those insights have never been completely lost—and indeed, they have led to a renewed interest in rhetoric by both skeptics and those seeking both to rescue interest in deliberative democracy.[37] And there is a long-standing suspicion of perceived antidemocratic efforts to make politics rarified and accessible only to the elite even within the context of formally democratic institutions, as Sheldon Wolin describes:

> It is no exaggeration to say that one of the, if not the, main projects of ancient constitutional theorists, such as Plato (The Laws), Aristotle, Polybius, and Cicero, as well as of modern constitutionalists, such as the authors of The Federalist and Tocqueville, was to dampen, frustrate, sublimate, and defeat the demotic passions. The main devices were: the rule of law and especially the idea of a sacrosanct "fundamental law" or constitution safeguarded from the "gusts of popular passions"; the idea of checks and balances; separation of powers with its attempt to quarantine the "people" by confining its direct representation to one branch of the legislature; the "refining" process of indirect elections; and suffrage restrictions. The aim was not simply to check democracy but to discourage it by making it difficult for those who, historically, had almost no leisure time for politics, to achieve political goals.[38]

Seen this way, the insistence on the primacy of deliberation can become just a new way to speak in the public's name without allowing many people to argue.

My aim is neither to rescue deliberative democracy nor to bury it but only to clarify why I am so insistently agnostic on the normative value of publicity. When I refer to "discussing" or "arguing"—terms that I will use roughly interchangeably, though I am mindful of the more contentious connotations of the latter and therefore employ it more often—I make no assumption that they are pale reflections of, or way stations to, deliberation; that they are rational; that they are more likely to occur in public or in private; or that they clearly distinguish between private and public interest, much less favor one or the other. And indeed, most of the time Islam is argued in the Arab world, discussion combines elements of the rational and emotional and of public and private interest. To say that arguing is occurring says nothing about who is talking and who is listening, nor does it require that all participants are equal.

But while remaining agnostic on norms and causality, I will seek to draw on some of the conceptual distinctions that have emerged from scholarly writings on the public sphere and deliberative democracy. When arguments occur in public settings, it matters how they are made; it also matters whether they are linked to decisions and how those decisions are made. For instance, Michaelle Browers has explored how political discussions among various ideological camps developed in the recent past (focusing largely though not exclusively on Egypt).[39] The dialogues were inclusive but were not connected to policy decisions. Discussions took place in newspapers, conferences, and workshops; Browers also shows how camps discussed issues through personal networks that developed over the years of dialogue. Difficult issues were discussed in settings that seemed to encourage deliberation. But they did not result in agreements, perhaps because they were unconnected to any mechanisms for decisions and not all differences could be bridged in a short time. The failure to overcome disagreements over issues involving gender and non-Muslims ultimately meant that when protest movements rose to public prominence, the participants could at most only bargain with each other to hammer out a thin opposition consensus. That consensus, of course, came apart quite quickly in Egypt. Limited deliberation may take place in the quiet of a workshop, but it is hardly likely to be helpful in the middle of street protests and the pressure of elections (as happened in Egypt in 2011 and 2012).

IN SEARCH OF LOST HABERMAS

Thus far, we have developed a general skepticism about appeals to speak for a single public interest in a rational-critical way. But there are aspects of Habermas's original analysis—and of the normative inquiries that have followed—that are still very helpful in understanding what happens in public. Our skepticism is justified, but it is not always shared by members of the public. We need to take the normative issues seriously because many of those who argue in public do so. In this section we will explore ways in which the normative concerns that motivate so much interest and activity can still help our analysis.

Returning or Imagining a "the" Back into the Public Sphere

Let us begin our recovery of parts of Habermas's original (and partially discarded) analysis by turning back to Mah's observation that what historians and empirical researchers have lost is the conception of the public sphere as a unitary thing. In Habermas's original formulation, the arguments taking place were not the sphere itself but made it possible, through critical and rational discourse, for a public sphere to be created and for its notion of the good to be identified. The public created itself and identified its interests and values through critical rational discussion.

When we discard this idealized notion of a single public, we lose (or discard) the word "the" in the phrase "the public sphere." I do not seek to return the "the" fully. But I do not think we can understand politics as public argument (and certainly not the politics of religion) unless we understand that the "the" looms very large for many of those arguing. Even as we discard it as analysts, those who argue can cling to it.

Our loss of the "the" is no accident—it is increasingly difficult to think of a single good that unites a society, and those common goods that are posited seem to be imposed by a part of a society pursuing its own particular conception on the entire whole. Habermas recognized that this could happen, but he deplored it; indeed, he saw the bourgeois public sphere as bourgeois but still public in a loftier sense; the tragedy was when private interests—generally the short-term material and even consumerist interests of various groups—invaded the public sphere and made it their own, perhaps tearing it apart in the process. What others have celebrated—the birth of a more pluralist conception of the public—Habermas in his earliest incarnation mourned.

And the ideal public sphere was not merely unitary and public spirited; it could be powerful. It was an entity that imposed itself on authority; the more corrupted and confusing public sphere by contrast is manipulated by private interests and is therefore not so much cause as it is effect.[40] Habermas himself was not systematic in his inquiry about how "the" public sphere could lead public opinion to impose itself, but he was very much alert to the ways in which specific structures (such as parliaments) might play a role (observing, for instance, how parliaments had been transformed from (in my words, not his) a structure that might serve such common purposes to one in which the public was reduced to a collection of material interests. Those interests were to be placated by politics preventing a publicity that ennobled politics.

I wish to be less judgmental. Thus in this book, we follow more recent usage and depart from Habermas while still drawing on his vocabulary. When we use "sphere" here we are referring to something that can exist in the plural, blends public and private, and may be ineffectual.

But current as we are with our usage, we still wish to draw on the older ideas in order to cultivate an alertness to the sensation that more than a plurality of private interests is involved; that there may be publics that sense themselves as "the" public; and that such a sensation might have very real political effects and indeed affect political outcomes. When I assure my listeners (perhaps with perfect sincerity) that I speak for "we" and "we" means the public, I not only cultivate that sense of "we" but endow it with loftiness, a sense of justice, and—perhaps just as important—inevitability. Religion may be especially likely terrain for a public to see itself as "the" public.

In short, many of those who argue in public see themselves as representing "the" public and if we move too quickly past that subjective sensation we may miss the moral force, mobilizing potential, and empowering aspects of the claim. And in reborn Arab politics (though hardly only there) such appeals based on a perception that "workers," "Muslims," "citizens," revolutionaries," or simply "the people," possess a unified will and voice can be powerful rhetorically—and perhaps (we hope to find out) politically as well.

But I do not assume such power will translate easily into policy. Indeed, I remain skeptical that we will find "the" Arab public sphere. We will find the power of the image of one—of a unitary "people" that each particular public claims to speak for. This book will vindicate our skepticism. Moreover, attention to specific mechanisms of translating public arguments into a single public policy—a major focus of the second half of this book—will uncover some of the critical features (and shortcomings) of Arab governance today. We will show not simply that many publics see themselves as "the" public but that public policy is actually rarely made by what is argued in public spheres precisely because of the weakness of institutional mechanisms designed to translate public discussions into outcomes.

Specialists, Religion, and the Public Sphere

And it is this identity between what we might otherwise see as a particular vision and the will of "the" public that makes religion a particularly fertile field for political argumentation. This leads us to another way that the normative concerns motivating the interest in public deliberation may have some empirical grounding through arguments among specialists. While specialist discourses operate very differently from discussions in the public sphere, because they are less accessible and operate by different assumptions and goals, these may resemble more closely what Habermas originally described as the public sphere. Religious discourse in particular may help close the gap between specialist discourses and real public spheres.

We might conceive of argument among specialists as somewhat different from public argumentation, though there can be considerable overlap. The latter requires some form of access for all who care to listen. Specialists, by contrast, may speak to each other in forums that are actually barred to the public (seminar rooms, private correspondence) or effectively inaccessible (through use of esoteric phrases, an uncommonly used language, or rarefied forms of communication). Public discussion allows and may (as we have just said) encourage efforts to cast arguments in terms of the interests, visions, or values of "the" public; specialists speaking to colleagues are virtually required to make some claim to be thinking in terms other than mechanical advocacy for their own personal or group interest.

It is precisely in this way that some religious traditions—and most certainly those associated with Islamic law—have engendered an extremely rich set of specialist discourses. In that way religion in general, and Islamic legal discourse specifically, can oddly take on some features of Habermas's original conception of "the" public sphere. Just as Habermas's bourgeois public sphere was elitist but still able to cast itself as devoted to the pursuit of the public good through critical-rational analysis, so religious specialists generally conceive of their training not as privileging their own interests but instead as enhancing their ability—and obligation—to serve far greater truths.

Such religious discourse also makes possible a bridge between specialist and public argumentation. Without getting too far ahead of ourselves, the boundary between the specialist and the fully public spheres may be eroding. A fatwa, for instance, may classically be a way for specialists to communicate not only with individual followers but also with each other; we will see how, in recent years, it has become a tool for those claiming expertise to reach out to mass publics.

A Look Forward: What We Need to Learn More About

There is much that we know about publicity and arguing that seems obvious when stated but has sometimes remained obscure because of normative explorations about what publicity could and should bring and about how arguments should be made. On publicity, we know that there is no single, uncontested public but multiple, shifting, overlapping, and conflicting publics; we know that "public" is not the opposite of "private;" even if the two are sometimes distinct, they are also frequently intertwined; we know that power and hierarchy are very much operative in the public sphere; and we know that doing things in public has many, sometimes contradictory effects. On arguing, we know that not all political discourse is rational and that the attempt to privilege certain forms of argumentation can be exclusionary even if it sometimes facilitates certain kinds of decision-making; we know that private concerns and emotional sentiments and passions are very much part of arguing (even when argument takes place in public). And we know that arguing religion in public will cross many of these boundaries that lie in the back of our minds when we approach the question solely from a normative perspective.

— 3 questions —

Thus, much of what we know will provide us with good questions—about the relationship among publicity, power, modes of argumentation, and policy outcomes—but fewer answers than we might have expected from the voluminous writings on subjects like the public sphere and deliberation.

And beyond those good questions arising from past writings, there are also three generally overlooked questions—ones that have not been posed enough but that will emerge as important in our inquiry.

First, we are now alert to the various ways that various public spheres might operate individually in reality—but what happens when they interpenetrate, intersect, or overlap? Such possibilities have provoked surprisingly little analysis[41]—but they have drawn attention, particularly in the Arab world. Indeed, from the beginning of the Arab uprisings of 2011, observers were immediately struck by the mutual dependence of various public spheres. Charles Hirschkind notes:

> This new relation between bloggers and other media forms has now become standard: not only do many of the opposition newspapers rely on bloggers for their stories; news stories that journalists can't print themselves without facing state persecution—for example, on issues relating to the question of Mubarak's successor—such stories are first fed to bloggers by investigative reporters; once they are reported online, journalists then proceed to publish the stories in newsprint, citing the blogs as sources, in this way avoiding the accusation that they themselves invented the story. Moreover, many young people have taken up the practice of using cellphone cameras in the street, and bloggers are constantly receiving phone film-footage from anonymous sources that they then put on their blogs.
>
> This event played a key role in shaping the place that the blogosphere would come to occupy within Egypt's media sphere. Namely, bloggers understand their role as that of providing a direct link to what they call "the street," conceived primarily as a space of state repression and political violence, but also as one of political action and popular resistance. They render visible and publicly speakable a political practice—the violent subjugation of the Egyptian people by its authoritarian regime—that other media outlets cannot easily disclose, due to censorship, practices of harassment, and arrest.[42]

Hirschkind's account is not only useful in showing how the spheres and the technologies and media prevalent at that time intersect but also how they bring events and arguments that may have previously been considered private to full public attention (further undermining the divide) and that the interpenetration is not merely an emerging trend but a conscious strategy on the part of those who wish to make their voices heard. In this book, I hope to begin to explore the implications of the increasing interpenetration of various public spheres—the way a salafi preacher's talk to his followers can, at one time, be posted by those who wish to ridicule him, circulated by his supporters by tweet, and set off a parliamentary discussion.

Second, we clearly need to ask how publicity and the nature of argumentation operate differently in the absence of a fully democratic setting. There have been some very promising initial empirical forays into understanding the nature of deliberation with strong normative implications for democratic theory.[43] In more complicated settings, there have been studies of the public sphere in the European Union (which combines democratic national governments with a far less participatory European public sphere and a structure of governance at the EU level which allows little role for representative structures).[44] In the Arab world, Marc Lynch has probed how the public sphere operated in a semiauthoritarian setting in Jordan and in a transnational manner after the advent of Arab satellite broadcasting.[45] Mark Beissinger has argued that a public sphere emerged in the latter days of the Soviet Union in language that shows parallels to what I refer to as the "revival" of Arab politics; he argues that this development had real effects on political outcomes.[46] But these remain fairly lonely attempts, and indeed, some of those interested in deliberation and the public sphere fall a bit too easily into an assumption that leaders must give reasons and are held accountable in democratic systems but not in nondemocratic ones where, by implication, the public sphere is irrelevant, nonexistent, or inconsequential. Of course, anyone who has lived under many of the various kinds of nondemocratic systems would be able to cite forms of public argumentation about politics; the kinds of semiauthoritarian systems that have emerged in the Arab world over the past several decades are ones which seem to be particularly hospitable to some forms of public argumentation (though cruelly and crudely inhospitable to others).[47] The influence of public arguments may be a bit more difficult to trace under such conditions, but when we probe debates over laws, curricula, and constitutions, for example, we will be focusing on political struggles that do have clear and identifiable outcomes.

Third, the two overlooked areas we have discussed briefly thus far (the linkages among the spheres and their operation in a non-democratic setting) suggest a third area that is far more worthy of our attention: how public arguments affect political outcomes in such countries. In fully democratic settings, there has been some interest in the effects of public argumentation and deliberation on policy and on specific structures and mechanisms by which such arguments become influential and shape legislation or policy. There is almost no attention to such mechanisms for nondemocratic settings. The few who have looked (such as Browers, as mentioned above) have found significant problems—even lively discussions that do not come to a conclusion that can bear much political weight, much less affect policy outcomes. Indeed, the most helpful view might be suggested by the title of Vickie Langohr's article, "Too Much Civil Society, Too Little Politics: Egypt and Liberalizing Arab Regimes,"[48] which we will come back to when we consider the specific forms of argumentation and the forums in which they occur in the Arab world, beginning in the next chapter.

One effect of the Arab uprisings of 2011, and the dramatic changes they wrought, was to divert attention from the regular mechanisms of governance to crowds, social movements, street protests, and massive expressions of public outrage and passion—phenomena that are of interest, to be sure, but should not completely edge out more formalized and institutionalized structures for pursuing change. We will turn to these issues far more fully in part 3 of this book.

NOTES

1. See, for instance, Jennifer Widner, Princeton University, "Constitution Writing & Conflict Resolution: Data & Summaries," first posted August 2005 and accessed at http://www.princeton.edu/~pcwcr on March 18, 2015. I met one very influential constitution drafter in Egypt (Justice Hatem Bagato, a member of the country's constitutional court and briefly a minister as well as an informal advisor to the country's post-2011 constitutional process) who used this project.

    Two other leading projects have been overseen by the United States Institute of Peace, http://www.usip.org/programs/initiatives/constitution-making-peacebuilding-and-national-reconciliation, accessed March 17, 2015; and the International Institute for Democracy and Electoral Assistance (IDEA) program Constitution Building Process, http://www.idea.int/cbp, accessed March 17, 2015.

2. See Salwa Ismail, "Islamism, Re-Islamization and Fashioning of Muslim Selves: Refiguring the Public Sphere," *Muslim World Journal of Human Rights* 4, 1 (2007): 1–21.

3. Jürgen Habermas, *The Structural Transformation of the Public Sphere: An Inquiry into a Category of Bourgeois Society* (Cambridge: MIT Press, 1989).

4. In this chapter, for drawing on this literature I turn primarily to the debate prompted by Amy Gutmann and Dennis Thompson, *Why Deliberative Democracy?* (Princeton: Princeton University Press, 2004). Most of the scholarship is primarily normative. However it should be noted that in recent years there have been some attempts to advance the normative debate by integrating empirical work in order to come to deeper understandings of how democratic deliberation could and should operate. See for instance John Parkinson and Jane Mansbridge, *Deliberative Systems* (Cambridge: Cambridge University Press, 2012).

5. For an example—actually only a small sample—of such work, see many of the contributions to Craig Calhoun, ed., *Habermas and the Public Sphere* (Cambridge: MIT Press, 1999).

    In the decades since Habermas introduced the idea of a distinct public sphere, all sorts of modifications have been introduced, some by Habermas himself. Rising interest in new media has given a powerful boost (often tinged with ambivalence) to inquiry into the possibilities of public deliberation. See, for instance, Judith Bessant, "The Political in the Age of the Digital: Propositions for Empirical Investigation," *Politics* 34 (2012): 33–44.

6. He does this most thoroughly in his *Between Facts and Norms: Contributions to a Discourse Theory of Law and Democracy* (Cambridge: Cambridge University Press, 1996).

7. Gutmann and Thompson, *Why Deliberative Democracy?* 3–4.

8. See, for instance, Jane Mansbridge et al., "The Place of Self-Interest and the Role of Power in Deliberative Democracy," *Journal of Political Philosophy* 18, 1 (2010): 64–100. For a systematic comparison of these approaches to others that tackle questions of the relationship among participation, public discussion, and decision-making, see Myra Marx Ferree, William A. Gamson, Jürgen Gerhards, and Dieter Rucht, "Four Models of the Public Sphere in Modern Democracies," *Theory and Society* 31 (2002): 289–324.

9. To be fair, some scholars have adopted creative approaches that try to combine expertise, deliberation, and mass democracy in ways that allow them to be mutually supporting. For some examples, see Josiah Ober, "Democracy's Wisdom: An Aristotelian Middle Way for Our Collective Judgment," *American Political Science Review* 107, 1 (2013): 104–122.

10. Joshua Gamson, "Taking the Talk Show Challenge: Television, Emotion, and Public Spheres," *Constellations* 6, 2 (1999): 202.

    For an extremely accessible presentation of various arguments along this line—of the inclusive effects of allowing spectacle, emotional, and seemingly trivializing modes of expression—see Alan McKee, *The Public Sphere: An Introduction* (Cambridge: Cambridge University Press, 2005).

11. Harold Mah, "Phantasies of the Public Sphere: Rethinking the Habermas of Historians," *Journal of Modern History* 72, 1 (2000): 181.

12. Mah, "Phantasies of the Public Sphere," 155.

13. Ian Shapiro, "Enough of Deliberation: Politics Is about Interests and Power," in *Deliberative Politics: Essays on Democracy and Disagreement*, ed. Stephen Macedo (New York: Oxford University Press, 1999), 29.

14. The difficulties facing political scientists interested in religion from a disciplinary perspective are difficulties not only for political theorists. For some thoughtful reflections and suggestions, see the conclusion to Ran E. Hassner's *War on Sacred Grounds* (Ithaca: Cornell University Press, 2009), 153–180.

15. For a comparison and critique of some of the most influential writings in this regard, see Roberto Frega, "Equal Accessibility to All: Habermas, Pragmatism, and the Place of Religious Beliefs in a Post-Secular Society," *Constellations* 19, 2 (2012): 267–287.

16. See, for instance, José Casanova, *Public Religions in the Modern World* (Chicago: University of Chicago Press, 1994); Mark Juergensmeyer, *Global Rebellion: Religious Challenges to the Secular State, From Christian Militias to Al Qaeda* (Berkeley: University of California Press, 2008); Craig Calhoun, Mark Juergensmeyer, and Jonathan Van Antwerpen, eds., *Rethinking Secularism* (Oxford: Oxford University Press, 2011); and Jack Snyder, ed., *Religion and International Relations Theory* (New York: Columbia University Press, 2011). Talal Asad's work has been particularly influential in several social sciences. See, for instance, *Formations of the Secular: Christianity, Islam, Modernity* (Palo Alto: Stanford University Press, 2003).

17. Gutmann and Thompson, *Why Deliberative Democracy?* 4.

18. Jürgen Habermas, *Europe: The Faltering* Project (Cambridge: Polity Books, 2009), 75.
19. See Felicitas Opwis, "Maṣlaḥa in Contemporary Islamic Legal Theory," *Islamic Law and Society* 12, 2 (2005): 182–223. A full consideration of the idea can be found in her book, *Maṣlaḥah and the Purpose of the Law: Islamic Discourse on Legal Change from the 4th/10th to 8th/14th Century* (Leiden: Brill, 2010).
20. Andrew F. March, "Rethinking Religious Reasons in Public Justification," *American Political Science Review* 107, 3 (August 2013): 529.
21. See Ethan Zuckerman, "New Media, New Civics," *Policy and Internet* 6 (2014): 151–168 (along with the responses from a variety of scholars).
22. Portions of this section are based on (and the ideas fully elaborated in) my article, "Reason, Interest, Rationality, and Passion in Constitution Drafting," *Perspectives on Politics* 6, 4 (2008): 675–689.
23. Adam Przeworksi, "Deliberation and Ideological Domination," in *Deliberative Democracy*, ed. Jon Elster (Cambridge: Cambridge University Press, 1998), 140.
24. Mansbridge et al., "The Place of Self-Interest and the Role of Power in Deliberative Democracy," 64–100.
25. Cass R. Sunstein, *Designing Democracy: What Constitutions Do* (New York: Oxford University Press, 2001), 9.
26. Martin Shapiro, "The Giving Reasons Requirement," *University of Chicago Legal Forum* 1 (1992): 179–220.
27. See Elster's discussion of "arguing" in his introduction to Elster, *Deliberative Democracy*.
28. Jon Elster, Claus Offe, and Ulrich K. Preuss, *Institutional Design in Post-Communist Societies: Rebuilding the Ship at Sea* (Cambridge: Cambridge University Press, 1998), 78.
29. There is now a substantial body of work on this subject, which I will make no attempt to summarize. For an extremely useful review, see C. Daniel Myers and Tali Mendelberg, "Political Deliberation" in *Oxford Handbook of Political Psychology*, eds. Leonie Huddy, David Sears, and Jack Levy (Oxford: Oxford University Press, 2012).
30. Jurg Steiner, Andre Bachtiger, Markus Sporndli, and Marco R. Steenberge, *Deliberative Politics in Action: Analysing Parliamentary Discourse* (Cambridge: Cambridge University Press, 2004). The authors seek to discover whether there is a European public sphere that has arisen around public matters involving the European Union. They find that there is indeed public discussion about EU policies, but it is dominated by governments. So official actors make themselves heard; those outside of government (political parties, social movements) are much less successful in meaningful participation.
31. Tali Mendelburg, "The Deliberative Citizen: Theory and Evidence," *Political Decision Making, Deliberation and Participation* 6 (2002): 151–193.
32. Adrienne LeBas, "Polarization as Craft: Party Formation and State Violence in Zimbabwe," *Comparative Politics* 38, 4 (2006): 419–438.
33. David Stasavage, "Polarization and Publicity: Rethinking the Benefits of Deliberative Democracy," *Journal of Politics* 69, 1 (2007): 59–72.
34. Philip N. Howard, *The Digital Origins of Dictatorship and Democracy: Information Technology and Political Islam* (Oxford: Oxford University Press, 2010).
35. Mendelburg, "The Deliberative Citizen," 152.
36. Iris Marion Young, "Justice, Inclusion, and Deliberative Democracy," in Macedo, *Deliberative Politics*, 155.

37. Bryan Garsten, "The Rhetoric Revival in Political Theory," *Annual Review of Political Science* 14 (2011): 159–80. See also Benedetto Fontana, Cary J. Nederman, and Gary Remer, *Talking Democracy: Historical Perspectives on Rhetoric and Democracy* (University Park: Penn State Press, 2004).

38. Sheldon Wolin, "Democracy: Electoral and Athenian," *PS: Political Science and Politics* 26, 3 (1993): 477.

39. Michaelle Browers, *Political Ideology in the Arab World: Accommodation and Transformation* (Cambridge: Cambridge University Press, 2009).

40. " 'Public opinion' takes on a different meaning depending on whether it is brought into play as a critical authority in connection with the normative mandate that the exercise of political and social power be subject to publicity or as the object to be molded in connection with a staged display of, and manipulation propagation of, publicity in the service of persons and institutions, consumer goods, and programs. Both forms of publicity compete in the public sphere, but 'the' public opinion is their common addressee." Habermas, *Structural Transformation*, 236.

41. The most notable exception is the interest shown by scholars of international relations in how democracies may operate differently since their leaders not only interact with other states but also must present policy arguments to their own constituents. For a seminal article that began this discussion, see James Fearon, "Domestic Political Audiences and the Escalation of International Disputes," *American Political Science Review* 88, 3 (1994): 577–592.

42. Charles Hirschkind, "The Road to Tahrir," *The Immanent Frame* (blog), http://blogs.ssrc.org/tif/2011/02/09/the-road-to-tahrir/ (accessed August 15, 2013).

43. See, for instance, Tali Mendelberg, Christopher F. Karpowitz, and J. Baxter Oliphant, "Gender Inequality in Deliberation: Unpacking the Black Box of Interaction," *Perspectives on Politics* 12, 1 (March 2014): 1–10.

44. Steiner et al, *Deliberative Politics in Action*.

45. See his *State Interests and Public Spheres: The International Politics of Jordan's Identity* (New York: Columbia University Press, 1999) and *Voices of the New Arab Public: Iraq, Al-Jazeera, and Middle East Politics Today* (New York: Columbia University Press, 2006). I should add that my interest on the subject of this book was sparked in part by his article "Taking Arabs Seriously," *Foreign Affairs* 82, 5 (2003): 81–94.

    Another work that specifically focuses on religion and publicity in an Arab context is Daniel Corstange, "Religion, Pluralism, and Iconography in the Public Sphere: Theory and Evidence from Lebanon," *World Politics* 64 (2012): 116–160.

46. Mark R. Beissinger, "How the Impossible Becomes Inevitable: The Public Sphere and the Collapse of Soviet Communism," Transformations of the Public Sphere, Social Science Research Council and Institute for Public Knowledge, http://publicsphere.ssrc.org/beissinger-the-public-sphere-and-the-collapse-of-soviet-communism (posted November 2, 2009; accessed March 19, 2015).

47. I have explored the nature of semiauthoritarianism in the Arab world more in *When Victory is Not an Option: Islamist Movements in Arab Politics* (Ithaca: Cornell University Press, 2012) and in "Dictatorship and Democracy through the Prism of Arab Elections," in *The Dynamics of Democratization: Dictatorship, Development, and Diffusion* (Baltimore: Johns Hopkins University Press, 2011), 46–63.

48. *Comparative Politics* 36, 2 (2004): 181–204.

PART 2
A Republic of Arguments

Bodies which are themselves in motion, produce noise and friction: but those which are attached or fixed to a moving body, as the parts to a ship, can no more create noise, than a ship on a river moving with the stream ... But sound is caused when a moving body is enclosed in an unmoved body ...

Aristotle, *On The Heavens*, ii.9

Do heavenly bodies make sounds—even music—as they move through the sky? Refuting those who claimed they did (and some who even suggested that extraordinary mortals could hear such music), Aristotle argued that without the friction caused by moving against something else, such bodies produce no sound.

Over the past generation, new worlds have opened up within Arab politics. And they appear to be very lively, very much in motion. In this section we will briefly explore some of them. But what is especially remarkable—if rarely noticed—is how those new worlds are increasingly affecting each other. It is when they are linked, and especially when they grind against each other, that the resulting noise is especially powerful. And as they interact in new ways, they foster new means to argue religious issues in public. This is the "republic of arguments" that we will probe in part 2 of this book.

It is precisely because of the ways in which various spaces for argument interact that Arab politics has become lively and religious debates so fraught. The linkages and clashes do not end hierarchies and authority, but they diversify them, most particularly by offering the possibility of detaching arguments from the speaker's control. When the boundaries between spaces and spheres are more permeable to arguments than to authority, politics and religion become noisier—and more interesting. Indeed, one of the most significant attributes of the linkages among the spaces is that they pry control over words from the hands of the speaker. Power and authority are not always fungible across spheres.

In part 2, I proceed in three steps.

In chapter 3, I explore the history of the various spheres. Drawing primarily on the research of others but supplementing it with my own work, I explore the various public spheres that have come to be so politically prominent in the Arab world, showing how they emerged. I also demonstrate that while they bear the heavy imprint of repressive regimes, they can no longer simply be seen as serving the functional needs of the political system; they now allow for a range of voices to be heard in public arguments about religion. And I add in two spheres that are of great public and political significance—even though they do not fully qualify as public as we are using the term—specialists' discourse and state authority.

In chapter 4, I probe the interaction among them, uncovering how the friction of these spheres sometimes produces noise that is music to some ears and a painful din to others. And I also fold in consideration of the two less-than-fully public spaces (specialist discourse and state administration) for political arguments about religion that interact with more public spaces discussed in the previous chapter.

Finally, in chapter 5, I integrate Islam into the analysis. I begin by focusing on the meaning of the term "the Islamic shari'a," showing how it lends itself to public argumentation. I then probe who participates in public debates about the Islamic shari'a, revealing increasing cacophony. Finally, I explore how the Islamic shari'a arises in public debates and the ways in which those involved in arguments agree and disagree about its implications for public affairs.

CHAPTER 3

The Music (and Din) of the Spheres . . .

The Italian papers were always ecstatically happy, as if they were written not by humans but by saints in triumph just stepped down from a Fra Angelico in order to celebrate the perfect social system. . . . Someone would make a monumental speech, and the people would enthusiastically applaud, at least according to accounts in the press.

Anal Szerb, *Journey by Moonlight*, p. 179

. . . in the absence of free and fair elections, democratic persons are nevertheless produced through quotidian practices of deliberation. These acts are not embellishments of democracy independently existing. They are the thing itself.

Lisa Wedeen, *Peripheral Visions: Publics, Power,*
and Performance in Yemen, p. 3

We often understand Arab politics as simply a function of existing regimes. I wish to depart from that portrait—to some extent. I have three purposes in this chapter. The first is descriptive or ethnographic—to portray the places where religion is argued in public in the Arab world. Second, I wish to give that description historical depth, to explore how those places have evolved over recent decades. Finally, I intend to show that while states and regimes leave a heavy imprint, the degree of their control varies quite significantly over time and space. This last claim will set the stage for chapter 4 where I will show how the various spaces are linked and how that enables what I am terming the "revival" of Arab politics—in the sense of lively public argumentation—in recent years.

It often seems that what politics exists in the Arab world is that which current authoritarian rulers allow. Such an image contains considerable truth if one relies on the public record, especially in certain periods (such as the 1960s and 1970s)—and it is what is said in public that concerns us. There were sharply authoritarian periods in the recent history of Arab societies in which the public record was largely dictated by—and served the purposes of—high officials. But public space is formed not merely by public authorities but also by members of the public. It is the emergence of a republic of arguments that I wish to explore in this chapter.

SEEING A BIT LESS LIKE A STATE

As I have stressed, the term "revival of politics" contains some exaggeration. Quotidian practices of deliberation (and argument) never died out completely. And in recent decades, looser (albeit nondemocratic) political forms have witnessed far more varied and extremely public arguments.

This makes such a purely functionalist approach to public arguments—seeing them only as serving the needs of the political system—even less useful. In this chapter, I will depart from a top-down view—or rather I will show how viewing public arguments from the perspective of the rulers increasingly needs to be supplemented by understanding the actions and words of those who do not sit at the apex of the state but are still able to argue in public.

I conversed once with an Egyptian I knew who lived on al-Mughrabilin Street—a north/south street just south of oldest part of the original Fatimid city of al-Qahira (Cairo) in what is today the middle of the sprawling metropolis. I made reference to a location about a mile or so north of his house, referring to it as being farther north on the same street. He was puzzled; he knew the location but insisted that was an entirely different street. The reason for the misunderstanding was that I was "seeing like a state," almost literally; he was seeing like a resident.[1] When Egypt's Fatimid rulers laid out the city of al-Qahira as a royal and military center in the tenth century, they seem to have planned a major north-south thoroughfare—one that exists to this day under different names but most generally as al-Mu'izz bi-Din Allah Street. Rulers constructing cities have often sought to impose a grid system (a model of urban planning spread in particular but not exclusively by the Romans), and Cairo was originally to follow suit. All that remains of the Fatimid grid is that street, which is the one I was referring to.

Over the centuries, the central planning of rulers has been completely remade by the accretions of later rulers and bureaucrats, but even more by residents. There are, to be sure, now two east-west thoroughfares through the area occupied by the Fatimid city that are creations of later ambitious rulers (Muski, often said to have been begun by Napoleon as part of an effort to allow his troops and their cannon the necessary mobility to control the populace; and al-Azhar Street built decades later in order to improve transportation). The older one, Muski, now bears few signs of central planning, but the newer one, al-Azhar Street, has been renewed as a major traffic thoroughfare by state authorities through the years.

Like Interstate 95, which retains its name and number as it moves up and down the east coast of the United States, the street I saw my friend as living on seemed to me an extension of the same thoroughfare—in this case, the millennium-old Fatimid north-south axis. He regarded his street instead through the eyes of someone who lived there. (Indeed, the postal address he gave me when I promised to write to him included not only the official street number but also the name of the man who had a kiosk next to his building. Even a state-run postal service would deliver mail most reliably if the house were described from the perspective of local residents.) To walk due north a mile, even if it was in a consistent direction when seen from above, was to enter a completely different neighborhood with its own residents and networks of interaction.

When I write of the "revival of Arab politics" in this book, I am referring to the way in which public argument about public affairs has become widespread after generations in which it had seemed to come close to dying out.

Seen from above—that is, from the perspective of questions of regime type—the change I am exploring might be generally described as a shift from full authoritarianism to semiauthoritarianism. For the rulers of such systems, politics never died. But sometimes it seems that it was their voices alone that could be publicly heard. When I first went to the Arab world in the 1980s, I read newspapers that seemed like those described by interwar Hungarian novelist Antal Szerb after visiting fascist Italy in this chapter's epigraph. Official ecstasy about diplomatic achievements and economic or construction projects was exceeded only by popular boredom and resignation from all I could see.

But over the past few decades, political arguments have emerged in some older forums, such as newspapers and in some newer ones, such as rapidly developing social media. Semiauthoritarian systems are those that allow the opposition some ability to organize and compete but deny them any possibility of forming the government.[2]

Seen from below, however, what is more apparent than formal opposition politics has been the greater ability to discuss and argue about public affairs outside of those channels narrowly controlled by the political and security authorities. A republic of arguments has grown up around the tyranny of semiauthoritarian regimes. Viewing matters from the perspective of the participants in politics rather than from that of the regime makes the revival of politics appear more opportunistic and far less systematic but therefore far more vital. And it is that vitality that we now probe.

THE SPACE BETWEEN COMES ALIVE: RED LINES AND YELLOW ZONES

Governance and politics in the Arab world might be seen in similar terms to urban landscapes. Yes, there were founding, transitional, or revolutionary moments in which the powerful drew up plans and implemented them; rules were consciously designed; institutions were built or radically reconfigured; and patterns deliberately set. The nineteenth and early twentieth centuries saw such moments for state formation and regime structuring in many Arab societies. The Arab regimes then constructed were often dominated by European states. Some were headed by a monarch of some sort; almost all were ambitiously systematizing and centralizing. Such regimes allowed and even enabled some new public spheres to be built—especially newspapers; they also sometimes reconfigured the urban landscape in a manner that allowed for public gatherings.

In the middle of the twentieth century, many societies passed through another such moment in which authoritarian regimes were built or rebuilt and public spheres were closed; such regimes closely controlled all aspects of public life—newspapers and broadcast media were state owned or sharply censored, and public gatherings were restricted to those sanctioned by the regime in order to support its policies. When one departed the company of small groups of trustworthy people, discussion and argument about public affairs became very constrained. This is the period when much politics in the sense of public arguments went into hibernation.

But between moments of creation, political systems changed more by accretion, contests, tactical adjustments, and trial and error than by central or conscious design. And those outside of the regime could often find ways and spaces in which to modify prevailing arrangements with the accumulation of individual actions that pushed limits, evaded rules, and flouted procedures. The cumulative effects of such incremental steps could be considerable indeed. And it should lead us sharply away from any attempt to understand Arab politics as solely a set of rules consciously and expertly designed to serve a coherent, conscious, and provident leadership.

Nothing better illustrates the ways in which politics developed than the uses and limitations of the expression "red lines"—widely used everywhere but also very misleading in the way it suggests clear and broadly understood limits of acceptable speech and activity. When Arab politics opened up, beginning in the 1970s in some societies, and by the end of the century in all but a handful, previously rigidly enforced taboos became relaxed—sometimes slightly and sometimes more significantly. Some topics—the positions of a few high public officials, clear policy initiatives identified with the head of state, the army and security services in general, and some foreign and security policies—were often treated by regimes as beyond permissible discussion and debate. The phrase "red lines" referred to those areas where public expression should not tread.

But the "red lines" were neither "red" nor "lines." They were not "red" because consequences for violating them were hardly clear. Sometimes harsh legal measures could be taken against violators, sometimes extralegal retribution, vilification, or harassment might be used. Or nothing at all might happen—and

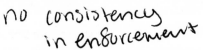
no consistency in enforcement

those who avoided sanction could only speculate if they had been noticed or not. Nor were these "lines" since they were not so much codified as discoverable through trial and error (though some transgressors I have met were informed a bit more directly through telephone calls or interrogations) and they seemed to vary from time to time, from person to person, and from subject to subject.

Of course, it could be argued that from a regime perspective, such "yellow zones" (a more accurate if unfamiliar term) might serve the function of policing dissent more effectively than clear red lines since their very unpredictability and apparent capriciousness encouraged a measure of self-policing and second guessing. But there is no reason to fall into a functionalist trap of understanding all political arrangements as serving the purpose of regime maintenance. Yellow zones likely resulted as much from the haphazardness of unaccountable authorities and the guerilla actions of those seeking to speak and act than from any act of deliberate design. And from the point of view of participants in debates, life in the yellow zones led to a period not only of self-censorship (though that occurred, to be sure) but more strikingly to a period in which opinions could be voiced and shared, voices other than official ones became audible, limits were hazy and could be prodded and probed, and attempts at argumentation and persuasion could be made in a variety of policed but still active public forums.

Thus the prevailing portrait of semiauthoritarian Arab politics—that there is greater freedom than in a fully authoritarian system but always red lines—may be helpful in the last analysis but still suggests too much clarity on both the degree of freedom and the clarity of the lines. And it is in the murky fog (or swamp) that has resulted that most people live their lives and form (and exchange) their views. Yes, there is greater freedom, but states still operate, police, own, and dominate; yes, there are officially enforced limits, but there is also considerable ambiguity in what can be said, who is setting policy, and who is responsible for particular decisions. The result is neither a war of maneuver nor one of position but instead an ongoing guerilla struggle in which (to mix a metaphor) clubs may be trump but all other suits are played.

But we are getting a bit ahead of ourselves. I have been referring to the "revival" of Arab politics and that suggests both that Arab politics was once alive; that it declined or fell into hibernation (or was murdered) at some point; and that it has now been awakened or reincarnated. Such an exaggerated picture is helpful, but only in a very general way. It is time to turn to the specific spheres in which discussion and argumentation took place and see how they evolved.

BIRTH, DEATH, AND RESURRECTION OF THE SPHERES?

We are interested primarily in the politics of Islam—how the religion is debated and discussed and how that debate and discussion affects political outcomes. In one sense, of course, Islam is hardly a stranger to the public realm. Public behavior is integral to most understandings of the religion. But many of the spheres in which Islam was formerly discussed tended to be either restricted to specialists or largely private.

There was, for instance, a very lively tradition of Islamic law, as will be explored in chapter 5. But this tradition was often understood historically as "jurists law"; to the extent that it was transmitted among regions in the Muslim world and over the generations, it was done through scholars and learned writings whose contents would have been inaccessible (both in the physical sense of not widely available and in the metaphorical sense of requiring specialized training to understand) for most believers. Indeed, some (though I am not among them) have gone so far as to identify the Islamic shariʻa almost fully with this specialist discourse, claiming that the way that states (and, sometimes, social movements) have wrested interpretive authority away from scholars or minimized it through codification, legislation, and sloganeering has led to the end of the Islamic shariʻa.[3] By contrast, I find the equation of specialist discourse with the whole of the Islamic shariʻa unhelpful. Moreover, as much at it has changed, the specialist discourse seems to me very much alive, but increasingly forced to operate in a world in which it has not only to compete with other spheres but also one in which it has become accessible to those who participate in other spheres. Specialist discourse has lost some of its insulation and all of whatever monopoly it may have possessed, not its vitality.

In the past, when non-specialists did show concern with the Islamic shariʻa, it was often in a private context. A believer who sought an interpretation of religious law from a scholar (a *mustafti* approaching a *mufti*) did so to understand his/her problem; when the answers (*fatwas*) were circulated, it was generally for the edification, comment, or education of other scholars.

To be sure, there were Muslim publics in the past; they are not a modern innovation. When they prayed communally, for instance, or gathered to celebrate a saint's birthday, the publics that assembled did so on religious terrain. For most Muslims, the meaning of prayer and the manner of its performance have always been determined, at least in part socially, one review of recent academic writing and traditional exegesis concludes about prayer that "its performance and supposed efficacy blur the rigid distinction between private and public spheres."[4] *Mulids* (saints' birthdays) have also served as a vital public sphere—one which (as many public spheres do) troubled some specialists precisely because there were so many people to be found there. Scholarly work on other ways that publics were created, expressed themselves, and were policed and licensed in the modern era is only beginning.[5]

But while these public spheres were real, argument about religion was not the central focus of most gatherings, with sermons the most significant exception. Many of those older spheres are still very much alive. But I am focusing particular attention on spheres that are not merely simply religious but are also political and argumentative. That is where politics went into—and emerged from—hibernation. I will examine three sorts of these spheres: small groups; public spaces; and media (print, broadcast, and social). For each of these spheres, I will briefly examine its history, the conditions of entry, and the modes of argumentation it allows and encourages. My focus will be primarily but not exclusively on how religion can be and has been argued in each sphere.

In general, I will show the pattern suggested in the title of this book: slow emergence of the public sphere; the ways in which authoritarian states worked to contain, monitor, and control the sphere; and the partial retreat of those trends in recent decades. But I will also show considerable variations in this general pattern. In chapter 4, I will show the same process not from the point of view of the separate spheres but from the perspective of the ties among them.

NEIGHBORHOOD AND NADWA: PRIVATE/PUBLIC SPACES

From above and from afar, the Arab world would appear to have few public places where people can safely speak their minds. And there are indeed few public places impervious to monitoring and policing. But when seen from the ground up, there are a number of spaces that might be seen as hybrid private/ public spheres where political and religious discussions can take place—where public issues can be argued in a setting that offers some of the protections of privacy; where people might not merely speak their own mind but change it (and that of their interlocutor) as well.

Residents of Arab societies have, of course, always been able to argue about religion. The public record of such arguments is extremely weak because they took place in private and through informal means.[6] Not only do we know little, but in the absence of knowledge, there is a natural temptation to see the realm of unwritten religious discussion as a historical constant, an unchanging realm impervious to public regulation.[7]

But to dismiss the public and political significance of such private arguments—because they were private or because they are assumed constant—would be a mistake because they certainly did come into contact with, inform, enact, and perhaps even subvert publicly expressed understandings. And their nature and vitality varied over time and place. Further, it would also be a mistake to miss attempts to formalize and publicize these private arguments, especially in recent years. Let us consider each of these features in turn—first, their public and political nature and second, signs of formalization.

The informal discussions and arguments I refer to take place among neighbors, friends, colleagues, and family members. Such discussions are based on

personal ties and networks. As such they do not merely reproduce local relations of power, in some sense, they constitute such relations. Any account of
neighborhood society will often highlight the role for small gathering places
(living rooms, coffeehouses, street corners, and other small public places) and
the vitality of the discussion that takes place. In Egypt, I often heard talk of
the rich social and neighborhood life of sha`bi (popular) areas, but the dense
network of socializing in cafes and other gathering places is hardly restricted
to the working class.[8] With urban locations sometimes informally segregated
by class (and sometimes formally so with the introduction of gated communities or residential quarters constructed by professional associations) and powerful (if varying) conventions on gender- and age-appropriate behavior, the
spaces for assembling in small groups are hardly egalitarian.

While the available record of discussions and arguments that take place in
such settings is scant, recent ethnographic work has richly documented specific manifestations of slightly more formal versions of such discussions. It
has also noted a trend toward conscious creation of group discussions around
religious themes—a tendency that is too diffuse to call a "movement" but
might better be described as a "piety trend."[9]

At first glance, the current piety trend would seem to represent a variety
of Islam that is simply neither political nor even "shari'a-minded," to revive
Marshall Hodgson's phrase. Participants would seem to be motivated more
by an exploration of faith and perhaps ethical conduct and much less with
the legal and political realm. Saba Mahmood, in her ethnographic account of
pietist preachers in Cairo, states that "reinstatement of the shari'a remains
marginal to the realization of the movement's goals, and few lessons address
the issue," though this is not tantamount to a "privatized notion of religion."
Instead the "movement" advocates a form of piety that brings religious obligations and rituals "to bear upon worldly issues in new ways."[10]

But while much of the pietist trend may not be oriented around an explicitly political or shari'a-based project, this is a restrictive way of conceiving of
the Islamic shari'a and the nature of the discussion. Not only does the pietist
trend entail a radical diffusion of interpretive authority—one with deep
political ramifications—but it is very much focused on correct social conduct.
And its members show signs of drawing heavily—if quite eclectically—from
shari'a-based discourses in their quest for answers to practical and ethical
questions. Indeed, a large part of the source of the "chaotic fatwa" phenomenon (explored more fully in chapter 5) that so frustrates the more tradition-
and authority-minded might be attributed to the pietist trend.

In one circle of Alexandrian women I met with, for instance, members
debated whether they were allowed to travel abroad without a male guardian.
Their research techniques would be familiar to a resourceful American under-
graduate, though their specific sources differed—they searched some popular
Islamic websites, read some sources available online, and consulted Al-Azhar

(the thousand year-old mosque that has grown into a vast complex of educational and research institutions) by telephone. In the end, the group member faced with a travel opportunity decided that it was permitted for her to travel alone so long as it was for a serious purpose, and she received the support of her colleagues. When they moved beyond personal issues to debate broader social and political questions—such as whether the Islamic shari'a prohibits women from serving as head of state or judge (a discussion occasioned by the appointment of a woman judge in Egypt as well as by Hillary Clinton's candidacy for the American presidency)—they did so in the same freewheeling spirit, one that drew on the various religious authorities available to them but treated none as definitive and reserved final judgment to the individual Muslim.

Participating in such discussions therefore has to be seen as public and political; as Salwa Ismail has argued, "the ethical formation of the individual as a public self has a bearing on the public sphere and public space."[11] Further "Muslim public self-presentation signals a change in the ideas structuring public discourse and in the practices and disciplines through which public subjectivities are formed and assumed. Specifically, these interventions shift the terms of public debate away from nationalist politics and secular conceptions of the project of modernization, proposing a redefinition of the community, its governing norms and its civilizational project."[12] And, to foreshadow slightly, the public and political significance of this sphere is heightened when it is linked to other spheres; Ismail found participants who "learnt about matters of religion and informed themselves of religious rulings, recommended conduct and so on. They sought self-discipline through extended prayers (tahajud), reading religious pamphlets, listening to sermons on audiocassettes, and some of them ventured into the classics of the tradition."[13]

The piety movement itself leads us to explore the second feature of small group discussions: attempts to formalize them in recent years. Two particular examples of this formalization are worth exploring: the *nadwa* and the *diwaniyya*.

The nadwa (perhaps best translated as colloquium or seminar) is a particularly notable trend in discussion among specialists and scholars but it is often open to the public: it may gather together academics, students, journalists, activists, and anyone else with the interest to attend. The format can vary greatly: roundtable discussion; public lecture followed by discussion and commentary; or debate. In a sense it is based in part on a formalization of discussion among specialists but also opens it to the public: nadwas are often advertised and open to all comers. There may be a featured speaker but other participants often feel free to expound their views; their comments are more likely to be labeled as "interventions" than "questions." Newspaper coverage suggests that nadwas (or similar practices such as the public lecture) are of varying ages in Arab societies; they are older in the established urban and intellectual centers and remain rare in some societies. But where they have emerged they often suggest a flourishing public intellectual life. They are also an important ground not simply for participants who share an orientation but also for cross-ideological participation.[14] Such slightly formalized discussions are perhaps the forum in which argumentation first might seem to come closest to the ideal of deliberation or rational-critical discourse: speakers are allowed to develop their arguments with some depth; they adduce reasons and interact; and those arguing work to persuade (and occasionally allow themselves to be persuaded). My own impression from participation in such discussions, however, is that while discourse is often polite, it is also rife with sloganeering, dialogues in which participants appear to be speaking more to express themselves than to persuade others, and heavy dependence on symbolic and charged language. And they can be policed. Authority, degrees, age, and status are very much factors in the discussion, but they are not dispositive.

The diwaniyya stands between the informality of a family or neighborhood discussion and a more formal, fully public gathering; it is most formalized in Kuwait (and indeed, that is where the word itself is used) but it sometimes has counterparts elsewhere (often known by different names, especially *majlis*) that are generally less formalized.[15]

In Kuwait, the practice of males gathering in diwaniyyas has become a focal point of national identity. The gatherings are often said to have begun as small group discussions among merchants or family members; as Kuwait grew wealthier, many Kuwaitis built structures adjacent to their houses in order to host such gatherings (generally on a weekly basis).[16] Since diwaniyyas became a place where friends, relatives, and colleagues could meet and discuss freely, they perhaps came to resemble Habermas's coffeehouse as much as any real coffeehouse that has ever existed. Indeed, their inviolability has generally been respected by the Kuwaiti state. Article 38 of the country's constitution protects domiciles, and the few times that police have entered (or on one occasion, attempted to surround) a diwaniyya, have provoked a strong storm of protest. In 1989, diwaniyyas were the central gathering places for an opposition movement centered on former parliamentarians demanding a full restoration of an elected parliament and suspended articles of the country's constitution.[17] The political role of the diwaniyya cuts both ways: not only has it thrust what might otherwise be seen as private discussions into the public realm, it has also raised public interest and concern about what happens in private homes—and the result has even lowered ever so slightly a strong gender bar against female participation.[18]

In sum, while the Arab world often appears to offer a bleak landscape for public discussions, there are a number of pockets where residents can gather in private but argue in a manner that has public impact. Some of these spaces take on some of the formality that we associate with public and political structures; others do not. Ones that are more oriented toward family and neighborhood tend to reproduce hierarchies of wealth, gender, and age, but not mechanically so. Those that are more intellectual or formal tend to reproduce hierarchies of education and official standing, but again not mechanically so.

The more formal, the more likely states are to survey and police the sphere. Indeed, a movement by a less formal group to link up to formal structures (for example, when an informal group becomes associated with an Islamist movement or a diwaniyya hosts an opposition parliamentarian) can provoke a hostile official response. In that sense, it appears that the public/private line is one defined and enforced by states that give their subject citizens the implicit message: "Talk informally among yourselves, but do not make a formal move."

But from a different angle, the public/private line might be better seen as one that is contested, defined, and manipulated as much by individuals as it is enforced by states. When participants move toward more formalization or link with other spheres that are more formal and public, they recast their private discussions as public ones—something of the sort seems to have happened with Kuwaiti diwaniyyas over recent decades. It is in this way that the small group networks of the Arab world can become the sinews of politics even—or especially—under semiauthoritarian conditions. And they can become even more: while there is likely considerable variation within Arab societies on this score, some of the surprisingly widespread (but highly variable) participation in the uprisings of 2011 was based in part on the ways in which residential areas and networks of friends and colleagues were able and willing to act politically against existing regimes and security forces.[19]

And there are other ways in which apparently smaller or more restricted gatherings can link or grow to become much more imposing—something of the sort seemed to have happened with the Cairo Book Fair, an annual event that dates back to the 1960s. What began as something of a trade fair in which books were displayed by publishers gradually grew into a major gathering for intellectuals, with seminars and debates; I remember attending in 1984 and finding a very crowded fairground, with more visitors congregating and socializing outside than perusing the exhibitions of books inside the hall. And the fair itself became the location of a tug of war—between opposition and critical opinions on the one hand and regimes attempting to police the written word on the other and also among various ideological camps. Islamists became a larger presence in the fair but also were active in criticizing some of the books presented.

The ability of the small group discussion to take refuge in the realm of the private undoubtedly preserved some continuous level of political discussion even in the harshest authoritarian moments. My own impression is that political discussions occurred even at such times, but they were characterized by considerable wariness and a sense of futility. In 1983, a year after the Syrian regime crushed an uprising in Hama with horrific violence, I found myself with two fellow-American students in the home of two Syrian brothers in

Damascus. One of them turned to me and asked in a hushed voice, "Did you hear anything about what happened in Hama?" Wishing to draw him out but myself very nervous, I responded vaguely, "Not really. I did hear something about it." He then quickly pressed me: "What happened?" Just as often, such discussions were likely truncated not simply by fear and lack of knowledge but also by boredom and a sense of pointlessness. There were often more interesting things to speak about.

But because such political discussions likely continued, some might object that politics never died. It may have simply disappeared from the public record. But that is precisely my point. It is when such private/public spaces became linked up with other forms of public argument that they became part of political life. But public space was more tightly patrolled. In a second conversation in Syria in 1983, a Syrian leaned forward to me in a public coffeehouse, glanced nervously over both his shoulders, lowered his voice and switched to English, apparently to avoid being understood by those at adjoining tables, and said to me, "Israel is very bad." The mere act of talking politics in a public place with a foreigner—even to mouth a very safe sentiment—required special precautions at that time.

MAYDAN AND MOSQUE

We have been speaking of public space in a less-than-fully metaphoric sense thus far to refer to physical locations where arguments can be made. Let us continue in this vein but return for just a moment to see Arab societies as a state would—as societies that are often arranged in such a way as to create venues for making political and religious arguments in public. Two particular places stand out most clearly for their potential for arguing religion: public squares (or other open places, such as wide boulevards or university campuses) where throngs can gather, and mosques. Both attract large numbers of the public—and also (for that reason) the attentions of states. Public authorities' interest in controlling, monitoring, and policing such spaces is real and is generally effective, but it is not always perfect and complete. The space between members of a crowd or worshippers at prayer sometimes appears filled in very different ways when viewed not from the vantage point of the state but from street level.

Let us turn first to maydans—public squares—and other large gathering spaces.[20] The physical geography of many Arab cities includes such places, but they often betray a strong imprint from past political struggles and state policing and regulation in some subtle and not-so-subtle ways. To leave an area clear of buildings is generally a conscious decision that reflects central political will: the destruction of a wall or other major public work; the leveling of an area or the destruction of a quarter. Most large public spaces in the

Arab world were founded as an official act. And that is often reflected in their names, official uses, and signs of commemoration.

Let us consider the most well-known such site, at least since 2011: Cairo's Maydan al-Tahrir. Often translated as "Liberation Square" but actually a large traffic circle in the midst of other open spaces and significant public buildings, the space was created in a series of conscious political decisions. The name for the area—adjacent to the earlier site of the main British military barracks in Cairo—refers to the liberation from those British troops. In its immediate environs are the Egyptian National Museum; the headquarters of the Arab League; the massive Mugamma` complex of bureaucratic offices; some palaces of members of Egypt's deposed ruling family (converted into a building controlled by the Foreign Ministry and another one by the American University in Cairo); and, less imposingly, the `Umar Makram Mosque, the beginning point for funeral processions for senior officials and other prominent persons. The mosque itself and the Mugamma` were completed immediately after the overthrow of the monarchy in 1952 (though their planning and construction began shortly before). The entire architecture and configuration seems to communicate the imposing and massive (if unattractive) nature of the post-1952 Egyptian state.

But Tahrir is not solely a state creation. Even before 2011, there were discordant elements. `Umar Makram, for whom the mosque is named (and who is featured in an unobtrusive statue near the maydan), is an Egyptian nationalist icon; he was al-Azhar educated and served as *naqib al-ashraf* (the leader of those in the country who were descendants of the Prophet Muhammad), a post of considerable social and religious prestige. While unquestionably a member of the country's elite, he is remembered today in Egyptian school textbooks as the leader of popular resistance against the French occupation of Egypt. In the period after the French left, he also seems to have been a thorn in the side of the country's rulers (an early backer of Muhammad `Ali, the founder of the dynasty overthrown in 1952, `Umar Makram later led resistance to the new ruler's fiscal appetites and was rewarded by being exiled from Cairo). In that sense, he is an easy symbol not only for the post-1952 regime's populism but for any popular mobilization.

And that is what the site has become—even before 2011, it was the site of pro-regime rallies but, when Egypt's rulers lost their taste for such things, for opposition gatherings as well. Indeed, when I first visited Cairo in 1983, I found the square a construction zone for an underground subway and sewer repairs then underway; on every subsequent trip, I noted (perhaps unfairly conspiratorially) that there always seemed to be some construction project obstructing or breaking up the space. As a site that could contain large crowds, it was attractive but also monitored and often seemed easy for state authorities to control. That ability collapsed in January 2011, however, when demonstrators seized the square, which then quickly supplanted other sites throughout the country as the symbol of a popular uprising against the regime.[21] 'Umar Makram's more unruly legacy momentarily won out; his mosque was used as a field hospital for the uprising and Mazhar Shahin, its imam, became something of a television celebrity as an advocate of the revolution and a religious figure who prided himself for speaking truth to power (and later for idiosyncratic support for power after July 2013). He spoke not merely from the pulpit: he addressed the crowds in adjacent Maydan al-Tahrir, appeared on television talk shows, and posted short statements on his Facebook page, expressing his positions with insufficient rigor and consistency and excessive flamboyance in the eyes of some of his colleagues. His proclivity for the public eye ultimately landed him with a promised television show—and his inattention to consistency led him to denounce the pernicious effects of social media on family communications.

While Tahrir Square was thus one of the primary sites and symbols of the January 2011 national uprising, over the ensuing months and years, security authorities gradually (and sometimes violently) restored the location to one for officially sanctioned purposes only.

Telling the story this way—one of ambitious, heavy-handed security-conscious regimes placing their stamp on large public places but occasionally facing mass unrest—is dramatic and worthy of attention but it can lead us to overlook a more small-scale guerilla battle between states and the society over urban space. And it can lead us as well to miss the slow emergence and evolution of public space.[22] Again, a street-level rather than a bird's-eye view often reveals an urban landscape heavily shaped by an accumulation of small-scale and localized popular actions as well as vocal entrepreneurs.[23] The contest for control is evident in urban landscapes, but usually one can walk right past these signs, quite literally. Graffiti and street art often mark territory, presenting a voice sharply different from those dominant in government and media; ritualized forms of protest (small demonstrations and marches; protest camps set up outside of official buildings) have become more common with the gradual shift from authoritarianism to semiauthoritarianism in many societies (including Jordan and Egypt); large crowds can gather for nonpolitical but still what might be seen as counterhegemonic purposes (most notably for festivals and *mulids*);[24] and religious icons might be unobtrusively but widely displayed.[25]

It must be noted, however, that there is nothing distinct about large public spaces that lend themselves only to religious argument. They certainly can be used for that purpose, but the kind of argument generally presented in such a setting is only that of a slogan, chant, banner, or placard; in general, it is the fact of the demonstration or the number of participants that is the primary content of the argument. Hortatory speech is enabled; dialogue is difficult.

The other significant assembly place, by contrast, is explicitly religious: the mosque. Control of mosques is continuously contested by states, specialists (preachers), and those who pray. The attempt by states to control mosques is clear: in most societies, states undertake the task of constructing many mosques and of staffing them. Ministries of religious affairs populate most states, and, while legal ownership is itself a complex topic, the ministries do act effectively as owners of many mosques. In Egypt, for instance, when a mosque is established, its legal ownership is held to have been transferred to God and is therefore outside of the control of the donor (though not of the Ministry of Religious Affairs which can be counted on to provide helpful assistance in administration in the absence of active divine management).

Thus states often appear domineering and heavy-handed.[26] And indeed they can be, though as we will soon see, in ways that are less complete and masterful than often appears. States control not only through constructing and employing but also by licensing those mosques they do not build and staff. They regulate in other ways as well, and it is not unusual to read about attempts to dictate the contents of sermons, close mosques between prayer times, insist that those allowed to give sermons pass an official examination, and place informers among the faithful to monitor what is said. Larger mosques are of course closely controlled, but even smaller mosques draw episodic attention. Indeed, in Egypt *zawiyas* (small rooms designated for prayer) are often singled out for public concern as minister after minister proclaims that zawiyas will be brought under full official oversight. In Egypt after the overthrow of President Muhammad Morsi in July 2013, the Ministry of Religious Affairs took great efforts to shut down unauthorized preaching and dismiss those who were affiliated with the political opposition (and even many salafis who departed from the Azhar-sanctioned approach).

In post-2013 Egypt, the campaign to regulate preaching was very publicly announced. And the Ministry of Religious Affairs trumpeted some of its more obsequious guidance, such as a comparison between the regime's project to enlarge the Suez Canal with the prophet Muhammad's command to dig a ditch which proved decisive in an early battle.[27]

In a visit to Egypt in 2015, I visited a mosque where I knew the imam and was surprised to find the door closed; it was not prayer time, he explained after admitting me through the locked front door. I spoke with several imams at that time, one of whom was close to tears about how tightly he was monitored; another who became visibly nervous when the conversation tilted in a political direction and made a zipping motion over his mouth. A third employed at a historic mosque sighed as he explained how the Ministry of Religious Affairs, the Ministry of Interior, and the Ministry of Tourism all demanded a say in how the mosque was administered. A year earlier, a religious official sympathetic with the new regime told me, "We definitely have to root out radical preachers. But we do not need an intelligence officer in every mosque."

At other times, much of this control is publicly visible but not reported and only occasionally does a heavy-handed measure draw attention, such as in December 2013 when the Saudi Ministry of Mosques, Preaching, and Guidance issued a directive to preachers not to violate the rulings of the Higher 'Ulama Council barring travel for jihad.

Mosques might be seen as a hybridized kind of space that is patrolled and policed but which also opens possibilities for religious argumentation, discussion, and socializing that shows some autonomy and even oppositional possibilities.[28] To ignore state control over mosques would therefore be naïve—but to view all preachers as simply state functionaries would also be a mistake for several reasons.[29]

First, they are engaged in something of a specialist discourse, so they are speaking not simply to those who meet for prayer but also to each other. Sometimes they compete—to show off religious knowledge, eloquence, or faithfulness. But they can also display professional deference. In a series of conversations with Egyptian imams in 2013 and 2014, I was struck by how they spoke about each other (and, in a few conversations I witnessed, with each other) in the kinds of respectful tones one might expect from those who were aware of differences but still interested in maintaining collegial relations. The difference in question then was political and it was fraught indeed: the Muslim Brotherhood had been tossed out of power and was being violently repressed. While public expressions of support for the Brotherhood were dangerous, the often unspoken fact was that of those who gathered regularly in mosques and among the imams themselves there was something like a fairly even split between supporters of ousted President Muhammad Morsi and incoming President 'Abd al-Fattah al-Sisi. Sometimes they resorted to polite or oblique language. When the imam of the 'Umar Makram mosque came up in another discussion with a group of imams I met with in central Cairo, it was because he had recently stated publicly that if one's spouse was a member of the Muslim Brotherhood that was legitimate grounds for divorce (the statement earned a rebuke from the leaders of Egypt's religious establishment despite its own hostility to the Brotherhood). In our discussions we referred to him genteelly as "an imam of a mosque not far from here" and the imams seemed to speak with a bit of polite condescension as of someone who had let media attention lead him astray from sound application of religious principles.

Second, control is incomplete and reactive. The constant proclamations of oversight by Egyptian ministers suggests the reality that they have never been able to exercise the control they promise. In conversations with preachers and religious officials in Egypt, Palestine, and Kuwait, I have been struck by how many seem to experience state guidance as crude and incompletely effective—it affects the content of what is said, to be sure, but not in a way that requires preachers to be mechanical mouthpieces. Instead, imams report that official concern tends to be episodic. It can be very bureaucratic—Egyptian imams reported to me prior to 2014 that the sternest and most specific language they receive about sermons was the time limit and indeed, some have been disciplined for verbosity. Another worshiper in Ramallah mosque complained about a preacher's salafi inclinations—he had been placed in a large mosque not because he was a regime sympathizer but simply because he was not affiliated with Hamas and inclined toward salafi interpretations that were deferential to rulers.

Monitoring varies even within the same regime over time in accordance with immediate political issues. (One Palestinian imam in Nablus I spoke with reported that under Israeli and Palestinian Authority rule he was fairly free in what he could say as long as he avoided obvious political subjects; the same was true when Hamas formed the government. But the government of Salam Fayyad, which served from 2007 to 2012, was much more restrictive.) Positive guidance (topics for sermons) in most societies generally tends to be vague, consisting of general themes (such as "problems of youth") to be addressed. Negative guidance can be much more onerous; some imams reported visits from security officials, especially if they gave a sermon that was interpreted as political—and the definition of "political" is itself very political, with one Egyptian imam observing wryly in the aftermath of a constitutional referendum, "If I endorse the constitution, that is not political. But if I oppose it, that is political."

And shifting politics can make the work of those policing sermons (as well as those giving them) a bit confusing. One prominent preacher in Egypt, Muhammad ʿAbd Allah Nasr, an Azhari dubbed the "preacher of al-Tahrir" for his sermons during demonstrations, seemed at first to be on the right side of the post-2011 political order. But he quickly turned against President Muhammad Morsi, denouncing him in a sermon in Maydan al-Tahrir as having "blood stained hands" and asking rhetorically if he wanted "the shariʿa of the Guide [of the Brotherhood], the shariʿa of [Israeli President Shimon] Peres, or the shariʿa of God."[30] He founded a brief coalition dubbing itself "Azharis for a civil state" and quickly came under strong verbal attack from Islamist forces (then waxing in influence) who went beyond disagreeing with his interpretations of religious teachings to suggest he was a communist. Morsi's overthrow did not bring an end to the controversy surrounding him, however; in August 2014 the public prosecutor opened an investigation into his statement that al-Bukhari, an authoritative collector of hadiths, made errors. The fact that it earned an expedited investigation from the public prosecutor rather than simply a rebuke from the al-Azhar leadership suggests that political considerations as much as religious ones were at work (at the time the prosecutor was routinely treating allegations from the security services with unlimited credulity; it was likely the shaykh's politically maverick nature that led to his targeting).[31]

Third, states simply do not have the capability to monitor every mosque or every preacher. It is common in some places for lay preachers to be invited to give sermons; those who endow mosques might themselves be given preferential treatment as well. I met one Egyptian salafi preacher who referred to "his mosque" because he had endowed it; from the point of view of the state, his sense of ownership was legally meaningless but it still allowed him to preach. I met another amateur preacher who was clearly opposition but allowed to speak because of his popularity as a rhetorician even among those who deeply disagreed with his politics.

Of course any such speakers can command the attention of either security or religious officials if they are outspoken, but they might also gain a following for precisely such reasons. Oppositional preachers can often operate within state-licensed and even state-operated mosques. Malika Zeghal has written of "peripheral 'ulama" who strike an oppositional stance even while some remain within the state-administered religious system.[32] As Charles Hirschkind has observed as well:

> The state's attempt to control da'wa has met two serious obstacles. One is grounded in the limited resources and capacities of the economically enfeebled Egyptian state. The second, on the other hand, owes to the very heterogeneity of the state itself. Many of the state-administered religious organizations include sizable factions sympathetic to the same religious arguments that their own institutions have been called on to officially denounce and combat.[33]

The struggle is an old one; Patrick Gaffney found in the early 1980s a similar kind of contestation among preachers in upper Egypt who manifested very different attitudes toward their work (including different political-religious orientations) as well as what seemed to be reactive and incomplete state attempts to police sermons.[34] And indeed, the political ambiguities of mosques, struggles over preaching, and the crossovers between official and unofficial sermons have manifested themselves in earlier periods in Islamic history.[35]

Seen this way, state control is quite real and often quite intrusive but also incomplete, variable, and reactive; security apparatuses and religious bureaucracies can monitor and shape what is preached but because the terrain is religious in nature, privileges specialist discourse, and involves members of the general public, the overall effect resembles far less a panopticon than a complex, multiparty, and multidirectional tug of war.

It also bears mention that the two spheres we have been examining— maydan and mosque—share a feature that is not immediately apparent but has potentially great significance: both are linked to the public/private hybrid spheres examined earlier in this chapter. Large public spaces are of, course, located in and around neighborhoods full of their own dense networks. But when they turn into major gathering places for a demonstration or march, those participating often are gathered in groups of friends, neighbors or family. What appears from the lens of a camera to be an undifferentiated mass is experienced on the ground as a set of momentarily united personal networks.

Similarly, mosques are located in neighborhoods and frequented by regular worshippers, individuals who are known for their piety or position or other personal attributes and ties. Just as significant, they can also provide a haven for study circles or a recruiting ground for Islamist groups (of the formal or informal variety) that are active in the area.

Paradoxically, when they metamorphose from amalgamations of public/private spheres into fully public venues for argumentation, both maydan and mosque become less interactive and less critical-rational rather than more. A study circle can debate and discuss; those who are reputed to have (or claim) more religious learning might dominate or lead the discussion but even then they might feel compelled to answer questions and respond to opposing views. Yet in a demonstration, march, or mass assembly, communication is limited to slogans and one-way speeches; these rely for their force on their emotional power and simplicity rather than their intricacy, erudition, or interactive nature. In a mosque, when worshipers gather to hear a preacher, the discussion is similarly one-way and combines logical argument with religious appeal. According to most I have spoken with, even lessons given after a sermon tend towards the didactic even if they are interactive.

MASS MEDIA, NEW AND OLD

In small public spaces and larger ones, argument depends on personal contact through physical proximity. An increasing variety of media allow such argumentation to take place using less immediate communication. In this section, we will consider in series three such collections of media: those based on the printing press; those based on broadcast; and those based on social media. The scholarly interest in all three has been enormous and nonscholarly interest has also been high (particularly in social media); our effort here is not to summarize the state of knowledge of each of these media but to briefly trace their trajectories as public spheres (with special interest in the way in which states can and cannot structure, police, and monitor them), especially with regard to religious argumentation. Once again, they all appear (and indeed are) closely policed but in recent years a ground-up view reveals a more varied set of spaces than a simple top-down image of state control might allow.

Press and Publicity: Illusory Intimacy

Most Arab countries have followed a similar pattern in the historical development of a periodical press. Originally introduced as a government mouthpiece—so that the public, at least as it existed in print, was simply official business—state sponsors were soon joined by private individuals who had the resources to make their voices heard by publishing items of public interest. In some countries, the press (especially in the form of periodical publications) came back under largely full public ownership through nationalizations, though a reverse trend toward privatization set in with the rise of semiauthoritarianism. Whether publicly or privately owned (or whatever mixture), official eyes were never far from the printed word. Yet genuine spaces have always been open for some unofficial voices, even under the most authoritarian conditions. And those spaces, as contorted as they sometimes appear, have grown unevenly in recent decades in much of the Arab world.

While the broad outlines of this trajectory can be traced for most countries, there is still considerable intra-regional variation. Two modal extremes can be identified in Jordan and Kuwait, on the one hand (where the press has been privately owned) and Egypt on the other (where the state-owned "national press" has been an outsized presence).[36]

A short presentation of these trajectories can illustrate the range of experiences in the Arab world.

In Jordan, an official press—largely for official notices—was founded almost the same time as the kingdom was established by a League of Nations mandate to Great Britain in the aftermath of the First World War. It was quickly joined by a private press, though one fairly anemic in nature. Not until 1949 and the annexation of the West Bank (including parts of Jerusalem, where an Arabic-language press had emerged under British mandatory rule of Palestine) did a more lively domestic press emerge; the press scene thereafter consisted largely of privately owned newspapers.[37] After a brief period of ideological diversity (in which a communist paper was briefly published), a marked turn toward authoritarianism began with a declaration of martial law in 1957. After that point, despite private ownership, the content of the Jordanian press resembled that of its neighbors with its combination of turgid official news, a narrow range of pro-regime opinion, and careful avoidance of most controversial or sensitive topics. (In a 1996 visit to the country, a Jordanian journalist asked for an interview with me because I was giving some public lectures on human rights and the rule of law; before turning on his tape recorder, he asked me plaintively, "Would you please tell me something I can write in the newspaper?")

The strict constraints on press discussion were supported by a series of practices: censorship; withdrawal of advertisers from those who strayed too far; private messages from security bodies; and, finally, in 1988, nationalization of two leading dailies. But at the end of the 1980s a period of uneven liberalization began. The nationalized newspapers were sold (with large shares generally going to state-owned or officially dominated bodies and leading officials). Weekly papers had already emerged in the 1980s and initially escaped the same degree of monitoring as the dailies; in the early 1990s they quickly staked out the less occupied ground of sensationalism and shrill political articles. Sometimes evading the law (for instance, by printing outside the country) and sometimes running afoul of it (and indeed earning brief suspensions on occasion), the newer, more daring newspapers attracted considerable readership (making commercial viability a seeming prospect). It was this period—the 1990s—and specifically the rise of the weeklies that appears in retrospect to be the height of a press-based public sphere in Jordan. As Marc Lynch observed, "Both the number of voices and their quality radically increased. The print public sphere allowed a wide, broadly representative spectrum of opinion to regularly engage in debate about specifically Jordanian issues. Furthermore, it could be reasonably assumed that all public sphere participants and many government decision makers regularly read this weekly press and took it seriously."[38]

A new, more open press law was promulgated in 1993, but some restrictions were reimposed from 1997 onward in order to rein in the new weekly press. A more ideological press (including an Islamist paper) also managed to establish itself in the shifting environment.

Perhaps the most innovative entrant to the Jordanian newspaper scene came in 2004 when a Jordanian-Palestinian businessman who had prospered in Kuwait founded a new daily, *al-Ghad*. He had earlier experimented with a free weekly that consisted solely of advertisements and his purpose in founding the new paper was similarly commercial. However, *al-Ghad* was designed to be lively without being sensationalist or seditious; indeed, it was so professional, youthful in image, and oriented toward business that it became attractive to potential advertisers. Quickly gathering or training the leading journalistic talent in Jordan, news coverage included sensitive areas (occasionally earning official ire and even pressure) while avoiding the shrillness and scandalmongering of other independent papers. Commentary was both diverse and freewheeling. The paper was commercially successful, though not spectacularly so.

The trajectory of the Kuwaiti press was similar to that of the Jordanian press, though it was comparatively compressed (with stable newspapers emerging only in the 1960s).[39] Daily papers were sometimes joined in the market by other periodicals (such as a left-wing weekly and an Islamist monthly); they tended to be respectful of the existing political order, but with a sometimes-active parliament, the Kuwaiti press had a more diverse set of opinions to relay than its regional counterparts. Two periods of parliamentary suspension (in the 1970s and 1980s) brought with them a more constricted environment, but the harsh methods used elsewhere in the region (such as nationalization) were never deployed. With the restoration of parliament in 1992 and the development of an increasingly outspoken and diverse parliament, the press opened up considerably and finally a new press law in 2006 pried some of the remaining restrictive tools out regime hands (for instance, the Ministry of Information had earlier simply ignored licensing requests for new papers; in the 2000s the number of papers rose quickly). For a small country, Kuwait quickly became characterized by a crowded press scene; while most papers had a political tilt they still tried to capture a broad audience with a range of news and commentary. Most taboos were broken, and with the political leadership increasingly fractious, the ruling family increasingly divided (and by the 2000s sometimes surprisingly willing to dish gossip and apparently self-serving accounts of family meetings), the press became lively indeed. With several newspapers apparently commercially successful, they attracted some businessmen; wealthy individuals showed interest, perhaps to further their political vision or at least amplify their favored voices (and a leading member of the ruling family bought one of the leading dailies after he was hounded out of a cabinet position with allegations of staggering embezzlement). In recent years, the profit motive has receded in the face of political motives for those wealthy enough to fund favored outlets. As a result, "the instrumentalization of privately owned media by ruling family members and the affiliated business elite" became "endemic."[40] On a few occasions, reminders of the heavy-handed restrictions of the past struck a sharply discordant note in the generally freewheeling media scene: a leading editor was jailed in 2010 (likely for some sharply worded comments about the prime minister that were actually not printed in the paper) and coverage of his trial restricted; in 2014, a paper was briefly shut for publishing a story regarding a leaked tape that appeared to show some members of the ruling family maneuvering against others.

If the Jordanian and Kuwaiti experience is one of a privately owned but officially constrained press scene, one with oscillations in openness, then Egypt has shown the harsher side of the Arab press experience. Egyptian papers started in the early nineteenth century as official publications that came to include some commentary as well as laws, regulations, and announcements. In the last third of the nineteenth century, a private press emerged that quickly engaged in coverage and discussion of a wide range of political issues. While commercially oriented, newspapers tended to take on a political slant and received backing (and, according to rumors, material support) from various political actors. When Britain occupied Egypt in 1882, its officials complained about some press coverage but they generally stuck to subtle methods of manipulation and persuasion (though outright censorship was imposed in World War I). The daily press was joined by a wide array of weekly and monthly periodicals, some with a particular focus (such as the arts); a small provincial press also emerged. In the 1930s and 1940s, newer, more ideological political forces entered the scene and political parties sponsored their own publications.

The press scene changed dramatically with the change of regime that came with the military coup of 1952. Existing papers toed a very cautious line at first; they also saw their ranks joined in 1954 by a daily (*al-Jumhuriyya*) edited by future president Anwar al-Sadat and clearly sponsored by the new regime. Over the following decade, the entire press was nationalized; much of the periodical press and the journalist syndicate was folded into the ruling political party. The result was a fully authoritarian press scene with newspapers used for official news and propaganda purposes; commentary varied from quietly to histrionically supportive of the regime.

The situation gradually liberalized beginning in the 1970s. Slightly more independent voices—or at least those who had fallen out of favor in the 1960s—were brought back to editorial positions. A gradual disestablishment of the sole political party necessitated the transfer of oversight of the press from the party to a press council and a newly created upper house of parliament. The overall result was to allow the "national press," as it came to be called, a bit more leeway; editors-in-chief were clearly approved by the president but they were allowed autonomy within their own realms. While loyal to the regime, some editors decided to allow a bit more openness especially in their commentary. But the press could still be startlingly sycophantic even on mundane occasions.

Yet the liberalization went far beyond the mild opening in the national press. In the late 1970s a limited opposition press emerged; some Islamist publications were allowed to open as well. For most of the remainder of the century the daily press was largely the preserve of the national press but weeklies and monthlies became far more varied. Licensing and harassment by security agencies (with regular warnings, occasional confiscations of publications, and arrests) were deployed to communicate the "yellow zones" referred to earlier in this chapter. And subtler methods were used as well—most newspapers depended on government-owned printing presses and on state-owned enterprises for advertising revenues.

In the first decade of the twenty-first century, the daily national press was finally directly challenged by a group of independently owned ventures. The first, *al-Masri al-Yawm*, initially resembled Jordan's *al-Ghad* for being lively, wide-ranging in commentary, a bit daring in political coverage while avoiding sensationalism—and apparently designed to be profitable. A series of political, business, and personal struggles among the paper's backers resulted in its changing tone to become more sensationalist in style, but that only seemed to increase its circulation and presence. Financial success was impressive even if (or perhaps because) professional standards were relaxed. It was soon joined by a series of other newspapers that seemed to base their viability more on their owners' egos and deep pockets rather than on any sophisticated business model.

The result put some mild pressure on the national press, which saw circulation and credibility (the latter never particularly high) go into steady decline.[41] The overall effect was to have a clearly pro-regime press (sometimes stodgy and often turgid) joined by an independent press operating in the yellow zone, sometimes earning quiet warnings or brutal harassment but allowing some space for critical voices.

The 2011 uprising initially seemed to auger significant further changes, with a post-uprising regime perhaps less willing to sink scarce public funds into the national press and less needy of such an extensive cheerleading apparatus.[42] Indeed, that press seemed initially directionless without a clear regime to propagandize for; the restrictions on the independently owned and partisan press initially seemed to evaporate. Yet the structural changes in the press scene were actually quite limited; even after the 2013 coup ending the brief experience of a Muslim Brotherhood presidency, the changes in the press were more in tone (with most of the press, national and private, joining in enthusiastic support for the post-coup order) than in structure. And in the aftermath of the coup, the privately owned and nominally opposition press became far more pro-regime in tilt; individual journalists who retained a critical stance were harassed and even imprisoned. Discordant voices could still be heard but they had to speak much more carefully lest they run afoul of the authorities.

The regional variation—with Jordan and Kuwait perhaps among the most liberal and Egypt often on the more authoritarian end of the spectrum—is considerable but still shows some common patterns. When words have been written in public in the periodical press, the first participants were generally state bodies that took the initiative in order to communicate their wills and directives, often in legal form. But that monopoly was quickly lost—not only was the dry and legalistic tone and content of periodical publications quickly drowned out by news and commentary but other actors joined in. Private individuals—though often ones with a significant amount of political influence and almost always those with some economic resources as well—were generally the pioneers. They were later joined by political parties and movements.

State actors intervened obviously and directly through censorship, nationalizations, and publishing their own periodicals. Even where they were less active in such obvious ways, they often policed less publicly by using pressure (sometimes quite brutally), legal, licensing, and regulatory tools, and economic inducements (such as placement of advertisements) in order to set (often hazy) boundaries, signal new directions, drown out or discredit critics, and steer arguments in a manner that supported official policy. Even those private actors who were involved in publishing entered a playing field tilted heavily toward those with wealth and political power—this was especially the case for those with deep pockets attempting to link the two.[43]

In sum, the periodical press—the public sphere most amenable to extended and rational discourse, and one that would seem exceptionally friendly at first glance for arguing religion in a manner that fully engages the complexity of the issues involved and the full set of intellectual traditions of Islam—is, at least at first glance, better seen as a platform for state actors, sometimes joined by wealthy individuals, to address the public in a one way "dialogue." Papers might at most occasionally print letters from readers in order to provide a feeble illusion of a more conversational medium.

But while newspapers and other periodicals are indeed hardly conversational and heavily shaped and policed by powerful actors, they are still a surprisingly vital site for public arguments about religion. First, the general pattern of loosening state control—the general regional shift from authoritarianism to semiauthoritarianism—has had the obvious effect of lessening the degree of repression and allowing greater range for opinion. Indeed, it is in the realm of published opinion where the shift is most marked and unofficial voices more remarkable for their presence. Islamist press, political party press, and trashy tabloids often led the way, sometimes influencing each other (my impression from being in Egypt when the mild opposition newspaper al-Wafd began as a weekly in 1984 was that it made its presence felt most effectively when it discovered that a steady diet of lurid crime reports might draw readers to its dryer political critiques).

But the general regional trend has a less obvious effect as well: no longer do the top layers of the regime patrol the entire state apparatus so thoroughly or effectively. When it comes to religious matters in particular, the existence of numerous state adjudicative, research, educational, praying, and preaching bodies means that the state no longer speaks with a single voice, even in the periodical press. As illustrated in chapter 5, the bureaucratization of Islam in the Arab world has led not merely to uniformity and control but also to subtle differences, rivalries, and pockets of dissidence and dissonance. Some of these state bodies can speak directly through the press—the head of a leading Islamic institution (such as a mufti) can generally command press attention; some bodies issue small specialized periodicals of their own (in Egypt, al-Azhar has a group of publications; until their abolition in 1955, even the shari'a courts had their separate law journal).

Second, religious voices outside the state apparatus have generally found an increasing ability to make their voices heard—or at least their words published. Samizdat publications were always (admittedly risky) possibilities. But the general liberalization of the press environment made it possible for alternative religious voices to be heard in more public settings. Those linked to formal political movements, such as the Muslim Brotherhood, generally found the largest obstacles placed in their path, but even when that happened, individuals who were affiliated with the movement or sympathetic to its views could often place commentaries in other publications.

Third, the placement of periodical press in an international media environment can sometimes open some critical spaces. Some religious publications cross state boundaries (Kuwait's *al-Mujtama'* became a leading Islamist publication in the region in the late twentieth century, for instance, protected by Kuwait's relative tolerance for its initially less political Muslim Brotherhood). And just as significantly, the rise of a transnational Arab press, especially from the 1980s on, allowed for a greater range of voices to be heard. This transnational press, often based in London, presented a fairly constrained and controlled space for argument and displayed all the idiosyncrasies of the privately owned press in individual countries—generally supported by those in privileged economic positions, often characterized by strong political ties to an existing regime, acting with political more than financial motives, and sometimes subject to pressure and even censorship if they stepped across vague boundaries of permissible speech. In a region unevenly awash in oil revenues, much of the transnational press naturally gravitated toward oil-rich political systems. But if far from politically neutral, this transnational press still introduced a degree of pluralism and professionalism along with an ability to forge linkages among intellectual elites in the region that eluded the nationally centered publications.

The end result, by the beginning of the twenty-first century, was a fairly lively scene for religious issues in which religious scholars, movements, intellectuals, and state officials could all work to persuade the broader public. Smaller niche audiences (salafis, Azharis, sufis, Brotherhood supporters, or preachers) could find more specialized venues to explore their favored issues. The liveliness was neither unlimited nor irreversible. In the spring of 2015, an overview of the Egyptian media (focusing on television but including written media) in the wake of the 2013 coup came with the ominous title "We Completely Agree," and described how public and private media all toed the official line with opposition voices and outlets shut out and suppressed.[44] Yet even after the most draconian set of controls placed on the press in several decades, dissident voices could be heard as time went on, and the existence of publications outside of Egypt—many of them available in web-based editions—made the full monotony of the 1960s impossible to recover.

Broadcast Media: The Public Sphere Enters Private Homes ... and Public Coffeehouses

Broadcast media in the Arab world betray strong similarities to print media: the first voices were those of states who used radio and then television to convey information and policies; when the sphere was born it was primarily states and high officials who had a public presence. But from the beginning there was also a significant space for popular entertainment as well. In recent years, the dreariness of news and official ceremonies has been broken by far edgier content and an erosion (though hardly an end) of regime hegemony. Again, the view from the top is one of control, but from a viewer's perspective, the result is a more complex scene and one that has been particularly friendly to religious programming of many different sorts.[45]

Initial broadcasting began on radio, generally in the 1950s, with broadcasting controlled by the state and generally part of a ministry of information. That broadcasting consisted largely of entertainment, news, and political propagandizing (such as speeches). If it was only states that spoke publicly in broadcast media at first (with a few minor exceptions), there were still some dissonant notes: radio waves crossed international borders and thus rivalries among regimes could be expressed vocally and sometimes vitriolically.[46] Television was added similarly, generally in the 1960s (though broadcast technology prevented it from being beamed across most borders until the 1990s; before that date, only entertainment shows were borrowed and rebroadcast by state-run media).

Indeed, in official broadcasting, popular entertainment generally dominated, but there was plenty of space for turgid news broadcasts; as mass rallies became less frequent even in the previously mobilizational authoritarian regimes, television became the primary medium for communicating policy statements and ideological pronouncements through speeches and formal occasions. Only in a few countries did private broadcasting emerge, and even then it was generally extremely tame when it came to any possible political subject. The effect of the broadcasting environment was hardly to provide any environment for serious political argumentation except that directed from regimes toward their populations; my impression is that at least by the 1980s most residents treated the resulting political and news broadcasts as background noise. Entertainment programs were far different, however, garnering significant audiences often engrossed in serials, sporting events, or (as we will see in the religious sphere), regular sermons or lectures.

Yet the boundary between ponderous news and more lively entertainment was broken in the 1990s with the advent of satellite television. Al-Jazeera was the most famous of the new broadcasters, though it was quickly followed by others. While transnational (and even global) in audience, these newer broadcasters were still anchored either in individual states or by wealthy individuals, some connected to (or members of) ruling families.[47] Yet they sought audiences not by lecturing and hectoring but by serving up a lively set of discussion, raucous debate, and aggressive commentary. The striking novelty of publicly airing such discussions led many watchers to refer to the "breaking of taboos" and an end to the patrolling of "red zones." Individual broadcasters, of course, had their clear limits (Qatari domestic politics, such as it was, received no coverage on Qatar-backed al-Jazeera) but that would often lead broadcasters who had different patrons to cross into their rivals' forbidden zones with particular glee.

The primary short-term effect was to create a broad Arab public sphere, susceptible to official manipulation to be sure, but under the control of no single actor.[48] A less noticed secondary effect was to force national broadcasters to enliven their own efforts. That was not difficult, as standard fare had been astoundingly turgid. But under the pressure of the new broadcasters, political talk shows and more diverse viewpoints seemed the best way for old broadcasters to regain attention.[49] In the new media environment, and with the spread in particular of satellite broadcasting, the strict licensing requirements of previous years no longer seemed sustainable, and transnational broadcasting was often joined with a far more varied domestic broadcasting scene. As with newspapers, individuals with deep pockets might sponsor their own broadcasters, less for financial reasons than for political or publicity-seeking motivations. And political talk attracted viewers.

Indeed, one of the most notable changes in Arab broadcast media during this period—though one I can only offer impressionistic support for—was that people started paying attention to what their televisions were telling them. Television sets had often been on in the background when I entered coffeehouses and homes. And some entertainment programming attracted very attentive audiences. But when it came to news and public affairs, my impression was that Arab broadcasting drew as much interest and respect as overly loud elevator music. But that changed, beginning with the Gulf war of 1990–1991 when the quickest news came from Western satellite broadcasters (rebroadcast by state-owned media at least in Egypt though without translation); with the advent of al-Jazeera, I noticed that such programming became a subject of normal conversation. While my circles are, of course, limited, the change among those I met was dramatic and profound.

The more unified national television audiences of the 1960s through the 1980s, and the more coherent transnational audiences of the 1990s and early 2000s gave way to a much more thickly populated broadcast scene by the second decade of the twenty-first century. Even the large transnational broadcasters split their efforts to some degree (with al-Jazeera, for instance, hosting not only the main news-and-talk station but also a special channel for sports and another one directed primarily at Egypt). Audiences were thus increasingly segmented along cultural, ideological, and, above all, geographic lines, as national boundaries remained strong.

And where did religious argumentation fit in this shifting media landscape?[50] There was space for religion even at the most rigidly controlled times. Some of this seemed primarily expressive or symbolic: recitation of the Qur'an or Friday preaching. My main impression of such broadcasting in various places I visited was that it was used to infuse the surroundings (a car, a home, or occasionally a store or even a market) with an atmosphere of piety; it seemed to constitute the equivalent of soft background music and the specific content seemed to matter less than the general ambience created.

But the opening of state-owned broadcasting to preaching led to the emergence of media-friendly preachers. Those who initially were given the limelight were hardly firebrands, nor were they likely to stray too far from the political lines of the regime. But they began to establish an independent presence for themselves and a hybrid manner of religious authority, combining specialists' knowledge with an ability to speak accessibly to a very broad audience. The most prominent preacher in the 1980s was Egypt's Shaykh Muhammad Mitwalli Sha'rawi, a figure very much from the religious establishment and one who managed to convey simultaneously an impression of tremendous learning with a very conversational style. Sha'rawy's focus on faith and practice combined with a message that Islam was a religion that was designed to help, guide, and assist the ordinary believer, not impose harm or hardship. With only a few exceptions, there were few implicit political implications from his preaching.[51]

Yet others soon followed, cultivating an ability to communicate religious authority with accessibility. Yusuf al-Qaradawi, for instance, a preacher originally from Egypt but based in Qatar, built up a significant media following, especially when he was allotted a program on al-Jazeera.[52] Such preachers were generally nationally based but some were very successful in crossing borders, with Egypt a leading exporter and Saudi Arabia a source for such preaching as well. Their ability to build strong followings (or sometimes niche audiences) on satellite broadcasters allowed some to venture more daringly into politics (though ethics and piety remained far more favored themes).[53]

The popularity of preaching led to the emergence of a separate genre: fatwa programs in which individuals submit questions to religious scholars. The format combines aspects of a newspaper advice column with religious instruction for a mass, non-specialized audience (most of the problems discussed involve the sort of personal and especially family relationships that populate both).

As a site of religious argument, television preaching and related programming have five notable features. First, the programming is successful to the extent that it can be attractive, entertaining, or enticing for viewers. This places a premium on those with either conversational or imposing styles. It allows those without formal religious training to enter the fray (most famously Egypt's Amr Khalid, who openly disavows any specialist knowledge); while the majority do pose as authorities in some manner, the genre frays the link between professional standing and authority. Indeed, the more successful such preachers likely prove exceptions to the general rule that broadcast media are rarely profitable.

Second, such programming cannot dwell on extended rational argument, though it might at times simulate it. The tools of persuasion are connected with dress, demeanor, affect, projections of piety, and sometimes varying doses of empathy and erudition. For the most part preachers and fatwa givers stay away from strong displays of emotion (though there are significant exceptions) preferring instead a homiletic or rhetorical style that makes use of quick, even facile, argument, homespun analogy, quoting of religious texts, definitive and self-assured delivery, and dress. In this last regard, most favor a wardrobe that is meant quite obviously to communicate the nature of their authority—the distinctive Azhari garb common in Egypt, the gown, beard and headdress characteristic of salafis, the jeans sported by youthful preachers, or even the suits preferred by those who seek to communicate earnestness and earthly success rather than formal training.[54] But there is variation even among the more stodgy figures. In an informal conversation I shared with an official of al-Azhar and a young Egyptian woman, the latter acknowledged under questioning that a recent appearance by an al-Azhar specialist (defending the institution against charges that it housed outmoded thinking)—clothed in a short-sleeve polo shirt that showed off not only his youth but also his muscular biceps—was designed to appeal to a youth audience more concerned with relevance and dynamism than book learning.[55]

Third, the communication is one-way. Occasionally a live audience might be introduced, a guest brought in for discussion or debate, or a questioner allowed to call in. Even more occasionally, preachers might refer to each other. But there is generally much more give than take in the genre.

Fourth, the forms used encourage a focus on personal conduct and ethical guidance. And that leaves a particular opening for salafi broadcasters, with their insistently textual focus on what Muslims should do in all aspects of their lives, to reach a wide audience beyond those who would normally see themselves as salafis. In some societies, the sense that such a focus on personal conduct is politically safe leaves many to suspect that the flourishing of salafi broadcasting has been anything but coincidental. But while such a focus may have been politically innocuous in most circumstances, it has had the unmistakable effect of creating a mass public as a religious body—not merely as voters and consumers but as a community of pious believers striving to live their lives in accordance with divine instructions.

Finally, it contributes to a transformation of the nature of the fatwa. Of course, fatwas have always taken many forms. But at its core, a fatwa has always been a question from a Muslim to a religious scholar. The answer is directed to the questioner; it might be more broadly circulated among specialists for educational or persuasive purposes. Some might be very elaborate in their argumentation; other times a very brief answer might be given. A television fatwa takes the same form but in a very different context. In speaking with one popular television mufti—one with extremely strong al-Azhar credentials—I was told that he felt compelled to issue approximately one fatwa per minute on his show. This leaves little time for discussion or argumentation, and the mufti had to acknowledge that his true audience was not the questioner but the vast number of viewers. The fatwa in this context is not a means for instructing an individual believer or teasing out a fine point of law or practice; it is a way of reducing proper Islamic behavior to an unending series of didactic aphorisms that can be heard and applied by a large audience.

As with print media, the story of broadcast media over the past couple of decades is not a linear one: there is greater variety and openness to be sure but there have also been serious—and sometimes brutal and successful—official attempts to police the new broadcasters. After Egypt's 2013 coup, Islamic broadcasters were either shut down or tamed (with salafi stations dropping any programming that might be suspect, filling the airwaves instead with programs about personal practice and even cooking shows and English lessons); some freewheeling television shows were canceled; and some broadcasters were harassed and arrested. The availability of external platforms required careful negotiation at times (pro-Muslim Brotherhood broadcasters, for instance, set up studios in Istanbul where a diaspora community developed but actually broadcast from London, presumably in order to take advantage of the freer legal environment and decrease their political exposure in Turkey).[56]

Internet and Social Media: Intimacy Regained ... and Watched

We come finally to newer spheres opened up by rapid developments in information technologies and social media.

Here the bottom-up view of openings and cacophony (rather than a top-down view of control and univocality) is far more obvious, perhaps excessively so. For here we run into formidable hurdles that stem not from our ability to study such developments and their effects but instead from three factors: the burst of enthusiasm for the subject leading to an outpouring of rapid analysis; the way in which the media themselves (as well as the ways they are used) develop and change rapidly; and the fascination with their potential for mass mobilization and even revolutionary movements.

The first difficulty is easy to trace. An early burst of enthusiasm for the new media and their political effects—that they broke taboos, enabled activist networks to be constructed, provided not merely a new public sphere but a very flexible one, and that they were therefore politically enabling—was followed by a wave of skepticism about their divisive effects, elite biases, and ephemeral nature. The uprisings of 2011 contributed to a trend in which strong claims rapidly outpaced empirical research. In this section, I will try to follow the advice of Henry Farrell to be alert to the way that the Internet (and, I would argue by extension, other newer communications and information technologies) can have different characteristics and effects; these may operate simultaneously in cross-cutting ways.[57] In other words, we should be less insistent in demanding that a unitary thing called the Internet or "social media" in the singular has one clear set of effects. Instead we need to become more attuned to the various ways the newer media and technologies may offer opportunities, impose costs, and carry specific characteristics when they are sites for politics.

The second difficulty is a bit more difficult to overcome but should sensitize us to the necessity for stepping a bit tentatively: the rapid changes in technologies and the creative ways in which they are used make categorical statements particularly difficult. There are great differences within the Arab world from country to country and from time to time regarding which newer technologies are used by various groups and in what ways; in such an environment yesterday's empirical finding may be outdated even before its accuracy becomes accepted.

Finally, the 2011 Arab uprisings as well as the color revolutions in Eastern Europe led to an understandable fascination with the roles social media and the Internet played in facilitating mass protest and even regime change. That is one potential topic, but we are focused here on more quotidian arguments about religion and daily life, public policy, ethics, and public life—and only a small portion of that discussion is aimed at revolutionary activity.

What follows in this section, therefore, is a set of four observations based on extant research supplemented by my own impressions from various pockets of Arab societies where I have a bit of familiarity. They are general characteristics relevant to our current inquiry rather than generalized claims about the nature of these spheres in all settings. My observations here do not give much specificity about the nature of religious debates, however; that will come in part 3.

First, and most obviously, whatever their diverse characteristics, newer social media and communications technologies allow for fairly unregulated communication. Many cultivate a spirit of spontaneity and free expression as well as a very individualistic spirit. To view them as solely the product of grassroots activism, however ignores the ways that they can be used by large-scale and formal movements, commercialized, and monitored by governments (as we will explore in a moment). And, as has been so frequently noted, it does not make the sphere egalitarian since access to the media in general and to large audiences in particular is highly unevenly distributed (as in most forms of public speech, no matter how democratic the political system). The media vary greatly, but many seem to privilege less a reasoned argument and more quick references to such arguments. Jokes and cutting remarks, impromptu and sometimes incompletely formed observations, and sloganeering are often more easily communicated than sustained reasoning. Habermas's coffeehouse patrons would be deafened by the roar and horrified by much of what they could make out. But most of these media are highly interactive and have great potential for individualization.

Second, the media can be—and have been—used by more than a collection of disparate individuals; they can support the efforts of self-conscious and strategic leaders and allow organizations and movements to work more effectively. As Paolo Gerbaudo has written, "despite their repeated claims to leaderlessness, contemporary social movements do have their own 'choreographers,' and these choreographers are not identical with the 'dancers' or participants."[58] Indeed, that is why they have attracted so much attention.

Here we have to be careful, however, since so much of that attention has been directed toward understanding their potential for mass mobilization against authoritarian or semiauthoritarian regimes. That potential is real; and though it is not our exclusive focus we should note that one characteristic of these media is their flexibility and the way they can be adapted by different groups for a wide variety of purposes. In the process of exploring successful oppositional mobilizations, scholars and activists alike have noted the tremendous power of such media; the phrase "public sphere" recurs continuously in such writings. Like Habermas's public sphere of the newspaper and coffeehouse, this new one is not democratic in the sense of allowing equal access, yet it easily enables its participants to see themselves as speaking for the common good. David Faris notes, "It is not that digital media necessarily have a democratizing effect in authoritarian countries. The quantitative evidence linking the Internet with democratization is spotty at best. Rather, under certain circumstances, digital media can serve as tools in the repertoire of dissidents. They also create alternative public spheres. These alternative public spheres function through the empowerment of individuals whose ability to express themselves and participate in politics is severely limited in other ways."[59]

Even those enthusiastic about their possibilities under such conditions have noted specific characteristics and limitations.[60] Mark R. Beissinger claims that "These new forms of networking—not face-to-face associations but digitally mediated social networks—have in a number of instances become vehicles for the organization of a 'virtual' civil society and the basis for organizing large-scale mobilizations that have challenged autocratic rule, providing for a civic activism even in the continued presence of anemic 'conventional' civil society association." But then he quickly notes that: "this mixture of weak 'conventional' civil society and robust 'virtual' civil society imparts a particular dynamic to state-society relations within autocracies."[61] More specifically:

> "Virtual" civil society may provide an effective basis for challenging autocratic regimes, but not necessarily for building effective political alternatives, leaving the streets as its main playing field.

"Virtual" civil society also tends to breed a false sense of representativeness within the opposition, an illusion that the opinions articulated through electronic networks mirror those of society as a whole. . . .

"Virtual" civil society can be quite effective in building ad hoc negative coalitions for challenging autocratic regimes. But whether "virtual" civil society is capable of sustaining a sense of solidarity beyond specific windows of contention and providing the kind of collective cohesion necessary for long-term governance is unclear.[62]

Perhaps that sense of being able to speak for the public good in a decentralized but hardly leaderless manner is what makes such media especially attractive to religious movements, including (but hardly limited to) Islamist actors. Sometimes this aspect can be used by formal movements,[63] though even then, the movements are often affected by the decentralized and youth-oriented tendencies of the sphere.[64] And much of the activity in the sphere that is of a religious nature is much more diffuse and allows users and activists to slide between the formality of organizations and the informality of loose ideological and religious tendencies.[65]

Third, despite such enabling features, the newer technologies are very easily monitored and manipulated by regimes and security agencies; they are less easily suppressed, but regimes do try (arresting bloggers, barring specific sites). The fact that such efforts are extremely haphazard, often clumsy, and sometimes little more than sporadically effectual does not diminish the fact that they have real and repressive effects and make online activism sometimes risky.[66]

Finally, for all their encouragement of individuals to elide between their own personal voice, that of like-minded people, and the common good (as in a classical public sphere), it is difficult to escape the impression that by facilitating contact among those with similar interests and ideas, many newer media and information technologies foster the development of self-referential communities. Indeed, they make it possible for marginalized groups to construct their own safer spaces for communicating among themselves.[67] Most such groups remain within state borders, supplement rather than replace other networks, and emphasize the personal. Of course, those within such bubbles interact with those outside. But much of that interaction seems to consist of insults and expressions of outrage. The overall effect of the decentralization and homophily on much religious argument is presented by Sarah Cowles Smith who claims that:

the Internet's tendency to democratize knowledge and encourage the formation of "echo chamber" communities of like-minded individuals, combined with the lack of functional systems of shari'a in the modern nation-state, will create a new normative discourse of fiqh in which personal knowledge and moral reasoning outweigh classical constructions of text-based authority. In practical terms, popular Muslim conceptions of shariʿa will become more individualistic, less likely to be derived from classical discourses, and more deeply rooted in personal experience and opinion.[68]

Yet what may be unusual is how much self-referential argument is occurring where everyone can see, hear, and read. In other words, when people discuss they do so in ways that are accessible to those who can overhear even if they are not invited participants. It is the public nature of this sphere that draws our attention—that is, circles may only be talking among themselves, but everyone can listen and use the words they hear for their own purposes, even ones very much at odds with the intent of the speakers. Indeed, such media facilitate greatly the ability to move words not only from one bubble to the next but from one public sphere to another.

Those translucent bubbles include those of the academics and analysts. Aware that their audience includes such figures—or that their followers might also be following the words of such scholars—some religious authorities have replied to writings about them. In my own time as a researcher at the Carnegie Endowment working on Islamist movements, we received two comments by Islamist leaders replying to articles that I had written; the replies were meant for publication on the Carnegie website. When my Carnegie colleague Georges Fahmi wrote an article on political salafism in Egypt and Tunis, he provoked a lengthy analytical reply from a salafi political leader, one apparently aimed at a Carnegie audience since it was devoid of religious formulas, Qurʾanic quotations, or moral exhortations.[69]

In this respect it is instructive to turn to an article that appeared in the *New Yorker* examining jihadist poetry. The authors—a literary critic and a leading authority on salafism—opened their presentation with a striking claim: "It is impossible to understand jihadism—its objectives, its appeal for new recruits, and its durability—without examining its culture. This culture finds expression in a number of forms, including anthems and documentary videos, but poetry is its heart. And, unlike the videos of beheadings and burnings, which are made primarily for foreign consumption, poetry provides a window onto the movement talking to itself. It is in verse that militants most clearly articulate the fantasy life of jihad."[70]

That horrific violence was meant for outsiders but poetry meant for insiders is itself anomalous. But what should also be noted is that the movement's quiet internal dialogue was being analyzed in the pages of an American weekly with a circulation of over one million. What is said in public can be heard by unintended audiences—with serious but unintended effects.

And that leads us to chapter 4—the real noise is often created by the friction among the spheres.

NOTES

1. James C. Scott, *Seeing Like a State* (New Haven: Yale University Press, 1998).
2. I have written on my understanding of semiauthoritarianism in the Arab world in "Dictatorship and Democracy through the Prism of Arab Elections," in *The Dynamics of Democratization: Dictatorship, Development, and Diffusion*, ed. Nathan J. Brown (Baltimore: Johns Hopkins University Press, 2011), 46–63; and in *When Victory is Not an Option: Islamist Movements in Arab Politics* (Ithaca: Cornell University Press, 2012).
3. Wael Hallaq has argued that the idea of a modern state that is based on the Islamic shariʿa is thus impossible. He has developed this argument most fully in his *The Impossible State: Islam, Politics, and Modernity's Moral Predicament* (New York: Columbia University Press, 2014).
4. Mun'im Sirri and A. Rashied Omar, "Muslim Prayer and Public Spheres: An Interpretation of the Qur'anic Verse 29:45," *Interpretation* 68, 1 (2014): 53.
5. See, for example, Adam Mestyan, "A Garden with Mellow Fruits of Refinement: Music Theaters and Cultural Politics in Cairo and Istanbul, 1867–1892" (PhD diss., Central European University, Department of History, 2011).
6. There are some areas that do admit more intensive historical investigation—for instance, Ralph Hattox, *Coffee and Coffeehouses: The Origins of a Social Beverage in the Medieval Near East* (Seattle: University of Washington Press, 1985).
7. For a provocative account of popular religion in Palestine that advances the view that "religion" has fundamentally changed meaning in the modern period, see James Grehan, *Twilight of the Saints: Everyday Religion in Ottoman Syria and Palestine* (Oxford: Oxford University Press, 2014).
8. See, for instance, Mark Allen Peterson, *Connected in Cairo: Growing up Cosmopolitan in the Modern Middle East* (Bloomington: Indiana University Press, 2011).
9. The most helpful work I have found focuses on the trend in Cairo; particularly instructive is Saba Mahmood, *Politics of Piety: The Islamic Revival and the Feminist Subject* (Princeton: Princeton University Press, 2005). Two other influential books cover related themes in a very helpful manner: Salwa Ismail, *Rethinking Islamist Politics: Culture, the State and Islamism* (London: I. B. Tauris, 2006), and Asef Bayat, *Life as Politics: How Ordinary People Change the Middle East* (Palo Alto: Stanford University Press, 2009).
10. Mahmood, *Politics of Piety*, 47.
11. Salwa Ismail, "Islamism, Re-Islamization and the Fashioning of Muslim Selves: Refiguring the Public Sphere," *Muslim World Journal of Human Rights* 4, 1 (2007): 5.
12. Ibid., 10.
13. Ibid., 16.
14. Michaelle Browers, *Political Ideology in the Arab World: Accommodation and Transformation* (Cambridge: Cambridge University Press, 2009).
15. The most helpful work here on the political nature of such practices, emphasizing their democratic nature, is Lisa Wedeen's *Peripheral Visions: Publics, Power, and Performance in Yemen* (Chicago: University of Chicago Press, 2008).
16. On Kuwaiti democratic practices in general, see Mary Ann Tétreault, *Stories of Democracy: Politics and Society in Contemporary Kuwait* (New York: Columbia University Press, 2000). On the diwaniyya specifically, it is a subject of

incessant talk in Kuwait (often in diwaniyyas themselves). An English language explanation of its origin and significance can be found in Mohammad Khalid A. Al-Jassar, "Constancy and Change in Contemporary Kuwait City: The Socio-Cultural Dimensions of the Kuwait Courtyard and Diwaniyya" (PhD diss., University of Wisconsin, Milwaukee, Department of Anthropology, 2009).

17. The 1989 diwaniyya movement is well covered in a series of articles that appeared in the Kuwaiti daily *al-Jarida* beginning February 5, 2009 by Jasim al-Qamis and Dari al-Jutayli.

18. Lindsey Stephenson, "Women and the Malleability of the Kuwaiti Dīwāniyya," *Journal of Arabian Studies* 1, 2 (2011): 183–199.

19. Salwa Ismail, "Urban Subalterns in the Arab Revolutions: Cairo and Damascus in Comparative Perspective," *Comparative Studies in Society and History* 55, 4 (2013): 865–894.

20. For a useful initiation into the politics and sociology of urban public space, see the collection edited by Marjatta Nielsen and Jakob Skovgaard-Petersen, *Middle Eastern Cities 1900–1950: Public Spaces and Public Spheres* (Aarhus: Aarhus University Press, 2001).

21. On the relationship between the uprising and Tahrir Square, see Atef Shahat Said, "The Tahrir Effect: History, Space, and Protest in the Egyptian Revolution of 2011," (PhD diss., University of Michigan, Department of Sociology, 2014). Also of interest is Dimitris Soudias, "Negotiating Space: The Evolution of the Egyptian Street, 2000–2011," *Cairo Papers in Social Science* 32, 4 (2014).

22. See, for instance, Leila Hudson, "Late Ottoman Damascus: Investments in Public Space and the Emergence of Popular Sovereignty," *Critique: Critical Middle Eastern Studies* 15, 2 (2006): 156.

23. Asef Bayat, *Life as Politics: How Ordinary People Change the Middle East* (Stanford: Stanford University Press, 2010).

24. Samuel Schielke, *The Perils of Joy: Contesting Mulid Festivals in Contemporary Egypt* (Syracuse: Syracuse University Press, 2012).

25. Daniel Corstange, "Religion, Pluralism, and Iconography in the Public Sphere: Theory and Evidence from Lebanon," *World Politics* 64, 1 (2012): 116–160. For a general treatment of the politics of a particular city, see Diane Singerman, ed., *Cairo Contested: Governance, Urban Space, and Global Modernity* (Cairo: American University in Cairo Press, 2011).

26. See the study by Amr Ezzat, *Li-man al-manabir al-yawm? Tahlil siyasat al-dawla fi idarat al-masajid* (Cairo: Egyptian Initiative for Personal Rights, 2014).

27. "Minister compares New Suez Canal to Prophet Mohamed's battle trench," *Mada Masr*, August 4, 2015, http://www.madamasr.com/news/minister-compares-new-suez-canal-prophet-mohameds-battle-trench, accessed December 30, 2015.

28. See, for instance, Aaron Rock Singer, "Prayer and the Islamic Revival: A Timely Challenge," *International Journal of Middle East Studies* 48, 2 (2016), 293–312.

29. For a rich but brief examination of this issue in recent years in Egypt, see Amr Ezzat, "Searching for the Church of Islam," *The Imminent Frame: Secularism, Religion, and the Public Sphere* (blog) Social Science Research Council, April 9, 2014, http://blogs.ssrc.org/tif/2014/04/09/searching-for-the-church-of-islam/, accessed June 3, 2014.

30. See "Friday Sermon Topples the Preacher of al-Tahrir," *al-Wafd*, November 30, 2012.

31. "The Public Prosecutor Opens an Investigation in the Accusation of the "Preacher of al-Tahrir" of Contempt of the Islamic Religion," *al-Shuruq*, August 10, 2014.

32. Malika Zeghal, "The 'Recentering' of Religious Knowledge and Discourse: The Case of Al-Azhar in Twentieth-Century Egypt," in *Schooling Islam: The Culture and Politics of Modern Muslim Education*, ed. Robert W. Hefner and Muhammad Qasim Zaman (Princeton: Princeton University Press, 2007), 107–130.
33. Charles Hirschkind, "Civic Virtue and Religious Reason: An Islamic Counterpublic," *Cultural Anthropology* 16, 1 (2001): 16.
34. Patrick D. Gaffney, *The Prophet's Pulpit: Islamic Preaching in Contemporary Egypt* (Berkeley: University of California Press, 1994).
35. Linda G. Jones, *The Power of Oratory in the Medieval Muslim World* (Cambridge: Cambridge University Press, 2012).
36. The best sources in English are Ami Ayalon, *The Press in the Arab Middle East: A History* (New York: Oxford University Press, 1995) and William A. Rugh, *Arab Mass Media: Newspapers, Radio, and Television in Arab Politics* (Westport: Praeger, 2004).
37. See the brief treatment in Ayalon, *The Press*, 101–102. I am very indebted to `Abd al-Wahhab al-Kayyali for collecting vital information on the recent history of the Jordanian press.
38. Marc Lynch, *State Interests and Public Spheres: The International Politics of Jordan's Identity* (New York: Columbia University Press, 1999), 63.
39. Given the liveliness of the Kuwaiti press, it is surprising how little scholarly attention it has received. The most comprehensive account in English is Kjetil Selvik, "Elite Rivalry in a Semi-Democracy: The Kuwaiti Press Scene," *Middle Eastern Studies* 47, 3 (2011): 477–496
40. Kjetil Selvik, Jon Nordenson, and Tewodros Aragi Kebede, "Print Media Liberalization and Electoral Coverage Bias in Kuwait," *The Middle East Journal* 69, 2 (Spring 2015): 255–276.
41. For some analysis of coverage and circulation, see Kenneth J. Cooper, "Politics and Priorities: Inside the Egyptian Press," *Arab Media and Society* 6 (2008). A useful account of the obstacles facing Egyptian journalists during this period can be found in Mohamad Hamas Elmasry, "Producing News in Mubarak's Egypt: An Analysis of Egyptian Newspaper Production during the Late Hosni Mubarak Era," *Journal of Arab & Muslim Media Research* 4, 2–3 (2012): 121–144.
42. I wrote on the post-2011 Egyptian press in "Can the Colossus Be Salvaged? Egypt's State-Owned Press in a Post-Revolutionary Environment," Carnegie Web Commentary, August 22, 2011, http://carnegieendowment.org/2011/08/22/can-colossus-be-salvaged-egypt-s-state-owned-press-in-post-revolutionary-environment/4ud2, accessed March 26, 2015. On analogous developments in Tunisia, see Roxane Farmanian, "What is Private, What is Public, and Who Exercises Media Power in Tunisia? A Hybrid-Functional Perspective on Tunisia's Media Sector," *Journal of North African Studies* 19, 5 (2014): 656–678. More generally, see Naomi Sakr, *Transformations in Egyptian Journalism: Media and the Arab Uprisings* (London: I. B. Tauris, 2013).
43. For how thoroughly such financial intervention can shape media even in the absence of a strong state presence, see Nabil Dajani, "The Myth of Media Freedom in Lebanon," *Arab Media and Society* 18 (2013).
44. Mohamed Elmeshad, "We Completely Agree: Egyptian Television Media in the Era of Al-Sisi," *Jadaliyya*, April 6, 2015, http://www.jadaliyya.com/pages/index/21305/we-completely-agree_egyptian-television-media-in-t, accessed July 14, 2015.

45. Writings on broadcast media in the Arab world have become very extensive in recent years. Rugh, *Arab Mass Media*, provides a very solid comprehensive look; another basic book that is useful is Naomi Sakr, *Satellite Realms: Transnational Television, Globalization and the Middle East* (London: I. B. Tauris, 2001). Also useful is Noha Mellor, *The Making of Arab News* (Lanham, MD: Rowman & Littlefield, 2005). More current work is available in the journal *Arab Media and Society*.

46. The radio wars among Arab regimes attracted great attention; in conversations with residents of the Arab world who grew up in the 1950s and 1960s, I have often heard mention of their listening to such broadcasts. My sense is that the political effects of the propaganda battles have yet to be seriously probed and might easily be slight.

47. Donatella Della Ratta, Naomi Sakr, and Jakob Skovgaard-Petersen, *Arab Media Moguls* (London: I. B. Tauris, 2015).

48. The best coverage of this new public sphere is Marc Lynch, *Voices of the New Arab Public: Iraq, al-Jazeera, and Middle East Politics Today* (New York: Columbia University Press, 2006). In a second work, *The Arab Uprising: The Unfinished Revolutions of the New Middle East* (New York: Public Affairs, 2012), Lynch shows this new sphere at work in a supporting capacity during the uprisings of 2011.

49. Indeed, even small countries were able to generate a considerable degree of local content. See, for instance, Mohamed Satti, "International Media and Local Programming: The Case of Kuwait," *Arab Media and Society* 18 (2013).

50. A particularly useful publication is Khaled Hroub, *Religious Broadcasting in the Middle East* (New York: Columbia University Press, 2012).

51. Jacqueline Jayne Gottlieb Brinton, "Preaching Islamic Renewal: Shaykh Muḥammad Mitwallī Shaʻrāwī and the Synchronization of Revelation and Contemporary Life" (PhD diss., University of Virginia, Religious Studies, 2009).

52. Bettin Gräf and Jakob Skovgaard-Petersen, eds., *Global Mufti: The Phenomenon of Yusuf al-Qaradawi* (New York: Columbia University Press, 2009).

53. This happened even in the more constricted space within Saudi Arabia. See Andrew Hammon, "Reading Lohaidan in Riyadh: Media and the Struggle for Judicial Power in Saudi Arabia," *Arab Media and Society* 7 (2009).

54. A particularly interesting analysis is provided by Yasmin Moll, "Islamic Televangelism: Religion, Media and Visuality in Contemporary Egypt," *Arab Media and Society* 10 (2010).

55. The subject at hand—the statements of a prominent broadcaster questioning an authoritative collection of hadith—could not easily be confronted directly. The broadcaster had implied that al-Bukhari, the scholar collecting the hadiths was fallible. The highbrow response—that infallibility of an individual human was of course accepted but that al-Bukhari's collection represents the best and most authoritative work and draws on rich individual and collective scholarship—would likely be ineffective if it came across as stuffy and obscurantist.

56. Personal interview with Muslim Brotherhood leaders, Istanbul, May 2015.

57. Henry Farrell, "The Consequences of the Internet for Politics," *Annual Review of Political Science* 15 (2012): 35–52.

58. Paolo Gerbaudo, *Tweets and the Streets: Social Media and Contemporary Activism* (London: Pluto Press, 2012), 159.

59. David Faris, "(Amplified) Voices for the Voiceless," *Arab Media and Society* 11 (2010).

60. For an assessment of the state of knowledge, see Marc Lynch, "After Egypt: The Limits and Promise of Online Challenges to the Authoritarian Arab State," *Perspectives on Politics* 9, 2 (2011): 301–310; also see Sean Aday et al., "Blogs and Bullets: New Media in Contentious Politics," *Peaceworks* 65 (2010), http://www.usip.org/sites/default/files/pw65.pdf, accessed June 23, 2014.

61. Mark R. Beissinger, "'Conventional' and 'Virtual' Civil Societies in Autocratic Regimes" (paper prepared for the 20th International Conference of Europeanists, Amsterdam, The Netherlands, June 25–27, 2013), 2.

62. Ibid., 24–26.

63. See, for example, Pete Ajemian, "The Islamist Opposition Online in Egypt and Jordan," *Arab Media and Society* 4 (2008).

64. Marc Lynch, "Young Brothers in Cyberspace," *Middle East Report* 37 (2007): 26.

65. Charles Hirschkind was an early scholar focusing on the emergence of a religious public sphere, especially in Egypt, involving newer media and information technologies. See, for instance, "Civic Virtue and Religious Reason: An Islamic Counterpublic," *Cultural Anthropology*, 16, 1 (2001): 3; and "New Media and Political Dissent in Egypt," *Revista de Dialectologia y Tradiciones Populares* 65, 1 (2010): 137–153.

66. See, for instance, Nicholas McGeehan, "Control, Halt, Delete: Gulf States Crack Down on Online Critics," *Al-Monitor*, 8 (August 2013), http://www.al-monitor.com/pulse/originals/2013/08/gulf-states-online-critics-crackdown-cybercrime-social-media.html, accessed June 23, 2014; and Lori Plotkin Boghardt, "Saudi Arabia's War on Twitter," *Policywatch* 2179 (Washington Institute for Near East Policy, December 9, 2013), https://www.washingtoninstitute.org/policy-analysis/view/saudi-arabias-war-on-twitter, accessed June 23, 2014.

67. On salafis in post-2011 Tunisia, for instance, see Kayla Branson, "Islamist Cyber-Activism: Contesting the Message, Redefining the Public," *Journal of North African Studies* 19, 5 (2014): 713–732. Also useful more generally is Geneive Abdo, "Salafists and Sectarianism: Twitter and Communal Conflict in the Middle East," paper (Center for Middle East Policy at Brookings, March 2015).

68. Sarah Cowles Smith, "Crowdsourcing Shariʿa: Digital Fiqh and Changing Discourses of Textual Authority, Individual Reason, and Social Coercion" (masters thesis, Georgetown University, Arab Studies, April 2011), iii.

69. ʿAbd al-Munʿim al-Shahhat, "Reply to the Research 'The Future of Political Salafism in Egypt and Tunisia," *al-Fath*, November 20, 2015, http://www.fath-news.com/Art/1086, accessed December 30, 2015.

70. Robyn Cresswell and Bernard Haykel, "Battle Lines: Want to Understand the Jihadis? Read Their Poetry," *New Yorker*, June 8, 2015.

CHAPTER 4

. . . Can Be Heard When Worlds Collide

In the end, the degree of critical rationality in the opinion space depends not on the arguments that are made within a single format, but rather on the ensemble of spaces and on the nature of critical dialogue that takes place between them.

Ronald N. Jacob and Eleanor Townsley, *The Space of Opinion*, 246

All spheres of life, from the most intimate everyday milieu through to large-scale global orga-nizations, operate within heavily mediated settings in which the meaning of messages is con-stantly changing and is often at odds with the intentions of their creator.

John Keane, *Democracy and Media Decadence*, 23

In the republic of arguments, people argue in many different ways in many different places. But what is heard?

In the last chapter, we saw how Arab societies are rich in locales—real, vir-tual, and metaphorical—for talking. And there are even broader spaces for listening. In this chapter we shift the focus away from specific spaces and more to the overall effect: how do the various spaces intersect, conflict, interpen-etrate, and interlock with each other? Like the last, this chapter is descriptive and historical. But it is analytical as well, showing the effect of the existence of various spaces that can be—and are—linked. That is, we present the evolu-tion of the interrelationship of the various spaces for discussing religion. This allows us to see the operation of the republic of arguments more clearly—and to understand its limitations. The interrelationship among media has grown considerably over time, leading to a complex but hardly harmonious blending of various public spheres.

And to make things even more complex, in this chapter we add two less-than-fully-public spaces for political arguments about religion to the public spaces discussed in the previous chapter. In addition to the various older and newer media, public spaces, and small group discussions already examined, we also consider less public but equally vital spaces—one of specialist discussion and one of state administration. The first involves scholars and religious officials and spaces where they speak to their followers. The second involves areas in which state officials and institutions make their determination about how religious matters are to be governed or inform the manner of governing. This chapter therefore helps sets the stage for part 3, in which we trace the effect of the revival, noting how the existence of linkages among the spheres allows arguments to be moved (and heard) with greater ease without the speaker's authority carrying with it.

We proceed in three steps. First, we consider the growing permeability of the divisions among the separate spheres for argument. Second, we turn to the political effects of this porousness and the way that authority operates (and is modified) when arguments are moved across spheres. Third, we add a historical dimension and trace the evolution of the republic of arguments. We see how it emerged by examining three moments with an eye to understanding how the spheres operated and interpenetrated over time.

Indeed, perhaps the most dramatic but underappreciated change in Arab political arguments is not how many spheres there are but how easy it has become in recent years to move among them. And that has worked all kinds of effects on Arab politics. But in the remainder of this book we will also see that authority moves far less easily than words. Sometimes authority can flow in strange ways; sometimes its flow is blocked or reversed. Indeed, one important effect of the increasing interpenetration of the various political spheres is to redistribute power—not to equalize it by any means, but to have it shift it in surprising ways (surprising, at least, to those used to exercising power in a specific sphere).

THE POROUSNESS OF THE SPHERES

In order to illustrate these ideas concretely, let us begin with a society with a particularly strong and well-earned reputation for political garrulousness: Kuwait.

The Kuwaiti parliament building stands on the shore of the Gulf, designed by a prominent Danish architect (Jørn Utzon, whose most famous building was the Sydney Opera House), who designed the roof of the main building to suggest a Bedouin tent. Most Kuwaitis I have spoken with—those who view their polity as having been founded not by Bedouins but by a collection of merchant families—seem to view the parliament building less as an oversized encampment and more of a national *diwaniyya*, the fixed gathering place generally adjacent to (or part of) a private home where Kuwaitis meet in the evenings, as described in chapter 3. The practice of meeting in diwaniyyas is traced back to gatherings among members of the same tribe, family, or group of merchants; Kuwaitis see its genesis as fully urban. The link between parliament and diwaniyya is not limited to the realm of metaphor but has grown quite close. Retail politics necessary to build a standing in parliamentary elections is conducted in diwaniyyas. (When I once quizzed a promising young Islamist on whether he would run for a seat in parliament, he replied, "Not yet. My diwaniyya is not big enough.") Campaign rallies are conducted in diwaniyyas or in capacious tents and halls designed to resemble large diwaniyyas.

In examining the relationship among the various spheres in which political arguments take place, the Kuwaiti parliament and the diwaniyya are very good places to start. Neither realm is free of internal hierarchies and displays of power and authority. And they are both enmeshed in broader power relations: in terms of their social and political significance, at first glance the parliament might appear to be an authoritative structure where laws are made and ministers questioned, while diwaniyyas are an informal structure with no relationship to political authority. Indeed, if we pursue our interest in the interrelationships among spaces for public argument, our first inclination might be that parliament and diwaniyyas are like a two-sided coin, with parliament the public and authoritative face of Kuwaiti politics and diwaniyyas the more private and informal one.

But the matter is a bit more complex. An issue discussed in a closed session of parliament (from which the public is barred) spreads very quickly to the general public as parliamentarians spend their evenings in various diwaniyyas and leak out their accounts. Journalists then write about what was the talk of the diwaniyyas the night before.

When I first visited Kuwait in 1994, access to the parliament building was uncontrolled and all members of the public could enter. I was able to wander the halls (designed by Utzon to resemble his conception of a Middle Eastern market) searching for the offices of parliamentarians I wished to meet. Diwaniyyas, by contrast, were only beginning to open to non-Kuwaitis. No formal bar existed and Kuwaitis boasted how anyone could enter, but as a non-citizen, I had to struggle to acquire invitations (unnecessary for Kuwaitis). Fifteen years later, the situation was reversed. Many of the more prominent diwaniyyas routinely hosted foreigners. By contrast, I found security at parliament extremely tight—it had become difficult to gain access not because of threats to the safety of the members but because of demands on their time. Constituents had learned to resort to their districts' MPs in any search for assistance regarding all kinds of private matters (everything from a driver's license to a scholarship for a family member). With the parliament building less accessible by day, constituents adjusted to ambush their MPs in diwaniyyas by night.

In that way, two different spheres have become closely linked, and private and public matters easily pass through the boundary in a manner that is confusing to the observer but seems natural to most participants.

We tend to think of publicity as empowering (for the speaker at least), and it can be. Those who can cast their words before the public are properly regarded as powerful. But publicity can also have very divergent effects, especially as various spheres are linked: one loses control of one's words very easily as those words are moved from one sphere to another. Unexpected things can happen when words and arguments travel stripped of their speaker's authority. Such a flow leads to many unintended effects—unintended, at least, by the speaker.

The resources that allow domination or that lend credibility in one sphere do not always operate in other spheres. A specialist giving a talk to colleagues or a leader giving a speech to followers might control the format and content of a discussion—but when a video recording is circulated to a less sympathetic audience, the speaker can lose such control in a dramatic fashion.

The effect is not simply to bring people together but often to drive them farther apart or encourage them to dig more deeply into already entrenched positions.

In June 2011, an Egyptian showed me—with a mixture of bemusement and horror—a video clip of a prominent salafi preacher explaining that anyone who entered a room saying "Good morning," rather than the Qur'anically enjoined "Peace be upon you," is effectively summoning Satan. The preacher's dire warning seemed designed for the context in which a small community of followers intend to follow the letter of God's instructions. In a more public setting—and after their forceful political emergence in 2011, many Egyptians who had ignored salafis for years suddenly began to swap the latest outrageous statements—the preacher's instructions sounded simply zany. When worlds collide, fear and ridicule are frequent responses (and they are not ones that I am above: after leaving the woman who showed me the video clip, I told her that I would have said, "Bye," but as I wanted to enter paradise, I would say, "Peace be upon you" instead.)

The results are not merely amusement and horror. A widely circulated video during the debate over the 2012 constitution in Egypt revealed a prominent salafi leader, Yasir Burhami, justifying the constitution to his followers by pointing to its Islamizing potential.[1] Shocked opponents inclined to see the document as an Islamist Trojan horse felt they had a smoking gun. To my viewing, the video showed something a bit different: a prominent salafi leader forced to sell his compromises to followers who had before them a document that only had a few clauses with any obvious Islamic content. The fact that he needed to persuade his supporters by using terms that alienated non-Islamists showed the kinds of dilemmas that face all politicians in settings in which the spheres collide.

A very similar story can be told about Rashid al-Ghannushi in Tunisia. Meeting with a group of Islamists during a time of constitutional controversy over the inclusion of a reference to the Islamic shari'a in the text, al-Ghannushi was videotaped arguing (seemingly with salafis) for a gradual approach to dealing with non-Islamist political opposition in the society and within the state itself. In one way the talk can be heard as an attempt by a leader to coax skeptical potential allies (but also potential spoilers) to be satisfied with a more conciliatory approach in order to support ultimate Islamist goals of a society operating in accordance with Islamic strictures. But when it was leaked, the tape was seized by al-Ghannushi's opponents as a blueprint for taking over the state through gradualism and stealth.[2]

Indeed, pursuing the case of the entry of salafis into public life may show how the new politics of porous, linked, and colliding spheres can impose some rude shocks. Perhaps one of the most jarring for the salafi rank and file is the rudeness of public political life itself. Salafis tend to treat their teachers with reverence due to their superior learning. But as they entered broader political life, salafis suddenly found such respected figures lampooned, ridiculed, and criticized in non-salafi spheres. Of course, some prominent salafis have been perfectly rude (and sometimes far worse) to their non-Islamist opponents, and that in itself may lead to a deeper unanticipated challenge of publicity, especially in a polarized environment. Many salafi movements that seek to lead the way to truth are successful in gathering some followers, but they often alienate many as well, with growing numbers repulsed by the salafi call.

Politics in a polarized environment has unwelcome effects for some, and indeed it has led to deep salafi resentment, not only that their scholars are mocked but that the public sphere and powerful institutions are arrayed against them. In January 2013, I met with a group of salafis who complained about the public atmosphere by repeatedly using what seemed to me an odd word—they complained that they were victims of racism ('unsuriyya). I resisted the urge to lecture them on the meaning of the word "race," because I realized it would have missed the point. What I sensed they meant to communicate was a feeling of exclusion and discrimination. There were places where they did not feel welcome or could not go, public bodies (such as the police) they could not enter, and public settings where they would not be treated with respect.

A century ago, most consequential arguments about religion and politics did not take place in such rough-and-tumble settings but instead occurred among specialists or within the state administration. The public spaces discussed in the previous chapter were far fewer in number and many, even when they came into existence, were far less active than they have become today. Over the course of the past century, of course, that has very much changed as those spaces have come very lively indeed—indeed, that is one way of understanding what is often spoken of as the democratization of religious authority. But of course, the public spaces discussed in the previous chapter have not supplanted the spaces of specialists or state administration. As we learned in the last chapter, states still play a powerful role in policing, regulating, and swaying public arguments. And specialists weigh in heavily—and are invoked—in such arguments as well.

But it is not merely that the public spaces stand alongside the specialist and state spheres nor that the specialist and state spheres affect the public spaces: the various spaces interconnect and interpenetrate and do so in increasingly complicated—but again, not always harmonious—ways.

FROM PUBLIC SQUARE TO CURTAINLESS WINDOWS

What are the political effects of this porousness?

The most common metaphors used for the public sphere often involve a physical space that is completely open, such as a public square, town green, or occasionally Hyde Park Speakers' Corner. Yet real "speakers' corners" are populated mostly by cranks (as speakers) and the curious (as bemused audience); most others in such space occupy it only briefly as they rush by, ignoring or avoiding the loudmouths attempting to harangue the public. There are places for serious and substantive argument in most societies, but they—and certainly the various spheres examined in the previous chapter—tend to be a bit more structured than a park and a soap box. A far better metaphor for the interlinked public spheres we are exploring might be a house with no curtains (and perhaps open windows) in which interactions among family members and friends are readily visible and audible to those outside who might use what they see and hear without the same discretion or shared understandings of those on the inside. Of course, those on the inside are generally aware that their words can be overheard and can try to use that publicity for their own purposes.

Focusing on links among the spaces is not new—indeed, it was central to Habermas's reference to "the" public sphere rather than a collection of autonomous and separate spaces—but it does move against the grain of some thinking on the subject. Early enthusiasts of newer media highlighted their distinctiveness rather than their linkages to old ways of communication. Yet some past explorations of the various spheres within the Arab world have frequently noted their interlocking nature. They have done so in a manner that highlights the ways in which groups—however loosely structured—can move messages and arguments through various channels in a manner that strengthens networks and seems politically enabling. For instance, Mark Allen Petersen writes of the Egyptian uprising of 2011, noting the way that social media could deploy the analysis and information of traditional media in support of their own arguments: "most links were accompanied by a brief framing message. That is, a message might point to a state media story about foreign influences and offer a mocking message such as 'Oh yeah, because the U.S. and Al-Qaida work so well together,' pre-framing the story for those who click on the link."[3] A group of scholars reporting on new media in the wake of the Arab uprisings noted how quickly enthusiastic claims about such media role outran empirical analysis but went on to note that "The key role for new media may be its [sic] bridging function: from an activist core to mass publics, from user-generated content to mainstream mass media, and from local struggles to international attention."[4]

Indeed, linkages among the spaces were hardly an innovation of the Arab upheavals of 2011—as any visitor to the annual Cairo book fair, described in the previous chapter, would have recognized in the 1980s or 1990s. Public debate among opposing points of view, display of newly published materials, traditional media coverage, and large crowds blended together every year in January in a mélange of forums where all kinds of public issues were argued.

The result can be extremely significant politically; it allowed, for instance, what Charles Hirschkind identifies as an Islamic counterpublic, one he found in Egypt but that was partly transnational and not contained within national structures; it was based on the linkages of several spaces: sermons, circulation of cassette tapes, personal conduct, and small group conversations:

> Da'wa is undertaken in the street, on public transportation, at the workplace, or in the home. It may take place between friends or coworkers, though also between total strangers. . . . From a liberal perspective, da'wa is seen as encouraging an unwarranted intrusion into the privacy of others, especially as it entails entering into what are considered to be personal matters of religious faith. . . . Da'wa for this reason constitutes an obstacle to the state's attempt to secure a social domain where national citizens are free to make modern choices, for it repoliticizes those choices, subjecting them to a public scrutiny oriented around the task of establishing the conditions for the practice of Islamic virtues.[5]

But what may have been insufficiently noted in past writings about such linkages is that not all attempts to move arguments from one space to the next are friendly. Most arguments can easily be made portable. In the process the one who initially makes it often feels his or her argument is taken out of context. The feeling is usually justified. Indeed, that is precisely the point. The portability of arguments removes control from the speaker.

This may indeed be the most democratizing effect of the spread of publicity—not only can it open access to new authorities, but often more significantly, it can help pry arguments from an authority's mouth and allow them to be deployed by both followers and adversaries in various ways completely unintended by the original speaker. The effect is to alter the ways arguments are used (often to ridicule or discredit the maker) but also to continue disputes in new spheres and make resolution more rather than less difficult.

Fatwas (as will be seen) are often well suited for such portability but the overall effect takes almost the opposite of the intended effect of a fatwa. Rather than amount to an authoritative (if unbinding) pronouncement rendering further discussion by nonspecialists unnecessary, a fatwa moving across spheres can become a political football, or, to use a different metaphor, a subplot in a long continuing soap opera in which continuing drama (and melodrama) trump resolution.

The ways that arguments can travel quickly does not amount to an end to privacy but instead to a loss of control over the terms of publicity. Leaks are the most obvious manifestation of this trend, and the various spaces are fruitful ground for reports of previously private conversations, real or forged, in which remarks intended for a small audience are broadcast to a larger one to discredit or expose the speaker. My impression is that the reliance of increasingly partisan and diverse media outlets on leaks has increased greatly in recent years and has extended to squabbles among leading members of the regime (such as those in Egypt after 2013, seemingly designed to discredit various high officials) or members of the Kuwaiti royal family (leading to public humiliation, embarrassment, and even allegations of bribery and sedition). Leaks, of course, are hardly the only way arguments travel.

The linkages among spaces do not often bring various groups together but can be used to entrench existing differences more deeply. Those who observe how strongly existing forms of authority (especially authoritarian rule) can still dominate and shape even the newer spaces often miss this fact. Yes, it is true that the press can be influenced, patrolled, and manipulated by rulers even in a more competitive environment, that social media can be monitored and policed, that reporters and producers for satellite channels can be arrested on laughable charges, and that political opinions in small group discussions can be reported to security officials. The terms of debate are never equal or free from control. But the increasing rapidity in which arguments can be moved makes them more difficult to chase.

The democratizing effects on religious argument seem to be especially noticeable. It is not that everyone can make an authoritative shari'a-based argument. But it is true that anyone can grab one and deploy it in a realm different from that of its original author. The interpenetration of the spheres empowers audiences—for it is generally someone listening (or overhearing) who moves the argument away from the sphere of the speaker's authority. Power, authority, and states have hardly disappeared, but as spaces have multiplied and boundaries lowered, their rules can be tested, evaded, and negotiated a bit more easily—or at least with much greater ingenuity.

Three quick examples involving Islamic law, all to reappear in subsequent chapters, can illustrate these points.

The first concerns *hudud*—a shari'a-based category involving criminal penalties. There is perhaps no area of Islamic law that more easily (and simultaneously) transfixes and repels shari'a opponents and skeptics than penalties for offenses like theft, adultery, or apostasy. And from a shari'a-based perspective, hudud penalties often seem less flexible since there are specific textual provisions suggesting certain punishments. But there is an argument available to those who seek flexibility on hudud—the early caliph 'Umar is said to have suspended the punishment for theft during a time of famine; similarly, one can say, if economic circumstances are hard (and they never seem easy), then the full panoply of criminal punishments should not be mechanically applied. I first heard this argument from Muslim Brotherhood leaders who wished to avoid a discussion of hudud, using it simply to forestall the answer of what they would do in office. But I later heard it from Islamists who argued against their more literal-minded salafi rivals and from the opponents of Islamists who sought religious arguments to buttress their positions. Used these varying ways, the argument likely does little to persuade the purported interlocutor but it does deflect criticism, parry attacks, or convince the user's own camp of the righteousness of the cause.

It should be noted that the rise of interest in the *maqasid* of the shari'a—a shari'a-based interpretive technique devised to guide specialists to the most appropriate interpretation by using the purported underlying purposes of the Islamic shari'a—has a similar effect; as much as specialists might cringe, the concept of *maqasid* can free its user of centuries of jurisprudence on the morally compelling grounds that the user is following God's own intentions rather than slavishly following the letter of the law in a small-minded manner.

Such arguments may travel easily but they do not travel everywhere: specialists are sometimes likely to use them but also regard them with some skepticism when placed in untrained hands; salafis are likely to be particularly suspicious of what would appear to them to be attempts to flee from clear meanings of the text.

A second example is the fatwa itself—a device for specialists to deliver pronouncements on Islamic law. Fatwas have been ways for specialists to communicate with each other; they could play a role in standardizing interpretations and applications among those within a community of scholars and judges; they might also serve as a mode of transmission over time as well as space.[6] They might allow nonspecialist believers to obtain guidance on a specific question and perhaps use it in a supporting fashion when involved in a dispute or a matter of guidance in an ethical quandary. And they can serve all those purposes today.

But as suggested above, they do more, especially with the rise and interpenetration of new spaces. They can be summarized and hurled against opponents; their advice (but of course not the full reasoning behind them) can be tweeted both by those who seek to use them and those who wish to ridicule them; they can serve as the functional equivalent of an advice column; they can be collected and bound in order to be placed on a bookshelf of someone wishing to construct a learned and pious atmosphere at home or office; they can be used by regimes and against them. <u>Once issued, they can become</u> public <u>property and detached from the particular circumstances that led to</u> their <u>being sought in the first place.</u> A fatwa could always serve some of these purposes, what is remarkable in the Arab world today, however, is how frequently and noisily fatwas can become simultaneously a tool of rhetorical battle and a field for contesting positions.

That leads us to a final example concerning a figure who will be discussed a bit more in chapter 7, Shaykh Salim 'Abd al-Galil. An Azhar-trained scholar, Shaykh Salim teaches and administers but is probably most widely known for delivering quick fatwas on television call-in programs. He draws on his Azhari training in ways that communicate his qualifications very effectively to a nonspecialist audience: he appears in the distinctive Azhari garb and broadcasts on a television station bearing the name of al-Azhar. (There is no formal affiliation with the institution, so when the station began broadcasting, al-Azhar's leadership complained and even threatened litigation but ultimately backed off). With a relentlessly cheerful manner, the shaykh's rapid-fire fatwas communicate very effectively that whatever problem befuddles a believer, there is a shari'a-based solution that is compassionate, practical, and just. The Islamic shari'a is a Muslim's friend.

But the shaykh found that his persuasiveness could be deployed by others for their own purposes. In the summer of 2013, as the army deposed President Muhammad Morsi of the Muslim Brotherhood and security forces moved forcefully against his opponents, a military department specializing in morale released a series of videos of religious figures praising the military and its actions. One such video featured separate appearances by Shaykh Salim and an utterly unrestrained Amr Khalid, a popular lay preacher. Shaykh Salim supported the coup (he was an opponent of the Brotherhood and the organization returned the sense of rivalry), but he made efforts to avoid polarizing rhetoric and was embarrassed by the way the video was used. Not only did he wish to stay outside of partisan politics but within pious circles, the pro-military position was controversial and one that he therefore preferred to espouse diplomatically. He complained that he had been asked to make some general comments denouncing violence and did not realize how they would be used; he cited the participation of some of his own relatives in the pro-Morsi demonstrations to illustrate that he wished to keep cordial relations with all sides. The statement, of course, was lost in the flurry of shrill post-coup propaganda; Shaykh Salim had been given an opportunity make his argument but he had discovered that having agreed to the recording, he had no control over who broadcast it and how it was heard.

THE EVOLUTION OF THE SPHERES

Adding a temporal dimension to our analysis can help in understanding the significance of the linkages among the spaces. In a sense, that will help show how religious arguments have moved (if the metaphor can be forgiven for such a weighty subject) from a game of tic-tac-toe to one of three-dimensional chess (with an unwieldy number of players). The result is a more confusing game where outcomes are harder to predict. We will leave those outcomes—and what we can suggest about them—to subsequent chapters. For now we will simply proceed with a snapshot of four moments. One dates from around the turn of the twentieth century, when spheres for influential discussions about religion and politics were primarily populated by specialists and state administrators who often spoke primarily among themselves. Our second snapshot will be from mid-century when some of the public spheres discussed in the previous chapter had either come alive or, if they were already extant, began to venture into the intersection between Islam and politics and broader publics became engaged. Our third moment is the 1980s, when authoritarianism prevailed throughout the region, but holes had opened up in many societies. And our fourth moment is the aftermath of the 2011 uprisings when cacophony and overlapping interpenetrated spheres have fully bloomed.

Turn of the Century: Mosque, Ministry, and Movements and a Restricted Public

At the beginning of the twentieth century, many of the spaces discussed in the previous chapter were in full existence; others were just beginning or had not yet been formed. But for most residents of the Arab world, even where the spheres existed, access was restricted and patrolled; links among spaces existed but were not always extensive; official and specialist forums (often distinct but always overlapping) dominated public life.

Physical gatherings in which public affairs were discussed were limited; congregational prayers were the main setting and sermons the primary ways in which views were expressed. We have little information on such sermons in normal times, though at periods of political turmoil (such as uprisings in 1919 in Egypt or 1925 in Syria), we have some contemporary accounts of fiery preachers aiming to mobilize. Indeed, one of the iconic images of Egypt in 1919, trotted out at any time in which national unity seems in question, is of priests being invited to ascend minbars in mosques to deliver sermons and imams being given the reciprocal honor in church pulpits.

Yet for all the image of a populist set of scholars, willing to voice the needs of the inarticulate and illiterate masses—the image that 'Umar Makram and others have been cited as embodying[7]—the more common stance of those with such positions in mosques and institutions of learning was to speak primarily *with* each other about matters of religious learning and to speak primarily *to* nonspecialists about matters of ritual, practice, and faith. Such specialists staffed judicial positions as well (though the precise nature of training and the jurisdiction of the courts varied over time and place), sometimes in courts of general jurisdiction but increasingly in personal status courts (where they were eventually pushed aside in some countries, including Egypt, in favor of those with training in schools of law rather than of shari'a).

Indeed, it was partly because of the feeling that such specialists were a bit isolated and not closely connected with social needs and realities that two other kinds of entrants to religious arguments were able to construct spaces for their own discussions. First, a group of prominent intellectuals found a growing interest in discussing religious issues outside of a specialist context. The trend began in Egypt in the 1920s as debates about religious issues (such as the controversy caused by 'Ali 'Abd al-Raziq's *Al-islam wa-usul al-hukm*) traveled outside of al-Azhar (where 'Abd al-Raziq was based) and into the popular press and parliament; by the 1930s, the debates about Islam (and its relationship to law and politics) became a staple of press (and book) discussion.[8]

While the participants in such discussions were members of an intellectual and political (and sometimes economic) elite, and they made their arguments in a form (the written word) not yet directly accessible to most people, we should not rush to assume that their audience was restricted. The little research that has been conducted on reading in the Arab world suggests that the audience for newspapers was far larger than their circulation because of public readings in which the literate shared newspaper contents orally; the joining of the coffee house and the newspaper were important devices for transferring the arguments of the elite to the general population and then to the male population more generally.[9] And there were certainly other public spaces where the ideas could be argued—in most countries professional associations and occasionally labor unions were founded during this period with specific bodies (especially bar associations) often hosting forums for public arguments about topics of political concern, sometimes edging into religious issues.

This public sphere was as close as the Arab world has ever produced to Habermas's bourgeois public sphere in more than the coincidence of newspapers and coffeehouses: it was highbrow, literate, and claimed to speak for the public not despite but because of its elitist nature. But it also gradually expanded in some societies to draw in or generate a public that was more broadly based.[10]

A second space was constructed by social movements, the most prominent and sustained of which was the Muslim Brotherhood. Again arising first in Egypt in the 1920s and 1930s, such movements also worked on the ability to build links among previously fairly discrete spheres: the small group (where recruiting for the Brotherhood was accomplished and the group constructed its more formal "families," the basis of its organizational strength) and the national political sphere (where the group was an active presence in social and later political life). While the Brotherhood was hardly alone, its ability to blend these two spheres and link them to the inculcation of its vision of a greater role for Islam simultaneously in public and in personal and family life gave it the ability to grow quickly and then later to sustain itself under harsh political conditions. In a sense, the model here had existed to some extent before—most notably in the form of sufi orders—but the Brotherhood (and similar movements) differed from those other organizations by insisting on making political participation a central part of its mission (though never the only one).[11]

These two innovations—the intellectual public sphere with an interest in religion and the social movement with religious ideology—spread out from Egypt to other Arab countries, generally in the 1940s and 1950s. Sometimes the influence was direct (with the spread of Egyptian newspapers and the conscious attempts of the Brotherhood to replicate itself in other settings) and sometimes it seemed to be based upon a similar set of social, economic, and technological changes (the spread of education, the growth of the middle class, urbanization, and the spread of new means of communication).

While there were some links among these spaces, they tended to be limited and operate slowly by the standards of later years. And despite the ways newspapers could be read and social movements could recruit members, access to participation in arguments was still limited and primarily one way—from elite or leadership out to an interested audience.

Yet if the spaces were limited in these ways, they were still influential through some of the mechanisms that resembled those in Habermas's bourgeois Europe. Most particularly, parliaments were far more notable for their characteristics as debating chambers for leading citizens rather than legislative bodies or arenas for electoral competition among competing parties. Arab political systems in the period, like those in early modern Europe, were generally monarchical (though many were under direct or indirect imperial influence or control) but there were elected parliaments in many of them. Election results were often manipulated but in a manner that still allowed for some competitiveness and plurality of views. Party systems tended to be very weak (at least outside of Egypt; Syria had a nascent party system developing as well). Thus, parliaments filled with independent deputies or those for whom party or ideological affiliation was weak. The result was to make parliaments weak bodies from the perspective of legislation or ministerial responsibility but far livelier bodies for debate.

Those debates mattered because they put pressure on governments. The most contentious issues often involved questions of sovereignty, and the public spheres that emerged in this period might be held partly responsible for placing governments in very awkward positions when negotiating treaties with Western powers; oil concessions often came under such public pressure as well. When it came to religious issues, missionary activity and legal privileges for foreigners (legacies of the capitulations in which foreigners were granted a form of extraterritorial status) could also be contentious issues, since they often blended religion and national concerns under the banner of state sovereignty. The social movements that arose during this period were often participants; they occasionally even moved pressure on governments from the parliament out into urban spaces with the possibilities of demonstrations and marches in a few countries.

Mid-Century: Authoritarianism and Hibernation of Politics

By the middle of the twentieth century, the political structure of most Arab societies had shifted considerably; the high point of a fairly rigid authoritarianism began in the 1950s and continued in most societies for several decades. On a formal level, pluralist party systems, parliaments (or at least ones incorporating a plurality of orientations and views), and competitive elections were generally shunted aside, suspended, or replaced by plebiscitary structures in which such mechanisms were reduced to a cheerleading role.

Outside of authoritarian formal constitutional procedures, the effects on Arab politics were equally severe. Newspapers and the press more broadly, as explored in the previous chapter, were brought under strict control and even state ownership; broadcast media (also presented in the previous chapter) came of age in this period under heavy-handed state control; restrictions on organizational life of all kinds prevented much open political discussion; and the vast internal security apparatuses designed to monitor and suppress dissenting political opinions were created in almost all states in the region. Most states strived to build ideological apparatuses that dropped any pretense to subtlety; they were designed not simply to inculcate identification with regime-defined conceptions of nation but to prevent articulation of any contrary ideological orientation or policy positions.

The result was not totalitarian in the sense of eliminating all sense of public life outside of the state; Iraq and Syria at their most repressive might have reached in that direction but they were the exception rather than the rule.[12] Much more common were regimes that policed each sphere carefully and became especially ferocious at the boundaries among them. In other words, there were spaces in which limited political discussions were possible, but any attempt to link those spaces—through a social movement, political party, or indeed any organization, formal or informal, was either closely controlled by the political, security, and ideological apparatuses of the state or suppressed.

The public sphere that had emerged in the previous era was reduced, captured, and constrained.

Intellectual production in most outlets was controlled and policed, with regimes either designing their own makeshift (and shifting) ideologies (Arab socialism being the most obvious, but varieties of religious and nationalist ideologies also appearing) or treating all ideologies as suspect and inappropriate for public airing. And when it came to religious argumentation specifically, the preference of most states in the region was to keep it under the watchful eye of official religious establishments or far away from political issues. Religious publications, for instance, either focused on faith and ritual or, in the more ideologically ambitious states, generated analyses linking the favored ideological orientation of the moment with the supposedly authentic nature of religious truth.

Social movements did not disappear. Some, like Sufi brotherhoods in some countries, thrived but maintained a virtual invisibility in political matters. Others, like those modeled on the Muslim Brotherhood were either suppressed (as in Egypt, Syria, and Iraq) or (in Kuwait, Jordan, and Palestine) gently or not so gently deflected into matters more removed from politics (such as education or social work).

And that may have been at the core of the near-death of Arab politics during this period: as soon as discussion left the realm of a restricted circle or edged into matters of public concern, speakers seemed to trip a wire. States patrolled the spheres with some vigilance but were especially insistent about blocking the interstices among them.

Cracks in the Dike or an Age of Osmosis

In the decades following its height, Arab authoritarianism retreated in most countries in which it had held sway. The change was slow and reversible. Polities as diverse as Egypt, Morocco, Algeria, Kuwait, and Jordan unevenly and fitfully liberalized with almost every step taken ambiguous and some reversed. Iraq and Tunisia took only limited steps and quickly reversed them, Iraq doing so with particular violence. In other countries, such as Syria and Saudi Arabia, changes were far subtler and only visible (and public) when an observer took a long-range view: private conversations could increasingly edge into public issues; salon conversations where public met private could be held with less nervousness.

As complex, limited, and subtle as it was, the retreat had several different dimensions that tended to allow older spheres to operate a bit more freely and newer ones to emerge. First, many states that had made extensive welfare commitments to their citizens sought to disentangle themselves from some of them, a process driven by fiscal pressures but still difficult to negotiate. Other states that had avoided extensive commitments still found that the economic changes in the region combined with the extensive developmental demands from their societies necessitated a turn toward a more permissive attitude toward private voluntary, community-based, and nongovernmental organizations, especially those involved in social service provision. These were not restricted to charitable activities and the poor; some of the greatest activity was located in, and sought to provide services to, the middle class.[13] In Egypt, Jordan, and Palestine, for instance, new organizations and groups found the political authorities a bit more relaxed, if still suspicious (and even repressive) when the new activities took on a political tinge. Religious groups seemed to be specially privileged to take advantage of the new environment since they often could build on preexisting informal networks based on family or piety; drew on symbolic and emotive themes with deep social roots; and offered a potentially nonpolitical view of their work that security apparatuses might wish to patrol and monitor but could often willingly accommodate. Even in wealthy states where social service provision did not retreat but rather expanded beyond even Scandinavian dimensions, the new atmosphere was one in which charitable groups, generally with a religious mission, offered new opportunities for crossing borders with philanthropy. As one salafi leader in Egypt explained to me with only a touch of humor, if a wealthy Qatari visits a mosque in Doha, the ranks of those praying is shallow and expenses are great; if he travels to inexpensive and crowded Cairo, he can see his dinars benefiting rows and rows of the pious poor.

A second dimension of the thaw in public life was the ideological retreat of the state. The sharp nationalistic and sometimes socialistic flavor of earlier decades gradually gave way to a less demanding (if still bombastic) official rhetoric that made fewer pretensions to grand or comprehensive visions and focused instead on providing support for existing policies, regimes, and individual leaders. The result was to allow for competing ideological camps to emerge more publicly among intellectuals; those who had been edged out or even arrested for being too far left, too reactionary, or too Islamist in earlier decades could often re-emerge and talk. One Egyptian academic told me at the beginning of the 1990s, "In Egypt today, you can think whatever you want; you can say whatever you want; and you can write most of what you want. You just can't do anything."

Third, some of the constitutional structures that had been undermined or become desiccated during the era of high authoritarianism stumbled back to some kind of viable life in many countries. Elections were generally restored where they had been abolished or suspended (such as in Kuwait and Jordan); they became a bit more competitive in those countries that had shut down competition (such as in Egypt) or a bit more open where pluralism had never disappeared (such as in Morocco). Parliaments increasingly were likely to seat members who could clearly be identified as opposition in some countries

(Egypt and even Tunisia) and showed increasing diversity where party life was weak and lines between pro-government and opposition deputies were a bit blurrier (Jordan and Kuwait). In some countries, judiciaries showed some ability to issue rulings that broadened political space (most notably with the administrative courts and Supreme Constitutional Court in Egypt, but even occasionally with the Jordanian High Court and on one utterly unexpected occasion even the Syrian Constitutional Court).

Fourth, the various media spaces profiled in the previous chapter showed some signs of life. Turgid official pronouncements, regime apologetics, and stultifying official news still dominated print and broadcast media, but there were some discordant (or at least slightly varied) voices, print media seemed to cross borders a bit more frequently, and religious media became a bit more varied even if they were generally discouraged from explicitly political matters. But even on that count there was variety. Kuwait's *al-Mujtama`*, for instance, inspired by that country's unofficial but still quite active Muslim Brotherhood, drew Islamist readers throughout the Arab world. Operating in what then passed for a freer media environment, the magazine allowed Islamists throughout the region to explore common ideas and views on political, social, moral, and religious questions.

Finally, other institutions and arenas opened up slightly as well—professional associations in some countries, the private business sector in others, and university campuses in a few (Egyptian universities stand out in retrospect in that regard—much of the organizational and ideological incubation of various Islamist approaches over subsequent decades took place among Egyptian students as well as those from other Arab countries studying in Egypt). This period is often seen retrospectively as one of the rise of the Muslim Brotherhood, and indeed, that was one of the most striking products of the changes in Arab public spheres. But the ferment was much more extensive and the Brotherhood hardly encompassed all or even most of the Islamic "awakening" (as its participants sometimes called it).[14]

Many specialists in authoritarian politics have tried to understand what I think is best described as a shift from authoritarianism to semiauthoritarianism, generally looking to regime motives and even the intentions of individual rulers. As mentioned at the outset of chapter 3, I am less persuaded that conscious design was always at work; the changes strike me as gradual and haphazard, the products of accretion, official misjudgments, declining capacity, short-term improvisations, and accident.[15] But what concerns us now are the effects on the first signs of the revival of Arab politics and their manifestations in the nature of religious argumentation about public affairs. In that respect, there are two specific implications for our inquiry that bear stressing.

First, the flourishing of an emerging web of Islamic organizations and spaces where they could argue did have the effect of creating the Islamic counterpublic that Hirschkind describes.

Second, as before, states in general and security apparatuses specifically stood on steady guard at the links among the spaces. Opposition voices might be permitted in some venues but when they attempted to link up to constituencies they found obstacles thrown (sometimes violently) in their path. The pious were welcome to pray and pontificate among themselves but not to hold rallies or leaflet in the public square. Yet the growing vitality of the discrete spheres allowed for some leakage; the pressure of arguments in one sphere could sometimes allow those arguments to spread by osmosis though the patrolled but sometimes permeable boundaries surrounding that sphere.

The way these developments worked their effects might be described based on three episodes taken from Egypt during the 1970s and 1980s.

First, in the 1970s, the regime was repositioning itself by downplaying its pan-Arabist and socialist claims and increasing its religious ones. As part of that process, a law professor and then speaker of parliament (and later briefly acting president under constitutional procedures after the assassination of Sadat in 1981) was given the task of developing a reformed civil code for Egypt, based on the Islamic shari'a. The committee may have taken its work a bit too seriously since it seemed to make progress on a draft—one that excited interest among some emerging Islamist circles who wished to ensure that it was truly faithful to the shari'a and not an attempt to wrap a code of non-Islamic origin in religious garb. Ultimately the committee's work was quietly shelved, but not before it set off a series of debates on the advisability of the project and of its consistency with the Islamic shari'a. The effect was to draw the new Islamist circles more directly into a national debate—not so much in official media (which were still sharply controlled) but in their own discussions and on campuses.[16] What is striking, in light of the political environment in preceding years, is how the newly emerging spheres were able to articulate alternative positions to those favored by the regime and force them onto the agenda in some mixed settings. No longer could they be so easily contained, and the entire project may have been shelved in part because the regime was losing its ability to control the debate.

A second episode—a personal experience—took place in 1984, when I was shopping for groceries in Suq al-Tawfiqiyya, a market in downtown Cairo. It was Friday and the market was bustling, but it was also time for the congregational prayer and sermon. An overflow crowd at a local mosque was accommodated by spreading mats in the street and setting up speakers so that the sermon could be heard. The result was that the sermon went far beyond preaching to the choir to inundate all the immediate area—including the market where I was shopping—with the booming words of a rather boisterous and flowery preacher. This was not an uncommon occurrence and most of the shoppers and shopkeepers acted as they usually did by treating the sermon as religious background music, as I did, perhaps like an organ played in a church before a service that infuses the atmosphere with a religious spirit without the necessity for those assembled to cease greetings and other interactions. On this occasion, however, I heard the preacher denounce "tourists" who come with their strange ways to Egypt and "enter mosques wearing shorts." Since I was clothed in long pants and not in any mosque, I did not take the remark personally though I quickly checked around me to see whether any listener seemed inclined to act on a very broad interpretation. My concern was baseless, but I was still struck at how the sermon (if my memory is correct) was clearly directed not simply against the tourists and their garb but against the political authorities who allowed such a practice, smitten by the approval and income such tourism offered. There was no blanket denunciation of foreigners or of rulers but a demand that officials require visitors to respect the religious teachings and practices of Muslim Egyptians. I do not know if the preacher was sympathetic to the increasingly public Islamist agenda, but the mosque was located in the immediate vicinity of the headquarters of the Brotherhood at that time. Almost literally, an argument was spreading from an office to a mosque and then out into the street in a manner that would have been unthinkable a decade earlier.

The following year a third incident occurred which almost escaped my attention, even though I was living in Egypt at the time. The Supreme Constitutional Court (SCC) issued a ruling in 1985 in a case involving assessing a penalty on unpaid debts that seemed—to punctilious shari'a-minded legalists—as amounting to a charge of interest. The challenge to the law—filed by al-Azhar after it had fallen delinquent in a debt payment—alleged that the provision mandating the penalty in Egypt's civil code violated Article 2 of Egypt's constitution stating that the main source of legislation was "the principles of the Islamic shari'a." The Court ruled that since the civil code antedated the text of Article 2, it was up to the parliament to bring legislation into line with those principles. The effect was to give a boost to those Islamist parliamentarians calling for "application of the shari'a," a task that the regime did not repudiate but handed over to torpid committees.

The resulting controversies in the parliament and press gave greater traction to Islamist arguments and galvanized Islamists into public advocacy. In the spring of 1985, a popular preacher, Hafiz Salama, proved a rallying point in Cairo for such calls. His pulpit—in the cavernous Masjid al-Nur—became a site for such groups, leading to crowds calling for Islamic law that made the regime extremely nervous, culminating in the dispersal of the crowds, dismissal of the fiery shaykh, and a series of legal battles over control of the mosque (the struggle did not end then but was rejoined after the Egyptian uprising of 2011 when Hafiz Salama and his supporters tried to retake the mosque).[17]

What was remarkable about the episode was how prominent the dispute was in Islamist circles; how opposition press that was not Islamist made only indirect or incomplete references to the "Masjid al-Nur incident" without specifying what it was; how President Hosni Mubarak felt called upon to address the issue obliquely himself, giving a speech prominently highlighted in the pro-regime press, repeating "I warn, I warn, I warn . . ." without making quite explicit what warning he was giving—in short, how a series of separate but linked discussions were occurring in which the various pockets of Egyptian public life—Islamist, opposition, and regime—were clearly linked but in very incomplete ways. The regime was sufficiently able to police public speech that it was difficult to piece together precisely what had happened or what the nature of the dispute was. To this day, I am not certain how accurate my account of the Masjid al-Nur controversy is, since I piece it together from my memory of distant public discussions that seemed oblique and to avoid engaging each other. Some details have been filled in by an interview with a former imam years after the events in question. Arguments among adversaries had become a powerful part of Egyptian public life but they were sometimes difficult to follow.

In short, what was emerging was something far less than Habermas's public sphere but still a qualitative shift in the nature of public arguments about religion. The emergence of new spheres, the ways in which religious themes were woven into many of them, and the forging of limited links among them had the effect of increasing the bandwidth devoted to religious discussions in public life. Some discussions were raucous; others were reasoned. Some were restricted to specific groups, but many began to spill outside of those groups. The overall effect was to give a greater religious flavor to public life and to change the nature of the way that arguments were made in front of national audiences—not only nationalist, developmental, socialist, or regime-approved arguments were heard, but oppositional and critical voices were audible and frequently cast their claims in terms that drew upon religion.

From Osmosis to Active Transport: The Revival of Arab Politics

We come then to the current period, the one that is the subject of the remainder of our analysis. The slow change of the late twentieth century was uneven to be sure, but by the twenty-first century it seemed to pass a qualitative threshold, what we are referring to as the "revival" of Arab politics. In the summer of 2006, I spoke to a Palestinian friend—herself on the left but also religious—about the emergence of Hamas after the Palestinian Legislative Council elections that year. She told me that one of the surprising effects of Hamas's electoral triumph was that many of the long-time supporters of the movements who had not spoken of their preferences before felt emboldened; while they had quietly spoken among themselves before they had little public presence. Suddenly it became clear that a wide swath of the society had inclinations that favored the movement.[18]

Hamas members themselves were stunned by their sudden entrance into new public spaces. In March 2006, I interviewed incoming deputy prime minister Nasir al-Din al-Sha'ir in a Ramallah hotel lobby where newly elected Hamas MPs had convened for the meeting of the Legislative Council in which they voted confidence in the new cabinet. Al-Sha'ir seemed a bit embarrassed by the fact that he now had several cell phones ("See? We are already corrupted!" he joked as he held up a phone to one ear to talk with a journalist while holding another to his other ear to consult with incoming prime minister Isma'il Haniyya over whether to encourage private business owners to take out advertisements in daily newspapers congratulating the new cabinet—Al-Sha'ir felt that discouraging the practice would alienate profit-minded newspaper owners). Over the course of the evening, Hamas deputies rose every hour on the hour to watch the same news clip on al-Jazeera of them voting in parliament earlier that day; they also assembled at prayer time having turned the lobby into a temporary mosque.

What happened quite suddenly for Palestinians happened more gradually in most other Arab societies (though the sort of sharp discontinuities experienced by Palestinians in 2006 could sometimes occur in other places, especially connected with upheavals in the political process, most dramatically in 2011). But the process was not merely a passive one of mutual discovery; it was one in which the various spheres that had grown up over the preceding decades were joined by newer ones, more fully described in the previous chapter. What was remarkable about the newer spheres was not that they could throw off some of the shackles of authoritarianism (they could to some degree, but to much less an extent than was sometimes perceived), but that they greatly increased the portability of arguments.

Indeed, newer social media were uniquely suited to just such a purpose: there was nothing new about a preacher giving a sermon; but over the course of the twentieth century the arguments voiced in the space of the mosque might spread more easily and quickly to an increasing number of other sympathetic spaces, generally ones receptive to the message through a steady but slow accretion of technologies (press, followed by broadcast media, and then cassette tapes). And in the twenty-first century, the process was accelerated and accentuated: such sermons might be tweeted; video links might be spread on Facebook; friends might coordinate by text message about where to gather for congregational prayer; journalists might follow such discussions; talk shows might be alerted to controversies, particularly ones that lent themselves to dramatic confrontations. And as arguments spread more quickly and widely, they fell into unfriendly hands with greater speed and ease.

Indeed, what was happening was not just that the boundaries among the spaces had become permeable; that was an old development and one closely monitored by most security services and regimes that viewed most forms of efficacious politics with significant suspicion and hostility. Instead, the new spaces and their characteristics seemed tailor-made not simply for osmosis but for active transport: individuals or groups who wished to move arguments from space to space could do so with more ease and much more speed; the term "viral" used to explain the most extreme form of this phenomenon was hardly unique to the Arab world but perhaps well exemplified the potentialities of the new environment for giving birth rapidly to widespread political discussion. Television interviews might be excerpted for YouTube videos; television serials might spark family discussions.[19]

Such active transport has been noted before, though its significance has not always been appreciated and the empowering aspects for opposition groups drew the lion's share of attention for two reasons. First, it initially left Islamists—who depended for their electoral success primarily on their reputations[20]—in a good position. Second, the benefits seemed to spread more widely in particular after the uprisings of 2011. The effects were certainly dramatic in that year and disorienting as well. As Mark Allen Petersen noted at the time:

> Egypt's media ecology is currently best characterized as being in an experimental phase, in which journalists, editors, military leaders, officials in old and new political parties, bloggers, and many others are seeking to find a new balance of roles and relationships. Every action—from the confrontation of a political leader on television, to the prosecution of a blogger—is an experiment whose political, economic and social consequences will shape subsequent experiments. These myriad contingent actions will collectively restructure Egypt's media ecology as the revolution continues to unfold. The revolutionary media ecology of Egypt—in particular the ways various media index, image and influence one another—suggests that, unlike in Iran, whatever the ultimate political outcome of the uprisings, the mediascape of Egypt post revolution will be significantly different from what it was before January 25.[21]

While the changes of 2011 were jarring on many levels, the landscape had changed more gradually than was clear before the uprisings of that year. Hirschkind's description of an "Islamic counter-public" has already been noted; in writings immediately before and after the 2011 uprising in Egypt he extended upon these by noting how newer forms could be less hierarchical and reach across what had appeared as entrenched divides. That they could.[22] But a view from a few years later would likely have led instead to a less rosy emphasis on polarization among camps that came to know each other a bit too well rather than bridges across the divide.

The new linkages among the spaces had some underappreciated but politically significant characteristics, some of which have been noted earlier in this chapter. Most notably, as explored above, speakers often lost control of their arguments as those engaged in active transport could use them for their own purposes.

The fate of Islamic leaders and movements in the new environment illustrates this most effectively. On the one hand, they could reach out to new constituents as well as build stronger links with old ones. On the other hand, there were several costs to the new environment for those who sought to lay claim to religious learning in the new public environment.

First, emotion, symbol, and drama are more transportable than sustained reasoned argument. Those only at home in the world of scholarly tomes might be left behind; those able to use powerful language, even weep, shout, or reduce arguments to quick retorts could have their voices heard across the spheres. Dress and demeanor became as important as text. (Should one appear in a suit? In the garb of a shaykh? Should one hector, coax, plead, or scold? Is an avuncular, placid, angry, righteous, humorous, or severe manner most helpful to communicate truth?) To be sure, few of the choices were entirely new nor were they ignored by generations of scholars and specialists who pondered such questions in the past.[23] But the choices seem more complex and numerous, the pressures stronger and more cross-cutting, the opportunities and risks both greater and harder to calculate (and perhaps to manage) in the new environment of interlocking spheres. The path was open for those who were bold enough to appeal more broadly, but it did not seem well marked.

But second, those who enter the fray can pay a reputational price by doing so—individual scholars sometimes seem to their colleagues to abandon respectability in a craving for popular audiences. Movements might come to be seen as too politically ambitious rather than spiritually driven.

Third, as noted earlier in this chapter, much of the trafficking in religious arguments was used less for religious preaching than for ridicule. Fatwas stood as a particularly potent weapon when grasped by hostile hands: when a prominent salafi leader in Egypt declared the symbol for Chevrolet forbidden for Muslims because it represented a cross, the effect was to inspire derision mixed with fear among non-salafis more than pious automobile preferences among the faithful.

When another salafi leader interrupted a television interview with a woman journalist with the peremptory command "Bring me a man!" in order to show his fealty to gender separation, he may have struck his followers as admirable for standing on principle but the line quickly became a subject of mirth among salafi critics, even sparking a widely watched musical video of a Muppet-like bearded puppet constantly interrupting a song with the "Bring me a man!" refrain.[24]

A vivid illustration of all these trends can be seen the battle among religious authorities in the wake of the overthrow of Egyptian President Muhammad Morsi in July 2013. The debate turned emotional, provoked grandstanding, and exposed venerated figures to ridicule in a rapid

rhetorical dissent that sidelined Islamic jurisprudence in favor of ad homi-
nem attacks with religious arguments appearing more of a prop than a pro-
peller of the dispute. The result resembled a shouting match after a traffic
accident more than a scholarly disputation—or rather it combined both
elements. David H. Warren describes the very public escalation between
the former mufti, ʿAli Jumʿa (a controversial figure but the object of considerable respect in some pious and scholarly circles) who supported the July 3
coup against Morsi, and Yusuf al-Qaradawi (a figure with a large popular
following and considerable influence), who spared no rhetorical effort in
denouncing the move:

> Their debate would rumble on for some weeks, with Jumʿa deriding al-Qaradawi
> as senile and suffering from Alzheimer's, and with al-Qaradawi responding in
> kind, aiming at Jumʿa's credentials and credibility as an ʿālim. This exchange and
> the personal invective involved can be seen not only as a demonstration of how
> deeply both parties were invested in the politics of ongoing events, but also as a
> result of the ʿulamāʾ's increasing use of utilitarian reasoning to intervene in the
> public sphere around social and political issues. Both Jumʿa and al-Qaradawi's
> legal discourses can be seen to resemble each other to a significant degree: they
> both claimed that al-Sisi and Morsi were the legitimate rulers supported by
> an authoritative consensus of the people, with al-Qaradawi citing the election
> result and Jumʿa the huge numbers of protesters that took to the streets on
> 30 June 2013 and remained there until the military intervention. Similarly
> their citations of the same hadith, "He who comes to you when you are united
> and wants to disunite your community, kill him," in support of their respective
> causes are equally nebulous.[25]

A year after the coup, al-Qaradawi and leaders of the religious establishment
in Egypt were still engaged in battles that included very heavy dollops of name
calling blended with light drops of fiqh (Islamic jurisprudence) over who was
serving the Palestinian cause and who was acting effectively as an Israeli agent.
Much of the debate took place on rival televised talk shows, some of which discussed fatwas (which were then written up in newspapers and shown in video
clips posted online, generally prioritizing the electrifying over the edifying).

To be sure, such histrionic argumentation is not restricted to the political
realm: Ron Shaham has probed the strange mixture of interpretative dispute,
erudition, and name calling between Yusuf al-Qaradawi and salafis, exploring
the decay of scholarly politesse in the modern period.[26]

In sum, we are now living in a period in which the fatwa has been transformed, in which emotion and symbol are mixed with reasoned verbal argument in new ways and in which arguments move with far greater speed and
force than they did earlier and in a manner which governments and speakers
can influence but not control.

The effects, then, are not simply limited to building bridges; it is so very easy in the new environment to burn them. And the effects are often felt within a single camp. In late 2013, I traveled to Egypt and spoke with two members of the faculty of al-Azhar. One began to refer to Morsi's overthrow by beginning with a reference to June 30 (the day of the largest demonstrations against him) then to July 3 (the date of the coup) and then, realizing that even his fixing of a specific date could be politically alienating even within a small group, simply said "the events of the summer," reaching for a neutral phrase. Americans discuss race relations with less nervousness about terminology than my Azhar interlocutor referred to recent politics—and the person whose ire he wished to avoid provoking (without knowing which minefield to avoid) seemed not to be me but his own colleague.

CONCLUSION

The vitality of the reemerged Arab politics, while often rambunctious, conflictual, shrill, manipulated, and patrolled, is thus very real. Citizens of the republic of arguments often find that they disagree with each other quite deeply. Their encounters seem at times less designed to persuade each other than to listen to their own camp.

The republic of arguments is a place in which unequal relations of class, power, status, gender, age, and training are very much real. As Salwa Ismail has written of the piety trend, based on grassroots activism and agency:

> They are not moved by something abstract called Islam, often projected as a puppeteer working behind the scenes moving Muslims to act in one way or another. Yes, Muslims reflect on their faith and on their lives in light of their understanding of their faith. They seek to use principles derived from Islamic traditions to guide them. However, they are touched by competing frames of reference and registers. Their ethical formation is shaped by their historical location. The agency they aim to recover is historically bounded.[27]

Yet if inegalitarian, all these spheres, intertwined and clashing as they are— are what amount to politics in the sense we have been using the term.

But what if we turn to the second (more common) definition of the word "politics" identified in chapter 2—one that focuses not on people arguing with each other but on formal institutions of state, mechanisms of governance, and attempts to influence those things, or in other words, one that focuses much more directly on power, formal authority, the state, and what is sometimes called "political society"? Does politics as public arguing affect politics as contest over policy?

In asking that question, we confront an immediate feature of Arab politics, especially in the semiauthoritarian era: most societies have readily identifiable structures of politics if by that we mean bureaucracies, law-making bodies, parliaments, parties, cabinets, presidents, and constitutions. But these structures seem to be designed to keep much of the public out of politics in this sense and to hollow out any mechanisms that link politics in the argumentative sense to politics in the policy-oriented sense. And in some countries, some of these structures exist only in name or are extremely weak.

The issue is partly state structures themselves—elections that are skewed, parliaments that are deprived of the tools of oversight, presidents who serve for life, other state institutions that are insulated from politics in almost any sense of the term—even in those systems that have liberalized sufficiently so as not to appear fully authoritarian. The issue is partly in what is sometimes called "political society"—those organizations and institutions outside of the state that organize constituencies, press for programs, ideologies, or policies, organize for campaigns or demonstrations. As Vickie Langohr aptly phrases the situation (using different terminology than we have here thus far), focusing on late Mubarak-era Egypt, the problem is "too much civil society, too little politics."[28]

But we should not conclude before fuller investigation that politics in the sense of public argumentation about religion does not matter. Instead we should investigate the effect of the reborn politics, alert not only to the ways in which it is ineffectual but also to the exceptions when it does have policy effects. And in part 3 we shall do precisely that in three areas: personal status law, constitution writing, and education. But first we will move to consider the substance of the arguments: what about Islam in public life is up for argument?

NOTES

1. "Salafi Leader Reveals Plot to Oust Azhar's Grand Imam," Al Arabiya English, December 25, 2012, http://english.alarabiya.net/articles/2012/12/25/256924. html. The full lecture can be viewed at www.youtube.com/watch?v=_xzsVgwG9-o. An edited excerpt of the segment in question can be viewed at: www.youtube. com/watch?v=tGbOM_4TJh4.
2. The video can be viewed (with the title "The Coming Threat to Tunis") at https://www.youtube.com/watch?feature=player_embedded&v=WuHi-O-PGhI, accessed March 31, 2015.
3. Mark Allen Petersen, "Egypt's Media Ecology in a Time of Revolution," *Arab Media and Society* 14 (Summer 2011). http://www.arabmediasociety.com/?article=770, accessed July 15, 2016.
4. Sean Aday et al., "Blogs and Bullets II: New Media and Conflict After the Arab Spring," *Peaceworks* 80 (July 2012).

5. Charles Hirschkind, "Civic Virtue and Religious Reason: An Islamic Counterpublic," *Cultural Anthropology* 16, 1 (2001): 12.
6. On the role of fatwas in transmitting Islamic legal thought, a useful perspective is provided by Wael B. Hallaq, "From Fatwās to Furūʿ: Growth and Change in Islamic Substantive Law," *Islamic Law and Society* 1, 1 (1994): 29–65. For an example of their social significance, see Judith E. Tucker, *In the House of the Law: Gender and Islamic Law in Ottoman Syria and Palestine* (Berkeley: University of California Press, 2000).
7. On ʿUmar Makram as a popular leader, see, for instance, Afaf Lutfi Sayyid-Marsot, *Egypt in the Reign of Muhammad Ali* (Cambridge: Cambridge University Press, 1984).
8. See Israel Gershoni, *Redefining the Egyptian Nation, 1930–1945* (Cambridge: Cambridge University Press, 2002), especially chapter 3, 54–78.
9. For an example of a historical account of reading newspapers, including the way they were read, see Ami Ayalon, *Reading Palestine: Printing and Literacy, 1900–1948* (Austin: University of Texas Press, 2010).
10. See Ziad Fahmy, *Ordinary Egyptians: Creating the Modern Nation through Popular Culture* (Palo Alto: Stanford University Press, 2011).
11. I have explored this more fully in *When Victory Is Not an Option: Islamist Movements in Arab Politics* (Ithaca: Cornell University Press, 2012).
12. For such a portrait, see Kanan Makiya, *Republic of Fear: The Politics of Modern Iraq* (Berkeley: University of California Press, 1998). Makiya's powerful but controversial analysis is based explicitly at points on Arendt and other theorists of totalitarianism; a useful alternative account of a neighboring regime (and, to some extent, a corrective), is Lisa Wedeen's *Ambiguities of Domination: Politics, Rhetoric, and Symbols in Contemporary Syria* (Chicago: University of Chicago Press, 1999).
13. Janine A. Clark, *Islam, Charity, and Activism: Middle-Class Networks and Social Welfare in Egypt, Jordan, and Yemen* (Bloomington: Indiana University Press, 2004).
14. For accounts of this period that take a more prospective approach (rather than a retrospective one centered primarily on the Brotherhood), see Carrie Wickham, *Mobilizing Islam* (New York: Columbia University Press, 2005) and Abdullah al-Arian, *Answering the Call: Popular Islamic Activism in Sadat's Egypt* (Oxford: Oxford University Press, 2014). The Brotherhood certainly makes a strong appearance in both works, but both portray a much broader sociological (Wickham) and ideological and organizational (al-Arian) scene.
15. I elaborate these views more fully in *When Victory is Not an Option* and in "Democracy and Dictatorship through the Prism of Arab Elections," in Nathan J. Brown, ed., *The Dynamics of Democratization: Dictatorship, Development, and Diffusion* (Baltimore: Johns Hopkins University Press, 2011).
16. See especially al-Arian, *Answering the Call*; a valuable contemporaneous account of the movement in al-Minya is contained in Patrick Gaffney's *The Prophet's Pulpit: Islamic Preaching in Contemporary Egypt* (Berkeley: University of California Press, 1994).
17. For a coverage of the 2011 events and some background, see Jonathan A. C. Brown, "Salafis and Sufis in Egypt," Carnegie Endowment for International Peace paper, December 2011.
18. Unexpected changes in mass political behavior—most generally in the upheavals of 2011—have led to interest in Timur Kuran's idea of the

consequences of "preference falsification" under authoritarian conditions—individuals do not reveal their true preferences until a few pioneers take the lead, making it safer for a larger number; the crowds expressing discontent can swell or cascade rapidly. See Timur Kuran, *Private Truths, Public Lies: The Social Consequences of Preference Falsification* (Cambridge: Harvard University Press, 1997).

My own view of semiauthoritarianism in the Arab world is that private preferences were far safer to reveal—and were in fact routinely revealed in small group and fully public settings. What was less clear was the likelihood that others would act or how they would do so. See my chapter "Constitutions and the Public Sphere," in *The Arab Uprisings Explained*, ed. Marc Lynch (New York: Columbia University Press, 2014).

19. On the latter, see Sarah A. Tobin, "Ramadan Blues: Debates in Popular Islam during Ramadan in Amman, Jordan," *Digest of Middle East Studies* 22 (2013): 292–316.
20. Melanie Cammet and Pauline Jones Luong, "Is There an Islamist Political Advantage?" *Annual Review of Political Science* 17 (2014): 187–206.
21. Mark Allen Petersen, "Egypt's media ecology in a time of revolution."
22. See "New Media and Political Dissent in Egypt," *Revista de Dialectología y Tradiciones Populares* 65, 1 (2010): 137–154, and "Beyond Secular and Religious: An Intellectual Genealogy of Tahrir Square," *American Ethnologist* 39, 1 (2011): 49–53.
23. See Linda G. Jones, *The Power of Oratory in the Medieval Muslim World* (Cambridge: Cambridge University Press, 2012).
24. I am grateful to Adel Iskander for bringing the video to my attention. It can be viewed at https://www.youtube.com/watch?v=B_qIr4HywI8, accessed July 15, 2015.
25. David H. Warren, "The 'Ulamā' and the Arab Uprisings 2011–13: Considering Yusuf al-Qaradawi, the 'Global Mufti,' between the Muslim Brotherhood, the Islamic Legal Tradition, and Qatari Foreign Policy," *New Middle Eastern Studies*, 4 (2014): 27–28.
26. Ron Shaham, "The Rhetoric of Legal Disputation: Neo-Ahl al-Ḥadīth vs. Yūsuf al-Qaraḍāwī," *Islamic Law and Society* 22, 1 (2015): 114–141
27. Salwa Ismail, "Islamism, Re-Islamization and the Fashioning of Muslim Selves: Refiguring the Public Sphere," *Muslim World Journal of Human Rights* 4, 1 (2007): 17.
28. Vickie Langohr, "Too Much Civil Society, Too Little Politics: Egypt and Liberalizing Arab Regimes," Comparative Politics 36, 2, (2004): 181–204.

CHAPTER 5

Charting the Islamic Way

A Guide for the Perplexed

Religious discourse, like all cultures, is fractured; consequently, scholars need to trace these ever-shifting and never-stable cultural and religious fault lines. If a religious discourse appears to have an essence or fixed meaning, then this is the result of politics, and the job of the scholar is to understand how this appearance was achieved.

Michael Barnett, "Another Great Awakening," in *Religion and International Relations Theory*, ed. Jack Snyder, 106

In June 2012, I went with a friend to the final presidential campaign rally of Muhammad Morsi, the nominee of the Freedom and Justice Party founded by the Muslim Brotherhood. Cairo has few central spaces for such rallies, but this one managed to cram a very large number of people into a square and streets around the front of 'Abdin Palace near the center of the city. We came to the rally shortly before it started but still tried to find seats near the front and immediately discovered a large section of empty chairs roped off. Those chairs, as it turned out, were not for us—they were reserved for Azharis. And sure enough shortly after our arrival a large contingent walked in, all dressed in the distinctive Azhari garb, seemingly giving a kind of official (because al-Azhar is a state institution) and religious (since al-Azhar is Egypt's premier institution of Islamic learning) imprimatur to the rally. When the speeches began, Morsi was preceded by Muhammad Abu Trayka, perhaps Egypt's most prominent soccer player (and thus an important national symbol) and Safwat Higazi, a firebrand preacher. Various sources of authority were on display, and they were deployed across several fields—religious learning, state authority, popular sovereignty, and nationalist iconography were all in play and the fields were public space, electoral process, and state apparatus. All seemed to be mobilized in support of a figure who would soon (if only for one year) serve as Egypt's first freely elected president.

The scene was remarkable for two reasons.

First, the various sources of authority seemed to operate in a uniform fashion and across a number of spheres—an illusion that was soon shattered by the realities of Egyptian politics. Within months, public demonstrations, electoral processes, al-Azhar, nationalist claims, and the state apparatus were all still operating but hardly in harmony and each one was the site of increasingly bitter battles.

Second, much of the meeting ground for these various sources of authority had religious coloration with preachers, Islamic social movements, al-Azhar, and religious symbols of various kinds present in abundance. This feature of the political scene was far less fleeting. Our task in this chapter is to lay the groundwork for understanding the confusing arguments over religion.

Specifically, in this chapter we will explore three questions. First, what is the Islamic shari'a? We will examine the meaning of the term itself, noting not only the extent to which it can be seen as public and legal in nature but also why that makes it the such a field for argument even in areas where there appears to be broad agreement. Second, who speaks for the shari'a? We will probe who participates in public debates about the Islamic shari'a, revealing increasing cacophony. Finally, how is the Islamic shari'a brought to bear on public issues? We will present how the Islamic shari'a arises in public debates and the ways in which those involved in arguments agree and disagree about its implications for public affairs.

In some sense these are distinct subjects, and we will try to disentangle them as best we can. But there is a limit to the usefulness of the distinctions we will make. As we work to understand the Islamic shari'a in public life in the Arab world, we will come to see that questions of content, authority, and the sphere in which debates take place are not simply related but woven tightly together. And all three have changed together, if not always coherently, in recent times. Thus, armed with the understandings developed in this chapter, we will proceed in part 3 to examine debates about the Islamic shari'a and public life in three areas—constitution drafting, personal status law, and education.

THE RELIGIOUS SPACE BETWEEN

The space between members of Arab societies who come together for any purpose is often heavily tinged with religious coloration. When they speak—to greet each other, to speak of the future, to exchange family news; when they gather—to throng in *mulids* (festive celebrations of saints' birthdays), watch television, or mourn at funerals; and when they act—to demonstrate, build, or even sometimes buy and sell—they often do so in a manner that involves religious language, rituals, and spaces.

Of course, I do not mean to imply that these societies are knit together only by religion; nor do I wish to suggest that irreverent thoughts are never expressed or that religious ideas are always on people's minds. I have no ability to peer into people's souls and I am privy only to a small number of private conversations. I have certainly met individuals who strike me as irreligious and heard impiety expressed forcefully in private conversations. But such thoughts are rarely stated in public. On the rare occasion when they are voiced, they often end discussion. Even in a small workshop I once attended—one focusing on the Palestinian constitution in 2000—a participant brought conversation over the religious clauses in a draft being discussed to a stunned halt with the question: "I am an atheist. What is in this constitution for me?" He received no response or even acknowledgment.

So, moving things into public spheres can place them on a terrain friendly to religious arguments.

But that observation is only the first step toward understanding. Religion does not end all arguments. Indeed, it often begins them. And while the arguments might have theological aspects, they are generally highly practical. When members of Arab societies argue about Islam today, their discussions are far less likely to focus on what to believe and far more likely to concern what is to be done. Public conduct, more than private belief, is at issue in most debates. Faith, doctrine, and creed are discussed to be sure—sometimes with great earnestness and urgency—and such matters are hardly divorced from public conduct in any case. But the most pressing debates focus on how individuals, families, communities, and entire societies should behave. What is the Islamic way of doing things; how should one act socially; and what guidance do religious teachings give to the course and conduct of public life?

When these arguments occur, two kinds of authority are often deployed. One is clearly religious in nature: what does the Islamic religion teach and who is most reliable as an authority on the subject? The second is political: speaking, writing, gathering, and acting are all regulated, monitored, and policed by political authority. Both forms of authority—religious and political—are contested, generally increasingly so. Neither kind of authority has disappeared or even diminished but both must operate—and can be deployed—in new ways. They are also often linked tightly together, though in different ways than they were in the past. The result, then, is not that authority has faded, far from it. But it is a bit more difficult to recognize and it is far less likely to speak in a single voice.

When the republic of arguments encompasses debates about Islam and public policy, it is chiefly through the Islamic shari'a.[1]

The term "Islamic shari'a" has subtly different denotations and sharply different connotations in Arab societies than it often does in the United States or Europe.[2] There is a reason many scholars insist that defining it as "Islamic law" (as it is often described in non-Muslim countries) is sometimes overly narrow.[3] Shari'a includes large areas of personal conduct not generally covered by legal rules in many societies (such as the regulation of prayer or ritual purity). Not only does it blend private practice, ethics, and public law, but it also includes categories such as *makruh* (detestable, but not prohibited) or *mustahabb* (desirable, but not required) that make perfect ethical but little legal sense.

So a more vague but more accurate translation of the term "Islamic shari'a" might be "the Islamic way of doing things."

That is the definition accepted by many who follow the Islamic shari'a. Such a translation makes clear why the Islamic shari'a in general is hard to oppose in many Muslim societies even by those who wish to question specific interpretations or provisions. It is, for instance, not so difficult to question specific *hudud* punishments (for serious crimes) derived from Islamic legal texts by claiming to wish to follow the spirit of God's instructions but not the letter of traditional understandings. It is far harder to proclaim that one simply prefers to do things in a non-Islamic manner or that Islamic teachings have no relevance to how we should treat each other. The latter could be as unexpected in many predominantly Muslim societies as US politicians claiming they prefer the "un-American way." Public opinion polls on the subject provoke the same response among the broader society.[4]

Of course, the Islamic shari'a is not merely the equivalent of a flag pin for a politician's lapel; it has enormous practical and not simply symbolic content. And it most definitely has considerable legal content—content to inform the process of governing and to be enforced by political authorities. But its breadth suggests that observers should not be surprised by the paucity of direct calls to abandon the Islamic shari'a in Arab political debates or the degree of apparent consensus that the Islamic shari'a is relevant to public affairs.

There is another terminological oddity that can shed some light on the connotations of the Islamic shari'a: following Arab usage, I often refer to "Islamic shari'a," a phrase that seems almost comically redundant in English, like referring to a "Jewish rabbi." A non-Islamic shari'a might seem to be something like a "Protestant pope." But in the Arab world, it is not at all unusual to seek to emphasize the Islamic nature of the shari'a being discussed or to refer to the shari'as of other religious communities. Muslims generally still regard the Islamic shari'a as superior—and indeed, as historically superseding those that came before—but they will sometimes refer to other religions' shari'as, especially to indicate non-Islamic provisions for personal status law (covering marriage, divorce, and inheritance).

But again, the Islamic shari'a does suggest a considerable body of legal rules even while it also has broader religious meaning. Exploration of its legal nature has led to over a millennium of intellectual inquiry into the law to be applied. Business transactions, criminal punishments, inheritance, and legal procedures, among many other areas, have been the subject of scholarship by those who probed religious sources to discover the ways that a community of Muslims should operate. And the Islamic shari'a also provides some guidance on how violations of the law must be treated—by compensation, penalties, or the voiding of contracts, for instance. Because of this, referring to the Islamic shari'a as law is not always misleading.

As with any intellectual tradition, opinions over the centuries have varied considerably about what God has required and what the earthly consequences are when a rule is violated. Recognizing, and sometimes even celebrating, that diversity among experts, Muslims will sometimes take pains to distinguish between the Islamic shari'a as unchanging divine guidance, and *fiqh*, or jurisprudence, as the fallible human effort to understand the content of that guidance. There is, in that sense, one shari'a but many different interpretations. Nor is the diverse nature of fiqh often presented as a problem; it is not uncommon to hear many Muslims today cite the multiplicity of interpretations in their legal heritage as a virtue, since it shows how attempts to discover and apply the Islamic shari'a naturally evolve with prevailing conditions and community needs.

In much of the Arab world, the twentieth century witnessed a broad democratization in shari'a-based discourse, accompanied by fundamental shifts in interpretive authority over the Islamic shari'a. Those trends had divisive—and sometimes even politically violent—results. In recent years, political violence over shari'a-based issues and grievances has receded and some signs of consensus on broad themes have unmistakably emerged. But that consensus, formed over decades, has frayed once again in the past few years and even when it prevails it frames rather than silences deep debates over the content of the shari'a, its role in society, and authority over its interpretation.

Ultimately, then, a call to apply or follow the Islamic shari'a will have to confront the questions of which rules to apply from this rich tradition of legal and ethical speculation and—perhaps more critically—who has the authority to decide which interpretations are to be enforced. A religiously based tradition that blends law and ethics, the personal and the political, can raise special complexities when public life becomes more active, the reach of the state becomes wider and deeper, and popular sovereignty becomes integrated into prevailing political ideologies.[5] These are difficult issues, but there are surprising areas of convergence on them in many discussions in the Arab world. Such convergence sets the terms for debates but it hardly resolves them.

WHO SPEAKS FOR THE SHARI‘A?

Who can say what the Islamic way of doing things is? A standard answer, especially in Sunni Islam, is confusing. On the one hand, all Muslims are individually responsible for their conduct and for finding the right answers. On the other, arriving at right answers is a difficult and uncertain process and is best pursued through training, the development of expertise in specific techniques, and deep familiarity with basic textual sources.

Combining individual responsibility with a specialized intellectual tradition means that arriving at a best answer often involves asking the right person.[6] Out of that specialized tradition arose a variety of individual scholars, guilds or schools, institutions of adjudication (courts), and academies of learning. The understanding of law tended to evolve (even when it appeared to be holding to fixed interpretations) and varied according to time, place, and scholarly approach.[7]

A recent study by political scientists of religion worldwide tells a story in very broad terms about the relationship between religious and political authority—one in which the two realms overlapped and showed some mutual deference but maintained some distinction for many years. But, according to this account, in the early modern era states began to assume more direct control over religion, often doing so initially with the support of religious authority. As state control grew, religion became more tightly controlled, contained, and subservient. In recent decades, however, democratic processes and the ability to build religious networks outside of state control (sometimes crossing state borders) have led to a resurgence of religious authority that can operate with some autonomy and even, under some circumstances, move to challenge or disrupt political authority.[8]

The breadth of this global argument is too ambitious to be useful to our regionally-based inquiry here, but there are two features that are notable. First, it is similar to the story that many religious scholars and leaders of religious movements in the Arab world tell about themselves and their history—of a religious realm that operated at some autonomy from governing, sometimes guiding and sometimes scolding rulers, until the modern era when rulers (or sometimes imperialists) sought to subjugate religion to their political needs. In recent years, however, scholars and religious leaders often hold that the deep religiosity of the societies has led to a resurgence of religious activism and attempts to rebuild religious authority with integrity and righteousness.

Second, even if the entire global story is too broad for our purposes, its latter parts do fit historical trends in the Arab world, however loosely.[9]

Religious authority was indeed nationalized in many countries and lost a good deal of its political independence.[10] And in recent decades, religious authority has hardly disappeared but it has grown more diffuse and fluid as well as a bit more difficult to identify.[11] Religious figures inside the state apparatus; those outside of it; and formal state structures (including fatwa-issuing agencies, ministries of religious affairs, parliaments, and ministries of education) offer interpretations of Islamic teachings that are often at odds with each other and contested both inside and outside the state. Religious movements have entered the fray, sometimes with an explicitly political and oppositional stance, other times seeking to avoid formal politics.

The twentieth century opened with the Islamic shariʻa established in specific legal and educational institutions in the Arab world; in most societies these institutions enjoyed a status that was rarely openly questioned. As a discourse, the shariʻa was a matter of technical expertise, specialist scholarship, teaching, and legal reasoning. Attempts by political authorities to reconfigure the social and political role of the Islamic shariʻa were undertaken in many places to be sure, but they were at most gingerly advanced and seemed designed more to supplement (and in some places contain) rather than directly challenge the older structures.

At that time, the Islamic shariʻa was most closely identified with three kinds of institutions in most Arab societies: an educational establishment, often led by mosque-academies (but with many local institutions to teach basic literacy in the Qurʻan); a set of leading scholars and legal advisors for state officials and individual believers (ʻulama and muftis); and courts of law whose jurisdiction often varied but generally included at least matters of personal status and sometimes were courts of general jurisdiction. These institutions generally operated with state license and support (though some were privately financed and even endowed), but even those that were a part of the state still had a degree of autonomy from high officials. This autonomy not only operated in a narrow organizational sense but also in a broader intellectual manner—all three participated in a specialized shariʻa-based discourse enabling them to posit their role as answerable not only to state authorities but also to more complete and timeless truths.

The autonomy accorded these institutions, however, was neither complete nor timeless. There had been considerable variation in how these institutions operated and their relationship to those who wielded political authority. Those societies under Ottoman rule did not escape the powerful Ottoman bureaucratization impulse. Ironically, it was those places that came under European control where high officials sometimes felt a bit more reticence in tinkering with religious institutions.

But however diverse the set of historical experiences in the past, and however varied the path in the modern era, the formation of modern states in the nineteenth and especially the twentieth century greatly reconfigured the political environment in which all religious institutions operated.[12]

This is true even though most ambitious states did not attempt a full frontal assault on religious institutions in the Arab world—even colonial powers favored deference and gradualism. As a general rule, in the nineteenth and into the twentieth century, states sought not to assert direct control over shari'a-oriented institutions so much as to contain them by constructing alternatives under direct state supervision, especially in the legal and educational realms. In a sense, treating religious knowledge as a specialized field that deserved state support allowed states to tolerate the reproduction of an autonomous body of religious scholars so long as those states could restrict the purview of shari'a-based institutions like schools and courts. An extensive nonreligious educational apparatus was erected in many countries; sets of courts adjudicating on the bases of legislated codes and texts were established. The older courts staffed by shari'a-trained judges were gradually transformed from bodies with general jurisdiction that relied heavily on shari'a-based rules and procedures (without being termed "shari'a courts") into specialized shari'a courts (sometimes labeled as such) applying Islamic law, but only in matters of personal status.

This trend—marginalizing shari'a-based institutions while maintaining their autonomy—was augmented over the course of the twentieth century by other broad, long-term political and social trends that further contained the role for many religious scholars. On a political level, state authorities in some countries increasingly sought to eliminate pockets of autonomy and moved to assert more direct control over the shari'a-based institutions. Religious universities were transformed from mosque/academies into large bureaucratized educational complexes under direct state supervision. Personal status law was codified and legislated in some countries from the 1920s on (Arab states could build on a late Ottoman effort in this regard); in some countries the personal status courts that applied that law were folded into the regular court system. There was tremendous variation in this regard: in Tunisia, for instance, personal status law was legislated and shoved to its most egalitarian extreme; in other countries far less egalitarian provisions were written into law; and in some other countries (such as Saudi Arabia) the law remained completely uncodified and was left to judges to interpret and apply.[13]

On a social level, the spread of education and the growing interest of some intellectual circles in matters related to Islam eroded the status of the Islamic shari'a as a specialists' discourse.[14] (Indeed, the distinction between specialists' discourse and fully public arguments about religion has begun to fade over the course of the twentieth century). Some of the public debate over Islam took a broadly religious character but some was specifically legal in nature. As the century wore on, discussions spilled over from general intellectual circles to the broad public, especially with the formation of the Islamist social and political movements (most notably but hardly exclusively the Muslim Brotherhood) and their forays into religious education and advocacy.

The first trend of greater state control seemed to bottle up the shari'a in terms regulated, licensed, and patrolled by political authorities; the second trend of spreading education led in the precise opposite direction of making the Islamic shari'a a subject of public argument. But both worked to circumscribe the role for religious scholars.

By the end of the twentieth century, states had often asserted direct control over the older legal and educational structures and invented all kinds of new ones to attempt to speak authoritatively in shari'a-based debates. This was the culmination of a long process in which education and willingness to argue had gradually spread out more widely among the public throughout the previous century. As this process advanced, the Islamic shari'a began to burst outside of the institutional frameworks where it had long been centered and become part of very broad public discussions.

As it progressed over the twentieth century, the democratization of shari'a-based discourse and the debates over the relationship between the Islamic shari'a and political authority came with a high price for political and social relations in some societies: beginning in the 1970s, shari'a-based debates became a matter of bitter contention and violent action in a few locations; these struggles spread to other societies by the 1980s and 1990s.

In the current century, much of the sharpness and violence of earlier debates initially ebbed, but they lost none of their vitality. Some of the ferocity may be returning in light of political violence surrounding the rise of the Islamic state and post-coup events in Egypt.

While residents of the Arab world continue to argue about the shari'a, and while the Islamic shari'a remains a central point of dispute in Arab societies, a degree of consensus emerged in the late twentieth century around a very general set of ideas (to be more fully explored below): that the Islamic shari'a provides some clear legal rules that should not be abrogated by the state; that the shari'a is not wholly identified with those rules but also provides more general guidance over social and political behavior; that debates about interpreting the shari'a among educated Muslims is healthy; and that the shari'a can provide a middle path that it is very much in the interest of individual believers and Muslim societies to follow.

Even liberals often draw on these ideas; non-Muslim members of predominantly Muslim Arab societies rarely directly challenge them.

Salafis, as will be seen, lie on the edge of—and sometimes outside—of this consensus; so do jihadists. But the jihadists whose actions seem almost designed to outrage—those in al-Qa'ida and the Islamic State—take great pains to justify their actions in shari'a-based terms and to pose as uncompromising in their dedication to authentic understandings of the shari'a.[15] While such movements do allow that Muslim rulers have some discretion, they charge that existing regimes have completely abandoned the Islamic shari'a with the complicity of co-opted scholars. Thus, even those who have exited the consensus (or charged members of the consensus with exiting from a true shari'a-based framework) still expend much intellectual energy engaging and attacking it. And disputations over law remain one of the primary battlegrounds; critics of the consensus use their understanding of the Islamic shari'a to reach Muslim publics.

The general consensus emerged over the past few decades in part precisely because of its generality. What I am terming "consensus" therefore expresses itself in paradoxically cacophonous forms. Arabs hewing to the consensus continue to argue about which shari'a-based legal rules are fixed, what the general principles are, how they are to be applied, who is qualified to speak in shari'a-centered debates, and what role the state should play. More subtly, Arab states have sometimes folded this cacophony into themselves by absorbing or creating several different—and often competing—centers for shari'a-based authority within their bureaucratic apparatus and set of governing structures.

In other words, even as differences have narrowed somewhat, the multiplicity of individual and institutional voices continues. And the state has moved not only to regulate but also to subsume many of these voices.

Thus, the Islamic shari'a, by the end of the twentieth century, has become highly politicized in two senses. First, it is often understood as providing the proper basis for the entire political order; the increasing tendency to focus on the shari'a as the appropriate source for specific legal rules to be enforced by the state has only heightened the connection between the shari'a and politics. Second, the shari'a was central to Arab political debates, as many contending forces claimed to be acting in accordance with its requirements. Sporadic violence in the 1970s and 1980s gave way to an insurgency in some countries (such as Egypt and, far more notably, Algeria) in the 1990s.

By the end of the twentieth century, the number and variety of participants in arguments about the Islamic shari'a had multiplied virtually everywhere in the Arab world. Of course, the old specialists remained—the 'ulama were still very much participants in public arguments; indeed, some found themselves able to carve out large public audiences for themselves rather than speak primarily through networks of other more local figures. But it was not only the 'ulama's audience who had been transformed—religious scholars themselves were trained in changed institutions. The construction of new Islamic educational systems—and the assertion of state control over older ones—produced religious knowledge in a very different process than in the past. No longer were there small circles of students clustered around individual scholars in mosques or schools; now there were official curricula, lecture halls, examinations, academic departments, and all the other accoutrements of formalized and bureaucratized higher education. The largest number of religious scholars—and certainly almost all of those who were professional scholars (in the sense of receiving a salary for performing a religious function, such as teaching, preaching, adjudicating, or writing)—were products of such institutions, but others with religious knowledge could also play an active role in public debates. In many societies, salafi movements were largely informally organized (though formal salafi organizations have most definitely been established as well). And some of those with salafi inclinations have gained a foothold in some otherwise non-salafi institutions (and are particularly influential in Saudi Arabia and some other locations in the Arabian peninsula).

But products of institutions like Cairo's al-Azhar or the numerous faculties of shari'a dotting the universities throughout the Arab world were not the only expert or academic participants in shari'a-based debates. University professors from other faculties—most notably law (where "shari'a" was often a required subject, though taught in a way that most more traditional scholars would likely find superficial and focusing on substance at the expense of method) but also social sciences. Other intellectuals and journalists, and sometimes jurists with a religious bent, often present themselves to public audiences as specialists as well.

The result can be confusing—to both the public and the specialists. In 2015, a leading Egyptian religious scholar (and indeed, the former state mufti), 'Ali Jum'a, was a guest on a television program and was asked about the requirement that women cover their heads. He explained that a Muslim woman was required to cover; when asked if one who rejected the principle that she should do so was guilty of disbelief (*kufr*), he said she would be—but then quickly added, in a rote (almost tired) recitation of a standard argument, that any punishment would require a trial before a judge. In that sense, his position was an evasion common in specialist circles: providing a demanding, even harsh, interpretation of the law but relying on a gaping loophole (the fact that it would be difficult to bring such a woman to court and that she would merely need to be silent or evasive to escape punishment) to avoid the possibility that the interpretation would be applied under any likely conditions. Yet what specialists would regard as an unremarkable but purely theoretical answer, when spoken on a television broadcast to an interviewer who pressed the point, excited public controversy. The nonchalant recitation seemed less evasion than threat to unsympathetic viewers outside of specialists' circles.

In the new environment, it is not only highly trained specialists and professionals who make their voices heard in shari'a debates. Many pious Muslims with high interest but little formal training have attempted to move from being passive recipients to active seekers of religiously based truths. The piety trend, referred to in chapter 3, takes many forms, from study groups to televangelist programs. But perhaps its two most striking expressions are the widespread popular followings of a wide range of preachers and the formation of small circles of friends who meet regularly to study and discuss religious themes in a group context. The trend is observable at all levels of society, but it is so varied as to be resistant to generalizations. The few remarks advanced here should therefore be taken as quite tentative.

In chapter 3, we considered the extent to which the piety trend is "shari'a minded," using Hodgson's phrase. For Hodgson, that expression indicated those whose sense of piety was expressed through attempts to understand divine instructions for individual and social conduct: "Every individual's life should be directly under the guidance of God's laws, and anything in society not clearly necessary to his service was to be frowned upon. Among both Sunni and Shi'i Muslims, a host of pious men and women who came to be called the 'ulama, the learned, worked out what we may call the shari'a minded program for private and public living centered on the shari'a law."[16] Participants in the current piety trend would seem to be interested more in an exploration of faith, perhaps in ethical conduct, and much less in the legal and political realms. Saba Mahmood, in her ethnographic account of pietist preachers in Cairo, sees the shari'a as a marginal element in the manifestations of the trend she studied.[17]

But while much of the pietist trend may not be oriented around an explicitly political or legal project, its members often participate in the consensual themes regarding the shari'a discussed below, with their emphasis on general goals and their turn away from a conception of the shari'a as primarily a legal corpus to be applied by the political authorities.

Of course, the debate over issues connected with the shari'a is hardly restricted to individuals who participate by virtue of their piety, interests, or training. Very significant institutions are quite active as well. In addition to pious Muslims and those with specialized training, a host of state actors intervene directly (and sometimes authoritatively) in debates. As will become clear throughout this book, such institutions are not merely participants, however. They are themselves battlegrounds in which those with contrasting visions of the shari'a and its applications see each other as potential adversaries, partners, vehicles, or implementers of their own approach. The most obvious institutional participants are official institutions dedicated to delivering interpretations of the Islamic shari'a, sometimes primarily for other state bodies. State muftis have become a normal part of the state apparatus in the Arab world.[18] And alongside such structures stand other fatwa-issuing bodies, sometimes attached to various other institutions such as ministries and state-sponsored research bodies.

But the existence of such specialized actors should not obscure how broadly and thoroughly the Islamic shari'a and religious understandings are woven into the fabric of so many parts of the modern Arab state. Ministries of religious affairs hire, license, and regulate religious space and religious officials; ministries of education decide how Islamic beliefs and practices are to be taught to children. Parliaments invoke shari'a-based norms, principles, and rulings while drawing up legislation; many government ministries do the same while drawing up regulations. Different court systems—constitutional, administrative, commercial, criminal, and, above all, personal status—are often called upon to adjudicate questions that involve the Islamic shari'a; individual courts and judges sometimes take up this task with enthusiasm and bring in shari'a-based norms and principles even when not specifically charged with doing so by a clear legal text.

And alongside such official actors there are also many unofficial ones—social movements, nongovernmental organizations, political parties, research institutions—that see themselves as full participants in shari'a-based debates.

What should not escape notice is that while some of these individuals or structures may claim political authority or superior learning, none can claim full doctrinal authority; even those state bodies that claim that their ruling must govern state (or nonstate) actors would not claim their interpretation is final and immune to contestation, discussion, or debate. A prominent scholar might regard other interpretations with contempt or as issuing from unqualified sources but none would claim that his or her own interpretation had sufficient authority that it had to be believed as the only true answer to a particular question.

A special note should be added here about two sometime participants in public arguments about the Islamic shari'a: salafis and jihadists. Both have stood at the edge of debates, sometimes as active, if distinctive, participants and sometimes excluded or ignored—but still relevant.

The salafi approach—with its emphasis on close textual study and correct practice based on the example of early Muslims—can manifest itself in several different ways with a variety of public roles. Salafi scholars, for instance, can easily present themselves as uncompromising in their fealty to religious truth, less willing to bend to social and political pressures and thus operating at some remove from general debates. Some salafi approaches view politics with disdain, often in conscious contradistinction to the approach of the Muslim Brotherhood which I have heard repeatedly derided by salafis as "more about politics than religion." This attitude sometimes has a doctrinal basis, connected to a spirit of deference to Muslim rulers.

Living in partial (and somewhat self-imposed) social and political isolation, salafis can be close to invisible even as they have gathered increasing numbers of adherents. The decision to distance should not be exaggerated—after all, the feeling that they are victims of "racism" mentioned in the previous chapter stems from resentment over restrictions on their activity in public life. But at times when they have entered public life more fully—such as in the aftermath of the Egyptian uprising of 2011 or in Kuwait since the 1980s—their numbers and forceful presence has become something of a shock to non-salafis.

A discussion of their full participation in constitutional debates will come later, but for now I should note the frequent question I heard Cairenes asking each other in the wake of a mass demonstration of salafis in July 2011 (dubbed "Kandahar Friday" by those astounded by the salafi presence): where did these people come from?

Yet for all their often limited public visibility, they have been a strong presence felt even by those who do not interact directly with them: in some ways the "wasati" trend—discussed in more detail later—can be seen as a response to salafis in that it insists on the flexibility of the Islamic tradition and its consequent relevance to the daily lives of today's Muslims.

A specific strain of salafism—one that emphasizes not simply correct personal practice but also the duties of jihad—has been a more forceful presence. Direct debate between jihadists and others has been rare but it does increasingly occur. In most public spheres, however, jihadist salafis (or sometimes those whose threshold for declarations of apostasy seems too low; i.e., takfiris) serve as an important foil for more mainstream authorities and they make their presence felt that way. And on occasion jihadist voices can be directly heard in public debates accessible to all. When I first visited Egypt in 1983, I heard about a series of televised debates between the ideologues supporting the 1981 assassination of President Anwar al-Sadat and mainstream official religious authorities. I never saw those debates or ascertained their precise nature, but what struck me was the contrasting ways they were described. For some, the surprising expertise of the radicals was the major lesson; for others, it was the way the more-establishment figures schooled their would-be rivals and showed how much damage a little learning could do.

For the most part, salafis and especially jihadists lurk at the edges of public debates but they have never been totally absent. Usama Bin Ladin, who made himself so well known internationally in the early 2000s, actually directed most of his stream of public writings and taped speeches to various Arab and sometimes broader Muslim publics (as did Ayman al-Zawahiri), sometimes addressing specific intellectuals by name. Those who recanted the more radical jihadist ideas—such as those who did so in Egypt in the first decade of the twenty-first century—sparked debates across the spectrum, with their former opponents probing their sincerity and their former allies implying they had been coopted.

And at specific dramatic points—such as the assassination of Sadat, the aftermath of the uprisings of 2011 in Tunisia and Egypt, or the rise of Islamic State—the radicals can impose themselves directly, participating in undeniable ways in public debates not merely with their missives but also by their actions—actions often designed to take the form of an argument about politics or doctrine in heavily expressive and active form (such as the destruction of idols).

In most Arab countries, few Muslims publicly question the idea that the Islamic shari'a should play a role in society and governance. Of course, the degree to which the shari'a is central to public concerns varies greatly among individuals and groups, but it is striking how those who harbor the deepest doubts about the wisdom of turning to the shari'a generally couch their public arguments in guarded terms. Arab politics today is about much more than the shari'a, but the salience of the shari'a has grown markedly along with a general increase in public forms of religiosity over the past generation. This is true at multiple levels—in the constitutional, legal, political, educational, social, and commercial realms, discussions are often infused with general themes related to the shari'a and shari'a-based discourse and arguments—ranging from the platitudinous to the technical—often invoked.

Recent public opinion polling has affirmed the centrality of the Islamic shari'a for many Muslims in the Arab world.[19] But what is the nature of the Islamic shari'a that has been invoked so often in public debates? And how is it to order politics, law, and society? For it is order—imposed public order—that is often at issue. Individuals and groups from a wide variety of perspectives generally display little discomfort with the idea of state power (so long as it is in the right hands) being used to enforce some morally and religiously based norms—or, as it is more often phrased, protecting society from animalistic behavior (with human society being defined by its adherence to such norms, norms that are themselves designed to protect, enhance, and elevate individual and communal life).[20]

While we will begin answering such questions by reference to five consensual themes, as has already been stressed, this should not be taken to imply that everyone (or even most) agree or subscribe to them—nor should it even be taken to imply that nobody would challenge them. The argument here concerns only apparent consensus in the public sphere. Salafis, jihadists, and secularists sometimes challenge the consensus in public. In private or restricted realms, of course, much more wide-ranging discussions take place.

But because our initial interest is with the public sphere, we will first examine the five themes in an almost disembodied way—as if the arguments are not made by specific individuals, institutions, or groups. Very soon, however, we will explore in some detail how these themes are deployed by advocates of different visions of society.[21]

A first consensual theme is that the shari'a encompasses specific rules, which fall into two categories. One category comprises those rules that are fixed and incontrovertible, sometimes referred to as those on which all scholars concur. These are incumbent on all believers; implicitly or explicitly they also bind political authorities in an Islamic society. Put differently, the political order is required to observe and even enforce a body of widely accepted shari'a-based rules. These definitive and binding rules are few in number, since the necessary scholarly consensus must span great historical and geographical distances. The second body of rules are less certain and can vary considerably according to time and place. It is widely acknowledged that the shari'a encompasses a broad tradition of religious inquiry that extends far beyond the few incontrovertible shari'a-based rules. But the guidance to the faithful that emerges from this broader inquiry is generally not definitive—it is dependent on human effort and prevailing social conditions. While the shari'a itself is of divine inspiration and unchanging, its application in most areas is not merely debatable and subject to multiple understandings but also quite flexible, responding to human needs.

A related idea that has emerged in some circles is the necessity to prioritize shari'a-based rules. The "jurisprudence of priorities" (*fiqh al-awwaliyyat*) has been introduced into widespread usage by Yusuf al-Qaradawi, a prominent Egyptian religious scholar (and media presence) based in Qatar, but the idea has been used by others, including the current mufti of Egypt, Shawki Ibrahim 'Abd al-Karim 'Allam. The approach asserts that those trained in Islamic law should weigh the relative importance of rules, an implicit criticism of the extreme textualism of the salafi approach.

The second consensual theme involves not specific rules but general purposes enjoined by the shari'a. While the shari'a is oriented toward prescribing (or sometimes encouraging) righteous behavior and prohibiting (or containing) iniquitous actions, it is held to do so within a framework that protects general principles. In other words, the shari'a cannot simply be understood as a set of rules but is deeply informed by set of moral goals. There is increasing stress in public discussions on the *maqasid* (goals or purposes) of the shari'a—a term from Islamic jurisprudence that has now passed into general usage to refer to the overriding goals that shari'a is said to pursue. The relationship between the maqasid and the fixed rules of the shari'a is not always explored—and, as will be seen, when it is explored it provokes disagreement. For some (especially credentialed specialists and trained professionals) an excessive or inexpert focus on the maqasid does not merely have a salutary effect of rendering shari'a-based discourse more reflective of divine intentions and responsive to the needs of the faithful but also carries a real danger as well, as some believers might be inclined to vague, even vapid, understandings of shari'a-based principles that allow freewheeling claims untethered by long accepted rulings.[22]

Again, the emphasis on the general purposes of the shari'a can be developed not only to be inclusive and relevant to daily life but also in contradistinction to what are seen as overly rigid interpretations, often of a salafi variety. One self-described Azhar-trained imam with a wasati bent explained to me that the salafi emphasis on dress—in which men wear gowns that come to mid-calf in emulation of the practice of the early Muslims—completely missed the point. The prophet favored such dress, he explained, since it was then considered ostentatious to display wealth by more flowing gowns (that is, those including more fabric). To insist on one's virtue now by wearing such a shorter gown completely subverts the point, since it is, he claimed, a sign of a slightly different kind of vanity (proud public displays of piety) rather than the true purpose endorsed by the prophet (personal modesty) that motivates salafi dress.

The effect of shifting emphasis from shari'a-based rules to general goals is marked—it would seem simultaneously to underscore the relevance but also the flexibility of the Islamic shari'a. Both trends—relevance and flexibility—are accentuated by a similar tendency to give great weight to the interest of the society in public debates about the shari'a. Those emphasizing *maslaha* (a term that generally means "public interest" though it has more specific technical connotations in Islamic legal thought) are simultaneously participating in a contemporary public debate and a historical discussion. The use of maslaha in efforts to derive legal rules in the absence of clear texts (and its linkage to maqasid) has a hoary history.[23] And while maslaha's role in broad public debates about Islamic law is a modern phenomenon, it betrays echoes of a long-standing debate over how it should be employed. This debate now seems to take the form of a sharp tension between approaches that use maslaha as a technique to make the shari'a more relevant and those that hold that it can be used to bend understandings of the shari'a to the whim of the users. Laid on top of this tension is a less obvious struggle over authority. As traditionally used, maslaha was a device for scholars, and it is still understood that way by some specialists. But the elision between the technical term "maslaha" and the broader concept of "public interest" in the less technical sense allows the populace and their secularly trained leaders to claim a role in the debate: while not expert in all aspects of Islamic law, they certainly seem to be on solid ground when demanding a role in determining the public interest. Or to put it in Arabic: *maslaha mursila* (the technical fiqh term with religious connotations) has metamorphosed into *maslaha `amma* (public interest) in general discussions without many people noticing. Specialists sometimes resist but at other times join in the elision; most other participants in the public debate show little awareness or interest in the conceptual stretching at work.

Third, there is a strong consensus that the state has a role in fostering and protecting moral values and codes of conduct with a religious provenance. As opposed to the other areas of consensus I have identified, this one is not always fully articulated precisely because it is so widely shared—it can remain largely unspoken until challenged. Challenges do occur, to be sure, from the fringes of public debate—from ardent secularists who press for a separation of religion from official structures; and, anomalously, from extremely pious groups who object less in principle and more in practice to existing states asserting control over the religious sphere and prefer instead to have religion left alone by current political authorities. For all those in between (and, indeed, sometimes even for non-Muslims who seek not secularism but state recognition of and protection for their communally based structures), the state should enforce public morality, foster religious knowledge and conduct in school children, adjudicate (at least in the realm of family law) on the basis of God's instructions, build mosques, pay preachers, educate religious scholars, and broadcast religious programs.

Fourth, the theme of *wasatiyya*—moderation or centralism—has gained increasing resonance in public discussions. Increased interest in the theme has expressed itself in conferences, tracts, and ideological statements throughout the Muslim world (and has figured prominently in international efforts to present Islam in a positive light). Hamas, al-Azhar, prominent intellectuals across the political and religious spectrum, popular preacher Yusuf al-Qaradawi, new political parties, older movements like Egypt's Muslim Brotherhood, and various liberals have all laid claim to the label. Salafis seem largely left out; everyone else seems to wish to claim the middle ground. Wasatiyya thus has several different connotations, but it is often linked to calls for persuasion and dialogue and against violence and perceived extremism. While "moderation" is an accurate translation, wasatiyya indicates something beyond political moderation as the term is used internationally and especially in the United States—indeed, some movements that would seem to be extremist by most political definitions lay claim to the wasatiyya label.

Few challenge the emphasis of wasatiyya, though some salafis have expressed concern that it leads to immoral compromises and adulterates good with evil. The term's religious overtones are often made explicit by reference to Qur'an 2:143 (which describes Muslims as forming a "middle" nation or community). Most of those invoking the term "wasatiyya" engage in little textual exegesis of the Qur'anic verse (which appears at first glance to be in a very different context).

Instead, the wasatiyya slogan is used with two different kinds of inflection. The first is to emphasize that proper interpretations of Islam should naturally incline against fanaticism or extremism; the second that those interpretations should incline toward those that are most sensible, appropriate, helpful, and even easiest for society (thus underscoring the increasing emphasis on maqasid and maslaha).

Finally, public discussions of the shari'a are often accompanied with expressions of distaste for *takfir* (charging apostasy) and "changing with the hand"[24]—a very marked departure from the 1980s and 1990s, when debates about such matters took place on the front pages of newspapers in several Arab states. Of course, radical groups still exist that claim a right, even a duty, to enforce shari'a-based rules themselves. Outside of radical circles, most reject the claim that individual believers are responsible for implementing change by force or that purportedly Muslim societies (or their rulers) have passed into a state of apostasy or unbelief. The rhetorical escalation in some Arab societies that came after the Arab uprisings of 2011—and especially the dramatic rise and fall of the Muslim Brotherhood in Egypt and the rise of Islamic State and similar movements—led to some revival of the language of takfir and direct action in some circles, however.

The overall effect of these consensual themes initially seems harmonious indeed when we put them all together. In the Arab world, many Muslims publicly agree that there are some shari'a-based rules that they are all bound by and which the state should enforce. At the same time, emphasis has shifted away from specific rules and enforcement to proper personal and social conduct and peaceful discussion of how to understand religious teachings. Public debates focus on how to realize the common good and practice ethical behavior in a social context. Indeed, debates seem to take place within a narrower range than they did two and three decades ago.

There are, of course, limits to the consensus. The turn toward general principles has taken some of the sharp political edge off shari'a-based debates. But it is not part of a process of converting the Islamic shari'a into a privatized ethical code; the emphasis is still very much on appropriate conduct within a social context, and the idea of a "wall of separation"—the famous Jeffersonian phrase—between the religious and state realms does not resonate in most Arab contexts.

More important, however, the reality of political discussions falls far short of harmony. Reference to these areas of general consensus cannot obscure the fact that deep differences still remain. The consensus described above emerged partly out of difficult struggles and the nitty-gritty of everyday politics: the defeat of radical jihadist movements; the tremendous reach of the modern state; the restrictions on formal politics; and the effort by state officials to regulate Islam and appropriate religious sources of legitimacy.

But the consensus also emerged because its central themes resolve so little—they allow for many different interpretations and can be deployed by various groups in sharply different ways. Each of the areas of emerging consensus mentioned contains within it substantial ambiguity and potential for difference and debate. In fact, the consensus is really just an agreement that certain words and at most concepts are central—but not on what they mean, how they are applied, and, most of all, who may interpret and apply them.

If, for instance, there are a limited number of definitive shari'a-based rules then what are they? Who determines them? Who enforces them? If the shari'a is flexible and subject to interpretation in other areas, who is qualified to offer interpretations? How is shari'a-based inquiry to be conducted? If maqasid and maslaha are to receive special emphasis, then who determines how such general ideas are applied? And are they a license for boundless flexibility, rendering the shari'a a collection of banal but pleasant sentiments? Or are they restricted and technical and thus inappropriate for public debate or less useful as tools for intellectual openness?

There are deep and abiding tensions even within these areas of emerging consensus, and many of those tensions are closely connected with different conceptions of interpretative authority. Those different conceptions vary along two dimensions.

First, there is a range of views over the relative importance of specialized training and personal piety in approaching the shari'a. Is interpretation of shari'a a complex task for those with the requisite education and knowledge or is it a task for all pious Muslims anxious to behave in accordance with God's guidance? The question is actually rarely posed this starkly. Those who stress specialized training—ensconced in official positions, bureaucratic offices, faculty chairs, and holding formal credentials—would hardly argue that their teachings are absolutely binding nor would they absolve individual believers of any responsibility for understanding Islamic teachings. Similarly, those who stress the role of individual believers—popular preachers, ordinary believers, political leaders, public officials, and intellectuals without formal religious training—do not deride the need for education or training or claim no need for seeking guidance from those who specialize in shari'a-based inquiry.

But even if the polar positions are avoided, there is a wide range of inclinations—perhaps best illustrated by prevailing arguments about the issuing of fatwas. Is there a crisis in Islamic belief and practice caused by a rapid multiplication in those who issue interpretations of the Islamic shari'a—or, as those concerned about the phenomenon often term it, a crisis of "chaotic fatwas" (fatawi 'ashwa'iyya)?[25] Or should Muslims look to a variety of sources until they find the appropriate guidance? Is the individual believer likely to be misled by amateur interpretation—or the lazy Muslim let off the hook, allowed to select whatever interpretation s/he likes in an unregulated market of religious opinions? Might state officials shop, cherry pick, cajole, and intimidate until they receive a blessing for a policy or law that is actually very dubious in religious terms? Or are pluralism and broad discussion signs of the vitality and relevance of Islamic teachings? Is the multiplicity of voices an opportunity for individual believers to educate themselves and draw on various perspectives and answers as well as a healthy sign that political, social, and religious issues are being explored increasingly in a shari'a-based idiom?

A second dimension of tension concerns the relative role of the state and the society. Which state bodies have roles to play connected to the shari'a and what are those roles? What are the relative roles of the individual Muslim, the religious scholar, official religious institutions, and state institutions (such as courts, the parliament, or the educational establishment) that are not primarily or even largely religious in their focus? If general principles—especially maslaha—are to be used in developing interpretations, then who may deploy the concepts and how? Is this a function for scholars, a prerogative of political authorities, or a field of discussion for all believers?

The state is not a religiously neutral actor anywhere in the Arab world. Few question its role in fostering religious values and knowledge and in encouraging and even enforcing some shari'a-based norms. Thus the state's accepted role inevitably requires officials to designate specific interpretations as legally binding or authoritative as a matter of policy (though rarely of belief). But who develops these interpretations and how?

These two tensions—over expertise and the role of the state—overlap but they are not identical. Those who stress the need for specialized training and knowledge and decry chaotic fatwas, for instance, might easily posit state-sponsored religious institutions as the answer. But they might just as easily hold the state responsible for contributing to the confusion by favoring weak interpretation and craven or unqualified authorities.

Thus the coincidence of emerging consensus and growing cacophony is less contradictory than immediately appears. And we can now go beyond characterizing the general areas of emerging consensus and disagreement and embody some of the voices that speak in shari'a-based terms in various ways.

In part 3 of this book, we will focus our attention on three areas. First we will examine the most abstract debate: constitution making. While constitutional texts do affect people's lives, they do so in ways that are often indirect and less predictable; debates can be (and indeed have become) increasingly intense but are often abstract and surprisingly divorced from considerations of implementation and enforcement.

Second, we will focus on an area with the precise opposite characteristic: personal status law, where personal concerns meet the political most forcefully. In legislating matters of marriage, divorce, and inheritance, states in the Arab world intervene not only in family life but also draw on religious teachings and religious authorities when they do so. This not only provokes argument, it also leads to actions, as those subject to these laws beat paths in their pursuit of their desires, preferences, and values in ways that conform to, shape, and evade the law. Indeed, there is likely no area where the language of religion (shari'a-based conceptions of family relations), the state (personal status codes), and ordinary conversation about such issues are congruent: words like ta'a (obedience) or darar (harm) might be deployed by a scholar, a lawyer, or a husband or wife with roughly the same meaning. And that leads to arguments that cross the boundaries of religion, law, policy, and human behavior.

Finally, we will examine religious education—a mandatory subject in schools in the Arab world and thus one where, at least in theory, religion and state speak in a single voice, thus provoking arguments about what that voice does and should say. Debates over religion and education are not only lively but contain an unexpected variety of participants. Various parts of Arab states— ministries of religion and education, institutions of religious authority, parliaments, and security agencies—might contend alongside parents, teachers, professional educators, political movements, and social reformers.

NOTES

1. I do not mean to suggest that Islam should be viewed only or primarily through the shariʻa. For a powerful critique of such a view, see Shahab Ahmed, *What is Islam? The Importance of Being Islamic* (Princeton: Princeton University Press, 2016). I do mean to suggest, however, that in the Arab world the revival of politics encounters religion chiefly through the Islamic shariʻa.

2. In this section I draw on and develop a guide I developed for the Carnegie Endowment for International Peace, "Egypt and the Islamic Sharia: A Guide for the Perplexed," http://carnegieendowment.org/2012/05/15/egypt-and-islamic-sharia-guide-for-perplexed, posted May 15, 2012; accessed March 20, 2015.

3. Most general overviews of the Islamic legal tradition show very clearly its breadth and its focus on method. Two more recent and particularly helpful guides are Wael B. Hallaq, *An Introduction to Islamic Law* (Cambridge: Cambridge University Press, 2009) and Bernard Weiss, *The Spirit of Islamic Law* (Athens: University of Georgia Press, 2006). Abbas Amanat and Frank Griffel, eds., *Shariʻa: Islamic Law in the Contemporary Context* (Palo Alto: Stanford University Press, 2009) provides a more current analysis on the meaning of the Islamic shariʻa.

4. Perhaps the most in-depth coverage and analysis of public opinion on this subject among others is available from the Arab Barometer Project, www.arabbarometer.org, accessed March 20, 2015.

5. See Andrew F. March, "Genealogies of Sovereignty in Islamic Political Theology," *Social Research* 80, 1 (2013): 293–320.

6. Predominant Shiʻi approaches are somewhat different, though the result is not always dissimilar. For the majority of Shiʻi in the Arab world, the task of an individual believer is to follow one of a limited number of leading authorities in matters of interpretation. In that sense, the authority of such scholars is determinative rather than advisory.

7. The evolving nature of Islamic legal approaches even within the dominant schools of law is not always appreciated by nonspecialists. A useful and influential set of detailed accounts of this subject illustrating this point can be found in Baber Johansen, *Contingency in a Sacred Law: Legal and Ethical Norms in the Muslim Fiqh* (Leiden: Brill, 1998).

8. Monica Duffy Toft, Daniel Philpott, and Timothy Samuel Shah, *God's Century: Resurgent Religion and Global Politics* (New York: W. W. Norton, 2011).

9. I am presenting an updated and condensed version of the argument I earlier made in "Shariʻa and State in the Modern Muslim Middle East," *International Journal of Middle East Studies* 29, 3 (1997): 359–376.

10. I do not mean to suggest a linear story in which ʻulama were independent and then lost their voice when religious institutions were taken over by the state. Such a story is frequently told by critics of either current regimes or of official religious establishment in the Arab world. And that story might bear some historical weight. But focused historical studies tell, at a minimum, a more nuanced and varied picture. See, for instance Meir Hatina, *'Ulama', Politics, and*

the *Public Sphere: An Egyptian Perspective* (Salt Lake City: University of Utah Press, 2010).

11. For a very sophisticated treatment of the role of religious scholars in the modern era, see Muhammad Qasim Zaman, *The Ulama in Contemporary Islam: Custodians of Change* (Princeton: Princeton University Press, 2007).

12. One prominent specialist in Islamic law has gone so far as to argue that the modern state and the Islamic shari'a are incompatible in their essences and that modernity has vanquished the shari'a as a system. See Wael Hallaq, *The Impossible State: Islam, Politics, and Modernity's Moral Predicament* (New York: Columbia University Press, 2013). A symposium in Perspective on Politics, to which I contributed, offers a series of critiques to Hallaq's argument; see Nathan J. Brown, "A Discussion of Wael Hallaq's Islam, Politics, and Modernity's Moral Predicament," *Perspective on Politics* 12, 2 (2014): 464–466. My own approach is to see the modern state as deeply intertwined with the Islamic shari'a but not to the extent that it has extinguished, conquered, or completely subordinated it. I am therefore far more influenced by Hussein Agrama, *Questioning Secularism: Islam, Sovereignty, and the Rule of Law in Modern Egypt* (Chicago: University of Chicago Press, 2012). Two other useful works that stress the role of the modern state without casting it as having completely subsumed the Islamic shari'a or destroyed it are Clark Lombardi, *State Law as Islamic Law in Modern Egypt* (Leiden: Brill, 2006) and Jocelyn Cesari, *The Awakening of Muslim Democracy: Religion, Modernity, and the State* (Cambridge: Cambridge University Press, 2014).

13. For an extremely rich study of the process in Egypt, see Kenneth M. Cuno, *Modernizing Marriage: Family, Ideology, and Law in Nineteenth- and Early Twentieth-Century Egypt* (Syracuse: Syracuse University Press, 2015).

14. The writings of public intellectuals on Islamic themes has been noted by many historians of modern social and political thought in the Arab world. See, for instance, Israel Gershoni's coverage of the islamiyyat literature in *Redefining the Egyptian Nation, 1930–1945* (Cambridge: Cambridge University Press, 2002).

15. See, for instance, Andrew F. March and Mara Revkin, "Caliphate of Law: ISIS' Ground Rules," *Foreign Affairs*, April 15, 2015, https://www.foreignaffairs.com/articles/syria/2015-04-15/caliphate-law, accessed July 16, 2016.

16. Marshall Hodgson, *The Venture of Islam*, Vol. 1, *The Classical Age of Islam* (Chicago: University of Chicago Press, 1977), 38.

17. Saba Mahmood, *Politics of Piety: The Islamic Revival and the Feminist Subject* (Princeton: Princeton University Press, 2005), 47.

18. Jakob Skovgaard-Petersen, "A Typology of State Muftis," in *Islamic Law and the Challenges of Modernity*, eds. Yvonne Haddad and Barbara Stowasser (New York: Altamira Press, 2004), 81–98.

19. Again, the most detailed data is from the Arab Barometer Project.

20. For a perceptive and helpful presentation of the way that Turks have grappled with issues of communalism and individualism while navigating among different orientations toward religion and nation, see Jenny White, *Muslim Nationalism and the New Turks* (Princeton: Princeton University Press, 2013).

21. An earlier but extended analysis of these themes is available in my chapter on Egypt in *Shari'a Politics: Islamic Law and Society in the Modern World*, ed. Robert Hefner (Bloomington: Indiana University Press, 2011), 94–120.

22. For a very helpful introduction to the concept of maqasid, its history, and its current use, see Andrew F. March, "Islamic Legal Theory, Secularism and

Religious Pluralism: Is Modern Religious Freedom Sufficient for the Shari'a 'Purpose [Maqsid]' of 'Preserving Religion [Hifz Al-Din]?'" Islamic Law and Law of the Muslim World Research Paper Series Paper No. 09-78; Public Law Working Paper No. 208 (Yale Law School, 2009).

March refers to *"complex* purposivism" (emphasis added) because the insistence on interpretations that are based on divine purpose is "constrained not only by the letter of revelatory texts, but also the accumulated tradition of positive legal rules, most of which crystallized before the advent of the theory of the maqāsid (or, indeed, before 'classical' legal theory) and thus acquired the status of authoritative and binding interpretations" (p. 22). What troubles some specialists is that overly enthusiastic use of the technique might not be complex at all but instead might be embraced by nonspecialists to evade long-accepted rules.

23. Felicitas Opwis, *Maṣlaḥah and the Purpose of the Law: Islamic Discourse on Legal Change from Islamic Discourse on Legal Change from the 4th/10th to 8th/14th Century* (Leiden: Brill, 2010)

24. The phrase "changing with the hand" is part of a commonly quoted hadith in which the Prophet is said to have instructed those witnessing something wrong to change it first with their hands, but if they are unable to do so, with their tongues, and if they are still unable, they should do so with their hearts. For a presentation of some of the interpretative tradition surrounding this, see Michael Cook, *Commanding Right and Forbidding Wrong in Islamic Thought* (Cambridge: Cambridge University Press, 2001).

25. For an analysis and critique of the debate about this phenomenon, See Alexandre Caeiro, "Debating the Chaos of Fatwas in the Arab World" (paper presented at the Annual Meeting of the Middle East Studies Association, New Orleans, 2013).

PART 3

Does Arguing Matter?

There is no life without dialogue. And in the major part of the world, dialogue has been replaced today by polemics. . . . Day and night, thousands of voices, each carrying on its own tumultuous monologue, pour out on the peoples of the world a torrent of mystifying words, attacks, defenses, and over-excitement.

Albert Camus, "The Artist as Witness of Freedom,"
Commentary, December 1, 1949

His mind was filled with thoughts that, taken one by one, were perfectly reasonable but in sequence did not quite make sense.

William Maxwell, *So Long, See You Tomorrow*, 112

WHAT HAPPENS WHEN THE REPUBLIC OF ARGUMENTS MEETS THE REALITY OF ARAB REGIMES?

We have seen in part 2 how and where religion is publicly argued in the Arab world. But what is argued? And what effect does arguing have? Does anybody ever listen? Do those arguing ever persuade each other? Do officials implement different polices?

Yes, but not very often.

I suggested at the outset that the problems caused by arguing religion are not tied so much to the issues being argued; while religion raises fundamental concerns, broad areas of consensus can be identified. Politics in the second sense of the term—focusing on policy outcomes—often requires building coalitions and crafting compromises. In important areas, perhaps the most important areas where politics treads, such compromises are possible. We shall see some possible areas for compromise and even common ground when we come to fundamental documents on governance (constitutions) and the most intimate sphere (the law governing relations between husband and wife).

But such agreements are rare and when they occur they are often shallower than enthusiasts of the public sphere would hope. Arab societies have grown rich with talk, but that talk only rarely leads to consensus, agreement, or policy change. Even where compromise seems quite possible in principle it is not often realized in practice. Tarek Masoud tackled the issue of Islam in the Egyptian state in the period between the overthrow of President Muhammad Morsi and the breakneck descent into political violence between state bodies and Islamists, noting that "Morsi's sin was not that he sought to Islamize the state—Hosni Mubarak had done a pretty good job of that himself, and the temporary constitution issued [in July 2013] by the new interim government includes all of the shariah-talk that liberals supposedly found so objectionable."[1] The conflict did not stem from the inability to find suitable constitutional language.

Public arguments about Islam persuade and effect policy change only on rare occasions. What explains the variation in persuasion and policy is not so much the issues involved as it is the structure of the state and of political life, with most political parties weak and unable to mobilize and effectively speak for constituencies, most parliaments providing platforms better designed for posturing than shaping policy, and most bureaucrats safely insulated from mechanisms that might force them to listen to their constituents.

That does not mean that the revival of Arab politics has no effect—it does shape how various groups view the political system and contributes to feelings of inclusion and exclusion. In part 3, we will realize these characteristics by proceeding inductively through three policy areas. We move from an area that is supremely and fundamentally political and garners international attention (constitution writing) to one that is clearly contentious and still has fundamentally political aspects (personal status law) and then finally to one that appears to be a bit less fundamental and apparently more narrowly a public policy concern (educational curricula).

As we move from the most fundamental area of political life through one that is fundamental but also very personal to one that seems primarily technocratic, we do not find a clear relationship between the issues at stake on the one hand and either the extent to which arguments lead to changes in positions through persuasion or affect policy on the other. Instead we find that when arguments have some authoritative audience—particularly when state bodies allow (and occasionally even encourage) interaction with those making public arguments—then public debates make a difference and there is some evidence on occasion that positions evolve as a result. In other words, it is the political framework more than the subject matter that leads to arguing making a difference.

We focus on constitution making in chapter 6, probing the effects of greater publicity in the drafting process, and we see that the primary consequences have been on the expressive parts of the constitution—those that set forth fundamental political values without necessarily having so much legal or political effect. Constitutional argument sometimes occurs within a narrow range, allowing for a large degree of agreement over much of the text—or at least allowing texts that most political actors can live with. But there is still considerable debate, and publicity has made a difference in those debates, actually deepening some of them—and particularly heightening debates over basic expressions of political community. Remarkably, arguments have their greatest textual effects on those clauses that matter less legally.

In chapter 7 we turn to personal status law, finding a set of arguments that are surprisingly only loosely linked to lived experiences. In limited instances—those in which a part of the state apparatus aims to accomplish a change—an agreement is possible but not so much by forging mutual understanding on principles as by an entrepreneurial state actor assembling support by spinning and manipulating reforms to gather widespread support.

Finally, in chapter 8 we will examine the politics of education curricula, witnessing heated arguments that are disconnected from any outcome—and that are especially heated precisely for that reason.

CHAPTER 6

Arab Constitutions, the Many Voices of the Public, and the Word of the One God

Islam is the religion of the State and Arabic is its official language. The principles of the Islamic shari'a are the main source of legislation.

Article 2 of the Constitution of the Arab Republic of Egypt

Tunisia is a free, independent, sovereign state, its religion is Islam, Arabic is its language, and its system is republican. This article may not be amended.

    Tunisia is a civil state based on citizenship, the will of the people, and the supremacy of law. This article may not be amended.

Articles 1 and 2 of the Constitution of the Tunisian Republic

CONSTITUTIONAL ARGUMENTS ABOUT RELIGION: DO PEOPLE CHANGE THEIR MINDS? DOES IT MATTER WHO WINS?

We will see that the legal effects of all the arguing that takes place in Arab politics are much less than might be expected, but the broader political effects are still deep since constitutional language can profoundly shape the attitudes that various groups take toward the political order.

    Constitutions are supremely public documents in many different ways—and they have become even more so in the Arab world since the first ones were written a century and a half ago. They are public in the sense that they are promulgated before the people and generally issued in their name; they also present themselves as constituting public authority. And they are increasingly public in that they serve as important markers of sovereignty before the world and before the people that they are said to govern: they are cited in speeches and quoted in textbooks; their clauses are invoked in public debates. They become still more public when they evolve (as they have in the Arab world) from being legalistic documents about the operation of state institutions to expansive ideological documents about the identity of a people.

But even further, in an uncertain but unmistakable trend accompanying what I am calling the revival of Arab politics, the process of drafting constitutions has become increasingly public in two additional senses: there is a general trend toward greater public interest in and attention to the process, and there are far greater expectations for formal public participation. Those expectations have grown in recent decades but burst forth with special force in some countries in the wake of the 2011 uprisings.

Each of these steps toward publicity has increased the overlap between arguments about the constitution and arguments about Islam. When the first drafters of constitutional texts for Arab political systems began their work in the second half of the nineteenth century, Islamic political concepts occasionally formed part of the backdrop for their efforts but rarely intruded into the foreground. When Islamic elements made their way into texts, the language was carefully crafted to excite little concern. So when religion entered constitutional debates, it usually drew little attention or scrutiny. For almost a century, beginning with Tunisia's 1861 constitution, explicit references to Islam were either close to platitudinous (preambular in spirit if not in location) or unemotionally technical and detailed. Legalistic clauses were sometimes written to protect a specific sphere for practices deemed Islamic, such as in personal status law or education, but hardly to construct a fully Islamic political order. Such a task was simply rarely seen as a constitutional one. Occasionally clauses connected with religion might excite a bit more attention but rarely led to sustained debate or crisis.

Yet in the second half of the twentieth century, the increasing publicity of Arab constitutions led to the growth of a slow process of Islamic inflation—constitutional clauses, while still often remaining either largely platitudinous or technical, grew far more fulsome and began to promise (quite vaguely) a more fully Islamic political order.[2] This inflationary trend was augmented by a significant change in the public debate: Islam gradually but quite forcefully moved into the constitutional foreground, alternately pulled in by bombastic regimes and pushed in by assertive social and political movements.

In the twenty-first century, efforts to draft new constitutions in more participatory processes—first in Iraq, then in Tunisia, Egypt, and Libya—set off emotional debates about the relationship between Islam and the political order. Similar but less fraught debates occurred in other countries including Kuwait and Syria.

Many who had lost interest in constitutional texts have regained it. Especially in the past two decades, earlier cynical doubts that constitutions can have any effect at all have given way in some contexts to greater hope (on brief occasions verging on giddiness) and expectations that the constitutions are significant documents for defining a political community and how it operates. I do not think this hope is entirely naïve, though it has generally been disappointed to date.[3]

In this chapter I will explore the nature of constitutions in the Arab world, focusing on the processes that produce them as arenas for argument and the documents themselves as outcomes in part of those arguments. I show the ways in which the changing and escalating forms of publicity have expressed themselves in constitutional arguments about Islam and the ways that has been reflected in constitutional texts. I will proceed historically, initially. After tracing the slow growth of both publicity and constitutional language concerning Islam in Arab constitution writing, I will then turn attention to the post-2011 experience of Tunisia and Egypt where Islamists became major political players but the expansionary tendency regarding Islam came to an end.

This presentation will then allow me to show the effects of arguing about Islam on three levels. First, the arguments have had a growing effect on the constitutional texts. If we ended our analysis there, we might see the arguments as efficacious. But second, I will also show, along the way, how the formulas that were developed did not always have much legal effect. In other words, if we turn our attention from constitutions as outcomes to constitutions as causes, we will see that the language adopted often seemed designed to placate various parties with preambles and platitudes rather than change policies or laws. That will lead me to close the chapter by presenting the third way the arguments had an effect: by shaping various groups' affective orientation toward the political system.

ISLAMIC INFLATION OBSERVED

Over time, Arab constitutions have tended to become more extensive in their public commitment to religion[4]. This trend can be understood as part of the processes by which constitutions themselves became more public documents in the various senses described earlier.

The Arab world's first written document that might be termed a constitution was the *qanun al-dawla al-tunisiyya* [Law of the Tunisian State or Dynasty] of 1861. It was followed by an Ottoman constitution in 1876 (which governed large parts of the Arab world and bequeathed its structures and clauses to many post-Ottoman constitutional texts in the Arab world) and an Egyptian Organic Law of 1882 (a less comprehensive constitutional document than the Tunisian and the Ottoman).

These documents were largely produced from within the state apparatus itself, as if structuring public affairs was a matter for state officials alone and not the concern of the public itself. Religious officials, scholars, and the administrative elite were often included in the committees drafting the documents and many such figures had significant education in what was then a largely religiously dominated curriculum for much of the education system—especially leading members of the bureaucracy, who generally comprised the vast majority of, and were and the driving force behind, the constitutional efforts. Thus it should be no surprise to find in the Tunisian document, for instance, an attempt to adapt some emerging constitutional practices by placing them within a framework described in religiously based and familiar terms—ones that were paternalistic and favored a conception of the people as a ward rather than a participant in governance. The 1861 constitution did not present itself as Islamic in any explicit way, though its authors expressed themselves in terms that drew on Islamic political vocabulary. Members of the newly established Grand Council, for instance, were referred to as *ahl al-hall wa-l-'aqd*; literally, the people who loosen and bind; and the population was generally referred to as *ra'ayana*; literally, our flock.

But that path was largely abandoned in later documents, following the Ottoman usage in the Empire's 1876 constitution. Islam appeared in that text, to be sure—in its designation as the official religion, for instance, or in connection with the educational system—and some religious scholars were still involved in attempts to ensure that any fundamental legal document be seen as true to shari'a-based norms. That issue occasionally spilled into public view. This happened most notably during the Ottoman drafting, which sparked some opposition from dissident religious officials. And, more so than the Egyptian and Tunisian efforts, it took place in an imperial capital with a burgeoning public sphere heavily engaged in debates about Islam and constitutionalism. But for the most part, constitutional arguing was a debate among officials and a few public intellectuals, often ensconced in the senior bureaucracy, in most of the region.

The collapse of the Ottoman Empire at the close of the First World War occasioned a wave of constitution writing. Some documents (such as those of the short-lived Syrian Arab Kingdom in 1920 or the incompletely independent kingdom of Egypt in 1923) came from political entities working to assert their independence in the face of imperial limitations; others (such as Iraq and Transjordan) were initiated and heavily conditioned by the existence of a European mandatory power.

Even the countries in the first category, those that were able to draft documents without direct foreign participation, still had to be mindful of an unfriendly international context (the Syrian Arab Kingdom was defeated by French forces on the eve of the creation of a League of Nations mandate; the Egyptian constitution of 1923 was drafted after Britain had unilaterally declared Egypt independent subject to four conditions restricting its sovereignty enormously on the Suez Canal, the Sudan, protection of foreigners, and defense and foreign policy).

Still, drafters could deliberate fairly openly among themselves on most domestic matters. The efforts sometimes took place in private (such as the 1923 Egyptian committee) and sometimes in public (in Syria in 1920, an assembly was primarily responsible). But while there was some public discussion, in all these earlier efforts, the bulk of the work was done by senior political figures who seemed to view their task as speaking for the people without necessarily listening to them. The drafters came from the political elite—senior bureaucrats, wealthy landowners, leading attorneys, and a smattering of religious scholars. In that sense, the constitutional discussions were taking place as a public sphere was emerging—perhaps the kind that most closely resembled Habermas's ideal bourgeois public sphere, though with a much higher concentration of public officials than his merchant coffeehouse habitués and thus one with heavy doses of official representation. The sphere also tended to be friendly to religion. Rashid Rida, a religious scholar and intellectual who came to be one of the most influential figures in Arab religious and political thought in the mid-twentieth century, was a leading member (and briefly speaker) of the Syrian assembly of 1919 and 1920.[5]

In the second category of cases (including Iraq, Jordan, Lebanon, and Syria after the imposition of the mandate), colonial officials were more directly involved and used the constitutional process as a part of the negotiations over the relationship between the imperial power and the nascent political system. Sometimes that moved all or much of constitutional discussion out of public view, but not always. The Syrian process of 1920 was shut down when the French defeated the nascent state and imposed their own system pursuant to the League of Nations Mandate. The mandatory power then publicly tussled with an elected constituent assembly whose members drafted a constitution; France accepted it only after excising clauses it disapproved of. Significantly, French concerns focused on provisions for territory and the Syrian government's authority; Islam was not mentioned in the document and religion was not much of an issue for any party.

But while these were generally elitist affairs taking place under a heavy colonial shadow, there were already some discordant notes. This could be seen most notably in Egypt, where a political movement had emerged in a 1919 uprising against the British occupation. That movement, the nationalist Wafd (meaning "delegation," so named because it claimed to be deputized by the Egyptian people to represent them at the Paris Peace Conference as a result of a nationwide petition campaign) rejected the conditions placed by the British on Egyptian independence and the constitutional process that followed it.

Significantly for our current inquiry, the Wafd's rejection was not based just on the continued British role or on the content of the document, but on the process—Wafd leader Sa'd Zaghlul famously condemned the drafting committee as the "Committee of Brigands."[6] Because the members were appointed by the Egyptian king without any popular participation or election (and the Wafd was justifiably optimistic about its electoral chances), the movement rejected the legitimacy of the document (only to embrace it later when it ran victoriously in parliamentary elections, leading the king to evade the document's provisions and even suspend it).

The Wafd had both partisan and principled reasons for its position, but its argument that the people should have a say in the document that governed them, that the ultimate source of constitutional authority is the popular will, was made a permanent part of the Arab constitutional scene. But as we shall see, the paradoxical results of the acceptance of popular sovereignty in constitutional matters until recently were to eliminate any genuine public role in composition.

Over time, Arab constitutions tended to ratchet up the symbolic commitment to Islam, often proclaiming Islam to be the religion of the state. They also began to tread slowly into detailed provisions on Islam in some other ways as well, such as personal status law and minorities. Often the head of state was required to be a Muslim. Minority rights were often guaranteed, sometimes with the intent of fending off European criticisms and intervention on the behalf of minority groups. But the effect was to ensure that all citizens who were not members of recognized minority communities fell under an order in the realms of personal status and education that was infused with Islamic norms, laws, and practices. In Iraq, for instance, the constitution recognized the shari'a courts as authoritative in personal status matters for Muslims.

Islamic concerns touched off some sensitive debates regarding religious freedoms, with various outcomes. Religious minorities secured a constitutional right to their own schools in 1925 in Iraq. In Egypt, a leading Islamic scholar involved in drafting the country's 1923 constitution unsuccessfully objected to a clause stating that "the state will protect morals and feelings of religions and creeds"; he complained that this would offend Egypt's existing religions. The other drafters rejected his argument, motivated not simply by liberal sentiments but likely as well by the desire to avoid giving Great Britain any excuse to intervene in order to protect foreigners and minorities.[7]

What is notable in all these efforts—most of them dominated by a small number of officials operating outside of the public eye—is that discussion was fairly practical. Drafters were concerned about big issues to be sure. They wished generally to achieve or protect national sovereignty, and none showed any sign of disloyalty to God or religion. But writing a constitution was not an exercise in jotting down everything that was good; it was a far thinner process of devising legal formulas that would guide the structures of government in the right direction. The concern with personal status law, for instance, stemmed not from an insistence on proudly proclaiming eternal truths about relations among family members; it was born out of a desire to protect one area of law still informed by the Islamic shari'a (at least for Muslims) while preventing foreign powers from using it as an opening to impose their protection of non-Muslims.

The resulting provisions, while increasingly detailed and carefully debated and crafted, had little effect on constitutional and political practice outside the very specific areas they were designed to affect. And even on a symbolic level, the provisions appear fairly modest in retrospect. Two issues that have since emerged as central to debates about Islam and the political order—the source of sovereignty and the relationship between positive and shari'a law—were not addressed, nor was this silence deemed particularly noteworthy at the time. Occasional voices of religious scholars suggested that humans were trespassing on sacred ground by writing fundamental laws, but such objections could be dismissed as cranky anachronisms by much of the political leadership.

Such reticence and silence can be explained by several factors. First, religious institutions (such as shari'a courts and institutions of learning) at that time tended to focus their attention on maintaining autonomy and jurisdiction over their existing realms rather than establishing hegemony over the political system as a whole; they had long accommodated themselves to a state structure they neither devised nor controlled.[8]

Second, most of the constitutions were written in an effort to establish or affirm independence from European rule. In that sense, the documents were drafted to shore up state authority internationally, not tie it down domestically. Those documents that were composed under conditions of limited sovereignty (such as Iraq, Transjordan, Lebanon, and Syria—written under British and French mandates—and even Egypt, with Britain retaining and enforcing a claim to limits on Egyptian sovereignty) still showed signs of battle over efforts to carve out autonomy for indigenous political institutions. (Extraterritoriality, for instance, was a major concern of the Egyptian drafters; Iraqi drafters inserted parliamentary oversight over treaties in a manner that complicated British efforts to retain influence in the country.[9]) There was not a strong perceived contradiction between this international focus on independence on the one hand and religion on the other. Establishing national sovereignty was generally not cast in religious terms by constitutional drafters, though it was still seen as generally consistent with and even supportive of the Islamic (and national) character of the society.

Finally, the constitutions written during the period generally restricted themselves to modest general statements about the political order followed by a lengthier list of specific procedural provisions. Extensive ideological and programmatic articles were a thing of the future.

That future came in the second half of the twentieth century, as states that had remained outside the orbit of formally constitutional states joined in the effort to craft fundamental legal documents, sometimes as a part of the process of achieving or asserting independence. Some of those states that already had constitutions embarked on a journey on which significant changes in regime or ideology were accompanied by new constitutional documents. Both contexts fostered the inclusion of sweeping ideological language.

These developments slowed in the last quarter of the twentieth century as Arab authoritarian regimes settled in, many gradually transforming into semiauthoritarian ones as explored earlier, but without the dramatic changes of regimes or bombastic gyrations in official ideology of the 1950s and 1960s. As the political orders in the Arab world grew stodgy, texts began to freeze a bit in place, changing little if at all until the upheavals of 2011.

But ironically it was in this undemocratic period that the argument initiated by the Wafd in 1923 finally won: constitutions were now to be written with full public participation. Sometimes there were formally elected assemblies; at other times there were appointed bodies but some of the work was done in public and occasioned public debate. In Syria in 1950 an elected assembly wrote a new text; in Kuwait in 1962 an elected body (joined by leading members of the royal family) did the same. The results were uneven—the Syrian constitution was replaced in three years, while the Kuwaiti is not only still in effect, unamended, until this day, but the mechanism by which it was created, with unelected members of a ruling family hashing out arrangements with a diverse group of elected citizens, remains the way that many Kuwaitis continue to understand the nature of their political order.

The effects were uneven in another way as well: the initial steps toward publicity began to have effects on the content of the documents. The Muslim Brotherhood was present in the Syrian assembly and managed to insert a clause providing that "Islamic jurisprudence (*fiqh*) is the main source of legislation." (The same article also hastened to protect religious communities in practicing rituals and placed matters of personal status on a sectarian basis.) A version of the clause migrated to Kuwait in 1962 where the Islamic shari'a itself (and not jurisprudence, a more specific term) was proclaimed "a main source" of legislation—leading some religious members of the assembly to question whether or not the Islamic shari'a should not instead be the mainstay of the entire legal order. We examine the transnational evolution of this clause later; for now it is enough to note that it was an outcome in part of publicizing the constitutional process.

But there was one aspect of introducing the public that ultimately overwhelmed and undermined all other aspects—or robbed them of practical effect: the ritualistic referendum. In the second half of the twentieth century, most Arab constitutions were presented for a vote in referendums and approved virtually by acclamation. And that step—formally giving the public the final voice in determining the fundamental law—seemed to combine publicity, popular sovereignty, and constitutionalism. But the reality was far different and fooled few people: regimes and leaders often ensconced in senior executive positions so dominated not only the state but also the public sphere during the fully authoritarian period that measures ostensibly giving the public a role vitiated their own spirit: allowing the people to speak in the Arab world often had the ventriloquist effect that results in us only hearing the voice of the rulers.

As a result, constitution writing evolved into a more public but less pluralistic project: it became one of regimes reconstituting themselves, incorporating participatory language but vitiating participatory procedures.[10] Small committees, generally including senior officials and helpful legal specialists working for them, crafted documents that spoke more fulsomely about the people's will (with "the people" as singular) while sheltering that people from any burden other than approving the final product. Press discussion and popular conferences might explore the officially sanctioned ideology with enthusiasm and perhaps expand on some of the increasingly extensive (even bombastic) ideological provisions, but the heavy lifting of investing (or robbing) meaning in the substantive and procedural clauses was left to top regime officials and technical legal drafters.[11] The minutes of the drafting committee for Egypt's 1923 constitution were published by the state; those for the 1971 constitution are kept in typescript in dusty cartons in a few official locations. There was no need to share them.

As Arab politics grew increasingly ideological, the symbolic provisions related to Islam often grew thicker. Islamic legal principles were often cited in constitutional debates.[12] Constitutional garrulousness meant that it was no longer enough to refer simply to Islam as the state religion, but lengthy catalogues of principles often grew to include references to Islamic values or heritage. The Saudi Basic Law of 1992 cites Islam and Islamic law in numerous provisions. In some cases—such as in the Libyan and Iraqi constitutions— newer provisions were as vague as the older ones. Occasionally, however, new, more specific elements were added. The Moroccan constitution of 1962 barred amendments diminishing the royal or Muslim nature of the state; the 1970 constitution specifically excepted these matters from parliamentary immunity.[13] Algeria invented a Higher Islamic Council in 1996 for its political system, specifically enjoined to exercise *ijtihad*. And specific steps were taken, especially in the states of the Arabian Peninsula, to mandate Islamic legal norms in specific areas. In the Kuwaiti constitutions for instance, Article 18 stipulates, "Inheritance is a right governed by the Islamic shari'a." Yemeni constitutions have probably been most ambitious and specific in this regard. The 1970 constitution, for instance, required enforcement of Islamic law in business transactions. The constitution further provided that "In cases heard by the Courts, the provisions of this constitution and of the State's laws shall be applied. If there is no precedent, the Courts shall pass their judgment in the case they are dealing with in accordance with the general principles of the Islamic shariʻa."[14]

Despite the increased salience of Islamic issues in constitutional debates, there was no question that the constitution served as the supreme law in the country and that it was a document designed to enable existing regimes and communicate its ideological preferences. There might be symbolic or institutional concessions to Islamic beliefs, practices, and law, but ultimate political authority remained elsewhere: theoretically in the constitution and in the people (with popular sovereignty proclaimed in most constitutions), and more practically in the head of state (formally in some royal systems and effectively in some republican systems).

THE PRINCIPLES OF THE ISLAMIC SHARIʻA AS "SOURCE OF LAW"—A TRANSNATIONAL AUCTION

Yet another set of provisions began to creep into some Arab constitutional texts that suggests a different relationship between the political order described in the constitution and the legal system enjoined by Islam. Again, the growing publicity of the documents and the drafting process helps explain the regional trend. A brief excursus into the history of these provisions—born in the last years before the full flowering of Arab authoritarianism and maturing in the period of semiauthoritarianism—is helpful not only for understanding the political and legal significance of the provisions themselves but also because they established much of the context for constitutional arguments about religion in the twenty-first century after the revival of Arab politics.

Beginning with the Syrian constitution of 1950 mentioned above, some Arab constitutional systems began to cite the Islamic shariʻa as a source—or more ambitiously the chief source—of law.[15] The 1950 Syrian constitution—the first Arab document to introduce thick ideological sections and catalogues of social and economic as well as political rights—was only in effect for a few years, and its provision regarding Islamic law had no noticeable effect.[16] But its innovation spread.

In Kuwait's 1962 constitution, a similar provision was introduced, in which "the Islamic shariʻa is a primary source of legislation." Periodic proposals to amend the constitution to make the Islamic shariʻa *the* rather than *a* primary source of legislation have thus far been unsuccessful, though at times there has appeared to be considerable popular support for such a change. Similar language has been adopted in other peninsular states (such as the United Arab Emirates and Oman); Saudi Arabia's 1992 basic law has a far more specific and detailed provision: according to Article 48, "The courts will apply the rules of the Islamic shariʻa in the cases that are brought before them, in accordance with what is indicated in the Book and the Sunna, and statutes decreed by the Ruler which do not contradict the Book or the Sunna."

In 1971, Egypt received its "permanent" constitution to replace the avowedly temporary documents of the Nasser years. That constitution's Article 2 went beyond mere declaration of Islam as the religion of the state; such a formula was deemed insufficient. It more ambitiously described the principles of the Islamic shari'a as "a chief source of legislation." Arguments in favor of still stronger provisions were rejected for the moment.[17] In retrospect, what is remarkable is that the debate occurred at all; it took place in part in a fairly diverse drafting committee (though one populated by many loyalists and operating under the watchful eye of a presidency that retained overall control of the content and process). It took place partly in public as well, though that public debate had no real effect on the content.[18]

The proponents of an even stronger Article 2 won a delayed victory as the constitution was amended nine years later to make the principles of the Islamic shari'a "the" chief source of legislation. (The amendment was likely introduced in order to attract voters to the polls to support a package of constitutional amendments that strengthened the positions and policies of then President Anwar al-Sadat, giving voters the opportunity to approve God's law and their president with a single vote. There is little evidence that much thought was given to the legal effect of the introduction of the definite article.) As amended, Article 2 of the Egyptian constitution came to proclaim: "Islam is the religion of the State, Arabic is its official language and the principles of the Islamic shari'a are the chief source of legislation". Thus Egypt had joined other Arab and Islamic countries in providing explicitly for a link between the Islamic shari'a and legislation.

In all the constitutional turmoil following Egypt's national uprising of 2011, only one thing seemed constant: the amended 1980 language. While there were some noisy attempts to tighten it, more timid attempts to water it down, and successful attempts to supplement it, the language itself seemed to be anchored in Egypt's constitutional order.

Such provisions can be taken to imply the possibility of a very different basis for the legal order than a Kelsenian view in which the constitutional text is the highest legal norm. Rather than the constitution sanctioning Islam as an official religion and observance of the Islamic shari'a in specific areas, these provisions might seem to imply that the shari'a itself stands prior to the entire positive legal order—including, potentially and by implication, the constitution itself. If the shari'a is a primary source—or even the primary source—of legislation, then it becomes possible to argue that it forms the fundamental legal framework. Indeed, it is noteworthy in this regard that constitutional texts tend to refer to the shari'a as a basis of legislation (*tashri'*) which would include all legal enactments (including laws, decrees, administrative regulations, and arguably the constitution) rather than as a basis of laws (*qawanin*) which would only refer to a specific category of legislation (laws passed by parliament or their equivalent).

But that is simply not the effect that the clauses have had. The growing publicity of constitution writings—augmented by the glimmerings of a transition to semiauthoritarian in which dissident voices could be heard—had the general effect of inflating the verbal commitment to Islam, but the resulting constitutional tinkering lacked much legal impact.

Why did Islam in general—and the Islamic shari'a specifically—increasingly intrude on Arab constitutional debates over the course of the twentieth century? In order to understand, we should realize that this story might be told a very different way. From the perspective of some of those taking the vantage point of religious institutions, the process was far less one of religion invading politics and much more of politics invading religion.

The initial disinterest of those with religiously informed perspectives in pulling Islam into constitutional debate and drafting was hardly surprising. Islamic institutions—schools, courts, mosques—operated in a different sphere, separate from the new political institutions being constructed. Even the Islamic shari'a was understood and pursued through a set of practices and institutions that stood at some distance from much of the process of governing. Thus, general obeisance to the Islamic nature of the society as well as some protection for critical shari'a-based institutions was sufficient to render constitutional architecture compatible with Islam.

Yet the unspoken mutual deference between constitutional state and scholarly shari'a decayed over the course of the twentieth century—and it was generally state institutions that initiated an incursion into the realm of the shari'a rather than the other way around. States asserted control over general education and then moved to incorporate religious education within their realms; religious endowments and the institutions they supported were nationalized and folded into ministries and other state structures; mosques were similarly brought under state ownership or licensing with preachers given weekly guidance on their sermons; state-constructed court structures assimilated shari'a-based judicial structures; and even matters of personal status, the area of law most associated with shari'a-based norms, vocabularies, and practices, became subject to legislated codification efforts in many Arab states.[19] The structure of the state was no longer primarily political or administrative; it was beginning to take on strongly religious implications.

The incursion was not merely institutional, legal, and fiscal: it was ideological as well. Earlier constitutional documents were thin documents primarily focused on laying down procedures for passing laws and developing budgets; they laid out the basic structures of rule and their interrelationship to each other. That function of constitutions actually declined over the course of the twentieth century as constitutional devices to ensure the separation of powers and the accountability of political authority were gradually hollowed out and the constitution became a device for entrenching executive domination. But if constitutions thus became less constitutionalist in spirit, they became increasingly fulsome and even bombastic in their ideological provisions. No longer were constitutions primarily about defining the mechanisms of governance; they increasingly became thicker platforms for espousing official ideologies and defining the nature and identity of the entire society.[20] And if constitutions were about declaiming on anything that was good, it was hard to exclude Islam.

But if states began the intrusion into the religious spheres, in latter decades of the twentieth century, new social actors began to return the favor with their own effort to insert Islamic provisions into constitutional texts. The trend was led by Egypt's Muslim Brotherhood, a religiously inspired (but always lay-led) reform movement, founded in 1928. Throughout most of its first two decades, the Brotherhood showed only sporadic interest in legal and constitutional issues, and indeed its political involvement was something that came only gradually.[21] But by the 1950s (perhaps with the entrance of former judges into leadership positions in the movement), the Brotherhood's interest increased. With the creation of a committee to draft a new constitution in 1954, the Brotherhood felt a call to spell out its position.[22]

The repression of the Brotherhood in Egypt was closely connected to the emergence of far more radical strains in Islamist political thought; one that spawned the radical political demands of Sayyid Qutb, and one that veered in a salafi direction. Such approaches generally did not articulate full constitutional visions, and indeed they often tended to show a lack of interest even bordering on contempt for written constitutional forms.[23]

But the bulk of Islamist movements focused (when allowed in the sharply constricted political environment that prevailed in most Arab states in the second half of the twentieth century) on a few constitutional provisions, notably those that spoke of the Islamic shari'a as well as the religious qualifications for the head of state. Public pressure and agitation from such movements may have had some effect in the Jordanian, Syrian, and Kuwaiti cases (most remarkably, perhaps in Syria, where disturbances broke out in 1973 in which demonstrators successfully insisted on retaining the requirement that the president be a Muslim and that Islamic law serve as the basis for legislation). In Egypt, it was less Islamist movements and more of a regime attempt to cloak itself in religious legitimacy that had such an effect on the 1971 constitution and the 1980 amendment to the second article.

The process of Islamic inflation was also assisted by the increasingly public nature of the constitution drafting effort discussed earlier. Public participation was introduced, generally in a ritualistic fashion with almost all the substantive work done in private, but still in such a manner that declarations of piety were encouraged as a form of populist sloganeering. The nineteenth century efforts had been largely concerns of the ruling elites; the constitutional documents of the first half of the twentieth century were generally drafted by committees working in private who presented their work to rulers for promulgation and to the people for enthusiastic ratification.

In the second half of the twentieth century, more participatory processes were gradually introduced—constitutions were sometimes drafted by elected bodies (as in Tunisia and Kuwait); they were also more routinely submitted to popular referendums (as in Egypt and Morocco). Such forms of participation were generally far from substantive (though not totally—the Kuwaiti assembly, for instance, does seem to have had some impact on the final text). It is for that reason that it is better to refer to the process as "public" rather than fully "participatory." The process of constitution drafting was designed to communicate the regime's orientation to the population and lend the political order a degree of popular legitimacy; the referendums in particular were in essence political spectacles that more resembled a mass loyalty oath than a mechanism for the people to speak in their own voices.

Yet it was precisely this publicity in process that gave such a boost to the Islamic inflationary trend in constitutional texts. Once a proposal was made to include Islam in some way, it became politically difficult to call for ignoring such ideas or eliminate such provisions. It was far easier to ratchet up religion than ratchet it down.

The publicity explains in turn why the trend had so little legal effect. The provisions were designed to communicate general orientations, not to change the political or legal order. Indeed, those legal and constitutional scholars who have scoured the provisions related to Islam to discern their possible impact and meaning may have been missing the point of these clauses: they are far more products of a political and constitutional environment than they are producers of it. To put it more simply, they are far more effect than cause.

What textual analyses often miss—and indeed, what much of the public discussion around such clauses often overlooks—is the frequent silence of Islamic provisions on matters of enforcement or interpretation. This was obviously true with those clauses that proclaimed Islam the official religion: it was never clear what practical effect such a declaration might have. But it was even true for the detailed provisions. Allowing matters of personal status to be decided in accordance with religiously based norms gave no guidance on how those norms were to be derived and who would apply them. Egypt's amended Article 2, proclaiming "the principles of the Islamic shari'a" as "the chief source of legislation" never explained how the shari'a's principles might be different from its detailed rulings, how they were to be discovered or discerned, and what the process would be for deriving legislation from them. Indeed, in practice, this process was left to the courts in general (with the Supreme Constitutional Court taking a particularly assertive role in measuring Egyptian legislation against its interpretation of

Article 2), the parliament (which had the authority to pass laws, dominated as it was by the president's party), the executive branch (which had the authority to issue regulations), and state controlled religious institutions (including al-Azhar and Dar al-Ifta'). (It was not until the aftermath of the 2011 uprising that attention was given to interpretive and implementing structures, and the very public debate about those subjects proved politically explosive as we will see later.)

In the drafting, it is therefore not surprising that the most difficult debates involved matters of principle divorced from any consideration of implementation. In 1971, for instance, advocates of women's rights on the constitutional drafting committee in Egypt clashed with Islamic scholars in a long series of discussions about provisions for gender and gender equality. The result of those discussions was a clause (Article 11) which reads as if it were designed by a committee attempting to offer something to everybody. And indeed it was: "The state guarantees harmony between the duties of a woman toward the family and her work in the society, [as well as] her equality with men in the fields of political, social, cultural, economic life without violating the rulings of the Islamic shari'a." Such an article provokes all kinds of question: What are these rulings? Who determines when they are violated? What does this harmonization mean in practice? But the text offers neither answers nor even any guidance on how such questions could be answered. Women were offered equality, Islamic scholars were offered the rulings of the shari'a, and Egyptians were offered a clause that could bear almost any interpretation.

Even some of the apparent attempts to ensure state respect for religion could just as easily be read as attempting to ensure state control over religion—and that is precisely the effect that some detailed clauses had. The Egyptian constitution, for instance, mandated religious education—and therefore implicitly but quite clearly made defining the faith and instilling it in schoolchildren a state function. And constitutional guarantees for religion are quite real but generally privilege communal rights in a manner that enhances the role of the state. Religious freedom clauses generally accorded respect to "creeds" ('aqa'id) and sometimes to "rites" ('asha'ir), terms that suggested something different from full freedom of conscience on an individual basis. Instead citizens are afforded the liberty to subscribe to a recognized (that is, state licensed) set of beliefs and practices—thus giving state bodies an effective authority to determine what is a legitimate religious sect, which are their true rituals, and which creeds and communities receive protected status.

By diverting attention from the question of who has religious authority to that of what the constitution stipulates about religion, the inflated constitutional clauses of the second half of the twentieth century could mask the largely expressive (but only vaguely legal) nature of the language. The passionate nature of symbolic constitutional debates is actually a global phenomenon; as constitution drafting has become an increasingly public process (and, in many places, a more participatory one as well), it is striking how much political energy is expended on preambles and basic proclamations of identity, sometimes it seems, even at the expense of finely grained discussions of how constitutional clauses will actually work in practice.[24]

Not all attention was on the expressive and religious aspects of constitutions, of course. Critics of existing patterns of governance learned, especially by the early 2000s, to look to the finer print of constitutional documents to notice how rights were promised in vague and ineffectual ways, judicial structures robbed of the structural requirements of independence, parliament deprived of any oversight, and most institutions left effectively subservient to an unrestrained executive. Such concerns led to concrete proposals in which an increasing number of intellectuals sometimes even reached across religious and ideological divides to advocate constitutional reform.

Most such efforts were ineffectual, though they drew increasing attention. In Egypt in the 2000s, the Muslim Brotherhood made a concerted effort to place itself squarely on the side of a constitutional reform agenda and explore links to other opposition movements. In Jordan in the 1990s and 2000s, the monarchy did not leave the issue to the opposition but instead called for a series of national dialogues and reform agendas, all of which were abandoned as soon as they produced concrete proposals. The ideas were shunted aside—in Egypt, Jordan, and elsewhere—until the uprisings of 2011 placed constitutional change very squarely on an extremely public agenda.

POLITICS REBORN AND CONSTITUTIONS REDONE—AND UNDONE

In March 2011, a scant month after the forced departure of Husni Mubarak, I visited Egypt. The immediate subject of my research was to understand how critical institutions of state were adjusting to the post-revolutionary environment. The atmosphere was celebratory and elated. Some sites of the uprising were festooned with banners, permanent camps, and periodic demonstrations. The sharp polarization that characterized politics soon afterward was not yet apparent; the cruelty and brutishness of the security agencies was held in check for a brief moment by popular mobilization. There was something unreal about the atmosphere. When I saw Egyptians standing in a line to enter a demonstration, my first reaction (with admittedly some exaggeration) was that both the existence of an orderly line and the demonstration were two startling innovations in nature of public space in Egypt.

In answer to my question of the way officials were reacting, I saw that state bodies were struggling hard to adjust to the new reality. I heard state radio playing songs by ʿAbd al-Halim Hafiz, the bard of the Nasserist years, since those were the only ones in their collection that celebrated revolution (I wondered how many listeners felt that those same songs idolized an earlier version of the very regime that had been overthrown).

Having read a newspaper article about disciplinary proceedings against an administrative court judge, Muhammad Fu'ad Gadallah (Jadd Allah) for political activity during the uprising (Gadallah had served as a legal and constitutional advisor for the demonstrators in al-Tahrir, helping to draft statements), I thought he might be a particularly interesting figure to meet. The demonstrations had a startlingly constitutional focus, with some central demands focusing on the authority of the presidency, the state of emergency, the use of military courts, and human rights protections. I contacted him and, while he had little time then for a direct meeting, he did invite me to a lecture he was delivering at al-Azhar University on the constitutional amendments that had just been drafted by a small committee. I met with Gadallah and the dean of the hosting college before the lecture and then we proceeded to a very large lecture hall crowded with students eager to hear and discuss the fine print of the text offered to voters.

Upon leaving the lecture hall, I was handed leaflets by several salafi student groups who supported the amendments largely (the leaflets made clear) in order to protect Article 2 (which would have been unchanged by the amendments). I chuckled a bit at the reasoning: rejection of the amendments would still leave Article 2 unchanged; and in any case, Article 2 had always been interpreted and applied in a manner that few salafis would recognize as consistent with the proper role of the Islamic shari'a in society. I was left with the general impression that the word "shari'a" was almost a talisman whose appearance could render a text worth defending.

From a legal standpoint, I was correct in my patronizing attitude. What I was partly missing was the enormous political significance of the moment. Constitutional issues were now central in Egyptian public life; they were closely linked to arguments about religion; and those arguments were being carried out in every conceivable sphere and moving among them with a rapidity that overwhelmed the ability of the political structures of Egyptian life to mediate and manage them. The constitution was becoming the major playing field for a political contest that was disconnected to a greater extent than I understood from legal issues.

And Egypt was not alone.

If the constitutions of the second half of the twentieth century were public but not participatory in their drafting, the post-revolutionary process in both Tunisia and Egypt promised a sharp departure. Not only were democratic mechanisms used to generate a constitutional drafting process, but the largest and most powerful electoral actors in both countries in the first elections were movements dedicated to enhancing the role of Islam in public life. This development, while striking, was not wholly unprecedented: in Iraq, Islamically oriented political parties played a similar role in drafting the country's post-invasion constitution. The Arab world was entering a new constitutional era—one in which participation edged out ritualistic publicity and Islamists were sometimes quick to fill the resulting political space. Did this have the effect of moving the religious provisions from the realm of political effect (a measure of the regime's desire to stake out religious claims) to cause (bringing about the Islamization of the constitutional order)? And did reversals to that trend—most notably with the ouster of Egypt's Muslim Brotherhood from power in July 2013 and the direct appointment of a new drafting body by an interim president himself appointed by the military—also roll back any changes?

Oddly, the variations in the influence and role of Islamist movements may not have had as much effect as might have been expected. In both Egypt and Tunisia, as their fortunes rose, Islamists played a subtler political game. The Islamist scene was surprisingly varied (in Egypt most notably, salafis joined the Brotherhood in the electoral arena), and the Islamist rise generated significant opposition. To be sure, Islamists sought to have Islam play a greater role. But the largest Islamist movements—the Muslim Brotherhood in Egypt and al-Nahda in Tunisia—focused far more on maintaining existing (largely symbolic) language than on expanding it. The rest of their constitutional energies were devoted to bringing about far more democratic systems, confident as they were of their popular standing. In that sense, they sought less to build explicitly Islamic structures than to breathe life into democratic and constitutional structures that had been hollowed out by the preceding authoritarian regimes and use the newly empowered tools to pursue their policy goals.

The shift in Islamist focus from constitutional to legislative process was actually apparent even before the revolutions in Tunisia and Egypt in places where Islamists gained substantial parliamentary experience. A focus on platitudes written in thick bold letters was replaced by an interest in the fine print written in a thin bookkeeper's pencil. In Kuwait in the mid-2000s, for instance, the Muslim Brotherhood's political arm, the Islamic Constitutional Movement, largely abandoned attempts to amend the constitution to refer to the Islamic shariʿa as "the" rather than "a" source of law but instead worked on specific pieces of legislation (such as its successful pursuit of a zakat law for corporations). When it did press for new constitutional language it asked that legislation be barred that violated the shariʿa, a far more specific formula (as well as one that would presumably empower a specific structure, the Constitutional Court, to apply it).

In the wave of mass politics during and after the Tunisian and Egyptian revolutions, the text of the constitution became a central focus, and Islam was hardly forgotten. As with the pre-revolutionary situation, the symbolic clauses generated passionate feelings. But those debates distracted attention from the legal heavy lifting done by the more procedural aspects of the document. And Islamist forces generally realized that. Those who paid attention to the loudest and angriest debates often tended to hear only those symbolic issues and overestimated their importance; those who listened by contrast to the quiet detailed discussions found processes that will likely have far more effect in shaping the constitutional developments of the societies in question.

Thus we come to the dramatically different constitutional context after 2011. Constitution drafting is still iterative, as it was before. Tunisians beginning the process in 2011 looked back at their older documents and processes as a starting point. Egypt's temporary military rulers suspended the entire 1971 constitution in February 2011 and then issued a "constitutional declaration" in March that borrowed very extensively from its clauses. When a constituent assembly finally began work on a new document in the summer of 2012, it very quickly went back to the 1971 constitution as a starting point, making changes of some symbolic but uncertain practical importance. And when the text produced by the 2012 assembly was suspended in June 2013, drafters of a very comprehensive set of revisions simply moved back to the 1971 document, seeking to entrench the way it had approached the relationship between religion and state more deeply.

So text did not differ nearly as much from the past as might have been expected. But political context had shifted dramatically—and the ground continued to shift under the feet of the drafters. When Egypt's drafters turned to Article 11 of the 1971 constitution (the tortured phrasing regarding gender equality and the Islamic shari'a discussed above), they first tried to adopt the old wording without much discussion. But they found that a problem that had been soluble in a small room now became a national crisis as the arguments contained to the drafting room in 1971 exploded in often shrill debates in all available public spheres. For the Islamists driving the process in 2012, that was not what they wished to spend their energies on. They had battles to fight, to be sure, but the constitutional meat was now in its thin procedural parts, and most of all it lay in the fine print.

What was so different? First, past constitutions had been written in the context of existing regimes and in fact initiated by those regimes. After 2011, by contrast, Tunisia and Egypt were both in a period of transition—the old regime seemed to have fallen, at least in part, leaving only provisional ones in place. Second, the rules for the process itself were contested: it was necessary for competing forces to work out (through a combination of negotiation, election, threats, popular mobilization, lawsuits, and even coups) precisely how the new documents were to be drafted and ratified. Third, no single political actor could dominate the process. Fourth, the issue of national sovereignty— so central to earlier efforts—had faded, giving more space to domestic political debates. Finally, there were strong demands for a public process—one carried out in public and with wide participation.[25]

Let us turn to each experience in turn.

Tunisia

In Tunisia, emotional debates about Islam not only pitted Islamists against their rivals but also led to deep quandaries within the Islamist camp. An ultimately successful project of writing a new constitution took three years in part because the public and its representatives were so badly divided—and so vocal—on the role of Islam in public life, as expressed in constitutional form.[26]

The constitution that Tunisians were replacing after 2011, which dated back to 1959, was remarkable for its brevity on identity issues as well as its taciturn reference to Islam. It was a product of a time when ideological provisions were just beginning to expand. There was a fleeting reference in the preamble to the people's determination "to remain faithful to the teachings of Islam," a declaration that the president's religion is Islam, and a short statement in Articles 1 and 2 that: "Tunisia is a free, independent and sovereign state. Its religion is Islam, its language is Arabic and its type of government is the Republic. The Republic of Tunisia is a part of the Great Arab Maghreb, an entity which it endeavors to unify within the framework of mutual interests." A series of amended constitutions over the years replicated this formula and indeed changed very little else except to enable the president to escape term limitations.

The impression one would gain from this history is that powerful long-term presidents only vaguely respectful of Islam were permanent parts of the Tunisian constitutional order. That impression would be largely accurate. Ruled from independence until 2011 by two presidents who showed a determination to control religious institutions, contain and then suppress religious movements, and even circumscribe the role of Islam in public life, Tunisia stood aloof from the regional inflationary trend.

It was therefore remarkable that when al-Nahda—an Islamist movement—emerged as the largest party by far in balloting for the country's Constituent Assembly in 2011, it decided not to make up for lost time but simply to make do with existing constitutional language.

It was not an easy decision for the Islamist movement. The reasoning was often explicit, steering in an almost secular direction: bringing state and religion too closely together had been a technique of the old regime to bring Islam under state domination. Al-Nahda leader Rashid al-Ghannushi spoke explicitly of an Anglo-Saxon (as opposed to French) model of religion-state relations in which the natural religiosity of the people could gain organized and public expression while escaping from official control. I was startled in my one meeting with al-Ghannushi in the summer of 2011 when he appeared visibly angry when discussing the "Francophones" (*frankufuniyin*), the term he spat out to denounce the country's old political and social elite; he made clear that his movement represented the true virtues of the people—who needed the government off their backs so that virtues would emerge spontaneously rather than an intrusive state that would coerce them to lead virtuous lives. It seemed to me his attitude was one part Sarah Palin and one part Robert Bellah.[27] The interest in Anglo-Saxon secularism was not merely for my benefit: he repeated it in television interviews when he traveled to Egypt that summer.

Yet al-Ghannushi's interest in Anglo-Saxon practice was not completely consistent nor was it shared by many of his movement's rank-and-file. And al-Nahda found itself not only pressed by its non-Islamist critics and international interlocutors to give reassuring signals but also by others (including a quickly politicizing salafi movement) that saw it as too quick to trade religious principles for political power. A Tunisian society that had seen religion circumscribed in public spaces prior to 2011—with Orwellian banners about "tolerance" far more commonly displayed than anything about religion during the Ben Ali years—suddenly found that religious actors and symbols were being deployed by social and political actors. Clashes on college campuses over cultural issues; calls to re-establish a religious educational network to supplant the state-controlled institutions that had preached a politically denuded religion for decades; and other aspects of a religio-cultural struggle, spilled out into public spaces all over the country. The newer public spheres that gained prominence in communicating messages among like-minded Tunisians during the uprising of 2010 and 2011 likely accentuated the struggle—a study of social media use during the period after the uprising found widespread usage. But social media users tended to view them as less reliable for general news and far more useful for coordinating action among groups whose members were originally pulled into involvement based on direct personal and face-to-face interaction.[28]

The existence of multiple spheres likely prolonged the entire process, as each group pursued its aims in the arena in which it could draw on its distinctive assets. With Islamists having a plurality in the assembly drafting the constitution, they naturally dominated the process. But the rules designed in the transition process required that they either garner a supermajority of assembly members or a majority in a national referendum. That tilted their interests toward a consensual process. Al-Nahda's opposition within the assembly could block such a consensus while those outside the assembly could mobilize demonstrators questioning the legitimacy of the process as it dragged on. The point of these efforts was largely to persuade already like-minded members of deeply entrenched camps rather than persuade others.

In the end, a compromise was reached that allowed a constitution to be completed and ratified after three years of argument. That compromise left the existing language on Islam largely in place. Yet different groups arrived at accepting that compromise through different paths.

Al-Nahda argued internally at great length before the top leadership (itself divided) managed to persuade the movement as a whole to drop any insistence on more ambitious language regarding Islam and the Islamic shari'a. Behind this attitude lay a supreme confidence that what was necessary to increase the role of Islam in Tunisian life was not a constitutional clause or even a set of legal provisions but instead the removal of the sharp restrictions on religion that had been enforced by the old regime. Of course, al-Nahda's strong electoral showing did provoke some within the movement to float the idea of more extensive constitutional provisions for Islam and the shari'a, and when the Constituent Assembly began meeting, some al-Nahda deputies strove to persuade the movement to reconsider its position. After an intensive internal party debate in the spring of 2012, the effort was turned back. This was hardly an abandonment of the Islamic shari'a by Tunisia's Islamists but only a savvy political (if symbolically difficult) judgment that their energies were better focused elsewhere. As the Tunisian constitution drafting neared completion, al-Nahda was satisfied with repeating the vague formula on Islam in the country's post-independence constitution (while entrenching the clause by making the official status of Islam unamendable) and inserting a vague provision allowing the state to protect those (unspecified) things that are sacred.

The liberal attitude of al-Nahda was controversial within the movement; indeed, it seems to have been imposed by some of the leadership on a base that was more enthusiastic about constitutionalizing the shari'a. The concession was deemed necessary to hold together the political process that promised far friendlier political terrain for al-Nahda than the pre-2011 regime ever allowed.

For al-Nahda's non-Islamist opposition, the compromise was initially not enough to allay fears about the movement's intentions, especially as salafis began to play a more prominent role, occasional political violence broke out, and a prominent non-Islamist political leader was assassinated. Yet there were also important political forces—a non-Islamist president less hostile to the Islamists; a powerful trade union movement—that could play a mediating role; they were able to negotiate a compromise by which al-Nahda surrendered its role in the interim government to technocrats and agreed to a clause designed to bar accusations of apostasy. The non-Islamist opposition outside of parliament also sensed (correctly) that al-Nahda could be electorally challenged. When the constitution was approved, there were few textual signs of the lengthy arguments about religion that had gone into its composition.

Egypt

The Egyptian case is far more complicated and contested than the Tunisian. Tunisia plodded along a difficult constitutional path—in the words of one expert always dancing on the edge of the cliff without falling over.[29] Egypt, by contrast, careened through a series of interim constitutions and constitution drafting efforts before arriving at a final document in 2014 (one that many of its own drafters thought might not last very long). During the process, Islamists played a varied political role. In 2012, Islamists in general, and the Muslim Brotherhood in particular, dominated the drafting process and were instrumental in passing a constitutional document at the end of the year. But that constitution was suspended on July 3, 2013 as the military intervened and security forces worked to suppress the Brotherhood's political activity (salafis also suffered some repression, but the main salafi political party limped along as an active participant in the post-July 3 political process). Tossing the Brotherhood out of the presidential palace and into prison reopened all constitutional issues. A thoroughly revised constitution was drafted by the appointed committee of fifty that contained only one member of the salafi party and one ex-member of the Brotherhood; no other Islamists were represented (though some academic specialists in Islamic law and members of state religious institutions did participate).

But surprisingly, in constitutional terms, all the political turmoil amounted to frantic running in place. The country's largest post-2011 political party, the Freedom and Justice Party (the political wing of the Muslim Brotherhood) neither sought to emulate al-Nahda's dalliance with an "Anglo-Saxon" model of religion-state relations nor sought to build an Iranian style system in which religious scholars oversaw the existing political system. Other Islamists (chiefly salafis) had stronger demands; non-Islamist groups came to resist these. Arguments were bitter but focused on only a few constitutional clauses. The final result in the 2014 constitution was fairly similar to the Tunisian case in one sense: existing constitutional provisions largely survived with only minor wording changes, sometimes to make the Islamic commitments more specific and sometimes to loosen them. Behind even these minor changes, the driving force behind those changes was not the Freedom and Justice Party but its Islamist and non-Islamist rivals.

Initial Efforts

In the year after the fall of Mubarak, there was some discussion about the role of Islam in the constitution, most of which centered on Article 2. Some suggested dropping the word "the" (added in 1980); others suggested adding some protection for non-Muslim religious communities to follow their own laws of personal status. But by the time drafting had begun, the focus had turned very much to practical issues of enforcement, and Egyptian political debate quickly developed a remarkable sophistication about such issues.

When salafi movements entered the political fray, for instance, in the aftermath of the revolution, they first showed a very limited familiarity with the political issues that had occupied the attention of their fellow citizens. In March 2011, as Egyptians voted on a series of constitutional amendments (eventually worked into a comprehensive "constitutional declaration" issued by the interim military rulers at the end of the month), salafi leaders recommended a "yes" vote simply because the text offered gave Islam official status and copied the wording of Article 2 of the suspended constitution. By summer, however, they had begun to become more demanding and discerning. Some began to explore ideas about constitutional text that was derived from (rather than just making a nod toward) Islamic legal principles and rulings.

Non-Islamists began to develop their own concerns, among them a fear that the electoral process would edge them aside. They therefore argued strenuously for a set of largely liberal "supra-constitutional principles" to guide any drafting effort. Salafi and Brotherhood leaders denounced the effort as attempting to tie the people's hands through an elite bargain. In a huge demonstration I visited in Tahrir Square in July 2011, I heard salafis chant "No principles above the constitution," a far cry from their earlier insistence that it was God's word, not human law, that should govern communal affairs.

Drafters set to work in 2012 and completed their work in December. In the assembly drafting the documents, Brotherhood members dominated, but salafis were a significant voice. Non-Islamists generally grew increasingly critical of the process and gradually pulled out, but for a while, the Brotherhood hoped to bring enough along so that it could present the result as a consensus document.

The 2012 Constitution

When the drafters turned from the procedure of drafting to the substance, the results reflected each side's understanding of its electoral position. Non-Islamists sought either to disrupt the process or to write in guarantees that would limit majoritarianism. Brotherhood members felt sufficiently comfortable about their future electoral chances to be willing to defer most religious issues to normal politics rather than the constitution. Salafis were also fairly optimistic about their electoral prospects but they were, in addition, anxious to show they were more faithful to the Islamic shari'a than the Brotherhood; they also showed more interest in the fine print than the Brotherhood being a bit less certain that they would be able to secure what they wished through the ordinary legislative process.

What is most remarkable about this debate is how quickly attention turned to very practical issues—and how much most participants preferred to focus on issues of judicial independence, executive-legislative relations, the removal of loopholes in human rights provisions, and the status of various state bodies (such as the press and al-Azhar). The Muslim Brotherhood's Freedom and Justice Party led the charge in most of these areas, leaving much of the debate over the Islamic provisions to others.

Why, when it stood on the brink of exercising a considerable measure of political authority for the first time in its history, did the Brotherhood back off an ambitious attempt to toughen constitutional language on Islam?[30] Oddly, it was precisely because of its politically powerful position. The Brotherhood felt it had the potential to set the legislative agenda, draft whatever laws it liked, recast the country's Constitutional Court, and even mold the enormous complex of Islamic educational, research, charitable, and didactic institutions under control of the Egyptian state. In short, the Brotherhood was likely be able to get far more of what it wanted (a greater role for Islam in public life) through majoritarian institutions than through rigid constitutional language.

As the Brotherhood General Guide Muhammad Badiʿ explicitly stated, "What is happening is a political competition. We have to defer to the ballot box. Let us compete with honor."[31] If the Brotherhood had a dispute with the Supreme Constitutional Court, for instance, it was not because of the Court's Article 2 jurisprudence—its decisions could have empowered elected authorities to push Islamization of law in a direction it liked--but because the Court dissolved the Brotherhood-dominated parliament in June 2012. Its members in the constituent assembly therefore explored ways of folding the Court into the regular judiciary rather than ask to have its justices schooled in Islamic law. They wished to bypass the Court through tools they were winning at the ballot box, not remake it in their own image. Similarly, the Brotherhood resisted calls to constitutionalize alms giving (*zaka*) on the explicit grounds that there was no need to insert such a clause in the constitution itself. As a prominent Brotherhood leader put it, "There is no difference among [constituent assembly] attendees, Muslim or Christian, on the duty of zaka. But the difference is whether or not to include textual provision in the constitution on it. We did not include a text on building mosques or the duty of the pilgrimage or the duty of fasting."[32]

Less convinced that they would win at the ballot box, salafi leaders tended to be more demanding on the text. But they also contented themselves with the assurance that Islamists of various stripes would play a significant role in drafting any implementing legislation. As discussed in chapter 4, a widely circulated video during the constitutional debate revealed a prominent Salafi leader, Yasir Burhami, justifying the constitution to his followers by pointing to its Islamizing potential.[33] Shocked opponents inclined to see the 2012 constitution as an Islamist Trojan horse felt they had a smoking gun. Whether or not they did, the video showed something else as well: a prominent salafi leader forced to sell his compromises to followers who had before them a document that only had a few clauses with any obvious Islamic content.

In the end a series of odd compromises resulted. On one issue—the provisions for women's rights carried over from Article 11 of the 1971 constitution—the drafters confronted the unbridgeable positions by simply removing both parts of the compromise arrived at during the earlier drafting process. Instead of addressing the issue with a messy and ambiguous compromise, they left the issue for the post-constitutional political process. (They attempted to placate women's rights activists only by sticking a general commitment to gender equality in the preamble.) Defenders of women's rights and defenders of the shari'a cancelled each other out in effect and the struggle was moved to the normal legislative and political arena.

A second area of controversy focused on provisions for religious freedom. Some Islamists in particular were worried about sanctioning heterodox forms of Islam or religions that some more conservative members would not recognize as legitimate at all (such as Bahai'ism). An absolute freedom of individual conscience would be legally difficult to codify in a country in which matters of personal status are governed by religious community—the effect of the Egyptian legal order (supported by religious leaders of almost all orientations) is to require all Egyptians to be members of one of a group of recognized religious communities, not to allow each individual to designate his or her own personalized set of beliefs and practices. Some Christian religious leaders demanded that some recognition be given to their right to be governed in accordance with their own law of personal status—a principle nobody opposed—but conservatives and some Islamists were wary about opening the door too widely. Hoping to bring along skeptics inside and outside the country, the draft offered stronger protection to specific groups than it did to the principle of religious freedom. The end result was to give recognition to Christianity and Judaism as "heavenly" religions alongside Islam—with the strange effect of according Egyptian Jews constitutional protection more than half a century after most of them had left (or fled) the country.

What of Article 2 and the commitment to the Islamic shari'a more generally? The outcome there was particularly complex, thought it was not clear what the changes meant.

Many non-Islamists were content with Article 2 as it had been interpreted but were nervous about any change in wording that might place the article's vague promises in Islamist hands. While a few sought to water down the wording, the majority seemed to accept it but insisted that the interpretation of Islamic legal principles be left to the country's Supreme Constitutional Court or perhaps entrusted to al-Azhar, the chief seat of Islamic learning, whose leader non-Islamists regarded as leaning toward liberal interpretations.

Salafis, however, grew increasingly demanding, arguing that Article 2 had delivered on none of its promise. Some wished to ratchet up Egypt's constitutional commitment to Islam still further by inserting the word *ahkam* (rulings) before making reference to the shari'a so that the constitution would make the rulings of the Islamic shari'a—a far more specific and exacting standard than the current "principles" of the Islamic shari'a—the chief source of legislation. Were such a phrase adopted, it would pack a potentially serious constitutional punch: it would make it difficult to avoid a whole host of specific shari'a-based rules. And salafi leaders were explicit in their reasoning: the current wording was too vague to be enforceable.

In the end, all parties seemed to get what they wanted—though some immediately drew back from the compromise when they saw how it might work. Non-Islamists kept Article 2 intact. A new article was added requiring that al-Azhar be consulted in matters of Islamic law and another one (Article 219) was added defining the principles of Islamic law in terms of traditional Sunni jurisprudence. The Brotherhood got a constitution that seemed to defer most matters to the political process; non-Islamists got Islamic law placed in hands they trusted; and salafis got some role for al-Azhar, an institution they did not trust but still saw as superior to Constitutional Court judges with no training in Islamic law.[34]

But the compromise, while adopted, proved problematic. Non-Islamists outside of the bargaining room came to fear that they had taken a step toward theocracy—not only was a religious institution (al-Azhar) empowered, but the provisions defining Islamic law, though difficult to understand for non-specialists, seemed potentially far more detailed than they would have wished. The Brotherhood found that al-Azhar took its role seriously, using the new text to insert itself into debates that the Brotherhood saw as parliamentary prerogatives. Salafis had to content themselves with a document that was not all that visibly Islamic and that would only move things in what they saw as an appropriate legal direction if al-Azhar became friendlier to salafi approaches (the existing leadership was hostile).

The 2014 Constitution

On July 3, 2013, the Egyptian military stepped in after massive street demonstrations and dismissed Muhammad Morsi, the first freely elected Egyptian president; a few days later the upper house of the Egyptian parliament was disbanded (the lower house had been disbanded a year earlier by court order). Oddly, however, despite the thoroughness with which they overturned the results of the ballot box, the generals merely suspended the 2012 constitution.

A quickly issued provisional "constitutional declaration" reproduced some (but not all) of its clauses on Islamic law. Even the language of Article 219 was retained in the provisional document, a clear attempt to keep the largest salafi political party on board.

But for the long term, the post-coup leaders promised only a tightly supervised process by which the 2012 constitution would be amended and then restored. The compromises of 2012 had come unraveled but it was not clear if new compromises could be struck. With the Brotherhood now shut out of the process—and with Islamists much less certain of their electoral standing—it was not even clear who would be trying to rewrite the text and what the goals of the various parties would be.

In the end, a group of senior judges was appointed to draft a set of amendments to the 2012 constitution; these proposals were then handed over to the appointed committee of fifty representatives of various state bodies, political parties, officially chartered unions and associations, civil society groups, and intellectuals. Marked by a determination to root out the effects of the brief period of Brotherhood rule, the committee of fifty went over every clause of the 2012 constitution and offered a series of amendments so extensive in number that they virtually amounted to a wholly new document; their proposals were presented to Egyptian voters in January 2014 in a referendum that bore more of a resemblance to the ritualistic plebiscites of an earlier era than a wide-ranging and inclusive national debate.

In a sense this was a return to the origin of constitution writing in the Arab world—the process was once again dominated by public officials. But the state bodies (including the military, the police, the religious establishment, and the judiciary) did not behave so much as representatives of the state as a whole but instead as actors who identified their institutional interest as so essential to the state and to the society that they acted as lobbies, seeking to insulate themselves from oversight not merely from the society but from other state actors.

While the drafters of the 2014 document took aim at liquidating some Islamist provisions, the actual changes they made were slight. Article 2 was retained intact; the constitutional role for al-Azhar was retained but the requirement that it be consulted in matters of Islamic shari'a was dropped. (The political effect of this was likely marginal: it might not be constitutionally necessary to consult al-Azhar but it would be politically very difficult to ignore the institution, especially as it consolidated its hold over other parts of the Egyptian religious establishment). Article 219, consisting of the complex formula defining the "principles of the Islamic shari'a" inserted in 2012, was dropped. And language was inserted into the preamble emphasizing the jurisprudence of the country's Supreme Constitutional Court on Article 2. But it was never clear that Article 219 would have led to any real changes in the way that the Islamic shariʿa informed legislation (indeed, in the Supreme Constitutional Court's one shariʿa-related decision issued under the 2012 constitution, its approach was unchanged and it made no reference whatsoever to Article 219). Gender equality was moved back from the preamble to the main text and the qualification in the 1971 constitution that it be enforced within the bounds of the rulings of the Islamic shariʿa was dropped. Religious freedom provisions were strengthened for existing recognized religions, but individual freedom of conscience received only a quick nod (and with most freedoms restricted to specified religion likely had little real protection).

NO GOING BACKWARD (OR FORWARD): A CAP ON ISLAMIC INFLATION (AND DEFLATION)

Thus the period of Islamist ascendancy brought at most mild furtherance of Islamic inflation (and sometimes not even that). When Islamists were evicted from power in Egypt in 2013, there was only limited deflation. Those religious figures most favorably inclined to the new regime (such as Mazhar Shahin, described in chapter 3) focused their attention on giving state authorities strong tools, some even calling for amendments to the 2014 document to bolster the presidency still further.[35] The Islamic shariʿa was not so much at issue. Rhetoric and even vitriol escalated but textual changes were not large. Process more than outcome was affected. Indeed, more public participation and debate made texts more difficult to change. Islamists were no longer likely to be satisfied either with vague promises or with majoritarian politics; non-Islamists were less likely to be trustful or amenable to compromise and indeed had begun to educate themselves on the implications of apparently subtle changes in wording. With the expectation that constitutions would actually mean something and that public participation was a necessary part of writing them, constitution writing was becoming more difficult—and drafters therefore tended to be reduced to tweaking the formulas of the past.

Even in calmer Tunisia, the more inclusive approach of al-Nahda was met with widespread opposition just as the drafting process was near completion. Again, there was growing mistrust on all sides regarding the willingness of rivals to play either the constitutional or the electoral game faithfully and fairly, and the result was seriously destabilizing and briefly threatened the constitutional process as a whole.

Egypt and Tunisia wrote new constitutions as they passed through prolonged periods of constitutional uncertainty. Indeed, that explains the sharply different shape of constitution drafting in those two cases, by regional standards. In a sense, society was far more democratic than in the past—there were more groups active, pluralism was greater, and popular mobilization was an important tool—but the political system had changed less and was still very much in flux.

In the early period of constitution writing in the Arab world, the process might be said to be mildly inclusive but not very public. A broad swath of officials and prominent scholars and specialists were given fairly unfettered leeway to craft much of the documents—within specific bounds, of course. Generally, existing rulers were insistent that their prerogatives be protected; international arrangements were also effectively mostly beyond the reach of the drafters. But for all their inclusiveness in that sense, the processes were often carried out in private deliberations, decreed by existing authorities rather than subject to extensive public scrutiny and debate, and the inclusiveness in question rarely reached beyond the political and intellectual elite to the general public. And they handled religion in a workmanlike fashion, writing in protection for existing arrangements (for personal status, for instance, and perhaps for education) where needed but largely treating questions of governance as separate from questions of religious teaching.

As that period gave way to a fully authoritarian era, constitution writing became the precise opposite sort of enterprise: it was very public but not all inclusive. Existing regimes took far greater interest in the documents as exercises to proclaim their ideological orientation and fundamental values. The result was religious hortatory of increasing reach and volume but rarely of much legal or institutional impact.

It is only in the current century, and then only in a limited number of cases (most notably Egypt and Tunisia, but arguably extending at least partially to Iraq, Yemen, and even Morocco as well), that constitution making has become both more inclusive and public. With many seats at the table and voices raised louder so that those outside the room can hear, and with enormous amounts of constitutional kibbitzing from all kinds of social and political actors, constitution writing has become a more fraught enterprise. The result has sometimes come close to paralysis, in which various actors argue in portentous terms before falling back on existing formulas. In Egypt after 2011, there were actual textual changes made along the way (though their significance was both untested and likely greatly exaggerated), but when the dust settled in 2014, something quite close to the pre-2011 set of provisions was the end result.

The overall impression is one of much motion and many emotions but very little legal movement: for all the increasing agitation, mobilization, polarization, and argument, most of the textual changes have been slight and with little obvious impact on the legal and political order. Is this then largely symbolic politics? Yes, though that is perhaps not the right word: it might be better to describe this as "expressive" politics, a term I have tried to use in this chapter to communicate what lies behind these constitutional controversies. The contest concerns statements of fundamental identity and moral principles;

various groups have come to see the constitution as a document that should directly express the purpose of public life.

Indeed, seen that way we can understand how tenaciously some groups cling to particular constitutional language (or are sometimes repelled by it). This is particularly clear in the Egyptian case. Egyptian Christians watched very nervously as the Islamist-dominated assembly wrote a constitution. Some insisted that stronger provisions be made for Christian personal status law—provisions that would seem to be unnecessary since they merely recognized existing arrangements that nobody had challenged. But without such clauses, some Christians felt excluded from full membership in Egyptian public life.

Salafis were part of a coalition that successfully inserted some new clauses. Their leaders, who had shown no interest in constitutional issues before 2011, suddenly began to regard the Egyptian state not as an inevitable but often thuggish and impious provider of order but rather as a state that was now publicly committed to an Islamic vision. As military and mob tore down that constitutional order in the summer of 2014, some salafis who had shown little appetite for politics in the past suddenly threw themselves into a defense of a constitutional text of human origin.

The unprecedented outburst of violence in July and August 2013—in which those resisting the coup violently attacked police stations and churches and occupied public squares, and military and security forces launched not only a severe crackdown but also mercilessly gunned down protesters and did so to much popular acclaim—might be explained in part precisely by the rising symbolic stakes. Various groups and institutions defined political community very differently and discovered those differences when arguing about the contents of the constitution. Hammering out a text led to verbal compromises in some cases but ones that had very limited legal and institutional implications. The result was to make Egyptians more aware of their differences without giving them tools to resolve them. Ultimately the battle turned murderous rather than consensual; public arguments in Egypt about what truths the constitution should express gave way to street battles showing how dangerous the republic of arguments could become.

NOTES

1. Tarek Masoud, "How Morsi Could Have Saved Himself," *Foreign Policy*, http://foreignpolicy.com/2013/07/19/how-morsy-could-have-saved-himself/, accessed July 19, 2015.
   Elsewhere Masoud has argued that the apparent great divides among Egyptian voters (as evidenced in swings in electoral outcomes) are not a product

of deep divisions on religious issues. See his *Counting Islam: Religion, Class, and Elections in Egypt* (Cambridge: Cambridge University Press, 2014).

2. I explore this in more detail in "Islam and Constitutionalism in the Arab World: The Puzzling Course of Islamic Inflation," in *Constitution Writing, Religion and Democracy*, eds. Asli Bali and Hanna Lerner (Cambridge: Cambridge University Press, forthcoming).

3. I explore this topic to a much greater extent in a book written at what might be seen retrospectively as the height of Arab semiauthorarianism, *Constitutions in a Nonconstitutional World: Arab Basic Laws and the Prospects for Accountable Government* (Albany: SUNY Press, 2001).

4. For more details on the early constitutional documents examined in this sections, see Brown, *Constitutions in a Nonconstitutional World*. This section is an updated and condensed version of the historical parts of that book.

5. See Elizabeth Thompson, *Justice Interrupted: The Struggle for Constitutional Government in the Middle East* (Cambridge: Harvard University Press, 2013).

6. The reference was to the *lijan al-ashqiya'*, administrative structures, notorious among Egyptian lawyers (of whom Zaghlul was a leader), constructed shortly after the British occupation to detain those with criminal reputations. See my article "Brigands and State Building: The Invention of Banditry in Modern Egypt," *Comparative Studies in Society and History* 32, 2 (1990): 258–281.

7. Majlis al-Shuyukh, *Al-dustur: ta`liqat `ala mawadihi bi-l-a`mal al-tahdiriyya wa-l-munaqashat al-barlamaniyya*, Part III (Cairo: Matba`at Misr, 1940), Part I, Discussion of Article 13.

8. See my "Shari'a and State in the Modern Middle Muslim East," *International Journal of Middle East Studies* 29, 3 (1997), 359–376.

9. I examine the debate in Iraq in "Constitutionalism, Authoritarianism, and Imperialism in Iraq," *Drake Law Review* 53 (2005): 923. Other far more comprehensive accounts of Iraq are Zaid al-Ali, *The Struggle for Iraq's Future* (New Haven: Yale University Press, 2014), and Haider Ala Hamoudi, *Negotiating in Civil Conflict: Constitutional Construction and Imperfect Bargaining in Iraq* (Chicago: University of Chicago Press, 2013).

10. I elaborate this argument in Nathan J. Brown, "Regimes Reinventing Themselves: Constitutional Development in the Arab World," *International Sociology* 18, 1 (2003): 33–52.

11. On ideological constitutions, see Saïd Amir Arjomand, "Constitutions and the Struggle for Political Order: A Study in the Modernization of Political Traditions," *European Journal of Sociology* 33, 1 (1992): 39–82.

12. In the debate over the adoption of the first Moroccan constitution, for instance, the opposition was able to cite the opinion of a leading Islamic scholar criticizing the document because it assigned a greater right in legislation to the state than should exist in an Islamic system. See Charles F. Gallagher, *Toward Constitutional Government in Morocco: A Referendum Endorses the Constitution*, report North Africa Series, Volume IX, No. 1 (Morocco), (American Universities Field Staff: 1963), 7. For a very different example see the discussion of women's suffrage in "Women in the Constitutional Committee" *Ruz al-yusuf*, October 19, 1953, 13. At that time, a committee drafting a constitution for Egypt considered the right of women to vote. Some committee members unsuccessfully cited Islamic grounds for opposing this right.

13. Ahmad Majid Binjalun, *Al-dustur al-maghrabi: mabadi'ihi wa ahkamihi* (Casablanca: Dar al-Kitab, 1977), 151–152.

14. Article 153. For the text, see Albert P. Blaustein and Gisbert H. Flanz, eds., *Constitutions of the World* (Dobbs Ferry: Oceana Publications, 2007); updated periodically.

15. On these clauses generally, see Clark B. Lombardi, "Constitutional Provisions Making Sharia 'a' or 'the' Chief Source of Legislation: Where Did They Come From? What Do They Mean? Do They Matter?" *American University International Law Review* 28 (2013): 733–774. Also very useful is Kristen Stilt, "Constitutional Islam: Genealogies, Transmissions and Meanings," http://ontheground.qatar.northwestern.edu/uncategorized/chapter-10-constitutional-islam-genealogies-transmissions-and-meanings, accessed April 1, 2015. For comprehensive coverage of Islam and constitutionalism, see Rainer Grote and Tilmann Röder, eds., *Constitutionalism in Islamic Countries: Between Upheaval and Continuity* (Oxford: Oxford University Press, 2012).

16. On the Syrian constitution of 1950, including Article 3 which described *fiqh* as the chief source of legislation, see Majid Khadduri, "Constitutional Development in Syria," *Middle East Journal* 5, 2 (Spring 1951): 137–160. Ironically, Syria later made Arab constitutional history when a constitution was proposed that removed the requirement that the head of state be a Muslim.

17. See Jamal al-'Utayfi, *Ara' fi al-shari'a wa-fi al-hurriyya* [*Opinions on the Shari'a and Freedom*] (Cairo: Al-hay'a al-misriyya al-'amma li-l-kitab, 1980); and the unpublished minutes of the preparatory committee for drafting the constitution for the Arab Republic of Egypt, 1971 (held in the library of the Majlis al-Sha'b, Cairo).

18. On press discussion, see Joseph P. O'Kane, "Islam in the New Egyptian Constitution: Some Discussions in al-Ahram," *Middle East Journal* 26, 2 (1972): 137–148.

19. I have written on this elsewhere in "Shari'a and State" and in "Consensus and Cacophony: Debating the Islamic Shari'a in 21st-Century Egypt," in *Sharia Politics*, ed. Robert W. Hefner (Bloomington: Indiana University Press, 2011), 94–121.

20. See Said Arjomand, "Constitutions and the Struggle for Political Order: A Study in the Modernization of Political Traditions," *Archives Européennes de Sociologie* 33, 4 (1992): 39–82.

21. I examine this pattern in *When Victory is Not an Option: Islamist Movements in Arab Politics* (Ithaca: Cornell University Press, 2012).

22. Hasan al-Hudaybi's short pamphlet, *Dusturuna* (Cairo: Dar al-Ansar, 1978) apparently dates from this period. I am grateful to Barbara Zollner for brining this to my attention. See her work on Hudaybi, in *The Muslim Brotherhood: Hasan al-Hudaybi and Ideology* (Abington: Routledge, 2009).

23. There had, to be sure, always been an anti-constitutionalist strain in some Islamist circles even before the Brotherhood's suppression. The Hizb al-Tahrir, for instance, grounded its call for an absolutist caliphate in traditional Islamic political thought.

24. I examine this issue in "Reason, Interest, Rationality, and Passion in Constitution Drafting," *Perspectives on Politics* 6, 4 (2008): 675–689.

25. In a private conversation, Donald Horowitz has persuaded me that consensus and inclusivity on the one hand and publicity on the other are often confused. For an account of a successful process that was consensual and inclusive while still having important parts carried out in private, see his *Constitutional Change and Democracy in Indonesia* (Cambridge: Cambridge University Press, 2013).

26. Two useful analyses of the process with a particular emphasis on religion are Monica L. Marks, "Convince, Coerce, or Compromise? Ennahda's Approach to Tunisia's Constitution," paper Number 10 (Brookings Doha Center Analysis, February 2014), and Pietro Long, "Islamic Constitutionalism and Constitutional Politics in Post-Revolutionary Tunisia," WP 03/23, Working Paper Series (UNILU Center for Comparative Constitutional Law and Religion, 2013).

27. Al-Ghannushi, personal interview, Tunis, July 2011.

28. Kevin Ivey, "Social Media and Contentious Politics: Tunisia 2010–2013" (master's thesis Elliott School of International Affairs, George Washington University, 2014).

29. I am indebted to Nadia Marzouki for the metaphor.

30. I base the information in this section on a series of personal interviews with Brotherhood and Party leaders during 2011 and 2012.

31. See Nada Hussein Rashwan, "'This is Not Politics, but Interests,' says MB Supreme Guide of Current Protests" *Al-Ahram Online*, December 8, 2012, http://english.ahram.org.eg/NewsContent/1/64/60059/Egypt/Politics-/This-is-not-politics,-but-interests,-says-MB-Supre.aspx, accessed August 6, 2013. See also "Badi` Video: Decision Now to the Ballot Boxes," *al-Wafd*, December 8, 2012, http://www.alwafd.org/%25D8%25A3%25D8%25AE%25D8%25A8%25D8%25A7%25D8%25B1-%25D9%2588%25D8%25AA%25D9%2582%25D8%25A7%25D8%25B1%25D9%258A%25D8%25B1/13-%25D8%25A7%25D9%2584%25D8%25B4%25D8%25A7%25D8%25B1%25D8%25B9%20%25D8%25A7%25D9%2584%25D8%25B3%25D9%258A%25D8%25A7%25D8%25B3%25D9%258A/323213-%25D8%25A8%25D8%25AF%25D9%258A%25D8%25B9-%25D8%25A7%25D9%2584%25D8%25A7%25D8%25AD%25D8%25AA%25D9%2583%25D8%25A7%25D9%2585-%25D8%25A7%25D9%2584%25D8%25A2%25D9%2586-%25D9%2584%25D9%2584%25D8%25B5%25D9%2586%25D8%25A7%25D8%25AF%25D9%258A%25D9%2582, accessed August 6, 2013.

32. See Wala' Na`mat Allah, Muhammad Hamdi, and Muhammad Yusif Wahba Amin, "Constituent [Assembly]: We Reject the Text on the Zaka Clause in the Constitution," *al-Balad al-Yawm*, November 13, 2012, accessed June 2, 2016, http://www.balad2day.com/site/News-15572-.html.

33. "Salafi Leader Reveals Plot to Oust Azhar's Grand Imam," english.alarabiya.net, December 25, 2012, http://english.alarabiya.net/articles/2012/12/25/256924.html. The full lecture can be viewed at www.youtube.com/watch?v=_xzsVgwG9-o. An edited excerpt of the segment in question can be viewed at www.youtube.com/watch?v=tGbOM_4TJh4.

34. For more on this compromise and its meaning, see Gianluca Parolin, "(Re)Arrangement of State/Islam Relations in Egypt's Constitutional Transition," Public Law Research Paper No. 13–15 (NYU School of Law, May 2013); Clark Lombardi and Nathan J. Brown, "Islam in Egypt's New Constitution," *Foreign Policy*, December 13, 2012; and Zaid al-Ali and Nathan J. Brown, "Egypt's Constitution Swings into Action," *Foreign Policy*, March 27, 2013.

35. See, for instance, Khaled Dawoud, "The Debate over Egypt's Constitution," Atlantic Council Egypt Source blog, November 24, 2015, http://www.atlanticcouncil.org/blogs/egyptsource/the-debate-over-egypt-s-constitution, accessed December 29, 2015.

CHAPTER 7

The Public Politics of the Private Realm

The modern 'ulama take a more expansive view of the powers of the state: the state must not merely let people live an Islamic life but should actively uphold and implement Islamic law; it must enable people to live according to such law, and it must allow nothing that contravenes it. Yet they also share with their medieval precursors an ambivalence towards the state. And as the power of the state has grown to encompass all facets of the life of its citizens, so too have the 'ulama's suspicions of it. But the ambivalence is not just that of the 'ulama. The power of the modern nation-state to intrude into and regulate all aspects of the life of its citizens means that religion occupies an uneasy place in any modern state.

Muhammad Qasim Zaman, *The Ulama in Contemporary Islam*, 100–101

Thus the rule of law, as part of the liberal regulatory state, constantly produces spaces of exceptions wherein it constantly expands. Distrust, suspicion, exceptions, and expansion are endemic to this distinctively modern process. When the Shari'a becomes subsumed under the rule of law, it may also begin to acquire some of these features.

Hussein Ali Agrama, *Questioning Secularism*, 35–36

How are private matters argued in public? With great vigor but also with tremendous complexities and sensitivities, since the issues are potentially so personal and public at the same time. In this chapter we will see not only the vitality of the arguments and how they link private and public but also ways in which private concerns and public policy are sometimes oddly disconnected. The republic of arguments can subsume the private realm in some quirky ways. The arguments that do occur can sometimes induce public authorities to change law and policy—but only if an actor within the state initiates and organizes the campaign.

Thus, in this chapter, I present how religion serves not merely as a meeting ground between public and private concerns but also weaves them together, making relations among family members a matter of public discussion and contestation. But I also show some odd disconnections between the republic of arguments and the world of policy and some unexpected agents in building bridges between them. I begin with some general reflections on the nature of personal status debates and then proceed in three additional steps, examining fatwas, courts, and parliaments in turn.

I first examine how the Islamic shari'a forms a starting point for individuals who seek to negotiate family relations in a variety of public settings, chiefly when they consult authorities for nonbinding moral guidance. More simply, I consider fatwas, showing them to provide an odd combination of public and private whose very moral authority stems from the fact that they are not authoritative in any enforceable sense.

I then turn to instances in which the binding and coercive public authority of the state is invoked in personal status matters by those who wish to have the law (generally based on Islamic categories and principles) applied or enforced and thus go to court. More simply, I examine judges and the adjudication of disputes. And I show that, paradoxically, private users of the courts tend not to try to understand public teachings about their own proper behavior (as fatwa seekers do) but instead to manipulate them to serve their own private interests.

Finally, much public argument takes place over the law which those courts apply and how it should be derived from the Islamic shari'a. So I will proceed in the last section to public policy and legal debates about personal status law, trying to probe the politics of the Islamic shari'a in the Arab world today. I will present the experiences of Jordan and Egypt in particular detail but will also examine Morocco, though more briefly. And I will present a strange pattern, where linkages between arguments and policy changes have been forged and where they have not been.

The private and public are intertwined, of course. But they are linked in a distinctive way. Arguments cross boundaries but politics and authority pass far less easily, and policy rarely at all. That is, when fatwas are sought and given, when lawsuits are filed and adjudicated, and when legislation is drafted, similar kinds of arguments are adduced by participants in debates. But the kind of authority that is trump in one realm is often devalued in another.

PUBLIC SPHERES AND PRIVATE LIFE

What is referred to—both in English and Arabic—as "personal status" (ahwal shakhsiyya) law is not simply where the private and the public come together but where all dimensions of both realms are so closely interwoven that they cannot be spoken of separately—ministries and official institutions, parliaments, courts, popular preachers, political parties, social activists, husbands, wives, children, and parents are all extremely active together on the terrain of family life; they act and call upon each other as litigants, quarrelers, question-ers, decision makers, law makers, adjudicators, teachers, counselors, admin-istrators, mobilizers, and lobbyists. Personal status is also the area of positive law most intimately connected with religious teachings in the Arab world.

In June 2013, as political activists were mobilizing followers to bring down President Muhammad Morsi and the Egyptian military high command was positioning itself to intervene to answer that demand, I found myself in an office attached to a mosque at a university campus located in a satellite city of Cairo. I had gone there to meet with Shaykh Salim 'Abd al-Galil because I was interested in the attempt by al-Azhar to begin its own satellite televi-sion broadcasting and I had heard his name as the director of the project. In fact, it turned out that 'Abd al-Galil indeed was directing (largely in an honor-ific rather than administrative sense) "Qanat al-Azhari" ("the Channel of the Azhari"); his main role was to lend the channel his name as director and to host a television program in which viewers submitted personal problems in order to solicit his shari'a-based guidance. As it turned out, this was not the al-Azhar channel I had heard about (that project, sponsored by the institution itself and in the planning stages for many years, has been more a topic for discussion than implementation). Instead it was a privately funded effort that presented itself as following the Azhari approach (and the shaykh, a graduate of al-Azhar, appeared on the show in the very distinctive dress of an Azhari). The leadership of al-Azhar, the shaykh explained, had originally been uneasy about the channel's use of the name, but he claimed that the law clearly was on his side (suggesting perhaps that the dispute had threatened to take a litigious turn before al-Azhar relented).

There were other mild surprises for me in my visit to the shaykh. When I arrived, he was sitting in a corner of the enormous office speaking quietly to an older man. The shaykh signaled me to wait in an adjoining chair while the man spoke. I could not make out what he was saying, and indeed made no attempt to do so, since the shaykh's other visitor seemed to be in some dis-tress and I suspected it involved a private problem. I felt somewhat intrusive; the discussion did not seem to be a public one. The shaykh, however, spoke more loudly and more clearly, invoking religious phrases and finally seeming to tell the man what he had to do. The man seemed both relieved and grateful and left.

Shaykh 'Abd al-Galil (along with his program) is fairly well known among Egyptians and it is not hard to discover the reasons for his popularity. Most of his attractiveness does not stem directly from the senior positions he has held (though those likely helped in securing backing for his broadcasting activities) but from his manner: he is energetic, cheerful, and engaging, with an extremely reassuring tone. With a smile perpetually on his lips, he is able to present the Islamic shari'a not as a set of legal strictures or as an inaccessible dialogue among scholars but instead as a compassionate, precise, and practical guide to intimate and difficult questions, delivered by highly trained experts. In my discussion with him, he reflected on the way he speaks to different audiences: among colleagues, in personal conversations, and on television. The requirements of the last medium were particularly confining: in a short program he must deliver something like a legal opinion every minute and none can come with anything more than a brief explanation; he must speak to the questioner but remain ever mindful that he is still addressing a broad public who can hear his words. He also recognized that he was invoking al-Azhar's name and that he had been a long-time senior official of the Ministry of Religious Affairs (having resigned when the Ministry changed hands after Morsi's election, returning only after Morsi was deposed after which he was sometimes mentioned as a candidate for holding the ministerial portfolio itself) and was regarded by some, with considerable justification, as a figure tied to the pre-2011 regime.

There are innumerable public forums where arguments about personal status take place—in parliaments, courts, televisions station, newer social media, seminar rooms, learned journals, and trashy tabloids. And of course in much of the intersection between public and private settings—neighborhood and family gatherings, most notably—particular relationships and policy matters are very much up for discussion.

It is these debates—the politics of personal status—that are most relevant to this book. But before plunging into legal and political debates—a step we will soon take—it is critical to remind ourselves what is at stake as members of Arab societies argue about matters of personal status. It might help to do so by steering away for a moment from the political sphere, narrowly defined as public discussions. In other words, we will begin this chapter not by focusing on policy and legal questions—though we will get back to them soon enough—but instead by probing the way in which personal status and public questions are so deeply linked.

In this regard, it is instructive to report a second conversation I had with a prominent public fatwa-giver, Muhammad Nuh al-Quda in Jordan, whom I met in the fall of 2014 at his office in Amman. A scholar who wore many hats, al-Quda was from a prominent family of judges originally from Mecca, some of whom had come to staff a wide range of religious positions in the Jordanian state as well as in some universities after the foundation of the Hashemite Kingdom there. He served briefly as a cabinet minister, earning him the reputation of being pro-regime but also giving him a role mediating with more radical forces (a mediating role that, according to rumor, cost him his ministerial position).

While he wore his family background and religious education with pride, I noticed right away that in most video clips, al-Quda was smartly dressed in a suit and tie. When I asked him why, he explained that there is no such thing as Islamic dress and that a preacher was part of the society and should dress in a manner that reflected prevailing social conventions. Only when delivering a

Friday sermon in a mosque did the occasion demand respect for less contemporary practice and he dressed accordingly (in a gown and head covering). But in most other appearances he stood out only for the smart cut of his suit and color coordination of the rest of his dress.

And his fatwas and sermons showed a similar concern for social relevance. His sermons stressed faith, fortitude, and rectitude, often by using religious stories that were designed to inspire the faithful to emulate their virtuous forbearers. When I observed that there was something quite general about his messages, that one could likely substitute Islamic names and stories with ones from different religious traditions and come up with a similar message, he appeared deeply pleased—not only because it meant that a visiting American academic could recognize something familiar in al-Quda's presentation of Islam, but also (I suspect) because he saw himself as the purveyor of practical but still universal lessons.

In his radio programs, al-Quda sped through fatwas with all the efficiency of 'Abd al-Galil. Like him, he dealt warmly with callers who brought their problems to him, again with an implicit message that the Islamic shari'a was there to help them live their lives and offer compassionate solutions, not onerous burdens. Al-Quda spoke in a friendly manner that bespoke learning without a trace of hectoring: his authority stemmed from his manner and his command of the material. But al-Quda also insisted to me that he would not supplant a different kind of authority: when faced with a caller who needed muscle more than helpful moral guidance, he would refer the caller to the courts. When it came to enforcement, al-Quda saw that state structures had an important role to play. Specialists in the Islamic shari'a could teach people the best path, but only courts and judges could enforce right conduct on those who would not willingly follow it in their treatment of family members. Islam was not merely a matter of personal ethics and conviction but also a way for ordering public life.

So we will turn to these two alternative sources of instruction on personal status issues, each in turn: first, muftis who explicate the teachings of the Islamic shari'a in response to specific questions; and second, judges who rule, generally on the basis of legislation based on the Islamic shari'a, in specific cases. Why do people turn to them and what kinds of arguments are involved?

MUFTIS AMONG THE FOREST OF FATWAS

Those who seek a nonbinding opinion on the Islamic way to deal with family members might consult a wide range of possible authorities. We will begin our exploration of religious authority not with those who turn to "authorities" in a political and legal sense—that will come in the following section—but to those who seek moral authority and religious instruction from muftis and preachers. We will focus especially on those who issue fatwas in public, through a variety of modern media, a transmutation of an old form (legal response) into a remarkable public form of propagating the faith and righteous conduct.

When it comes to the figures who deliver such teachings, one of the most remarkable developments in many Arab societies over the past generation has been how public the search for religious guides has become. While religion and various forms of celebrity have blended in the past, the phenomenon of popular preachers, speakers, and scholars reaching followers through multiple media—rallies, television programs, social media—has been sufficiently widespread to have engendered a term: the "new preachers" (al-du'a al-judad) in pubic discussions.

While the term suggests strong commonalities among the preachers, what is actually more striking is the great diversity within the group. Some senior religious officials and scholars (such as 'Ali Jum'a, former head of Dar al-Ifta' in Egypt) have extensive popular followings garnered through social and broadcast media; one religious scholar, Muhammad al-Ghazzali of Egypt, has a considerable social media following somehow created and sustained by his devotees two decades after his death. In addressing their audiences, such figures (at least the ones still alive) tend to dress and act in a manner consistent with what one might expect of personages of dignity and stature, though they often deploy informality (or, in al-Quda's case, sharp Western dress) in order to communicate approachability, practicality, success, or charm. Others have little formal religious training and make no pretensions to authority in that sense. Some answer direct questions regarding the Islamic shari'a; that is, they serve as muftis. Others make no pretension to any authority to deliver fatwas but instead give gentle moral guidance and coaching to viewers or listeners.

All address a wide range of topics—often focusing on matters of faith and virtue, but with heavy doses of personal behavior and conduct under circumstances of difficulty (such as interpersonal relations, human appetites, or even stress surrounding the annual secondary school examination). Politics might emerge for some preachers, either in a very general and platitudinous way (deciding among presidential candidates on the basis of qualifications and rectitude) or in a far more specific manner (addressing a current controversy such as participating in a particular demonstration). Others approach such topics obliquely if at all.

Two such personalities—'Abd al-Galil and al-Quda—have already been introduced, but they are joined by a vast array of preachers and muftis. It may help to review some of them, if only briefly and anecdotally, merely to illustrate the range of figures offering guidance.

Ahmad al-Shuqayri is a fairly young Saudi without advanced religious training; he appears in short videos wearing jeans and heavily relying on fancy visual aids to make his points; his exhortations have significant moral and ethical content but not always explicit religious instruction or language. He can move from topics such as Ramadan to how *jihad* can be pursued in all manner of individual ways. While he steers clear of politics, he can refer to social ills such as gambling and homelessness found in the United States (implicitly holding up Islamic teachings and family life as an alternative to steer his viewers away from vice and the problems it brings).

Tariq al-Suwaydan is a Kuwaiti with religious credentials and an affiliation with the Muslim Brotherhood; he can also pursue broad themes but has less of an aversion to politics and can mix talks about faith, fortitude, and personal conduct with the clash of civilizations or current political and social controversies.

Mustafa 'Adawi is an Egyptian salafi trained in the Arabian Peninsula; a bit more severe in manner, he answers callers' questions with dispatch and without doubt. Some of his callers get slightly detailed answers to direct questions (can a man in his twenties teach the Qur'an to a woman in her twenties?); responses are succinct and definitive (in this case, it is unambiguously wrong).

The range of orientations on those issues that are specifically religious—salafi, modernist, Brotherhood, Azhari—seems endless, as does the style and content of the preaching. Most preaching is national in scope, sometimes implicitly in the message (in that many use the colloquial language of their home country or make references to events and places that fall within national boundaries) and sometimes in the mode of broadcasting and the nature of the audience. There are a few preachers whose following is transnational, (such as al-Suwaydan). Yet far more frequent is the practice of someone like Al-Quda, who rattles off names of Jordanian places associated with the early history of Islam to bring a vivid, immediate, and local sense to the timeless truths he imparts, or 'Abd al-Galil, who can dismiss a rival opinion simply by describing it as "not Egyptian, not Azhari" almost as if "Egyptian," "Muslim," and "Azhari" were synonymous for his viewers.

And the range of media they use can be breathtaking. Some have a following that is developed through only one medium (such as broadcast television), but most are able to communicate through a variety of channels—starting on broadcast media, using twitter and Facebook as they come in fashion, preparing themselves for newer media as they are invented; participating in talk shows and then posting clips on YouTube; writing books and hawking them on the television appearances; holding public rallies or appearing in front of sizable live audiences (appearances that are, in turn, tweeted or featured in Facebook posts). Questions and responses may take the form of television or radio broadcast; questions might be submitted by live callers or posted on Facebook with answers then recorded and posted.

But if the new preachers appear to be operating in a very open marketplace of religion in which they brand themselves according to manner and message, there are three general commonalties: the way they tend to minimize dialogue; the role they play for their followers; and the way they deploy the Islamic shari'a.

First, most speak directly to their followers (or appear on interview programs where they listen to and respond to questions from hosts or guest callers). Not only does that mean that communication with followers is unmediated; it also means that little dialogue takes place between leader and followers. Programs sometimes involve only the preacher or mufti taking calls and responding; sometimes there is a host who follows up, gives brief framing remarks, and introduces topics and callers. Most callers are allowed to pose their question and sometimes stay on the line for a quick follow-up but the conversations remain largely one of a questioner and an expert who gives definitive answers.

Nor is there much direct dialogue among the various preachers, at least in public. Preachers and especially muftis will sometimes argue indirectly (for instance, a caller may ask about a different approach she has heard from another scholar). There are exceptions—joint appearances, for instance—but even those take a form that might be called parallel preaching more often than direct dialogue. Al-Quda described to me with pride about how he participated in a series of such appearances in football stadiums in Jordan he termed "Come on Board!" (*Irkab ma'ana*). He directed me to the video recording in which he and three fellow preachers ('Ayd al-Qarani, a Saudi leaning far to the most liberal end of the Wahhabi spectrum, Mahmud al-Masri, an Egyptian salafi, and Mustafa Husni, an Egyptian with a bit lighter and more generic touch) were each greeted almost like an arriving wrestler; they joined in the middle of the playing field to take turns preaching, each one in his distinctive style.

Interaction among preachers takes a second, indirect form as well: the participation of multiple preachers in addressing the same controversy, often sparked by a notorious incident or controversial personality. For instance, a debate after 2012 about lowering the marriage age in Egypt (set off when a salafi deputy in parliament mentioned the subject) led to multiple authorities weighing in. Other societies have seen intermittent sets of discussions about the repercussions of delayed marriage (because economic hardship makes it difficult for grooms to provide what they are expected). A scandal surrounding an elopement (or alleged kidnapping or how to distinguish between the two) may set off a string of pronouncements as various authorities are pushed or pulled into stating their opinion.

A second common feature is the way these communications—especially those that are broadcast—are used. Followers or viewers do sometimes pay attention to content, but very often their sermons and broadcasts play the role of religious background music; a television might be on in a private home, or occasionally an office, broadcasting religious talk while other conversation and work takes place. Yasmin Moll observes that just the act of having the broadcast on is itself a pious gesture:

> Indeed, for many Muslims tuning into an Islamic channel is considered a virtuous act, a deliberate choice to improve the self through a shunning of non-Islamic media that might be morally corrupting in what they project on the screen (scantily-clad women, sex-scenes, glorified violence, and so on). It is necessary to take this choice—and the Islamic satellite channels that make it possible—seriously in order to understand the cultural politics animating the Islamic revival in Egypt since the millennium.[1]

A final common feature of these broadcasts is especially germane to our current inquiry: the way they present the Islamic shari'a. The muftis (a category generally reserved for those preachers who give answers to questions on proper practice, a group that consists of those who make some claim to authoritative training) give answers that often in their content and almost always in their manner convey the attitude that the Islamic shari'a is a friendly force. Even the preachers who do not play the role of muftis convey a similar general impression: God, faith, and the Islamic shari'a deserve awe and respect but reward those who follow them handsomely: religious, personal, and social virtues interlock and indeed are difficult to disentangle.

In this respect, the manner is often the message. Muftis may intersperse smiles, reassuring nods, and chatting with interjections of much more formal language, Qur'anic verses, and hadiths. Salafis do tend to be much more austere in appearance but can sport a smile even when giving stern answers. They rarely give concrete reasons for their answers but the answers themselves are often clear and draw for their authority on the knowledge and understanding of the mufti.

The effect is at once friendly and commanding. Muftis enter into details to be sure, but those details tend not to be reasoned ones but instead detailed explanations: it is as if they are giving directions on how to perform a mildly complicated task or operate a machine rather than explaining why to do so or how the machine works. In the process, they will often presume a level of knowledge of technical terms, especially those connected with personal status, marriage, the body, and morality; expressions like *sinn al-tamyiz* (the age of discernment when a child bears greater moral responsibility) or *'awra* (those parts of the body that should be kept covered for the sake of modesty) are used without definition. Sexual matters are often discussed without hesitation or embarrassment.

In the fatwa broadcasts, listeners generally hear a question and a response along with a short explication of the relevant principle or text but nothing like an extended reasoning and rarely a consideration of multiple approaches or an appreciation of ambiguity. Preachers who avoid fatwas—or scholars who give fatwas but also deliver more general homiletic answers—may step back and approach matters far more generally. Al-Quda, for instance, has posted a lengthy discussion of marriage in which he explains it is about complementarity, not competition or equality. God has created husband and wife with their male and female particularities and one would not apply the same rules to both just as one would never use an Opel manual to operate a Mercedes, he explains.

Callers are often emotional, with words tumbling out of their mouths, though others are calm and direct. Regardless of the manner, the mufti demonstrably listens carefully, often with a smile and reassuring nod and perhaps a quick follow-up question or two if a legally critical detail is missing from the way the question is phrased. If the caller goes on too long, the mufti (or, if the program is hosted, the host) might send the question forward with dispatch with a quick sympathetic rendering of the problem.

The mufti is generally responding to the caller but it is clear from the rapidity with which questions are processed, follow-ups discouraged, and discussion kept succinct, the mufti is indirectly but consciously addressing a much wider audience. The logic of such programs is not simply that the Islamic shari'a gives guidance for the most intimate question and difficult problem. The broadcasts presume that such answers are accessible to ordinary believers and that turning to an educated authority is likely to result in helpful and clear advice and instruction. To be a Muslim, to live a virtuous life, sometimes requires a little guidance from a friendly teacher but that guidance is sensible, uncomplicated, easily available, and makes life easier and more certain, not more difficult and confusing.

The world that emerges from these programs is one in which Muslims are beset by problems and pressures but also one that is infused with a shari'a-minded spirit. The frequency with which the perplexed pious pepper respected figures with questions on the most intimate details of their lives—and the popularity of the programs and the preachers—might seem to be testimony to the shari'a-mindedness of the society; it would seem to be very good news for the religiously minded that when so many Muslims think about their problems and cast about for solutions, the language they speak is that of the Islamic way of doing things.

But in fact, just the opposite feeling seems to be afoot: that there is a crisis of religious authority, a cacophony of fatwas in which ordinary believers are bewildered by the vast array of opinions they are exposed to on any question. The fact that such programs take a form very different from that of specialist discourse means that entry into the world of public fatwa-giving seems based more on personal characteristics than on scholarly credentials. Talk of *fatawi 'ashwa'iyya* [fatwas that are haphazard and without order; the same adjective is used for shantytown housing] has grown thick. Those who use the term generally do so to suggest that outlandish fatwas or those based on spurious readings easily mislead the naïve, that pious people need some guidance in deciding which self-proclaimed authority needs respect. They worry not only that believers will be misled but also that the entire enterprise of fatwa-giving will be brought into disrepute.

But it is only slightly uncharitable to suspect that what bothers many religious authorities is not so much that people turn to muftis for guidance but that they turn to the wrong muftis. As one Azhari official once explained to me in a private conversation, believers will be confused if offered many interpretations, so they should just receive one—and that one is logically delivered by al-Azhar. The claim is not that al-Azhar (or any other favored source) can issue binding opinions, only that it offers the best ones.

But there are sources of binding authority, at least in particular cases. Popular muftis may wield tremendous moral and didactic authority but it is judges, who may or may not have moral authority, who clearly speak with the authority of the state.

PUBLIC AUTHORITY AND ADJUDICATING PRIVATE MATTERS

In moving from muftis to judges, we would seem at first glance to be shifting from the informality and privacy of fatwas to the formality and public authority of court rulings. There is a shift to be clear, but it is paradoxically often in the direction opposite to the one we might expect.

It is true that when they take their private problems to personal status courts, litigants are attempting to invoke public authority in support of their position; they are moving not merely into the realm of the state but also to a setting in which sessions are supposed to be public and disputes settled on the basis of a law that is issued by public authorities. As Baber Johansen noted in the wake of some apostasy rulings in Egypt:

> The analysis of one apostasy judgment of the highest Egyptian court shows that the court understands belief and apostasy as objective facts that can be separated from the person who professes or denies them. The court effectively claims the role of the highest instance in questions of belief and unbelief. Apostasy thus becomes a depersonalized objective fact without any relation to the intentions of the individuals concerned. The court's sentence presents a radicalized version of the opposition between the individual's interior forum and the courts' exterior forum: the first loses its connection with the second. The court's definition of apostasy serves to control the ideas that can legitimately be discussed in the public sphere. It denies bold reinterpretations of Islam, but implicitly also a number of political persuasions and theories, the right of access to the public space and assigns them the private sphere as their legitimate abode.[2]

Courts present themselves as a realm hostile to private haggling, and indeed, judges in the Arab world tend to frown upon such out-of-court bargaining, viewing it as a way in which the dominant can escape their legal obligations and the weak can be pressured out of availing themselves of their legal protections. The task of judges is to adjudicate in a realm in which truth, justice, and law are supposed to prevail, not private agreements among unequal parties.

Yet something quite different actually happens when disputes enter personal status court. People can use the law and courts in many different ways—sometimes all at once.[3] And judges regularly make concessions to private negotiations even while insisting on the role of the law in very complicated and personal family disputes. Informality, privacy, and bargaining are very much at play in legal disputes, much more than in the realm of public fatwa mongering.

In the mid-1990s, I went to a Kuwaiti courthouse to meet a judge who was then assigned to personal status court. As I entered the room where he was working, the scene was not all that different from that which I saw in Salim ʿAbd al-Galil's office two decades later. The judge sat not on a couch but at a desk; he was speaking to a man and woman (from the Arab world but not Kuwaitis) while I sat uncomfortably in a chair on the other side of the room. What I was witnessing seemed to be something a bit less formal than a court session but something more than a casual conversation—as the judge explained later, it was a meeting in which the couple wanted to have their divorce officially registered with the court in a manner that would allow the wife to remarry without additional waiting. The husband spoke in hushed, plaintive tones. The judge, holding the husband's identification card in a gesture that implied he was ransoming it (and with it the husband's legal status in the country) in return for truthful answers, asked and re-asked a question (had the husband been alone with the wife at all since the divorce) whose answer would determine whether he would register the divorce on the date requested.

What the scene shared with the one in ʿAbd al-Galil's office was its informality and odd combination of elements of a private discussion (hushed tones, back-and-forth conversation, discussion of intimate matters) without exclusion of all public elements (an American academic, after all, was in the room; in addition, I recall a couple of other people waiting for their turn with the judge). But there were differences: the couple sought a legal move, not moral guidance. Coercion—or at least a form of pressure—was implicit (with the brandishing of the identity card); moral suasion was absent. The veracity of the couple's statements was clearly doubted rather than accepted at face value. I suspect there was some prior bargaining and agreement between the husband and wife which was leading the husband to seek to allow his ex-wife to remarry immediately.

What explained these differences between the mufti's office and that of the judge? It was not that the latter relied only on the law. The judge's implied threat with the identity card was not legally sanctioned. Nor was it the public nature of the judicial proceedings as opposed to the private nature of a fatwa. Indeed, fatwas are often delivered in front of mass audiences. More generally, personal status courts in the Arab world often regularly violate the law precisely in the matter of publicity. In Qatar and Kuwait, when I asked to attend a supposedly public personal status court, I was very politely refused on the grounds that private matters would be discussed. Hussein Agrama has found more generally that regardless of the letter of the law, normally punctilious judges in Egypt insisted on hearing personal status cases in private.[4]

Indeed, Agrama points us to the key difference between the mufti and the judge: the fact that court proceedings are connected with political authority. The faithful go to muftis voluntarily for moral guidance on how to live their lives; litigants go to judges to have their rights enforced. The skepticism involved in a formal legal proceeding is greater not simply on the part of the seekers, but also on the part of the authorities: the statements of litigants are greeted with more skepticism (since they are assumed to be pursuing their own interests) than those of fatwa seekers (who are assumed to be seeking moral guidance).

In his conversations with those who delivered fatwas in comparison to his observation of courts issuing judgments, Agrama noted an odd phenomenon that becomes less puzzling in light of the differing nature of scholarly and judicial authority: those who sought fatwas often asked for more demanding interpretations, frustrated if the muftis seemed to be making things too easy for them; litigants tailored their appeals in such a way as to obtain the most favorable ruling. Those who fail to get a favorable court ruling might appeal; those who seek a second fatwa (not a common occurrence) do so in the precise opposite circumstances: "if people ask different muftis the same question, it is often not because they are seeking advantage, but because they are uncomfortable with a past decision that *is* to their advantage."[5]

In speaking with those who deliver fatwas in the Arab world, I have asked about this phenomenon noted by Agrama and been told similar stories, with muftis often feeling forced to teach the questioner that the Islamic path is rarely the more difficult one but instead designed to meet the needs of the believers. Those given easy answers seem suspicious that they are not given the right ones.

Judges, by contrast, betray suspicions of litigants, seeing them as more likely to evade rather than welcome burdensome rulings, and insist that they need to question carefully and search for signs of shaving the truth and deception.

In the 1990s, I conducted research on how Cairenes resorted to the courts in personal status cases.[6] Egyptian personal status law is based on Islamic law and a shari'a-based conception of marriage as a contractual agreement between a husband who pledges support and a woman who pledges obedience. The law has been codified since 1929 (with a law of procedure actually codified earlier in 1897) and has undergone some substantial changes since then. Even as codified in 1929, the law gave substantial rights to a wife to divorce from her husband if he failed to provide support or caused her harm. The husband's right to divorce his wife is virtually without substantive restriction, although Egyptian personal status law does include procedural requirements designed to ensure that he will not do so recklessly. (Technically, a husband can directly divorce his wife and ask that it be officially recognized; a wife does not directly divorce her husband but asks a court to order divorce.)

In 1979, President Anwar al-Sadat issued a decree-law giving the wife stronger guarantees; when the Supreme Constitutional Court ruled in 1985 that al-Sadat had exceeded his constitutional powers by failing to submit the decree to parliament, a new, slightly diluted law, was duly passed. Two of the principle changes adopted in 1979 and 1985 were to make it easier for a wife to claim that she has suffered harm (and thus was eligible to request a court-ordered divorce) if her husband married a second wife and to require that the husband provide housing for his divorced wife and any children still under her care. A further change implemented gradually in the 1960s and 1970s related to *bayt al-ta'a* (literally, "house of obedience"). A husband whose wife has left his house (as will be seen, joint property is virtually unknown and housing is usually is provided by—and belongs to—the husband) can ask a court to order her return. Formerly, such an order could be forcibly implemented by the police. Over the past half-century, that practice has virtually disappeared, but a wife who ignores a bayt al-ta'a order will forfeit many of her legal rights.[7]

The impact of the law can only be understood in the context of Egyptian customs and bargaining related to marriage. Since husband and wife retain separate ownership, much of the premarital bargaining concerns what each side will bring to the marriage or pledge to the other. In general, a husband is expected to provide an apartment and major appliances. A wife may provide some of the furnishings. A husband also is required to pay a *mahr* (bride-price) to his wife (or to her family to hold in trust for her), often consisting of two separate amounts. The *mahr muqaddam* (advance bride-price) is paid at the time of the wedding. A *mahr mu'akhkhar* (delayed bride-price) is also some-times pledged to be paid in the event of divorce (or death). A husband is also expected (and required by law) to provide financial support for the family; so long as the husband provides the proper home and support, a wife is expected (and required by law) to live with her husband.

These arrangements leave tremendous room for bargaining and protracted financial negotiations to precede (and often prevent) a wedding. With housing scarce and expensive and financial resources tight for all but the very affluent, the families of the bride and groom are generally very anxious to ensure that the needs and interests of their side are guaranteed; they are also careful to safeguard the interests and property of their side should the marriage end in divorce. The social standing of the two sides, the earning power of the groom, and quality of housing he can provide all affect the outcome. As a result, although the law would seem to give a husband far greater divorce rights than a wife, the situation in practice often depends on the arrangements made in advance of the marriage and the nature of the marital difficulties. If a wife can show harm—perhaps because of physical or verbal abuse (or, since 1979, because the husband marries a second wife)—she will not only be able to divorce her husband, but may also be able to demand the *mahr mu'akhkhar*, child support, and housing. If, however, she leaves her husband and is unable to satisfy a court that she is justified, she may face a bayt al-ta'a order giving her the choice of returning to the home she fled or forfeiting most of her financial rights.

The result is that a troubled marriage often erupts in a tangled web of public lawsuits and even criminal charges, which in turn provoke formal and informal attempts at private mediation. For instance, in order to substantiate charges of harm, a wife will sometimes go to the police to swear a statement that she was subject to physical or verbal abuse. A husband will seek to gain an advantageous legal position by filing a *bayt al-ta'a* suit to threaten the wife that she will face potentially disastrous financial consequences unless she drops her grievance. A creative spouse can find a variety of ways to invoke personal status, civil, and criminal law on his or her behalf; such attempts generally provoke a similar set of moves by the other spouse.[8] What is especially noteworthy is the wide variety of forums that are employed, often simultaneously. Husbands and wives will deal directly with each other, use the mediation of relatives and friends, and use the criminal, civil, and personal status courts in complex strategies to obtain (or prevent) a divorce on the most favorable terms.

While it is impossible to ascertain the extent of physical violence in family relationships, the courts tend to take allegations seriously. Battery is not simply grounds for divorce but also a criminal offense; if a wife charges battery she exposes her husband to criminal charges even while strengthening her rights to a divorce. A husband might also charge that a wife's family has beaten him. Thus, criminal and civil cases often are intertwined.

Working-class and middle-class Cairenes tend to be very aware of the provisions of the personal status (and other relevant) law, and this affects their actions both before a marriage and in the course of a marital conflict. Thus some of their strategies are essentially preemptive—to gain a stronger bargaining position in case marital difficulties occur. This takes the fairly obvious form of carefully recording the material obligations of both sides in a written marriage contract, but it can also take subtler forms. In one instance I encountered, a fiancée's engagement seemed about to collapse in an argument over finances and her prospective groom's wish to travel to Saudi Arabia to work. She therefore insisted that he write her a check for the value of the household furnishings he had pledged to provide. (In Egypt, checks are often used not to exchange money but as guarantees of good faith, or they are postdated and used as promissory notes.) He agreed, but when the engagement finally collapsed he withdrew the money from the bank account. She took the matter to the police, because writing a check without sufficient funds is a criminal offense punishable by a jail sentence. Her family then used the criminal case to increase their bargaining power.[9]

The extensive use of the courts by working- and middle-class Cairenes in marital disputes suggests that the formal legal system is hardly seen as the forum of last resort. With the prolonged nature of litigation surrounding divorce (according to one estimate, the average life of a divorce case in the courts is seven years) early resort to the courts is almost necessary. Yet the courts are hardly seen as a forum of first resort either. The various methods for settling marital problems—formal and informal, direct and manipulative, obvious and inventive—are all used, very often simultaneously. (Perhaps this characteristic of personal status litigation in Egypt was most dramatically on display in one of the most prominent court cases of the last quarter century in Egypt—that of Nasir Hamid Abu Zayd, a Cairo University professor whose writings on Islam prompted Islamist critics to secure a court decision dissolving his marriage on the basis that he was no longer a Muslim male and therefore could not be married to a Muslim female.)

The courts and the legal system have become part of the social landscape, not simply accepted but actively sought out by those with severe marital difficulties. Once the courts have been introduced into a dispute, their role tends to escalate partly because of the actions of the parties themselves: suits provoke countersuits; criminal charges are filed to buttress a civil claim; appeals and delaying tactics ensure that the matter can be postponed for a momentarily disadvantaged party. And Egyptians are aware not only of the provisions of the personal status law available to them but also other legal provisions (including the criminal code) whose relevance to marital dispute is made obvious only by the ability of litigants to invoke them. Hardly passive actors, even those with a relatively weak legal position devise tactics to make their claims on property, spouses, or custody of children.

For Cairenes involved in marital problems, the legal system can be less an alien, hostile, or terrifying presence than a potential ally or set of tools. Some of these tools are generally helpful to one side and some to the other, but all are used, sometimes early and sometimes often. The nature of the way these courts operate—in a manner that takes the form of authorities delivering binding pronouncements after receiving all the facts but actually facilitates all kinds of bargaining and maneuvering—is hardly unique to Egypt.[10]

Judges and muftis—and the way that they are used—therefore share a series of similarities. Both present themselves as authoritative dispensers of truth based on their mastery and application of authoritative texts. But both operate simultaneously (and, at least in private, quite frankly) almost as social workers, conceiving their role as applying truth in a compassionate and just manner sensitive to the needs of the confused, vulnerable, or troubled. Both give reasons for their decisions, but there is a limited role for argument or exchange and reasoning is often very brief, designed less to walk the untrained through a decision and more to communicate the technical mastery of the authority (though both judges and muftis might balk at this description). Both rely on a combination of publicity and privacy and of formality and informality.

And both apparently operate in a one-way fashion (as authorities dispensing truth and justice to those who seek them). But in reality, those who invoke their authority are hadly passive. They have a variety of other tools to use singly or in combination—they can choose a forum, combine forums, and solicit the intervention and mediation of courts, police, friends, and family—and some of these tools (especially family bargaining and mediation) are actually encouraged by the authorities.[11] Some procedures offered are protracted but indeed they do end and result in a decision or settlement that is accepted or imposed. In all the to and fro, there is much room for inventiveness but much less for intellectual give-and-take. It is rare that any of the tools involve much critical-rational exchange between authority and seeker of truth and justice. Authorities give reasons not to engage in an argument but to end one.

But we have also discovered one critical if unexpected difference between the fatwa and the court judgment. In previous chapters we noted the ways in which spheres collide, in which arguments can be detached and travel from one sphere to the next. In this chapter we have stumbled on another aspect of the two spheres (Islamic shariʻa and state court) that applies more generally: arguments move more easily than authority; the membrane separating spheres is much less permeable to authority than it is to ideas and words. A questioner can rely on a fatwa's reasoning in preparing a legal case but the fatwa itself is not binding. A disappointed litigant can bring a question to a mufti who might question a court judgment's justice but cannot reverse it.

Indeed, for the particular pair of mufti and judge we have found that the fact that authority is not fungible is very much detected by seekers of truth and justice—and actually augments the distinctive authority of both. A questioner goes to a mufti voluntarily and is therefore more willing to defer to the mufti's authority. And a litigant is likely to go to a court when desiring to have a ruling enforced, even if the search for such a ruling comes at some sacrifice to the search for a morally correct one. We have called muftis and judges both "authorities" but the nature of their authority almost belies our use of the same word to describe the nature of their arguments and abilities. A mufti's words derive a good part of their force from the fact that they are sought voluntarily and are not enforceable; a judge's words derive a good part of their force from the fact that they can be imposed on those who neither sought nor accepted them.

Is there any way that moral and state authority can coexist and even reinforce each other? Yes, and the place where they most commonly do so is the quintessential public sphere: parliament. It is in parliaments and debates over public policy that various actors make arguments designed to turn their understandings of right and wrong into enforceable norms. Because parliaments involve both talk and law making, those who argue that personal status law should be changed direct their attention there. But the translation of arguments about personal status into public law is not as easy as this might make it seem; the use of public authority to enforce private conduct is more effective when it involves less publicly accessible parts of the state.

PUBLICLY DEBATING TURNING THE ISLAMIC WAY INTO THE LAW OF THE STATE

Our interest in public arguments about Islam and their impact on public life draws us quite naturally to debates over personal status law in parliaments. As Léon Buskens has noted about Morocco:

> The Moroccan debate shows that in order to understand Islamic family law, we should analyze it as a political phenomenon. I treat the current debates in Morocco as an example of how family law and gender serve as powerful political symbols in the modern Muslim world. In many Muslim societies it is impossible to speak about family law except in terms of Islam. Many people understand the legal status of women as a sign of the direction that society at-large should take. Every codification of family law entails a selection, interpretation and re-creation of classical fiqh norms. The content of the law is a social construction, shaped by political considerations. Hence, public discussion about family law raises larger questions, e.g., who may participate in politics and what views about Islam may be expressed in the public sphere?[12]

It is precisely in this context that those arguments about family life developed in other settings might be translated into public policy outcomes—that those who believe that the Islamic way of conducting family relations is knowable and should be supported (and even enforced) by public authorities would find an appropriate venue through the legislative process for coming to a common set of understandings and write those agreed-upon beliefs in legal form.

In fact that happens to a degree, but with a series of important qualifications that greatly lessen this idealized picture of parliaments, public law, and private life: only some arguments are rendered into publicly debatable form; arguments often do not produce common understandings; and parliaments are not the most important state actor in producing and enforcing any such understanding. Given the justifiably cynical views that prevail of political systems in the Arab world, the gap between the idealized role for parliaments and the actual nature and impact of public arguments should be no surprise. But the patterns of that departure are distinctive and worthy of analysis nonetheless, and there are indeed ways in which public arguments do affect outcomes even if the idealized portrait is never met.

As we have seen above, personal status law is an area in which those governed by it not only have an acute personal interest but also a familiarity with the legal terminology as well as underlying conceptual foundations. With all elements of family life informed by such terms and concepts, this familiarity is no surprise. What may be more of a surprise is how little these terms and concepts are contested.

Shariʿa-based personal status codes display three elements that are at variance with more liberal or individualistic legal frameworks. First, they are frankly inegalitarian. Of course, all legal frameworks recognize distinctions among individuals: they distinguish between the rights and obligations of parents and children or of those who can act on their own behalf and those who need guardians. Shariʿa-based systems also distinguish based on gender. The reasoning is clear: men and women both have rights and obligations but they are not identical: they have fundamentally different roles in a family and in society; they also differ in power. This can, of course, place wives, mothers, and daughters in a disadvantageous legal and material position when compared with husbands, fathers, and sons. But the reasoning behind the distinction is based in part on the belief (firmly and sincerely held, it seems to me, by scholars, judges, and many participants in public debates) that weaker parties need legal protection and that a framework based on divine wisdom and mercy will provide precisely that.

Formal equality in an unequal society can rob the weak of their rights, an apologist for shariʿa-based systems might argue, echoing Anatole France's ironic dismissal of bourgeois law "which prohibits the wealthy as well as the poor from sleeping under the bridges, from begging in the streets, and from stealing bread." That apologetic view is so broadly accepted as to be virtually unspoken among many members of Arab societies; it is generally directly deployed only in an attempt to persuade those from other societies that shariʿa-based systems are just and fair despite their insistence on distinguishing rights and duties by gender.

Second, shariʿa-based systems are based on the religion of those concerned—that is, the laws are applied to those regarded as Muslims based on their membership of a community of Muslims. Adherents of different recognized religions are generally allowed to have their personal status governed by their own religious communities, though precise arrangements vary.

In that sense, personal status law is based on a conception of religious freedom—though the freedom inheres in communities more than it applies to individuals. Of course these legal systems operate within a world structured internationally far more on conceptions of nationality and citizenship than religious community. Within a shari'a-based legal order there are often acknowledgments of that broader international context in that noncitizens are often treated in accordance with the laws of their home countries rather than their religion. Citizenship laws (absent from shari'a-based legal traditions) also intersect with personal status laws to make the latter operate quite differently (a noncitizen wife might lose access to rights that she would get if she were a citizen).

Third, membership in a religious community is not completely voluntary. An individual born to a Muslim father is presumed Muslim; no profession of faith or affirmative decision to accept the religion is necessary. Membership in a nonrecognized religious community is just that—not recognized. In such cases, it is often the case that the law of the state—a codified version of Islamic legal norms—is the law applied by default. (A codified version of Islamic law is often the law of the state with exceptions allowed for specified communities—if a community is not specified as one having its own legal mechanisms, then the shari'a-based state system applies.) A renunciation of the Islamic faith is possible, of course, and such an act of apostasy might often carry no official penalty. But the rejection of apostasy is so deeply embedded that it is virtually impossible to implement it in any legal manner—officials might refuse to register it and courts might not recognize an individual's embrace of a non-Muslim religious community.

These aspects of shari'a-based legal systems may render them distinct; they also provoke frequent discomfort and even harsh opprobrium from external observers as well as occasional outrage-generating international news coverage. But those who seek changes in personal status law or other areas related to gender and family life rarely challenge the ideas underlying them. There are some aspects of prevailing social practice—female genital mutilation in some societies, honor killings in others—that they will challenge precisely because their basis in shari'a-based norms are so weak. But by doing so, they are implicitly affirming the appropriateness of the shari'a-based system.

But if the underlying conceptions are uncontested, virtually all aspects of their application can be. There is vigorous argument indeed—among specialists, individual activists and intellectuals, and political movements—and while many positions and gradations are possible, debates can sometimes become highly polarized. The question of how to deploy state authority in support of appropriate family relations is a staple of political debates in the Arab world, also a place where positions can be easily translated into policy prescriptions and legislative texts. Those texts are drawn up inside various parts of the state apparatus—parliaments, ministries, legal bureaucracies, official religious structures. Once set into legislative form, state structures—judges, prosecutors, police—are expected to enforce them. Even in systems that are highly authoritarian, those structures possess a degree, however circumscribed, of professionalism and autonomy. This creates spheres of specialist debate, in which lawyers, judges, and religious officials discuss among themselves.

There are important participants outside of the state—social movements, political parties, women's groups, human rights organizations, intellectuals—who advance their understandings of the proper content of legislation. Those debates still tend to be restricted in nature. In my private conversations in the Arab world (especially but not exclusively in Egypt), those who speak of their own family relations generally accept the law as it is written as a given. They may complain about other family members and their manipulation of the law, about slow and uncertain legal procedures, about the attitude or behavior of judges or lawyers, but I rarely hear calls for a change in legislation that arise in such private conversations about personal experience. Those who take part in debates are motivated by principles—principles informed very much by practice but not necessarily by personal experience. The husbands, wives, and others who resort to judges to have personal status law enforced generally have not formed well-organized mass constituencies for specific kinds of changes. When it comes to personal status, everybody talks about it, but only officials, specialists, and activists work to change it.

Precisely because such actors are involved—entrenched officials, scholars, social movements, and prominent activists—but security concerns and entrenched economic interests are less in play, debates about personal status are less constrained by authoritarian politics. Even official actors seeking changes find that they are operating in a crowded field, with their moves provoking strong reactions from actors able to articulate their views.

The phenomenon we have noted thus far—that arguments cross from one sphere to another with increasing ease but that authority finds the barriers among them less permeable—applies with special force when it comes to personal status law. Specialists in the Islamic shari'a—scholars and officials—tend to argue in terms that are very much rooted in the conventions and terms of shari'a-based inquiry. The range of opinions is wide and the variety of arguments that participants in those debates use are likely very greatly expanded from those of their counterparts a century ago. Yet even when greatly expanding the interpretive and argumentative tools available to them, and even when arguing for what appear to be fairly innovative approaches to personal status questions (such as greatly enhancing divorce rights), specialists unsurprisingly feel bound to the terminology and conceptual categories of the shari'a. But by introducing fairly general concepts (*maslaha; maqasid al-shari'a*) and a wide range of arguments in their discussions with each other—and by airing some of those discussions in newspaper columns, television talk shows, and books for the general public—they make them available to a range of actors. Intellectuals, activists, and officials all can use expert views in ways that strike the specialist as opportunistic, amateurish, and clumsy. But specialist arguments, sometimes stripped down to aphorisms, remain effective tools for non-specialists to cast their arguments in recognizably shari'a-based terms. A debate, for instance, on child support or divorce rights, can be framed not simply in terms of individual rights and equality, but in terms of the Islamic way of doing things. And those are debates for which specialists forge tools that they are no longer alone in wielding.

Another boundary is also porous: participants in debates on family law can cross the divide between official and unofficial status. Two particularly significant ways involve powerful participants in debates about personal status. First, Islamist movements are certainly unofficial and even oppositional with only occasional bouts of participation in cabinets in a few scattered Arab countries. And yet they often draw from the official religious establishment (with preachers and professors in state-operated institutions often among their ranks) and have a disproportionate share of supporters among students and faculty in some state-run schools and universities. (In conversations in various countries, I have found a range of views among religious officials and scholars about Islamist movements, with many viewing them as amateurish and ambitious political organizations and others regarding them with far more sympathy). The result is that what are seen to be fairly conservative positions on personal status law are often developed in spheres that are fully public (with seminars, conferences, books, and newspaper columns being key locations for discussion) but generally restricted (partly by self-selection to be sure) to those who, regardless of their official position or lack thereof, see themselves as defenders of a shari'a-based order.

Similarly, supporters of more generous interpretations for women are often sprinkled throughout the intelligentsia, high officialdom, and prominent political activists. Like the guardians of the Islamic shari'a, such individuals can develop their arguments through a variety of spheres, with conferences, newspapers, and talk shows among the most publicly visible.

Can participants in the various debates—liberals, Islamists, and others—argue and reason with each other in public about private matters? Can they find ways to agree that affect legislation and public policy?[13] Based on the Arab experience, we can say: yes, but they rarely do. They talk among themselves, even when they appear to be talking to each other. But there are important exceptions: they can (though rarely do) talk with each other through state actors.

In debating family law in the Arab world, two contrasting bodies of norms are invoked: international human rights norms that are anchored in a host of international instruments (such as the Convention on the Elimination of All Forms of Discrimination against Women) and those that are anchored in the constructs and norms of the Islamic shari'a. Different parties—civil society organizations, political and social movements, independent activists, rulers, social and political leaders, state officials, and members of the state-supported religious establishment—have been involved at various times in these debates. And those debates occur not only in the press but also in the parliament, responsible for legislation on such issues. Indeed, to some extent they cross national boundaries; because of the tremendous international interest in women's rights in the Arab world, the issues are debated among states, in international forums, and even in an internationalized civil society for such issues.

Our interest in this chapter is both on the legislative outcomes in such cases and the nature of the debate. Do defenders of shari'a-based norms cast their arguments in terms of international human rights standards or constitutional norms and rights that do not derive from religious origins? Do advocates mix and match arguments, seek to use or engage norms from their adversary's camp, attempt to craft political alliances that cross ideological divisions, or use arguments primarily to mobilize their own followers? How do those within the state (parliamentarians, members of the official religious establishment, or senior state officials) navigate these ideological waters—when do they craft intermediate positions, use norms selectively or instrumentally, avoid participation, attempt to build bridges, or stay within the confines of their own spheres?

In order to answer these questions, we will focus on three controversies regarding family law in the Arab world[14]—in Jordan over *khul'* divorce (a controversial legal device by which a wife obtains divorce in return for a financial payment, often amounting to the original *mahr* she received; other payments, such as the wedding expenses and even *nafaqa* or support can be included as well); in Egypt over personal status changes that awarded women more divorce rights (including khul'); and (much more briefly) in Morocco over a similar series of reforms to the personal status law.

We find that activist groups rarely talk to each other in public, and when they do they generally quite intentionally talk not only to but past each other; the primary purpose seems to be mobilizing support within their own camps. As such, they seldom reach ideological consensus or bridge divides between camps. The groups do reach out, but not to their ideological adversaries but instead to real and potential friends. Those inclined toward Islamists and those favoring women's rights groups each seek separately to form alliances with specialists (intellectuals, scholars, judges), the media, parliamentarians, government officials, and members of the royal family in order to influence decision-making processes and outcomes. It is not surprising to find that high officials play a defining role in such debates. Religious officials can play an especially prominent role. Because debates are often framed using the Islamic shari'a as a reference point, religious authorities attached to the state are not merely an audience or target, they can emerge as significant actors in their own right.

Advocates of women's rights can sometimes make strong arguments for their desired outcomes based on elements within the Islamic legal tradition and indeed sometimes search for interpretations and practices in that tradition that support their claims. Similarly, Islamists and Islamic legal scholars can sometimes argue for shari'a-based practices in terms compatible with international human rights instruments. But there are areas, especially regarding family law, where the tension between the two sources for norms seems more pronounced. Bridging arguments between the two normative orientations can still be made—but sometimes they are rejected as sophistry, insincere, or misleading.

In recent decades, there have been a series of efforts by Islamists and non-Islamists to reach across their ideological divide and explore commonalities. But as Michaelle L. Browers notes after studying such efforts:

> Rather than ideological convergence or end, what these examples of cross-ideological alliances and the discussions at the National-Islamic Conferences over the past decade represent is a significant attempt at rapprochement and accommodation, one that reveals both the increasing impact of liberal discourse on a wide variety of groupings, and the persistence of various illiberal oppositional frames that both enable cross-ideological collaboration and limit the formation of a more progressive political opposition.[15]

The two camps talk in a variety of settings but while some fairly limited, perhaps even shallow, understandings have been possible, they have been shorn of practical effect by their limited nature, the narrow circles involved, their restriction to the intellectual realm, and the fact that most of those involved hail from opposition movements. There have been a few limited efforts at electoral and programmatic collaboration among opposition parties of various stripes,[16] but they have realized limited success and in the wake of the Arab uprisings of 2011, the gulf between the camps has surely become much larger.

However, there have been instances in which the debates left conference halls and seminar rooms and entered parliaments—where various contesting ideological positions had to grapple not merely with conceptual arguments or electoral slogans but actually tried to affect the course of legislation. It is to three such instances that we now turn.

Jordan

In October 2014, I was in the living room of Muhammad Abu Faris, a leader of the Muslim Brotherhood in order to speak with him about his position on personal status law in Jordan. Abu Faris had been a member of parliament and continued to serve as a professor of the Islamic shari'a specializing in personal status law. He was thus an ideal person to speak about debates on the subject. But he was also a firebrand (a leader of the "hawks" within the Jordanian Muslim Brotherhood) who had spent time in prison after visiting the funeral tent set up for Abu Musab al-Zarqawi. Earlier, he had described the Jordanian state as "kafir" (non-believer) for its failure to govern in accordance with the Islamic shari'a. Abu Faris was formal and hospitable in his manner but spent some of the conversation harshly denouncing the United States and implicitly holding it responsible for the violence perpetrated by the Islamic State in Iraq and the Levant then dominating the headlines. This did not come as a surprise. I had expected him to combine personal agreeableness with political stridency as experienced by Rana Husseini shortly after the Jordanian parliament balked on khul' divorce:

> Some one hundred protesters, including myself, demonstrated a week later in front of Parliament. We carried banners and handed out pamphlets and intercepted deputies' cars. Whenever I managed to stop one, I told the MP to remember their female relatives when they voted on both articles in the future. Most drove on quickly, leaving their windows firmly rolled up.
>
> MPs Mohammad Abu Fares and Mahmoud Kharabsheh stopped to talk to us. They reassured us they would always work to see the Khulue law rejected because it contradicted the "Islamic Sharia and women will destroy the family if divorce was in their hands."
>
> When I told Deputy Abu Fares that Egypt's Grand Mufti from al-Azhar had approved Khuloe in Egypt as part of Sharia since March 2000, his answer was: "Al-Azhar's Mufti is an agent for the Egyptian government."[17]

Indeed, when I met him at his house, Abu Faris was personally agreeable, answering all my questions directly, but also quite strident in many of his opinions.

But when it came to recent changes in Jordan's personal status law, ones that allowed something quite close to khul', he surprised me by indicating his acceptance of the legal validity of the recent Jordanian legal changes and failed to cite any shari'a-based objection to it. I left the house laden with his writings on personal status law; one book explicating reformed Jordanian law mixed Qur'anic quotations with very detailed provisions on marriage and divorce.[18] The treatment of the law was respectful, even when it came to its liberalized provisions for divorce rights for women—provisions that had the sometimes-ambivalent support of activists who had been stopping MP cars a decade earlier. Abu al-Faris clearly accepted the law and, while he expressed reservations about some of its provisions, set himself the primary task of explaining the legislation's roots in Islamic jurisprudence.

What explains this unexpected convergence of views? Why did the state, an Islamist firebrand, and women's rights advocates all express general satisfaction?

In fact there was no convergence of basic outlooks; what direct argument occurred was largely confrontational in nature. Instead a slow process of negotiated change had occurred, but critical elements of the consensus-building effort, incomplete as they were, succeeded because they took place in discussions that were private and indirect, mediated by a state actor with its own ideological and institutional interests—the shari'a court judiciary.[19]

In 2001, senior officials in Jordan took up the cause of personal status law reform. The new king, Abdullah II, had succeeded his father two years earlier and embraced liberal socio-economic policies directing the country into what was intended to be a more progressive and modern path, in response to domestic, regional, and international pressures and stimuli. Economic reforms included measures such as privatization and combating public bureaucracy, while social reforms aimed at breaking taboos and upgrading Jordan's modern image, specifically at the international level. In 2001, the king dissolved the parliament and waited for two years before calling new elections. In the interregnum, legislative authority for emergency matters passed to the cabinet—a constitutional provision that the Jordanian regime used regularly to push through legislative changes when the parliament was likely to balk. Any decrees with the force of law issued by the cabinet would remain in effect until and unless a later elected parliament rejected them.

Thus, in 2001, a former prime minister, Ahmad Obaydat, acting on a royal initiative to reform the judiciary (including the shari'a courts), asked the Qadi al-Quda to prepare modifications to the personal status law. (The "Qadi al-Quda" refers simultaneously to the chief justice of the shari'a courts, the shari'a court of appeals, and the administrative body overseeing those courts; the request was essentially for the chief justice to have his office develop proposals.)

The suggestion was to find ways to reform the existing law to enhance women's rights as related to marriage, divorce, and visitation. Such modifications were favorably viewed at that time by senior Jordanian officials as part of an all-inclusive process of judicial reform and changes in gender relations that targeted the shari'a-based legal system dominating in matters of personal status.[20] One specific proposal was to allow a woman a khul' divorce, a provision that had just been adopted in Egypt.

The khul' modification sparked immediate controversy. Since it was issued by decree as an emergency measure in the absence of parliament, the Jordanian constitution required that it be submitted to the parliament when that body met. When the parliament was finally elected in 2003, the issue had achieved public prominence. Some regime loyalists, liberals, and women's rights activists vocally supported the reform. Islamists and their allies among more conservative forces opposed the changes. The latter camp did not reject all modifications but was critical of the khul' law. A possibility for dialogue between the two camps was not realized (unless the attempt to stop MPs' cars is considered a form of deliberation). The palace had pushed for the reforms when they were initiated but was curiously diffident when they were publicly debated, perhaps because of the intense controversy at a time when it was hard pressed by security and foreign policy issues (the US-led invasion of Iraq, the Palestinian uprising).

Thus the debate passed into the public realm with supporters and opponents mobilizing their camps.

Islamists were not satisfied with the khul' modifications. The involvement of religious authorities (including the Qadi al-Quda) in developing the reforms did not immunize the changes from attack but may have softened the reaction—the law was promoted within a shari'a-based framework by its architects. But the reforms still irritated and provoked the conservative and tribal actors in the government, the parliament, the media, and Islamist forces, especially the Muslim Brotherhood-inspired Islamic Action Front, which publically took up the issue when the party participated in the parliament elected in 2003.

In this controversy, critics of the law did not claim it was an absolute violation of the Islamic shari'a, but they criticized its provisions and effects as inconsistent with a religious and shari'a-inspired social order. They managed to discredit the term "khul'" so effectively that later changes in the personal status law (in 2010, to be discussed below) used the term *iftida'* instead.

When the debate moved so forcefully into the public and parliament, the opponents of the reforms found that they were operating on favorable terrain—they had conservative, tribal, and Islamist deputies (seven from the IAF alone) in their camp, and they could block parliamentary action. Ultimately parliamentary leaders close to the palace managed to bottle the matter up. The law was rejected by the lower house, but the upper house simply failed to act. Such a tactic made it impossible for the parliament to reject the law and thus left it on the books but the maneuvre of silence by the parliament left the measure very suspect in the eyes of many it was supposed to govern.

At that point, the Qadi al-Quda quietly took up the matter on its own and worked on a new draft. This time it was not content with modifications to the existing law of personal status (dating back to 1976) but instead wished to draft an entirely new law. The work began in earnest in 2007, but it was accomplished outside of parliament and actually issued by decree at a time in 2010 when parliament had been dissolved. (It was submitted to the parliament after the body was reconvened; the parliament looked favorably upon the decree-law as a whole but dragged its heels on full approval while it considered some possible modifications).

Yet while at first glance the pattern of legal change from above seems a familiar one, in fact, this initiative was dramatically different from the previous one in several respects. First, it was initiated not by activists, the royal court, or high officials in the regime but instead by the Qadi al-Quda itself. Second, there was virtually no public controversy surrounding the law—while it provoked plenty of discussion, that discussion took place between the Qadi al-Quda and various interested groups, mostly in private sessions in which leading judges worked to satisfy various constituencies that the legal change was in their interest. Third, the change was not one that pitted advocates of international standards against those who grounded themselves in the Islamic shari'a—instead, it was presented as consistent with both. There was one common element between the 2010 law and the earlier khul' controversy, however—there was little direct dialogue between the two camps. There was talk aplenty, but it tended to occur between the camps and the Qadi al-Quda; the rivals rarely dealt directly with each other.

In general, the Qadi al-Quda seemed to select the most liberal interpretation that would be recognized as legitimate to most shari'a-minded scholars and activists. Formal adoption of khul' was avoided; instead, wives were given more leeway in showing the sort of harm that would allow them to ask a court to grant a divorce (one that would not have them surrender their material claims and in that sense might even be more favorable than khul').

Most remarkably, perhaps, was the way that a judicial body worked to consult with all interested groups, including religious scholars, judges, women's rights activists, some associated with the Muslim Brotherhood, and even a salafi scholar. While many private dialogues were held, they tended to be between like-minded participants. Very rarely did women's rights activists enter into direct dialogue with Islamists.[21] The effect was to allow the Qadi al-Quda to spin the proposed reforms to opposing camps in such a way that all walked away feeling they had won.

Overall, the Qadi al-Quda played a dual role: it served as a mediator but also as the final decision maker in matters of religion and flexibility. Islamists were satisfied as were allied conservative forces. Women's rights activists expressed some satisfaction. Each side continued to apply pressure for more changes, suspicious of the intentions of the other. Yet the overall effect was to persuade even women's rights activists to shift their focus: they still pressured the parliament, but as a result of the changes, they began to treat the Qadi al-Quda as the real authority on religious issues affecting women's rights.

The struggle over rights and personal status law in Jordan might have taken one of two forms. First, very sharply contrasting conceptions of the source of rights—whether they are rooted in divine instructions according to Islamic texts and interpretative traditions or in a set of universal values as codified in a transnational, largely liberal discourse—might result in a political battle among rival camps. Second, a possible common set of understandings—perhaps a mere modus vivendi, but also more ambitiously a Rawlsian "overlapping consensus" or perhaps even a syncretic liberal-Islamic tradition—might emerge through dialogue, political practice, and philosophical exploration.

The experience of Jordan over the past fifteen years suggests that the first path might be the norm but there are unexpected possibilities for the second path. The first path was the most likely outcome when the two camps dealt directly with each other. When direct discussions between the two camps took place, it was rarely productive and indeed, participants seemed primarily to be speaking to their own supporters and potential allies even while addressing the other side. While each camp did dip into vocabulary and argumentation developed by the other camp, it turned out that this was done more for rhetorical effect (to suggest that the other camp was hypocritical or did not faithfully apply its own principles); the effect was not to persuade but to argue. There is little evidence that either camp modified its position as a result of incorporation of the arguments or views of the other side.

Yet some common understandings were possible when state actors got involved. Those actors were not the ones that might initially have been expected. In an authoritarian monarchy, one might look to the monarch and its agents and supporters to impose a common understanding, excluding other views from public discussion. But in Jordan, the role of the regime and the royal family has not been what one might expect in an authoritarian system—they do intervene but their intervention generally sets off controversy rather than resolves it; their initiatives did not bridge gaps but accentuated them.

A second potential actor would be the parliament—a body that, after all, is the subject of much interest on those who look for a Habermasian public sphere. Jordan has a parliament that was very much involved in the arguments over the issues covered in this paper—but again, it hardly resolved these debates or provided a bridge for common understandings to emerge through deliberation among the camps. Instead its very public nature ensured that it would only be the locus for grandstanding, digging entrenched positions, and makeshift solutions.

The Qadi al-Quda, by contrast, was able to bridge gaps not by getting the two sides to reason with each other but by opportunistically talking to each side individually. Not only did both sides get a deal they could live with but the Qadi al-Quda emerged as a powerful institutional actor. Through deliberating separately with the two camps, the Qadi al-Quda proved capable of defining and pursuing its own interests even while it persuaded others that it was protecting theirs.

Egypt

A very similar set of stories could be told in Egypt (and indeed, Egypt provided a model for the Jordanian attempt to liberalize divorce law). But the actors were a bit different and the full flowering of politics in the two years after the 2011 uprising actually made policy change more difficult rather than less.

In the 1970s, the difficulties existing personal status law (codified since the 1920s) posed for women emerged as a topic for discussion among the intelligentsia; a controversial popular film (*Uridu Hallan*) portraying a woman stuck in a marriage with a philandering husband generated considerable attention for the issue. A move to make changes to the law gained the support of Jihan al-Sadat, the wife of President Anwar al-Sadat. Her identification with the cause was such that the decree-law issued by the president to increase women's divorce rights was generally referred to as "Jihan's law." It increased women's custody rights and gave wives a far stronger claim for a court-ordered divorce if their husbands married a second wife. The law was issued at a time when a growing religious trend in Egyptian society led to far greater attention to the "application of the shari'a" and it was in this period that a president-appointed committee drafted a civil code that was based on its interpretation of the Islamic shari'a (the project was later shelved) and the constitution was amended to make the principles of the Islamic shari'a *the* (rather than *a*) chief source of legislation.

While the matter generated some debate, the politics surrounding the legislative change was anemic by later standards. The president issued the decree-law in the absence of parliament precisely in order to avoid debate. And the changes were ones that attracted criticism from conservative and Islamist forces, but were not generally the focus of their attention. The most effective opposition to the law came from within the state apparatus itself—in 1985 the Supreme Constitutional Court (SCC) rejected the law on very bold grounds, but not ones connected with the debate over the personal status law. Instead it ruled that the president had used his decree power unconstitutionally since his authority applied only to matters that could not admit delay, and this was not such an emergency.

The parliament proved reluctant to deal with the issue—it was coming under pressure to be more faithful to Islamic jurisprudence from an opposition group of Islamist parliamentarians and many social and religious regime supporters. Thus the matter lay dormant for a decade while top officials displayed a reluctance to allow debates about Islamic law have much impact on legislation or policy. But in the late 1990s a new, politically savvier coalition had emerged out of a community of activists that had formed after the 1985 SCC decision; they had used the years to work quietly on a new model marriage contract designed to allow prospective brides and grooms to insert some new provisions; they also turned their attention toward developing a number of changes in existing legislation. But this time they reached out to supportive officials, lawyers, and religious scholars, essentially enrolling important parts of the state as well as intellectuals in their efforts.[22] They received strong support again from the president's wife and a top legal official close to her,

Fathi Nagib. In 2000, they won not only endorsement of the new contract but also many of the legislative changes they sought, including khul' divorce. The success of that effort was heavily dependent on an engagement with leading religious scholars. Many important scholars within the official religious establishment were suspicious of the changes, but key members were not—and contrary to Abu Faris's claim to Rana Husseini in front of the Jordanian parliament, it was not merely those scholars associated with the regime who endorsed khul'. Important oppositional figures (some of whom retained official positions) were brought on board.[23] And shortly after the legislative change was made, Fathi Nagib was appointed chief justice of the SCC, which upheld the law when it was challenged.

The coalition that pursued the law, therefore, thoroughly crossed any state-society division. As with the Jordanian legal change, indeed, it was state officials supportive of the effort who took on much of the task of drafting, strategizing, and consulting religious officials. The involvement of intellectuals, activists, and then parliament ensured that the parts of the process were carried out in full public view and the later stages in particular took on something of the nature of a campaign, with efforts to put the issue in full public view and generate broad support. As in Jordan, there was no true meeting of the minds among liberals, feminists, high state officials, and religious scholars, but the direct contact among them was probably more sustained and serious.

Yet for all its publicity and ability to engage diverse groups, the coalition encountered a bit less success in practice than it may have achieved on paper. For all the public debate and the successful efforts at legislative change, when it came to litigants acting on the basis of law, attorneys appealing to it, and judges ruling in accordance with its provisions, one early study found that the results were slow and meager. Since many marital disputes involve the threat of action (and thus the change could have impact without having many court judgments actually issued), and the study reflects the situation only a few years after the amendments were made, the assessment may be premature.[24] But indeed, these findings and the qualifications only serve to underscore the degree to which public arguments about Islam and private practice, even when they concern the same subject, can seem a bit disconnected.

The critical role of a coherent group of state-based actors in turning debate into policy and legal change was illustrated in the years after the Egyptian uprising of 2011. Immediately after the uprising and for the next three years, I interviewed a varied group of imams of Cairo mosques, mostly official though occasionally I met with those who gave sermons on an unofficial basis (a practice greatly curtailed after the overthrow of Muhammad Morsi in 2013). While their political and religious orientations varied considerably, all evinced a mixture of excitement, concern, and disorientation at an environment in which those attending expected political topics to be addressed. Imams now had to find words in a society in which mosques proved a major public gathering point (though one skewed, naturally, to the pious end of the spectrum) but also to speak in the midst of a sudden reversal from a situation in which officials discouraged political talk to one in which the assembled demanded it. This was a need easy to fill when the public spoke with one voice, but as that unity dissolved in bitter acrimony in the months and years following the January 2011 uprising, mosques became literal battlegrounds and physical contests for pulpits were not unknown. In 2013, a post-Morsi leadership sought to purge oppositional preachers and by 2015 the Ministry of Religious Affairs went beyond policing oppositional speech to attempting to enforce loyalist sermons.

While Islamist political actors were prominent in the period between the January 2011 overthrow of Husni Mubarak and the July 2013 overthrow of his successor, Muhammad Morsi (winning both parliamentary and presidential elections), and while that prominence greatly increased the attention to personal status law in public debate, the major effect was to increase the heated nature of discussion without shedding light on new possibilities. In 2012, as a new parliament was elected, a salafi deputy denounced the marriage age decreed in the personal status law suggesting that the Islamic shari'a allowed for girls to marry at a much younger age. The Brotherhood—which largely controlled the short-lived 2012 parliament, ignored the suggestion and from a procedural parliamentary perspective no motion was introduced, no further discussion occurred, and of course no votes were taken and no legislative changes made. The matter died with the deputy's provocative remark. But it lived on in public debate as it soon became accepted among the Brotherhood's non-Islamist opponents that there was a move afoot to lower the marriage age to nine years old. This was an odd debate: it concerned a legislative proposal that was on no agenda and it was an argument generally only on one side, most Islamists having little interest in pressing the matter.[25] Debate even about law was disconnected from the legislative process; this was a public political debate held without reference to policy and legislative procedures.

That feature of Egyptian personal status debates continued over the next couple years in large part because the coherence of the state apparatus disintegrated.[26] The leadership of al-Azhar, the presidency, other parts of the official religious establishment, and various other state bodies each pursued their own approach to issues of family law without any substantive changes being placed on the legislative agenda. And the family debate among state institutions was played out in full public view. In one particularly dramatic moment, the internecine squabble took the international stage. In March 2013, the UN Commission on the Status of Women concluded its meeting by issuing a lengthy set of recommendations that would likely have gone unnoticed in much of the world had Egypt's Muslim Brotherhood not decided to issue a harsh denunciation of the Commission's document. It is not clear why the movement decided to speak so forcefully, though it may have had something to do with the fact that the head of the Egyptian National Council of Women—a state body—was invited to address the same meeting and used that opportunity to denounce the country's constitutional process in a manner utterly at odds with the soothing message of the Egyptian president's own representative at the same meeting. The Brotherhood's attack on the document, while unofficial, led the Shaykh of al-Azhar to step in, concerned that the Brotherhood's harshness would be taken as the Egyptian position. Accordingly, he asked al-Azhar's Body of Senior Scholars to take up the matter, and that body eventually developed a statement that was far less confrontational in tone.

What was remarkable about most of these battles was not merely their intensity but also their remove from any legal or policy change. There were only occasional exceptions in which legal change was at issue during this period, and they tended to involve less passionate issues, far removed from family law. The Brotherhood-dominated upper house of parliament did attempt to write a law governing *sukuk*, the functional equivalent of a bond in shari'a-compliant finance. The Brotherhood-dominated leadership wished to enable the Egyptian state to use the device, convinced it would help alleviate intense fiscal pressures. But the Islamists found that their own judgment on what was appropriate in Islamic legal terms was not automatically accepted. When the matter was taken up by a parliamentary committee, al-Azhar was invited to submit its views but considered that kind of participation beneath the institution's dignity. Instead it insisted that the law should be formally submitted to its "Body of Senior Scholars" specified in Article 4 of the country's short-lived 2012 constitution so that it could conduct a review on its own. Impatient and worried that this would drag things out, the Freedom and Justice Party bloc rushed ahead with the sukuk law, leading to howls of protests from some salafi deputies, embittered al-Azhar officials, and elements of the opposition who claimed that the failure to consult al-Azhar violated the constitution.

Oddly, the overthrow of the Muslim Brotherhood and the wave of repression in Egyptian political life did not restore full coherence to the state apparatus on such matters. In 2014, Mazhar Shahin, the state appointed imam of the ʿUmar Makram mosque in Tahrir Square (see chapter 3), publicly advised spouses of members of the Muslim Brotherhood to seek divorce; more senior scholars in the religious hierarchy, while equally hostile to the Brotherhood, made clear their professional discomfort by quickly if laconically responding that the advice was at variance with Islamic law, which did not include Brotherhood membership as among the justifications for dissolving a marriage.

Morocco

As in Jordan and Egypt, Morocco also changed its personal status law in a manner that enhanced the rights of wives as part of a contentious and protracted process in which critical state actors pushed through reform by navigating a polarized environment and placating or coopting some of the opposition. The

Moroccan case was distinct in three ways, however. First, the religious apparatus of the state was initially badly divided. Second, while public demonstrations were not unknown in Egypt and Jordan, Morocco saw mass marches—a kind of public politics that is mobilizational, designed to rally supporters around a position and impress those who do not share it rather than to persuade or argue in any critical fashion. Third, the parliament was far more of a scene of action, though it was hardly the most critical one.

Morocco's law of personal status was written at the time the country gained independence from France; it was far from egalitarian in some matters but did allow for women to receive some divorce rights. Toward the end of the twentieth century, reform of the law in order to widen women's rights became a topic for intellectual conversation, one that, as in Egypt and Jordan, anchored itself in part in international instruments regarding human rights. As Buskens notes, "It became the new intellectual fashion to discuss claims for family law reform as a struggle for human rights, which could be explained by referring to international conventions. 'Human rights' became one of the key notions in the modernist discourse that seeks to criticize the current social and political situation in Morocco."[27] But while the debate was fairly wide-ranging, legal changes were limited, since they were kept under the watchful eyes of the king and religious officials. But when a new king took the throne in 1999, he publicly committed himself to advancing women's rights, and over the next few years, the issue of personal status law became increasingly prominent. Advocates of reform organized marches, and Islamist movements—then increasingly able to mobilize their supporters—organized counter-demonstrations.

While the tactics and some of the language were increasingly confrontational, the positions of the supporters and opponents of the reforms were not diametrically opposed. Advocates of reform wished to increase women's rights and anchored their advocacy in international standards. Opponents tended to claim that they objected not to change by itself, but instead insisted that it be accomplished with greater respect for shari'a-based understandings and criticized the reliance on external standards as bowing to external imposition rather than Islamic standards. Writing at the time of the struggle, Buskens noted: "Nongovernmental organizations (NGOs) for women's and human rights, Islamist movements, and political parties are all engaged in a national debate in which every faction fiercely defends its right to speak in public about its proper understanding of Islamic law."[28] But just as remarkable as the participatory nature of the debate was the way in which state officials and bodies joined in: the king seemed to tilt the playing field in favor of reform but not in a way that conveyed a stance above the fray that most political actors were willing to accept; and senior religious officials expressed strong concerns about the tenor and content of the proposed reforms.

The confrontational public debate took place during a time of increasing political liberalization in Morocco with far freer parliamentary elections held in 2002 that gave the Islamists a stronger perch to raise their objections to the issue. A public commission prepared change for the new parliament to consider; it came under pressure from the various parties. However, in May 2003 a series of bombings created a crisis atmosphere in the country with the Islamists suddenly on the defensive in public debates. During that period, according to Rania Maktabi, a royal thumb in the scales combined with the bombings swung the debate in the favor of reform advocates:

> The king, however, showed his support by attending two working sessions in November 2001 and March 2002. Eventually, the "Casablanca bombings" in May 2003 tipped the scale in favor of reform. The women's movement intensified its pressure, while Moroccans—numbering up to a million—marched under anti-terrorism slogans. Barely six months later, on January 16, 2004, parliament approved a new mudawwana, after an extensive debate where 110 amendments were made to the 400 proposed articles before the assembly unanimously approved it.[29]

The Islamists, of course, denied any retreat. They claimed that what had changed was the process, not their position: the commission had carefully consulted with Islamic legal scholars.

In the most extensive and sophisticated examination of the debate, Dörthe Engelecke has noted that there were various positions within the camps so that the image of total polarization is likely overdrawn (and it might be added that the same could be said for Jordan and Egypt).[30] It still took place in an authoritarian context in which the king ruled even when he appeared to be merely reining.

But there was still a sense in which the public spheres in Morocco had a clear political effect: reform in personal status law was a cause that grew up in an emerging public sphere in the era of limited liberalization; at the turn of the twentieth century, opposition to reform arose that seemed at first to outmaneuver the advocates, with the force of the arguments second to the numbers they could mobilize; the role of the king and of the security atmosphere surrounding the bombings forced opponents into a stance more amenable to negotiation; and in the end, an agreement was reached—one backed perhaps by the monarchy and the threat of a crackdown on Islamists, and therefore a rare instance which married semiauthoritarianism with deliberative politics and haggling to produce a clear policy change.[31]

CONCLUSION

In the three realms we have examined—fatwas, court judgments, and legislation—we can see a lot of argument. Many of the issues are the same, and the arguments made in support of various positions can be similar. Some of the authorities involved in various realms (judges, muftis, parliamentarians, intellectuals) are pushed or pulled into public debates with each other, though they rarely are able to bring the authority of their home base with them when they do so. And sometimes the same issue or question is debated—when a prominent court case sets some off in search of fatwas or generates a parliamentary debate, for instance.

But there is much less overlap among these realms than might be expected. A troubled spouse might seek a fatwa or a court judgment, and occasionally he or she may seek both, but rarely is such a spouse able to use the fatwa in court and, of course, a court judgment would not likely persuade a mufti.

Most striking, however, is the way in which these two realms so poorly intersect with the third: one might expect all the fatwa and judgment seeking to lead to concerned, disappointed, aggrieved, or offended citizens mobilizing for a particular legislative change. But when laws do change—and they do—popular mobilization is certainly not a sufficient condition nor is it even necessary. Private litigants and fatwa seekers do not form a public; the judges and muftis who answer them do sometimes take part in public debates, but their voices are not always heard. When mobilization does take place—and it sometimes does—it tends to be restricted to middle- and upper-class citizens who advocate for but do not seem accountable to those whom they claim to represent.

Indeed, the necessary actor for legislative or policy change is the state itself—or rather, a part of the state. Because of how highly fraught personal status issues are, because they are ones which all members of the society can understand personally as applying to their own lives, even a powerful state actor often needs to show a spirit of political entrepreneurship in order to assemble a coalition to secure a desired change. In doing so, such actors often reach outside of the state for support, not so much to build a deeply unified constituency as much as to pick up tactical supporters or pick off potential opponents one-on-one.

In these ways, the private debates are disconnected from the public ones; the use of public authority to decide private cases does not generate a strong sense of a public. And while arguments do cross from one realm to the next, they tend to get reduced and homogenized in the process, turned into slogans that are not used to persuade opponents but to motivate the committed to act.

Parliaments—the talking and legislative bodies—serve in such instances as a rubber stamp, though not in the way the term is often used for them in the Arab world. When it comes to security matters, most parliaments do indeed do what the head of state or security apparatus say is necessary.

But when it comes to matters of personal status, parliaments tend to ratify matters that are carefully (and sometimes privately) negotiated among disparate forces elsewhere.

More strikingly, the struggles over policy and law do not draw very heavily on the experience or energy of those who seek fatwas or court judgments. Mass constituencies affected by a specific policy are rarely organized or mobilized. Instead, policy is the realm of state bodies, penetrated sometimes by specific elites but only rarely by fuller constituencies; the interests of citizens are brought into policy debates but citizens rarely speak for themselves unless asked to do so. Even on rare occasions when the republic of arguments is brought into policy making, various camps of citizens do not speak so much to each other (except to disagree) but instead state actors pursuing change coax each group of citizens separately. Argument leads not to principled agreement among the public but to practical proposals among policy elites. And that is when change occurs.

NOTES

1. Yasmin Moll, "Islamic Satellite Channels and the Ethics of Entertainment in Egypt" *al-Sada*, April 21, 2010, http://carnegieendowment.org/sada/2010/04/21/islamic-satellite-channels-and-ethics-of-entertainment-in-egypt/6bpg, accessed October 16, 2014.
2. Baber Johansen, "Apostasy as Objective and Depersonalized Fact: Two Recent Egyptian Court Judgments," *Social Research* 70, 3 (2003): 688.
3. I explored this in a chapter, "Popular Uses of the Courts," in *The Rule of Law in the Arab World: Courts in Egypt and the Gulf* (Cambridge: Cambridge University Press, 1997).
4. Huessein Ali Agrama, *Questioning Secularism: Islam, Sovereignty, and the Rule of Law in Modern Egypt* (Chicago: University of Chicago Press, 2012), 76–82.
5. Ibid, 117. But see chapters 3–5 of Agrama's book for a careful if complicated argument questioning the helpfulness of a simple law/coercion–fatwa/voluntary binary opposition.
6. The information and presentation in this section is based on a short portion of my earlier book, *The Rule of Law in the Arab World: Courts in Egypt and the Gulf* (Cambridge: Cambridge University Press, 1997), chapter 7.
7. On personal status law and courts in Egypt, useful background can be found in Yuksel Sezgin, *Human Rights under State-Enforced Religious Family Laws in Israel, Egypt and India* (Cambridge: Cambridge University Press, 2013), John L. Esposito, *Women in Muslim Family Law* (Syracuse: Syracuse University Press, 1982), chapter 3; and Enid Hill, *Mahkama! Studies in the Egyptian Legal System* (London: Ithaca Press, 1979), chapter 3. See also Ron Shaham, "Judicial Divorce at the Wife's Initiative," *Islamic Law and Society* 1, 2 (1994): 217.
8. Opportunities for creativeness in the use of litigation are not new. Ron Shaham has documented the workings of the law (and the ways that judges applied the law) in the shari'a courts that had jurisdiction in personal status cases until their abolition in 1955. See Shaham, "Judicial Divorce." See also Shaham, "Custom, Islamic Law, and Statutory Legislation: Marriage Registration and Minimum Age at Marriage in the Egyptian Shari'a Courts," *Islamic Law and Society* 2, 3 (1995): 258.

9. For more systematic analysis of the use of postdated checks and other devices, see Christine Hegel-Cantarella, "Kin-to-Be: Betrothal, Legal Documents, and Reconfiguring Relational Obligations in Egypt," *Law, Culture and the Humanities* 7, 3 (2011): 377–393.

10. In John Bowen's *A New Anthropology of Islam* (Cambridge: Cambridge University Press, 2012), the role of bargaining in courts is similarly noted; see in particular chapter 7.

11. Sezgin, *Human Rights*, notes that the existence of forum shopping and epistemic communities shapes the way that authorities are able to apply texts.

12. Léon Buskens, "Recent Debates on Family Law Reform in Morocco: Islamic Law as Politics in an Emerging Public Sphere," *Islamic Law and Society* 10, 1 (2003): 71.

13. I explore this question for the Jordanian case described here in greater detail in Lamis El Muhtaseb, Nathan J. Brown, and Abdul-Wahab M. Kayyali, "Arguing about Family Law in Jordan: Disconnected Spheres?" *International Journal of Middle East Studies* 48, 4 (2016). A very useful overview of a similar issue in Egypt can be found in Marwa Sharafeldin, "Islamic Law Meets Human Rights: Reformulating *Qiwamah* and *Wilayah* for Personal Status Law Reform Advocacy in Egypt," in *Men In Charge? Rethinking Authority in Muslim Legal Tradition*, Ziba Mir-Hosseini, Mulki Al-Sharmaini, and Jana Rumminger, ed. (London: Oneworld, 2015), 163–196.

14. This section on khul` in Jordan is based heavily on El Muhtaseb et al, "Arguing about Family Law."

15. Michaelle L. Browers, *Political Ideology in the Arab World: Accommodation and Transformation* (Cambridge: Cambridge University Press, 2009), 16.

16. Schwedler, Jillian, and Janine A. Clark. "Islamist-Leftist Cooperation in the Arab World." *ISIM Review* 18 (2006): 2.

17. Rana Husseini, *Murder in the Name of Honor: The True Story of One Woman's Fight against an Unbelievable Crime* (Oxford: One World, 2009), 78–79.

18. Muhammad `Abd al-Qadir Abu Faris, *Al-ahwal al-shakhsiyya: al-ahliyya, al-wilaya, al-wasaya, al-arath* (Amman: Dar al-Qur'an li-l-nashr wa-l-tawzi`, 2012).

19. Extremely useful, and far more detailed on this, is Dörthe Engelcke, "Processes of Family Law Reform: Legal and Societal Change and Continuity in Morocco and Jordan" (PhD diss., St Antony's College, University of Oxford, 2014).

20. Interview of Judge Wasif al-Bakri by Lamis El Muhtaseb, August 2014, Amman, Jordan. I am very grateful to her for sharing her notes from the interview with me and helping me secure my own interview with him some months later.

21. Personal interview, Judge Wasif al-Bakri, Amman, Jordan, October 2014.

22. The story is told by Diane Singerman in "Rewriting Divorce in Egypt: Reclaiming Islam, Legal Activism, and Coalition Politics" in *Remaking Muslim Politics: Pluralism, Contestation, Democratization*, ed. Robert Hefner (Princeton: Princeton University Press, 2005), 161–188. A very useful account of the debate and the way that the law was implemented is Nadia Sonneveld, *Khul` Divorce in Egypt: Public Debates, Judicial Practices, and Everyday Life* (Cairo: American University in Cairo Press, 2012).

23. See Rania Maktabi, "Female Citizenship in the Middle East: Comparing Family Law Reform in Morocco, Egypt, Syria and Lebanon," *Middle East Law and Governance* 5 (2013): 280–307. She mentions Muhammad al-Ghazzali, a

sometime MP who was associated at times with the Islamist opposition, and
Jamal Qutb, an Azhari scholar very critical of state domination of al-Azhar.

24. The author of the study specifically notes these limitations. See Nadia Sonneveld,
"The Implementation of the 'Khul` Law' in Egyptian Courts: Some Preliminary
Results," *Recht van de Islam* 21 (2004): 21–35. A fuller account is available in her
Khul` Divorce in Egypt.

25. There were exceptions. See, for instance, the response of salafi preacher Mustafa
al-`Adawi to a viewer's question in which he denounces the law fixing the
marriage age at eighteen as "forbidding male and female Muslims what God
permits them," and links the 2000 changes to the internal coalition described by
Singerman and international hands, https://www.youtube.com/watch?v=vaQ-
nOFJ-F8, accessed February 6, 2015.

26. Parts of this section are based on Zaid al-Ali and Nathan J. Brown, "Egypt's
Constitution Swings into Action," *Foreign Policy*, March 27, 2013, http://
foreignpolicy.com/2013/03/27/egypts-constitution-swings-into-action/,
accessed February 6, 2015.

27. Buskens, "Recent Debates," 78.

28. Ibid., 72.

29. Maktabi, "Female Citizenship," 293.

30. Dörthe Engelcke, "Processes of Family Law Reform".

31. For another very useful and thorough account—one that emphasizes the
mobilization of movements on the issue—see Zakiye Salame, *Between Feminism
and Islam: Human Rights and Sharia Law in Morocco* (Minneapolis: University of
Minnesota Press, 2011).

CHAPTER 8

Arguing about the Children; Arguing in Front of Them

Take two men who meet and find that some common need calls on them to remain together rather than to part company. Neither knows the language of the other. As far as communication goes, these two, both men, are worse than two dumb animals, even of different kinds. For all its identity in both, their human nature is of no social help, so long as the language barrier makes it impossible for them to tell each other what they are thinking about.

St. Augustine, *City of God* XIX, 7

WHAT HAPPENS IF EVERYBODY IS ARGUING AND NOBODY IS LISTENING?

In the previous two chapters, we saw instances in which public discussions in the republic of arguments had some effects on policy even in nondemocratic regimes. Listening was limited and rarely led to persuasion, but it did produce some compromises and coalition building in limited cases. With constitutions, the effect was mainly on expressive clauses of constitutions. In addition, various actors' affective orientations toward the political order were shaped as a result of arguments and policy outcomes. With personal status law, the effect was limited to cases in which official actors (though not necessarily anybody else) listened (for echoes of their own preferences) and fashioned coalitions.

In this chapter we will turn our attention to educational curricula, where arguments are sometimes fierce but officials show little sign of listening—and indeed, the disconnect between public argument and policy outcome actually makes arguments fiercer. Actors deprived of responsibility over outcome are more likely to argue irresponsibly.

To the extent that non-officials have any impact—and they do, though it is not large—it is enabled by their ability to operate less publicly.

Schools in Arab states have become sites where states show their abilities to centralize, monitor, and control. Children are required to go to school, and those schools work to shape them over many years through a curriculum devised by state officials, taught by state employees, and reflecting the state's values and authoritative interpretation of everything from history to trigonometry; children are tested and teachers inspected by state officials; official books are memorized and the disorderly are disciplined by teachers and others hired or licensed by the state. Education is a public concern, a matter of public policy, and a place where public authority is exercised and enforced.

But education and schools are not designed to be places for public political activity: education is still seen largely as the reserve of an authoritarian state that harks back to fully authoritarian orders that edge out politics.

Such an image is accurate and fair on one level. And that is the level at which I begin this chapter. But then in the rest of the chapter I peel pack a series of layers that tell a slightly more complicated story—one in which the public is able to argue, partly because of the revival of Arab politics and partly because the public is able to act publicly by partaking of the private.

Thus, in the first section, I examine the way in which states appear to act in an authoritarian and authoritative manner in education. In the next section I turn to public debates about what to teach the children about religion. I show those debates to be lively, though without much appreciable effect on what children are taught. In the third section, I show how the public but semi-secluded nature of the classroom allows for potentially more efficacious debates that actually involve the students. In all parts of the chapter, I draw examples primarily from those Arab societies I have studied most (Egypt and Palestine) but include other countries, such as Jordan and Morocco as well.

THE UNIVOCAL STATE

Educational systems in the Arab world are very highly centralized. With only Lebanon an exception, the bulk of the educational apparatus is either directly controlled by the state or very tightly regulated. In practice, some latitude for pockets of autonomy sometimes have come to exist for private schools in many settings, especially for those that have been able to anchor themselves in an international context or a recognized religious minority. But for the vast majority of the population, there is a unified school system with an even more unified curriculum; and that curriculum includes religion as a mandatory subject. Religious and moral lessons creep in across other parts of the curriculum as well, from composition topics and handwriting to arithmetic and history. The content of those lessons is designed in ministries of education, often with the participation or guidance of the official religious establishment. This is not merely the divine speaking through the schoolbooks but doing so through the words chosen by the state. In Arab schools it might be said that *vox principis, vox Dei.*

Arab states set these principles out in the most authoritative public form available: their constituting documents. Article 39 of the Tunisian constitution provides:

> Education shall be mandatory up to the age of sixteen years. The state guarantees the right to free public education at all levels and ensures provisions of the necessary resources to achieve a high quality of education, teaching, and training. It shall also work to consolidate the Arab-Muslim identity and national belonging in the young generations, and to strengthen, promote and generalize the use of the Arabic language and to openness to foreign languages, human civilizations and diffusion of the culture of human rights.

The 2014 Egyptian constitution elides among moral development, education, religion, and the strong state role in all levels of education. It provides (in Articles 19 and 24) that:

> Every citizen has the right to education. The goals of education are to build the Egyptian character, preserve the national identity, root the scientific method of thinking, develop talents and promote innovation, establish cultural and spiritual values, and found the concepts of citizenship, tolerance and non-discrimination. The State shall observe the goals of education in the educational curricula and methods, and provide education in accordance with international quality standards. . . .
>
> The State shall supervise education to ensure that all public and private schools and institutes abide by its educational policies. . . .
>
> Arabic Language, Religious Education and National History, in all its stages, are core subjects in public and private pre-university education. Universities shall teach human rights and professional values and ethics of the various academic disciplines.

More specialized educational documents similarly blend state and religious authority. Laurie Brand describes an authoritative 1995 document from the Egyptian Ministry of Education that "listed the following as its top objectives: deepening children's affiliation to their homeland, its history, and civilization; upholding national loyalty; affirming faith, religion, divine and social values, and respecting others' needs, rites, and holy places."[1] The Palestinian curriculum plan approved by the Palestinian Legislative Council (PLC) in 1997—and in continuous operation since—mandates "faith in God" at its center.

And having granted itself such a powerful and authoritative voice, what does the state use it to say? One group of studies of textbooks throughout the region found some common patterns in Arab educational textbooks about religion.[2] They tend to teach it in a univocal manner, not as a set of texts that believers must grapple with to discover meaning and proper conduct but instead as a set of certain moral truths to be believed and followed. Critics often charge that textbooks in the Arab world are not designed to cultivate critical thinking; certainly the overriding message when it comes to religion sometimes seems to be: "Behave!"

In the Palestinian textbooks, for instance, the sixth grade "Islamic education" text explicitly diagrams Muslim "belonging" as a series of concentric circles: individual, family, town, governorate, state, Islamic world.[3] This general message is communicated directly and consistently throughout all of the textbooks: religion, family, school, and nation are portrayed as mutual reinforcing authorities. Being a good student, son or daughter, Palestinian, Arab, and Muslim are identical. The first grade Islamic Education book displays correct practice in prayer, ablutions, donations, washing dishes, crossing in the crosswalk, and cleaning the yard of a school decorated with the Palestinian flag.[4]

More generally, religion in school is nationalized in the sense that prevailing ideologies and national identities are presented not merely as congruent but as virtually indistinguishable. Religious differences within Islam are minimized, giving a homogenized impression of the religion—at least inside national borders. A sense that Islam is under attack, misunderstood, and operating in a less-than-friendly world creeps into the official textbooks in several countries to varying degrees, from the concerned and resentful to the paranoid.

Anecdotally, those with whom I have spoken who were taught in schools in various locations in the Arab world describe a pattern that seems to replicate in the classroom what occurs at a national level: a severe teacher for religious subjects, often doubling in Arabic language instruction, who lectures and hectors religious and moral truths.

ARGUING ABOUT THE CHILDREN

Ministries of education also seem to be places constructed to allow a few specialists and officials speak with each other, insulating them from public debate. The specific institutional patterns that develop in various states of the region owe their basic contours to official attempts to manage the opposition, govern, and propagate supportive ideologies.[5] While those patterns evolve in ways that sometimes allow the opposition to have some impact, curricular content seems to remain largely (though not completely) an official preserve.

This insulation is not for lack of controversy, as shown perhaps most dramatically in the case of Palestinian textbooks. With the possible exception of Salman Rushdie's *The Satanic Verses,* perhaps no set of books have inspired more ire among those who have not read them. American presidential candidates, European parliamentarians, Israeli politicians, Islamist intellectuals, and Palestinian parents have all leveled their criticisms. Yet in periodic visits to the Palestinian Curriculum Development Center in Ramallah—and one to the Ministry of Education in Gaza—I was struck by how much of the noise seems not to faze the officials responsible for the books themselves. The debate has effects, to be sure, but the dominant attitude among Ministry of Education personnel was that the attacks were political rather than pedagogical and many could be ignored as ill informed and irrelevant to the task of educating children.

But the revival of Arab politics has led to many debates, and education has become a frequent subject of them. Those who have witnessed textbook wars in other settings would find much familiar: adults arguing over issues of identity and definitions of the nation, clashing over moral visions and political programs, aghast at the religious views of their fellow citizens, and suspicious that education authorities are insinuating inappropriate values through teaching young children. Public arguments have few points at which they can affect the policy process, which often does little to lessen their edge (and often even heightens them by removing the arguments from practical applications).

In many Arab countries, a trenchant critique of existing educational practices has developed in recent years. That critique is centered in two locations: among some educational specialists and in public intellectual circles. In both, a similar set of complaints is sometimes heard: the existing educational system is overly centralized and authoritarian, focusing on transmission of information rather than cultivation of critical thinking. Such critics charge that educational materials and approaches are authoritarian both in content and pedagogy, outmoded and incapable of preparing students either for the requirements of citizenship or the needs of the economy, and too deferential to religious authority. It is not uncommon to hear such ideas in discussions among intellectuals at conferences and in newspapers. Ministries of education and other authoritative structures are not devoid of such voices and occasionally a figure with a strong reformist reputation will take on a senior official position (such as when Ibrahim Badran served briefly as minister of education in Jordan in 2009–2010 or Khalil Mahshi served with the Palestinian Authority's Ministry of Education in the late 1990s). While sometimes popular in intellectual and specialist circles, however, these ideas often strike little resonance among broader publics.

Indeed, if they are heard, they often spark opposition. There are political forces that often find education a fruitful issue on which to appeal to their potential supporters, especially on religious and nationalist grounds. Prolonged international critique of Arab educational practices among Western policymakers have probably augmented the ability of politicians to grandstand against foreign interference on the issue of schoolbooks. Parliaments often offer a particularly effective venue for airing such critiques, sometimes buttressed by press and social media campaigns: a change in a text can be attacked as undermining religious truths or carried out at the instigation of foreign patrons.

The hostility is often returned: intellectuals and some officials who see themselves as progressive advocates of critical thinking and curricular reform often take specific aim at Islamists as their opponents and seem suspicious of existing religious education curricula as possible Trojan Horses for Islamist groups to inculcate a new generation; when they feel forced to choose between undermining political or religious authority, the second often receives priority.[6]

There would seem to be no logical contradiction between teaching critical thought on the one hand and religion on the other; religious education (at least at the advanced level) is, in many contexts, often predicated on Socratic-style questioning, consideration of multiple meanings, and weighing of alternative interpretations. Those kinds of pedagogies suffered in part because of the tremendous expansion of education in the twentieth century and the insistence of states on supervising and overseeing education in general and, as time when on, most sites where formal religious education took place.[7] Centralized states with few resources built educational systems to serve mass needs, making it difficult to replicate older, more interactive, techniques and pedagogies in many Arab societies.

So the tension between centralized official educational establishments, progressive educational ideas, and religion may be a creation of the political circumstances of Arab politics. But it is real and we can see it played out in three settings: fairly extensively in Palestine over civic, religious, and national education; in shorter analyses of arguments in Egypt over religion before, during, and after the country's brief experience with a Muslim Brotherhood presidency; and in Jordan over testing.

Palestine: God, Nation, and People (but no State)

The signing of the Oslo Accords in the mid-1990s allowed for the construction of a set of Palestinian administrative bodies—which participants saw as the infrastructure of a state—to oversee the civil affairs of Palestinians residing in the West Bank and Gaza.[8] The Palestinian National Authority (PNA), as Palestinians came to call it, assumed control over education in the 1994 school year, with schools up to that point having used Jordanian and Egyptian textbooks subject to Israeli censorship. The PNA secured international funding for an effort to write its own curriculum and formed a committee headed by a returning diaspora intellectual, Ibrahim Abu Lughod, and including a number of educators and intellectuals, in order to design a new curriculum.

That committee was operating at a time of relative political freedom—Israel had stopped policing most Palestinian political activity and the PNA's security bodies, while heavy-handed, were only beginning to learn how to manipulate and police political debates. What had been a political field largely confined to nationalist issues suddenly turned partly inwards, and very lively debates quickly erupted about a host of domestic issues.

The curriculum committee sought to establish a far more open and participatory method for designing the curriculum than had existed in the past. It jealously guarded its autonomy from the Ministry of Education and other structures of the PNA. In consulting with teachers, for instance, the committee reached directly to teachers themselves rather than going through the Ministry or school bureaucracy.[9] The committee conducted comprehensive surveys of teachers and studied the results, citing them in support of its arguments for radical reform. It also scheduled a series of meetings with teachers. ʿAli Jarbawi, an intellectual and academic who served with Abu Lughod, goes so far as to claim that most of the committee's ideas came from teachers themselves.[10] The committee sought out other audiences—students, recent graduates, and religious figures—to discuss their impressions and present initial ideas. The work—and the prospect of a Palestinian-authored curriculum—generated considerable public interest and excitement.

While social media were only beginning to develop and older media (broadcast and print) tended to be a bit stiff (reporting on the issue, for instance, by simply providing summaries of meetings), the curriculum committee took it on itself to organize a series of public meetings (with Abu Lughod taking credit for introducing the "town hall" and "empowerment" to the Palestinian political lexicon[11]). In the period, the quantity of public discussions was such that a visitor to some Palestinian cities (most notably but not exclusively Ramallah) would be forgiven for concluding that Palestinian politics had moved from the stage of armed resistance to the stage of talking in seminars and workshops.

Yet for all its emphasis on openness, the committee found itself running up against two sacrosanct subjects: God and nation. On religion, the leaders of the committee were progressive intellectuals who came close to a secular orientation: while they accepted that religious sensibilities were powerful in large parts of Palestinian society, they regarded religion as of marginal relevance to most of the curriculum and distracting (as educators squabbled, for instance, on the relative proportion of covered and uncovered women in textbook illustrations). Ultimately, they sidestepped the issue of religious education altogether, noting without endorsing proposals to shift to education focusing on ethics. And while the committee members saw themselves as staunch nationalists and their task as a vital national project, they also did not want to allow curricular and pedagogical issues to be drowned out by debates over maps, borders and history on which Palestinians (and committee members) disagreed. Palestine's unsettled position made it virtually impossible to speak an uncontested truth.

When their work was presented to the Ministry of Education, the officials there made significant modifications. Most significantly, perhaps, the "intellectual basis" of the entire curriculum plan developed by the Ministry was now said to be faith in God.[12] And when it came to the nation, Abu Lughod's committee posited a fairly cosmopolitan Palestinian identity, consisting of three elements: international, Arab-Islamic, and specifically Palestinian. The Ministry of Education plan paid far less attention to the international dimension, and designated the Islamic dimension as distinct (rather than combined with the Arab).[13]

Anxious to imbue the plan with full political legitimacy, the Ministry submitted it to the cabinet, which approved it in December of that year. The proposal then went to the PLC, which approved it in March 1998. While there was great interest in the idea of a Palestinian-authored curriculum, there was surprisingly little interest in the details. Members of the Legislative Council did show concern but focused almost all their attention on the sensitive nationalist issues. On most other matters (such as religion and budgetary exigencies) PLC members supported the Ministry with little discussion. There was greater unease on matters like the geography and history of Palestine, on which the Ministry's plan gave little guidance.[14] Only a small number of minor changes were introduced, most with political implications (for instance, the phrase describing Palestine as a "peace loving state" was changed to "a state loving a just peace").[15]

The process of curriculum and textbook writing then passed largely out of public view, handed over to subject teams who operated with only loose guidance from the Ministry on sensitive matters (one team leader told me of receiving general suggestions that they should "be careful" without any specifics); the closed nature of the process was accentuated when in 1998 an Israeli NGO issued a report on the Jordanian and Egyptian books then used in Palestinian schools and Israeli, American, and European politicians took up the cause of combatting "incitement." Feeling under attack, the Ministry attempted to insulate the process from prying eyes. When new textbooks were issued beginning in 2000, they tended to reflect the existence of different specialist committees: Arabic language books tended to be highly nationalist; Islamic education books to be fairly conservative; and civic education books to be strikingly progressive.

Perhaps the most daring book to date has been the eighth-grade civic education text issued in 2002. The committee writing the book was dominated by intellectuals and activists sympathetic with the progressive educational vision; they therefore sought to engage students directly in thinking about gender roles, democracy, human rights, and pluralism. This was done not simply through the textual material but also through what might be termed a progressive hidden curriculum—illustrations showed women (with bare-headed and covered women together) marching; homework exercises and classroom activities provoked students to think hard and debate prevailing social relations and practices. Students were told to "choose a case of family violence from a story we heard, read about, or lived," then "select a judge, a prosecuting attorney, a defense attorney, and a jury" in order to hold a fair trial. They were to consider whether a woman prevented from working outside the house by her husband is a victim of violence and instructed to draft three clauses they would want to see included in a Palestinian family law.

In May 2003, an Islamist research center, the Al-Buraq Center,[16] held a workshop on the new book, presenting its own critique and inviting some of those who had been involved in its composition.[17] The Center's director, Adib Ziyada, began the discussion by claiming that the texts should draw from a single *marja'iyya* (reference point) so that students are not confused and filled with contradictions. Two al-Buraq researchers criticized the book for its negative portrayal of men and eschewal of Islamic sources. Others found in the balance between uncovered and veiled women tilting toward the former a preference for Western terminology (democracy) over Arab and Islamic (*shura*).

A member of the textbook team acknowledged that "the general philosophy of the curriculum tried to satisfy Islamists, liberals, donors, negotiators, and leftists. The general philosophy of the curriculum is a complete cocktail that has no connection with an intellectual base and unified theory that the entire curriculum is based on." Much more pugnaciously, a member of the Teacher Creativity Center, a progressive educational NGO, asked "Do we want a civic education program or not? If we want one, we have to realize that it is not simply an Islamic program; that is only one of its bases. Civic education in its essence contradicts religion, whether that religion is Islam, Christianity, or Judaism. For instance, there is no doubt that civic education opposes polygamy and wife beating, and Islam permits these things." This prompted the al-Buraq director to retort that his progressive colleague saw the West "as the source of existence."[18]

The workshop came to no conclusion; the Islamists held fast to their critique and the progressives insisted that civic education could not be taught appropriately in the way the Islamists wished. In the end, the member of the textbook team attending the workshop offered what seemed like a political compromise but was also an accurate description of the multiple approaches of the emerging Palestinian curriculum: "Civic education is not religious education. In religious education you will find all you want about divine laws, rights of women, polygamy, the family, and so on. The team composing was told that the policy of the Curriculum Development Center in civic education is related to international documents. Yes, there is a contradiction. For civic education, there is one law, and that is the one laid down by an elected parliament."[19]

The truce over the eighth-grade civics curriculum did not end the contest—in fact, al-Buraq returned to the fray a few years later. In 2006, when Hamas won in parliamentary elections, the movement put Nasir al-Din al-Sha'ir, the older brother of one of al-Buraq's researchers in place as minister of education and deputy prime minister. Al-Sha'ir denied being a Hamas member but did acknowledge he was an Islamist (if an unusually curious one: his doctoral dissertation at the University of Manchester compared daily prayer rituals in Islam and Judaism with a special emphasis on the role of women).[20] Under watchful international and domestic eyes, al-Sha'ir and Hamas decided to pick their public battles and pledged to keep the existing books in place.[21] Instead they pursued much less publicly visible measures to shift the curriculum. (Al-Sha'ir increased the hours devoted to religious instruction by ministerial order, thus necessitating the hiring of more religious teachers; he also used the opportunity provided by the failure of the Ministry to secure funding to print all textbooks to license the use of a religious book produced by the al-Buraq Center).

The brief experience of Hamas leadership of a unified PNA set a pattern that survived the Palestinian civil war of 2007 that split the PNA into rival Gaza and West Bank branches. Hamas, now only in control of Gaza, was limited in the changes it could make to the curriculum by fear of public criticism that it was dividing Palestine. Thus rather than lead to a split between the two educational systems, the Palestinian curriculum proved to be one of the last links that held the two halves of the PNA together. Hamas discovered to its disappointment that other Arab states would not recognize diplomas signed by its Minister of Education and had swallow its pride by maintaining the curriculum as written in Ramallah if it wanted its graduates to be able to enter universities in Cairo or Amman. The split, for all its bitter nature, was deeply unpopular in Palestinian society, leading Hamas to drop any idea of developing its own curriculum and Ramallah to avoid unilateral changes that might provoke division.

So the two halves of the PNA entered into quiet but definite cooperation on educational issues. The Education Ministries were virtually the only structures straddling the Gaza-West Bank split that were on speaking terms. And they were forced to speak on two issues. First, and most notably, they had to coordinate the annual *tawjihi* exam, taken by graduating secondary students and determining their success and placement at university. A divided tawjihi was politically unthinkable; neither side was willing to pay the enormous price to go its separate way with the exam. This created a need to coordinate the exam between the two halves of the Ministry, which in turn required that the curriculum (on which students were to be examined) be kept in place.

They cooperated as well in a limited process of curriculum review and revision.[22]

This is not to say that Hamas's vision of Palestinian education is similar to that of the West Bank leadership's. Discussion of educational and curricular issues in pro-Hamas newspapers[23] and websites show a special interest in religious issues and a focus (that the progressives would likely find both old-fashioned and authoritarian) on fostering respect for religious and national values; there is much less of a stress on individuality, creativity, and citizenship. Yet the Hamas government's vision of education cannot be pursued systematically without dividing the two systems, so no real attempt has been made.

Thus, after the 2007 split between the West Bank and Gaza, the tawjihi and diplomas were virtually the only things holding the PA together. Even that connection threatened to fray in 2012, when the Gaza government introduced a new education law[24] and promised curricular changes. The effective steps were quite modest—the new law criminalized "normalization" that did not take place in Palestinian schools; it also mandated gender segregation in a manner that was already effectively enforced for all schools. The new curricular steps were ones that affected "National Education" for two grades only at the preparatory stage. The overthrow of a supportive Egyptian regime in July 2013 likely stopped any further steps by Hamas and actually led it back to exploring possibilities for reconciliation.

Thus, for all the public interest and debate, the main effect of public arguments about education was to constrain educators: to hew closely to God and nation when writing textbooks and to continue using a unified set of books even when Palestine was deeply divided over every single issue. In private discussions with Palestinian teachers, former students, and parents, I have consistently heard one other severe critique of the curriculum that is not well reflected in the public record, and it is one which makes officials nod in acknowledgment without budging: those who use the new curriculum consistently complain that it is too hard.

Egypt and Jordan: Firestorms in Teacups

In Egypt, it is possible to find similar actors, arguments, and spheres—but with an official educational establishment even more isolated from any impact of public discussion with the result that the reborn Arab politics has had virtually no discernable impact on policy, though it has brought educational debates through some emotionally difficult terrain and allowed education to be a site for bitter expressive conflicts.

The Egyptian curriculum and textbooks are drawn up within the region's most massive educational bureaucracy. On paper, the system is highly centralized, with a single curriculum for the entire country and a single matriculation examination, the *thanawiyya 'amma* (General Secondary Examination, the equivalent of the tawjihi), making only limited allowance for literary, scientific, and vocational education at more advanced levels. But in reality

different streams have formed. Al-Azhar, for instance, oversees its own educational apparatus of primary, intermediate, and secondary schools with its
own thanawiyya ʿamma (with a bit more religious content); it is still, however, a part of the state. A variety of private schools offering an emphasis on
foreign languages, foreign (generally European) curricula, or an international
baccalaureate have blossomed as many middle-class Egyptian families in
major cities strive for upward mobility through their children's education and
cosmopolitan and elite families are anxious to obtain education of perceived
international quality in a country where the regular state education system
has been designed to serve the needs of a poor and densely populated society. State monitoring of such schools seems episodic. As we shall see shortly,
such pockets are important sites of variety and innovation, but often they can
serve that role because they operate a bit out of the public eye.

Over the past couple decades, intense educational debates have often
arisen and political or ideological opposition forces have sometimes found a
specific educational issue—such as the modification of a textbook—to be an
opportunity to press a broader critique. Islamists in particular could use parliamentary seats for such purposes, having some success in raising controversies but much less in affecting educational content. Other intellectuals would
look to other kinds of settings—such as workshops and media discussions—
to launch critiques of existing educational practices. For many officials, these
contributions appeared to be less trenchant and incisive critiques than the
chatterings of self-appointed guardians of national or progressive virtues
unaware of classroom realities, fiscal constraints, and capacity shortcomings.
The result was a predictable sense of alienation, as Fatma Sayed noted:

> The Egyptian intellectual elite is to a large extent distant from the decision
> making process, and their participation in official conferences and workshops
> launching reform programs often turns out to be purely ceremonial. . . . Indeed,
> complaints of exclusion from participation in the general process of decision-
> making are not only limited to national experts with Islamist or leftist inclina-
> tions, but also extend to others who are distant from the centers of power.[25]

Sayed speculates that a tendency for "conspiracy theory"—attributing education decisions to shadowy foreign funders—can flourish in such a context;[26]
it is also likely that such charges can burnish the nationalist and religious credentials of those making them.

With the election of Muhammad Morsi as president of Egypt, the patterns
were set, therefore, for a highly charged ideological debate that was not always
tethered to specific empirical realities or well-designed policy options. The
Ministry of Education was headed for most of Morsi's presidency by a nonpartisan curricular specialist with no previous service in the state. However, the
fact that the Brotherhood had moved into the presidency led its critics to be

vigilant about any "Brotherhoodization" of the state and the state educational apparatus, accustomed to sycophancy toward those in authority but also experiencing a prolonged period in which combating Islamism was an objective of senior officials, struggled to adapt. In visits to Egypt during the period, I would hear press discussions about specific examination answers in which, it was alleged, students were required to regurgitate the virtues of the Brotherhood or their new president or other ways the Brotherhood was revamping Egyptian education. In fact, however, very little was changed, as Patrycja Sasnal found:

> Even experts base their opinions on what they think happened and not on what actually happened. Some experts are certain that the Muslim Brotherhood "changed everything" in the textbooks, including adding their own history, while others claim that MB wanted to introduce such changes but did not have enough time and, despite Morsi, the lower echelons of the ministries remained intact. Both statements are only partially true. The authors of the textbooks remained mostly the same in the school years right before and after 2011. The only textbooks that the MB could have had an impact on are the 2012/2013 or 2013/2014 versions. The contents, however, compared with 2011/2012 hardly changed, and even these changes do not seem to be imposed by the MB.[27]

Following the overthrow of the Brotherhood in July 2013, Ministry officials explained without much elaboration that they were rooting out any incitement to violence in the curriculum and removing offensive passages. While they promised comprehensive curricular reform there was little sign that there was much reconsideration of the highly nationalistic tone, its praise of the military and other state institutions, and the elision among nation, family, morality, and religion long engrained in textbooks. The only dramatic public step was taken in April 2015 when education officials in Giza discovered books not authorized by the Ministry in a private school which had recently been taken over by the state because of its alleged affiliation with the Muslim Brotherhood. In their enthusiasm to cleanse the school, and citing the backing of security bodies, Ministry officials photographed themselves holding Egyptian flags and burning the books in question. (Some of those burned included a work by Egypt's leading modern jurist, ʿAbd al-Razzaq al-Sanhuri as well as one by Rajab al-Bannaʾ, a leading pro-regime journalist of the Mubarak era, perhaps because his name may have inaccurately suggested a family tie to Hasan al-Bannaʾ, the founder of the Muslim Brotherhood.) Less in the public limelight, officials eliminated passages in religious textbooks they found noxious or, in their views, sympathetic to extremism, leading to loud but ineffectual complaints especially from salafi circles. In addition, material lauding the new regime's accomplishments (such as the Suez Canal project) was included with little public discussion.[28]

In short, there is not much evidence that public arguments about education had much direct effect on policy outcomes.[29] But that did not rob the arguments of intensity; just the opposite: it may have increased the emotional valence of political discussions linking education, nation, and religion. That linkage had political effect in allowing politicians in opposition before 2011 to mobilize supporters and state officials after 2013 to purge the schools of Islamist influence.

As in Palestine, there is a major subject of public discussion of education that is far from such concerns but perhaps even more pressing: the difficulty of the thanawiyya ʿamma. The annual examination is, among other things, a media event, with programs devoted to helping students study, numerous interviews with students and officials about the exams, and noisy debates about its difficulty and appropriateness. As with more policy-centered debates, arguments about the examination's difficulty attract a lot of attention but there is not much evidence that officials do much more than acknowledge the resulting noise.

In Jordan, a somewhat different dynamic emerged. The Education Ministry came to be regarded as something of an Islamist and conservative preserve in the latter decades of the twentieth century, especially for a cadre of teachers and mid-level Ministry officials. From 1970 to 1973, a leader of the Muslim Brotherhood (Ishaq Farhan) served as minister of education (though the movement suspended him when he accepted the post); the movement also held the Ministry briefly in the early 1990s. The Jordanian regime has often (and thus far successfully) resisted attempts to form an independent teacher's union for fear that it would become an Islamist preserve. Nevertheless, some with a more liberal orientation—and implicitly or explicitly, an anti-Islamist agenda—have served on occasion in high levels in the Ministry.

The curriculum is overseen by a body attached to the cabinet; it has independent figures and government officials; and it operates out of the limelight. In this restrictive atmosphere, there still have been a series of specialist bodies charged with drafting plans for educational reform. The overall effect has been to give more liberal educational reformers a few points of entry generally outside of a peering public eye—for instance they made an effort to abandon the process of using a single state-authored textbook and instead issue guidelines that private book providers would meet, allowing schools to choose from a menu; that proposal ran against the centralization built into the system and was dropped.[30] In recent years, they have secured a comprehensive rewrite of textbooks to include values of tolerance and pluralism in a very general way— though including too many details of the beliefs of those to be tolerated (such as Christians) has generally been seen as pushing too far.

As in other countries, the curriculum and content of textbooks is sometimes occasion for noisy political debate; the presence of a parliament with a strong Islamist opposition offers opportunities for politicians to strike out strong positions and suggest that the government is insufficiently supportive of religious or national values, currying favor with international donors, or surreptitiously attempting to de-emphasize the Palestinian cause. And as with other countries, such debates attract press attention but do not necessarily result in significant changes.

They may make change more difficult, however. The experience of one reform-minded minister, Ibrahim Badran, may illustrate the point. Badran, an academic, served on an educational reform commission raising his prominence; in 2009 he was appointed minister of education. Parliament at that point was not in session, allowing him a bit of a freer hand. However, he clashed early on with Islamists and with teachers (partly on the issue of a teachers union and partly on his plan to begin teacher training programs outside of the ministry). The confrontation was a public one carried out through the press; Badran reports that his personal relationship with Islamist leaders was cordial; he describes them as "frenemies" and notes that there was little attempt on either his part or theirs to argue or discuss the issues directly.[31]

Badran's critics first seized on a religion book that apparently referred to an Islamic story narrated in the Qur'an (the battle of Badr) as "legendary," which they took to be dismissive. That allowed them to mobilize some of their supporters, but in the absence of parliament the controversy remained largely within Islamist circles. But Badran also had plans to revamp the Jordanian tawjihi. While unable to develop those plans fully, in his time as minister the tawjihi was toughened, partly as a way to manage burgeoning university enrollments. That provoked a national controversy since the much higher failure rate reached into many families. Unlike in Palestine and Egypt, the controversy was not merely the subject of complaint, the outrage in Jordan may have had more effect; with an accumulation of teachers, Islamists, bureaucrats, students, and parents upset with him, Badran found himself out of office in 2010. Only in 2014, with the rise of the Islamic state, did advocates of educational reform find the political support necessary to undertake a quieter, but still controversial, curriculum review.

PRIVATE POCKETS OF EDUCATING THE PUBLIC

Overall, the image of the politics of curriculum development is broadly consistent: various intellectuals and movements debate what is taught, parliaments sometimes provide platforms as do newspapers, nadwas, and broadcast media; parents and pupils complain about examinations, and ministries carry on their work, generally oblivious to the public debate.

And yet there is one public/private site that is completely omitted from this picture: the school. The univocal state may resonate oddly within the walls of the classroom for several reasons.

First, there are schools that can escape close state control. Elite schools generally are required to use state-mandated texts, but they can supplement them. Some elite schools also might teach their students using various kinds of foreign curricula. In the nineteenth and early twentieth centuries, such schools were especially common and sometimes, because of the capitulations (legal arrangements effectively granting foreign-controlled institutions extraterritorial status) or other indirect forms of European imperialism, such schools escaped any state oversight. That extreme independence gave way in the second half of the twentieth century to a variety of less obvious forms of autonomy in which some schools carved out freedom for experimentation with curricula and especially pedagogy. A variety of political circumstances made this possible. In Palestinian schools, for instance, the first intifada is remembered as a time not only of educational crisis (since schools were closed for long periods) but also, in some circles, of educational innovation (with students meeting sometimes in private houses and teachers developing new techniques to teach in unpromising settings). Some educators in Gaza (in the schools run by the United Nations Relief Works Administration [UNRWA]) have carved out space provided by their control of a set of schools somewhat autonomous from the Hamas-run Ministry of Education to introduce a human rights curriculum whose content is supplemented by an unusually interactive pedagogy. (Indeed, in my only visit to a school in session in the Arab world in 2012, I was startled by how much a ninth-grade girls class in Gaza studying human rights departed from my expectations of an authoritarian environment with an extremely free-flowing and participatory discussion and set of class activities.)

Of course, not all such schools are creatures of elites or international organizations. Religion itself sometimes provides islands of partial autonomy. In some Arab countries, Christian schools are common; in a few, such schools attract non-Christian students because of the reputed quality of their education. Most notable in recent years in some countries has been the expansion of private Islamic education—in Egypt this has been a particularly noteworthy phenomenon.[32] Alongside such schools there exists an entire network of schools run by al-Azhar, the mosque/university/research complex that has dominated much of official Islam in Egypt. While clearly part of the Egyptian state, al-Azhar does have some autonomy and its network of schools have sometimes been the subject of a tug-of-war between the Ministry of Education and al-Azhar and even provincial governors.

Such pockets of autonomy appear all over, even if they rarely can escape curricular supervision; Linda Herrera found a school operating in Egypt in the 1990s that kept within ministry guidelines on the books but still had students sing a religious substitute for the national anthem and (as with the salafi shaykh mentioned in chapter 4) taught students to avoid "good morning" in favor of "peace be upon you" as a greeting.[33] Gregory Starrett makes the case more generally about the space opened up by states through the practice of using schools as sites for inculcation of a state-endorsed view of religion:

> In documenting the role of the contemporary school in teaching Islam, I hope to show how the expansion and transfer of religious socialization from private to newly created public sector institutions over the last century has led to a comprehensive revision of the way Egyptians treat Islam as a religious tradition, and consequently of Islam's role in Egyptian society. . . . As part of this institutional transformation, programs of mass public instruction conceived in the nineteenth century as cost-efficient means of social control have instead helped generate the intellectual, political, and social challenges posed by the country's broad-based "Islamist" movement, the most significant political opposition to the current Egyptian government.[34]

One study of educational reform in Morocco, initiated as a response to global pressure after the attacks of September 11, 2001, in the United States and the May 2003 Casablanca bombings, found that Islamic education teachers actually welcomed changes as allowing them to engage in a more active pedagogy.[35]

Of course, what happens in the classroom is very much a concern to states in the region. Hamas's mini-state in Gaza showed great discomfort with UNRWA's human-rights curriculum.[36] When Egyptian President 'Abd al-Fattah al-Sisi lectured al-Azhar leaders in December 2014 about how to teach religion, the Ministry of Education followed up by reviewing the curriculum in al-Azhar's schools (as well as carrying out the book burning mentioned above); it also sought to increase its monitoring of curricula (and extracurricular activities) in "international" schools.[37]

For all their efforts, states and educators struggling for autonomy also continuously confront another obstacle: students. In conversations with young adults in the Arab world, I have heard all sorts of accounts of their own experience with religious education, few of which focus on content but rather on the personality of teachers (often lampooned as rigid and less educated) and ways in which a subject can be devalued if it is not included in the tawjihi (with state practice varying in that regard).

Thus education provides a number of pockets where religion can serve as a point of contestation among states, schools, teachers, and students. But it is critical for our current purposes to note that these are pockets that survive because they partake of the private: they are places where access is difficult to varying degrees for the prying eyes of state officials, parents, and politicians. States in particular are limited in the extent to which they can control and fall back on crude devices—the tawjihi itself being a major one—to police the schools. The subversion that takes place in some classrooms is not only conditioned on (and by) but just as much limited by its sub rosa nature.

CONCLUSION

As with the other areas examined in the previous chapters, Arab politics of education is lively in the sense that there is engaged public argument about the purposes and content of education. States control curricula very effectively but they are far less able to control what people think and say about them. The debates have limited effects on outcome and the effects that they do have tend to occur partly out of public view—narrow discussions among specialists that might occasionally be heeded by sympathetic officials; surreptitious decisions by local school officials to supplement or subvert the state-mandated curriculum; and, of course, students using the content of what they are taught as an opportunity for derision.

And yet the fierceness of some debates—in particular, the contest between Islamists and their opponents—is still striking. In that sense, education curricula might seem much like a catalyst in the technical sense of the term: an element in a reaction but one that remains fundamentally unchanged at the end.

NOTES

1. Laurie A. Brand, *Official Stories: Politics and National Narratives in Egypt and Algeria* (Palo Alto: Stanford University Press, 2014), 102.
2. Eleanor Abdella Doumato and Gregory Starrett, eds., *Teaching Islam: Textbooks and Religion in the Middle East* (Boulder: Lynne Rienner, 2006). There are many alternative ways to teach Islam—see for instance Robert W. Hefner and Mohammad Qasim Zaman, *Schooling Islam: The Culture and Politics of Modern Muslim Education* (Princeton: Princeton University Press, 2007).
3. *Islamic Education*, Grade 6, Part I (Ramallah: Curriculum Development Center, Palestinian National Authority), 69.
4. *Islamic Education*, Grade 1.
5. Sarah J. Feuer, "Religious Establishment and Regime Survival: The Politics of Religious Education in Morocco and Tunisia, 1956–2010" (PhD diss., Brandeis University Politics Department and Crown Center for Middle East Studies, 2014).
6. See the example of Kamal Bahi al-Din, minister of education in Egypt in the 1990s, in Linda Ann Herrera, "The Sanctity of the School: New Islamic Education and Modern Egypt" (PhD diss., Columbia University, 2000), chapter 4.
7. The process was not uniform. For an examination of different trajectories in North Africa, see Feuer, "Religious Establishment."
8. I have written of this effort in a number of writings, including *Palestinian Politics after the Oslo Accords: Resuming Arab Palestine* (Berkeley: University of California Press, 2003).
9. `Ali Jarbawi, personal interview, Ramallah, January 2000.
10. Ibid.
11. Ibrahim Abu Lughod, personal interview, Ramallah, October 1999.
12. Palestinian National Authority, Ministry of Education, *First Palestinian Curriculum Plan* (Ramallah: Ministry of Education, 1997), 7.

13. Ibid., 26.

14. Personal interview with Dalal Salameh, member of PLC and of its education committee, al-Bira, February 2000.

15. Report of the Committee on Education and Social Affairs on Palestinian curriculum, unpublished document submitted to PLC and approved, March 31, 1998.

16. The Al-Buraq Center was later closed by Israel and some of its personnel have been arrested by both the PA and Israel. Israel and the post-2007 PA have apparently concluded that al-Buraq was affiliated with Hamas. I visited the Center in 2006 and collected some of its material. My impression was that it was clearly Islamist in orientation but I did not see any evidence that it had any clear partisan affiliation. Since Hamas is not a legally recognized organization, it is sometimes difficult to tell where it begins and ends, but I did not see any evidence that the connection between Al-Buraq and Hamas went beyond political sympathies and ideological inclinations. One of the most extravagant (and quite likely inaccurate) claims about an employee of al-Buraq turns up in Mossab Hassan Yousef's *Son of Hamas* (Carol Stream, Il: Tyndale House, 2010). Yousef, an Israeli collaborator and the son of Hamas leader Hasan Yousef, suggests that ʿAziz Kayid, then a researcher working for al-Buraq, was the clandestine leader of Hamas in the West Bank. Kayid himself forcefully denies the claim (ʿAziz Kayid, personal interview, Ramallah, June 2010).

17. Al-Buraq Center for Research and Culture, "Proceedings of a Workshop Concerning the Curriculum for Civic Education for the Eight Elementary Grade in Palestinian Schools," unpublished manuscript, Ramallah, May 24, 2003.

18. Ibid.

19. Ibid.

20. Al-Shaʿir personal interview, Ramallah, March 2006.

21. Al-Shaʿir, personal interview, Ramallah, June 2006.

22. In periodic visits to the Ramallah Ministry after 2007 and in a visit to the Gaza Ministry in 2012, I heard of tense and sometimes minimal but generally business-like relations and cooperation on curricular matters.

23. The daily *Filastin* and the weekly *al-Risala* were both Gaza newspapers with a pro-Hamas line.

24. "Qanun al-taʿlim al-jadid bi-ghaza," http://www.msar.ps/8174.html, accessed October 31, 2013.

25. Fatma Sayed, "The Contested Terrain of educational Reform in Egypt," in *Education and the Arab 'World': Political Projects, Struggles, and Geometries of Power*, eds., André E. Mazawi and Ronald G. Sultana World Yearbook of Education 2010 (New York: Routledge, 2010), p. 90.

26. She explores the subject of international influence and educational reform more fully in *Transforming Education in Egypt: Western Influence and Domestic Policy Reform* (Cairo: American University in Cairo Press, 2006).

27. Patrycja Sasnal, "Myths and Legends: Modern History and Nationalistic Propaganda in Egyptian Textbooks," report, Polish Institute of International Affairs, May 2014.

28. See, for instance, "We Publish the Changes in the Social [Studies] Curriculum in All Stages of Education," *al-Shuruq*, July 29, 2015, http://www.shorouknews.com/news/view.aspx?cdate=29072015&id=36b97659-4dc5-4e03-a40e-ce6d3c4a5102, accessed December 29, 2015.

29. For a general portrait of educational debates in Egypt emphasizing its responsiveness to an elitist orientation somewhat estranged from prevailing religiosity, see Bradley James Cook, "Egypt's National Education Debate," *Comparative Education* 36, 4 (2000): 477–490.
30. Victor Billeh, personal interview, August 2014.
31. Ibrahim Badran, personal interview, October 2014.
32. See Herrera, "The Sanctity of the School," for a wide-ranging analysis of the phenomenon.
33. Ibid., 116.
34. Gregory Starrett, *Putting Islam to Work: Education, Politics, and Religious Transformation in Egypt* (Berkeley: University of California Press, 1998).
35. Ann Marie Wainscott, "Defending Islamic Education: War on Terror Discourse and Religious Education in Twenty-First-Century Morocco," *Journal of North African Studies* 20, 4 (2015): 635–653.
36. In a 2012 visit to the Ministry of Education in Gaza, I heard the curriculum criticized not for its content but for the failure of UNRWA to coordinate with the Ministry and accept its authority over educational content.
37. See "[Ministry of] Education: Decisions are Issued to Organize Work in International Schools . . . and Saluting the Flag and the Anthem are 'Obligatory,'" *al-Shuruq*, September 15, 2014.

CHAPTER 9
Politics and Policy; Affect and Effect

Finally, at least the European Parliament is supposed to establish a bridge between the political battles of opinions in the national arenas and the momentous decisions taken in Brussels. But there is hardly any traffic on the bridge.

Jürgen Habermas, *The Lure of Technocracy*, 3.

Saying something to another: how can we expect it to affect anything? The current of thoughts, images and feelings that flows through us on every side, has such force, this torrential current, that it would be a miracle if it didn't simply sweep away and consign to oblivion all words anyone else says to us, if they didn't by accident, sheer accident, suit our own words.

Pascal Mercier, *Night Train to Lisbon*, 137

Residents of the Arab world argue with each other in many different ways in many different forums. They do so in ways that are much livelier than in the recent past and that pull in increasing numbers of speakers and larger audiences. The arguments even occur in a few ways that let audiences argue with speakers.

The republic of arguments is built out of a combination of all sorts of spaces that have emerged using all sorts of technologies, new and old. These spaces operate under the watchful eyes of security services; all privilege some voices over others; many are better at one-way communication from leader to follower than true give and take; and all allow those with advanced training or superior resources to speak in highly amplified voices. Their arguments do not serve as a substitute for violence nor does their existence suggest an end to oppressive state authority. Violence and oppression are profoundly rooted; they are sometimes woven into the fabric of public argumentation rather than undermined by it.

All this has been visible and audible for a while. But in this inquiry, we have also seen how the new environment not only allows for many voices but also allows those voices to carry—they cross the boundary from one sphere to another. Actually, the voices are consciously carried more than they carry themselves, and portentously it is often not the speaker but his followers and critics who transport words and arguments from one sphere to another. In the process arguments are often stripped down, lampooned, reduced to a slogan, and taken out of context. And that is the point—it is often the transporter rather than the speaker who determines the context.

We have seen that often the authority of the speaker carries (or is carried) far less easily than her words.

Nobody would call most of these arguments ideal political speech. Sometimes specialists do argue among themselves in a way that might be sufficiently genteel to earn the term "deliberation," but the necessary degrees of rationality and politesse are enabled by the restricted nature of those discussions. When the same scholars argue in more public settings, they can descend into name calling and sloganeering designed more to motivate, provoke, activate, or titillate their own supporters than to persuade their colleagues or opponents.

Not only are there arguments in public; there are many publics that argue with each other and they do so in a manner that often makes it even more difficult for the many publics to become *the* public—though they often do not make that distinction themselves. As Marc Lynch has observed, "Even at its height, there was always something a bit ominous about the populist conviction of the Arab public sphere. Commonplace assertions of what 'the people' want are almost always wrong—indeed, such claims should be taken as a signal of either ignorance or a partisan agenda."[1]

We have seen in this book how these various publics argue about religion in specific issues areas. By probing the publics as they really exist and the spheres as they really operate, we have seen that their arguments are increasingly lively but their efficaciousness is far less impressive. We conclude, then, by probing this paradox a bit more in order to both summarize our findings and to understand their implications.

First, we have seen that religion is surprisingly amenable to public arguments; indeed, its heavily public nature in the Arab world is in part because it is so woven into structures of governance. The interpenetration of religion and the state raises the salience of religious arguments and the stakes of how issues are decided. We will revisit the question of whether religion is distinctive as a subject for arguments and, if so, how and why.

Second, we have seen that the arguments have effect on public policy only under specific circumstances—but we will also highlight in this conclusion how the arguments matter even in the absence of identifiable policy impact.

Finally, we will probe how the revitalized Arab public arguments do offer some limited possibilities for political orders with real virtues, though not ones that will mitigate, much less overcome, the deep structural problems within existing regimes as they are experienced by those they govern. In that respect, we will conclude by considering a glimmer of hopeful possibility—one that is not based on a denial of the realities of the Arab world today but still finds a limited degree of cheer.

IS RELIGION DIFFERENT?

Does it matter that the arguments are about religion? It may seem that religion offers a particularly fraught field for public argument because it involves ultimate truths and may be less amenable to many political arts of compromise and creative ambiguity; indeed, some of the most powerful arguments for separating religion and politics—that is, for privatizing religion and evicting it from public space—are founded precisely on the fear that religious arguments involve absolutes and are therefore exclusionary and resistant to compromise and mutual accommodation. This is what generates the ironic phenomenon that intolerance of religious arguments in public seems so defensible in the name of tolerance.

In the opening of the book, I expressed some skepticism about such views. Indeed, the fear that religion is not amenable to politics, however normatively strong in some settings, does not seem to fit empirical realities in the Arab world. Human fallibility in interpretation is a widespread presumption for even deeply religious discourse. It is sometimes stunning how much argument about religion there is and how much acceptance there is of the idea that religion is a subject for discussion. Raising religious dimensions of public issues generates discussion; it does not end it.

There are special challenges posed by religion but they do not stem from the irreconcilability of different versions of ultimate truth. Religion is fraught because it ties the personal, even the intimacy of marital relations, so insistently to the public, and because it brings together competing sources of authority that do not always blend easily.

Those who examine religion from the perspective of social sciences shaped by the modern European historical experience might unconsciously incline to a view of religion that emphasizes doctrine and individual faith. Of course doctrine and faith are important to many Muslims, but the public arguments about religion that are heard may make more sense if we understand them in the context of a view of religion that gives much greater emphasis to social practice and to the communal, if we view religion in part as a set of practices and structures that shape or even govern the ethics of interpersonal behavior. It is precisely these elements of religion that are highlighted in public debates and matter most for political purposes.

When it comes to politics and religion, what matters may be less what is held in the heart and more how people interact with each other—an emphasis that is very much part of shari'a-based discussions. Apostasy, for instance, may be seen as repugnant to God, but many shari'a authorities suggest that God will know best how to deal with the offense and the matter can be left to Him if it is a purely private affair. Public apostasy—that is, proudly renouncing Islam and mocking it—by contrast is seen a threat to the social fabric, an offense against God and humanity, and it is society that must respond by punishing the offender.

Religion is thus above all a public matter and therefore we should not be surprised to find it woven into the structure of the modern state: ministries of education write religious textbooks; ministries of religious affairs administer mosques; state muftis offer interpretations of religious law; courts of personal status guide husband and wife and parent and child in ways to conduct their interactions in what they see as the Islamic way. And religion is a language for people to communicate about matters of morality and justice.

Of course, some of the emphasis on practice and community may be traceable back to Islamic doctrine, the experience of early Muslims, and core beliefs derived from sacred texts. But in their particularities—even in many of their most general features—those emphases and institutional patterns are rooted much more in the process of modern state formation. State muftis are largely a nineteenth- and twentieth-century innovation. Ministries of religious affairs and the nationalization of *waqfs* (endowments) and *zakat* (alms) are historically recent creations as well. The entire category of personal status law—perhaps the most essential element of the shari'a as Islamic law for many adherents—simply did not exist as a distinct body before the nineteenth century. There is no doctrinal reason to claim that conducting marital relations in an Islamic manner is more important to God than trading goods in an Islamic way, but for reasons having to do with what colonial and later independent states strove to do and chose to ignore, marriage, divorce, and inheritance emerged as the one area of law where states tread most carefully, taking only measures that can be expressed in the terms of older Islamic jurisprudence.

So religion is distinctive in distinctively modern ways. And the way that it is argued is of even more recent origin, traceable to what I have called, with some exaggeration but not complete hyperbole, the revival of Arab politics. Do the arguments matter? Does the politics of religion have any practical effects?

DOES POLITICS MATTER? BEYOND HABERMASIAN DISGUST

Of course, while the kind of politics I have examined here is new to the Arab world, at least in its intensity, it is hardly unique to that region. What is striking in the Arab world are the loose connections between the republic of arguments and the realities of governing.

The same kind of blending of specialists' dialogue, interpenetration of the spheres, transportation of arguments stripped of authority, and more than occasional shrill results are a feature of many societies. In 1989, the Stux Gallery in New York held an exhibition including the photographic works of Andre Serrano. The artist had earlier gained fame outside narrow circles for one of the photographs then on display, his "Piss Christ," which showed a crucifix in a beaker of Serrano's own urine. A review of the exhibit in the New York Times gushed:

> Mr. Serrano struggles against inhibitions about the human body. His use of bodily fluids is not intended to arouse disgust but to challenge the notion of disgust where the human body is concerned.
>
> It is possible to see Mr. Serrano's use of bodily fluids as pure provocation. But you can also believe that Mr. Serrano views them as a form of purification. The fluids make us look at the images harder and consider basic religious doctrine about matter and spirit.[2]

The element of purification eluded some viewers and aroused the disgust the reviewer thought Serrano did not intend to provoke. More significantly, the photograph provoked a much larger body of the public that did not ever view "Piss Christ" but heard about it. Some reacted to the discussion not by questioning religious doctrine so much as federal arts policy, since Serrano's work had received some public support. The National Endowment for the Arts, the granting agency, based its response to such calls on the fact that Serrano's work earned the respect and admiration of those in the artistic community; in essence, it passed peer review. But many in the broader public arrived at a fairly harsh judgment not only about the author's oeuvre, focusing as it did on imaginatively blending the sacred with bodily fluids, but also about the artist himself. Senator Jesse Helms, for instance, was trenchant and personal: "I do not know Mr. Andres Serrano, and I hope I never meet him. Because he is not an artist, he is a jerk." In remarks from the Senate floor, Helms reached for avian metaphors including calling Serrano "this bird" and his work as "horsefeathers."[3]

There were few changes in United States federal government arts funding directly as a result of the controversy and Serrano's "Piss Christ" was still publicly exhibited (in privately owned galleries) over two decades later. But the effects of the controversy were real in terms of the atmosphere for the arts, the desire of some bodies to avoid controversy, and the mobilization of constituencies. There were authoritative political structures that were linked to, influenced by, and helped to shape the sometimes distasteful and rarely enlightening arguments. Politics in the sense of public argument and politics in the sense of policy process were connected.

Public arguments as they are really made will generate Habermasian nausea among many members of many different publics. Will they do anything more than disgust? Do arguments about religion make policy different in the Arab world?

The short answer—a summary of what we have seen in constitution writing, personal status, and education—is that the policy effects are limited but do occur and under some slightly unusual circumstances. In order for public argument to have a direct policy effect, state bodies need to become actively involved as agents and not simply as tools or arenas. They do so by making themselves accessible to public debate and by sponsoring some kind of change (as we saw most directly in the case of some reforms in personal status law). Those conditions are in short supply in the Arab world. Publics lack the structures and avenues of pressure to impose themselves on state bodies.

The second sense of the word politics that we have been using here is simply very weak in the Arab world. That is the case, for instance, with the definition offered by Bernard Crick: "Politics, then can be simply defined as the activity by which differing interests within a given unit of rule are conciliated by giving them a share in power in proportion to their importance to the welfare and the survival of the whole community."[4] Various state bodies are not designed and do not operate as political in that sense.

Those schooled in Habermasian views of politics sometimes distinguish between a public sphere of deliberation and debate and a political sphere where decisions are taken and policy is made. Parliaments are meeting grounds where public deliberation can be translated into political decisions. I have generally eschewed such specific distinctions here because I think they offer too much clarity in a murky political world and tilt the analytical field a bit too far in favor of normative at the expense of empirical concerns. But I will briefly draw on such a framework here to say that the problems of Arab politics stem not just from the weakness of the public sphere but from the poor nature of its connections with the political sphere. The failure to connect arguing to governing enhances polarization, gives little space for persuasion, and provides few rewards for compromise or attempts to forge agreement.

But if Arab arguments have only limited policy effect, they have tremendous effect on affect: the feelings of belonging or alienation by various publics can be understood in large part by the degree to which there is some way in which their voices are heard and reflected in official actions. We saw this most clearly with constitution drafting, in which tremendous arguments produced minor textual changes and those changes in turn produced little institutional, legal, or policy change—and yet debates and their outcomes still deeply affected attitudes toward the political system, general political atmosphere, and who felt invested in (or excluded from) the polity.

So policy is sometimes changed by public arguments and, much more often, people sometimes feel differently as a result of the revival of Arab politics. But does anything get better?

A FEW CHEERS FOR A POLITICS WITHOUT CHEER

A few years after the uprisings of 2011, there seemed to be two very unattractive alternatives paths for the reborn politics.

One was a reborn authoritarianism in which public argumentation was sharply constricted by a muscular and abusive security apparatus and a newly vigorous official media on the one hand (and, in Egypt, more than a touch of intolerance in public toleration of dissent).

The second was state disintegration. A wave of political change that began in 2011 as a challenge to Arab regimes metamorphized in some societies into a decay of the entire state.

In a period in which state institutions throughout the Arab world passed through severe crises, it is remarkable how much mechanisms of coercion—militaries and internal security forces—seemed to be able to find their balance, sometimes surviving even as the rest of the state decayed.

The Arab world seemed to face a vicious palindrome: Sisi or ISIS. Yet the republic of arguments survived both. One Egyptian remarked to me in the fall of 2015: "If you criticized Mubarak, he would beat you up. This man kills you." The violence of post-2013 politics he referred to was real. But the remark was made by someone I had just met; I could not imagine a similar frank comment made to a foreigner who was a total stranger when I first visited Egypt in 1983.

Political scientists have approached the question of regime type in less apocalyptic but still excessively binary terms. On the one hand stands democracy, a regime type in limited supply in the Arab world. On the other stands authoritarianism and its numerous gradations and variations, all united by their failure to provide (or their corruption of) democratic mechanisms. What we have found does not change the image of Arab governance as predominantly authoritarian, but it has highlighted the existence of political life and its sometimes ugly but still impressive vitality. And it challenges the image of authoritarian politics as simply the projection of the will of the ruler or the regime.

The revival of Arab politics is reversible. The portrait of politics that I have drawn here is not always attractive, but it does seem better than the alternatives presented by the vicious palindrome. In visits to Egypt after the military coup of 2013, I came across one religious figure who tearfully told me that the contents of his sermons was dictated and his words were monitored for political content. Another pious but nonpartisan person I had met earlier was unable to meet with me—he fled the country fearing his religious and political opinions would transfer him from welcome lay preacher in a state-regulated mosque to inmate in a state-run prison.

And that was in Egypt where the state remained viable—indeed, there was a bit too much state for safe politics. In some other places in the Arab world I would not have even felt comfortable visiting—such as Iraq, Syria, or Yemen—the claimants to state authority were even more brutal but utterly ineffective at governance.

Is there anything other than this unappetizing menu of alternatives to recommend the politics that has emerged in the Arab world? Has the revival of politics brought about anything good?

Of course, there is the vitality and liveliness of public debates which can be their own reward for the intellectually hungry.

From the viewpoint of the pious, there is something else that might be seen to cause cheer: the fact that so much public argumentation takes place on Islamic turf.

From an Islamic viewpoint, many participants in public debates have suddenly realized they are speaking the prose of shari'a. For even those whose preference might be to avoid such talk still sometimes feel constrained to adopt it. Depending on a speaker's orientation, that can be exhilarating, empowering, oppressive, or depressing. Significantly, however, even this religious grounding of arguments brings little cheer to those who might be expected to greet all the shari'a talk that can now be heard. The more common sentiment expressed by the pious is not delight that everyone is speaking shari'a but that too many discordant and inexpert voices are heard and that believers are easily led astray by those who lack authority (often defined as those whose orientations are different than the speaker's).

But our focus in this book, on real publics and their real arguments, offers one other cause for limited cheer, and not merely for the pious. It suggests the possibility of modifying, though hardly eliminating, the experience of authoritarianism. As befits an approach predicated on understanding the world as it is and not only as it should be, I will therefore close with a note of realism on what those modifications will look like and why they are limited.

While the revival of politics is not completely irreversible, it does have some striking and well-entrenched effects. New spheres are hard to dismantle; authoritarian regimes (or regimes attempting to rediscover their authoritarian roots) can work to suppress the republic of argument, but what they often wind up doing is not so much eliminating the spheres but isolating them: a campaign of sustained repression (such as in Egypt after 2013 with some Islamist spheres) cut down on the numbers of those who participated and shut down some locations where discussions took place (such as newspapers and some broadcasters), but arguments very much continued in social media, face-to-face groups, and even demonstrations and graffiti.

Similar public spheres in nonliberal settings have been noticed elsewhere: in China, an economic liberalization associated with rapid growth has been cited as a contributing factor in such a phenomenon.[5] In many Arab societies, state retreat has been a factor in promoting public arguments but not economic success. In much of the region, the state has failed large portions of the population. In education, health, employment, housing, a variety of private solutions have sprung up because state services offer so little; those who depend on them consign themselves to ill health and downward mobility. Many of the spaces for argument emerged in that context. After the upheavals of 2011, some of those spaces were more sharply constricted but they rarely disappeared.

The result was lively argument, though polarization was also an all too common result. It was not inevitable; Berna Turam found in Istanbul and Berlin "important counterexamples" in which "Urban space that is deeply divided by ideology and identitarian clashes generates new alliances over freedom and rights."[6] My more superficial impression of Cairo after the 2013 coup was not quite as happy: where there were differences of orientation, I heard not of alliances but of topics that were unspeakable, family tensions, and even physical altercations. State repression did not provoke repudiation as much as replication. The effect was to make the bubble around Islamist discussions an even less permeable membrane, isolating Islamists from the rest of politically engaged society and effectively facilitating deeper polarization, demonization, and even violence.

What this inquiry has highlighted is why arguments are divisive: not because of gaps among the people but because of the gaps in governing orders in the Arab world. The problem is not a dearth of politics or of ideas; the problem is a weakness of institutional mechanisms to translate public discussions into public policies. Before he became famous for his idea of "clash of civilizations," Samuel Huntington was best known for his work on "praetorianism," centering on his claim that "The primary problem of politics is the lag in the development of political institutions behind social and economic change."[7] Huntington might say the same thing about the reborn Arab politics: too much public participation in words; too few institutional channels for translating public words into policy outcomes. It should be no surprise that rhetoric spins out of control if it finds no traction in policy outcomes. Huntington's own approach seemed to prioritize order over justice (and be insufficiently attentive to possibilities of building orders that are more enduring because they are seen as just).

But even a softer version of this argument would still highlight the need for order: "If all discussion, conflict, rivalry, struggle, and even conciliation is called politics, then it is forgotten once more that politics depends on some settled order."[8] The problem in the parts of the Arab world analyzed here is that order when provided is of a kind that is seen as impervious to public voices and that has ironed in some very bad habits.

We have seen that under some circumstances, entrepreneurial actors within the states that sprawl so widely throughout Arab societies can draw on public arguments and marshal them for their purposes. This is not democracy, but it can be participatory; it can also build the functional equivalent of consensus on specific issues; and it can translate public arguments into changed outcomes. As parts of the state jostle against each other, public voices can sometimes be heard—and actually listened to. The arguments are not always without effect.

The underlying problem—of people speaking but states only hearing when they wish—will not be easy to fix. Until and unless it is fixed, states may find their citizens resentful and full of complaints, and their grumbling will have deep foundations. Residents of the Arab world are discovering how complicated things become when real people—with all their insights, insecurities, passions, preferences, predilections, prejudices, altruism, and egoism—barge into public places.

NOTES

1. Marc Lynch, "The Rise and Fall of the New Arab Public Sphere," *Current History* 114, 776 (December 2015): 332.
2. Michael Brenson, "Andres Serrano: Provocation and Spirituality," *New York Times*, December 8, 1989.
3. "Comments on Andres Serrano by Members of the United States Senate," *Congressional Record*, May 18, 1989, http://thomas.loc.gov/cgi-bin/query/F?r101:89:./temp/~r101txU1Ji:e6261, accessed April 8, 2015.
4. Bernard Crick, *In Defence of Politics* (Chicago: University of Chicago Press), 21.
5. Sebastian Veg, "New Spaces, New Controls: China's Embryonic Public Sphere," *Current History* 114, 773 (September 2015): 203–209.
6. Berna Turam, *Gaining Freedom: Claiming Space in Istanbul and Berlin* (Palo Alto: Stanford University Press, 2015), 11.
7. Samuel Huntington, *Political Order in Changing Societies* (New Haven: Yale University Press, 1968), 5.
8. Ibid., 30.

BIBLIOGRAPHY

Abdo, Geneive. "Salafists and Sectarianism: Twitter and Communal Conflict in the Middle East." Paper. Center for Middle East Policy at Brookings, March 2015.

Abu Faris, Muhammad `Abd al-Qadir. *Al-ahwal al-shakhsiyya: al-ahliyya, al-wilaya, al-wasaya, al-arath*. Amman: Dar al-Qur'an li-l-nashr wa-l-tawzi`, 2012.

Aday, Sean, Henry Farrell, Marc Lynch, John Sides, and Deen Freelon. "Blogs and Bullets II: New Media and Conflict After the Arab Spring." *Peaceworks* 80 (July 2012).

Aday, Sean, Henry Farrell, Marc Lynch, John Sides, John Kelly, and Ethan Zuckerman. "Blogs and Bullets: New Media in Contentious Politics." *Peaceworks* 65 (September 2010), http://www.usip.org/sites/default/files/pw65.pdf, accessed June 23, 2014.

Agrama, Hussein. *Questioning Secularism: Islam, Sovereignty, and the Rule of Law in Modern Egypt*. Chicago: University of Chicago Press, 2012.

Ahmed, Shahab. *What is Islam? The Importance of Being Islamic*. Princeton: Princeton University Press, 2016.

Ajemian, Pete. "The Islamist Opposition Online in Egypt and Jordan." *Arab Media and Society* 4, (2008).

Al-`Utayfi, Jamal. *Ara' fi al-shari`a wa-fi al-hurriyya* [*Opinions on the Shari`a and Freedom*]. Cairo: Al-hay'a al-misriyya al-`amma li-l-kitab, 1980.

Al-Ali, Zaid. *The Struggle for Iraq's Future*. New Haven: Yale University Press, 2014.

Al-Ali, Zaid and Nathan J. Brown. "Egypt's Constitution Swings into Action." *Foreign Policy*, March 27, 2013.

Al-Arian, Abdullah. *Answering the Call: Popular Islamic Activism in Sadat's Egypt*. Oxford: Oxford University Press, 2014.

Al-Hudaybi, Hasan. *Dusturuna*. Cairo: Dar al-Ansar, 1978.

Al-Jassar, Mohammad Khalid A. *Constancy and change in contemporary Kuwait City: The socio-cultural dimensions of the Kuwait courtyard and Diwaniyya*. Ph.D. diss., Department of Anthropology, University of Wisconsin, Milwaukee, 2009.

Al-Shuyukh, Majlis. *Al-dustur: ta`liqat `ala mawadihi bi-l-a`mal al-tahdiriyya wa-l-munaqashat al-barlamaniyya*. Cairo: Matba`at Misr, 1940.

Amanat, Abbas and Frank Griffel, eds. *Shari'a: Islamic Law in the Contemporary Context*. Palo Alto: Stanford University Press, 2009.

Arendt, Hannah. *The Promise of Politics*. New York: Schocken, 2005.

Arjomand, Saïd Amir. "Constitutions and the Struggle for Political Order: A Study in the Modernization of Political Traditions." *European Journal of Sociology* 33, 1 (1992): 39–82.

Asad, Talal. *Formations of the Secular: Christianity, Islam, Modernity*. Palo Alto: Stanford University Press, 2003.

Ayalon, Ami. *The Press in the Arab Middle East: A History*. New York: Oxford University Press, 1995.

———. *Reading Palestine: Printing and Literacy, 1900–1948*. Austin: University of Texas Press, 2010.

Bayat, Asef. *Life as Politics: How Ordinary People Change the Middle East*. Palo Alto: Stanford University Press, 2009.

Beissinger, Mark R. "'Conventional' and 'Virtual' Civil Societies in Autocratic Regimes." Paper prepared for the 20th International Conference of Europeanists, Amsterdam, The Netherlands, June 25–27, 2013.

———. "How the Impossible Becomes Inevitable: The Public Sphere and the Collapse of Soviet Communism." Transformations of the Public Sphere, Social Science Research Council and Institute for Public Knowledge, http://publicsphere. ssrc.org/beissinger-the-public-sphere-and-the-collapse-of-soviet-communism, posted November 2, 2009; accessed March 19, 2015.

Bessant, Judith. "The Political in the Age of the Digital: Propositions for Empirical Investigation." *Politics* 34, 1 (2012): 33–44.

Binjalun, Ahmad Majid. *Al-dustur al-maghrabi: mabadi'ihi wa ahkamihi*. Casablanca: Dar al-Kitab, 1977.

Blaustein, Albert P. and Gisbert H. Flanz, eds. *Constitutions of the World*. Dobbs Ferry: Oceana Publications, 2007.

Bowen, John. *A New Anthropology of Islam*. Cambridge: Cambridge University Press, 2012.

Brand, Laurie A. *Official Stories: Politics and National Narratives in Egypt and Algeria*. Palo Alto: Stanford University Press, 2014.

Branson, Kayla. "Islamist Cyber-Activism: Contesting the Message, Redefining the Public." *Journal of North African Studies* 19, 5 (2014): 713–732.

Brinton, Jacqueline Jayne Gottlieb. "Preaching Islamic Renewal: Shaykh Muḥammad Mitwallī Shaʿrāwī and the Synchronization of Revelation and Contemporary Life." PhD diss., University of Virginia, Religious Studies, 2009.

Browers, Michaelle. *Political Ideology in the Arab World: Accommodation and Transformation*. Cambridge: Cambridge University Press, 2009.

Brown, Jonathan A. C. "Salafis and Sufis in Egypt." Paper. Carnegie Endowment for International Peace, December 2011.

Brown, Nathan J. "Brigands and State Building: The Invention of Banditry in Modern Egypt." *Comparative Studies in Society and History* 32, 2 (1990): 258–281.

———. "Can the Colossus Be Salvaged? Egypt's State-Owned Press in a Post-Revolutionary Environment." Carnegie Web Commentary, August 22, 2011, http://carnegieendowment.org/2011/08/22/can-colossus-be-salvaged-egypt-s-state-owned-press-in-post-revolutionary-environment/4ud2, accessed March 26, 2015.

———. "Constitutionalism, Authoritarianism, and Imperialism in Iraq." *Drake Law Review* 53, 4 (2005): 923–941.

———. *Constitutions in a Nonconstitutional World: Arab Basic Laws and the Prospects for Accountable Government*. Albany: SUNY Press, 2001.

———. "A Discussion of Wael Hallaq's Islam, Politics, and Modernity's Moral Predicament." *Perspective on Politics* 12, 2 (2014): 464–466.

———. "Islam and Constitutionalism in the Arab World: The Puzzling Course of Islamic Inflation." In *Constitution Writing, Religion and Democracy*, edited by Asli Bali and Hanna Lerner. Cambridge: Cambridge University Press, forthcoming.

———. *Palestinian Politics after the Oslo Accords: Resuming Arab Palestine*. Berkeley: University of California Press, 2003.

———. "Reason, Interest, Rationality, and Passion in Constitution Drafting." *Perspectives on Politics* 6, 4 (2008): 675–689.

———. "Regimes Reinventing Themselves: Constitutional Development in the Arab World." *International Sociology* 18, 1 (2003): 33–52.

———. *The Rule of Law in the Arab World: Courts in Egypt and the Gulf*. Cambridge: Cambridge University Press, 1997.

———. "Shari'a and State in the Modern Muslim Middle East." *International Journal of Middle East Studies* 29, 3 (1997): 359–376.

———. *When Victory is Not an Option: Islamist Movements in Arab Politics*. Ithaca: Cornell University Press, 2012.

———, ed. *The Dynamics of Democratization: Dictatorship, Development, and Diffusion*. Baltimore: Johns Hopkins University Press, 2011.

Buraq Center for Research and Culture, Al-. "Proceedings of a Workshop Concerning the Curriculum for Civic Education for the Eight Elementary Grade in Palestinian Schools." Unpublished manuscript, Ramallah, May 24, 2003.

Buskens, Léon. "Recent Debates on Family Law Reform in Morocco: Islamic Law as Politics in an Emerging Public Sphere." *Islamic Law and Society* 10, 1 (2003): 70–131.

Caeiro, Alexandre. "Debating the Chaos of Fatwas in the Arab World." Paper presented at the Annual Meeting of the Middle East Studies Association, New Orleans, 2013.

Calhoun, Craig, ed. *Habermas and the Public Sphere*. Cambridge: MIT Press, 1999.

Calhoun, Craig, Mark Juergensmeyer, and Jonathan Van Antwerpen, eds. *Rethinking Secularism*. Oxford: Oxford University Press, 2011.

Cammet, Melanie, and Pauline Jones Luong. "Is There an Islamist Political Advantage?" *Annual Review of Political Science* 17 (2014): 187–206.

Casanova, José. *Public Religions in the Modern World*. Chicago: University of Chicago Press, 1994.

Cesari, Jocelyn. *The Awakening of Muslim Democracy: Religion, Modernity, and the State*. Cambridge: Cambridge University Press, 2014.

Clark, Janine A. *Islam, Charity, and Activism: Middle-Class Networks and Social Welfare in Egypt, Jordan, and Yemen*. Bloomington: Indiana University Press, 2004.

Cook, Bradley James. "Egypt's National Education Debate." *Comparative Education* 36, 4 (2000): 477–490.

Cook, Michael. *Commanding Right and Forbidding Wrong in Islamic Thought*. Cambridge: Cambridge University Press, 2001.

Cooper, Kenneth J. "Politics and Priorities: Inside the Egyptian Press." *Arab Media and Society* 6, (2008).

Corstange, Daniel. "Religion, Pluralism, and Iconography in the Public Sphere: Theory and Evidence from Lebanon." *World Politics* 64, 1 (2012): 116–160.

Crick, Bernard. *In Defence of Politics*. Chicago: University of Chicago Press.

Cuno, Kenneth M. *Modernizing Marriage: Family, Ideology, and Law in Nineteenth- and Early Twentieth-Century Egypt*. Syracuse: Syracuse University Press, 2015.

Dajani, Nabil. "The Myth of Media Freedom in Lebanon." *Arab Media and Society* 18, (2013).

Della Ratta, Donatella, Naomi Sakr, and Jakob Skovgaard-Petersen. *Arab Media Moguls*. London: I. B. Tauris, 2015.

Doumato, Eleanor Abdella, and Gregory Starrett, eds. *Teaching Islam: Textbooks and Religion in the Middle East*. Boulder: Lynne Rienner, 2006.

El Muhtaseb, Lamis, Nathan J. Brown, and Abdul-Wahab M. Kayyali. "Arguing about Family Law in Jordan: Disconnected Spheres?" *International Journal of Middle East Studies* 48, 4 (2016).

Elmasry, Mohamad Hamas. "Producing News in Mubarak's Egypt: An Analysis of Egyptian Newspaper Production During the Late Hosni Mubarak Era." *Journal of Arab & Muslim Media Research* 4, 2–3 (2012): 121–144.

Elmeshad, Mohamed. "We Completely Agree: Egyptian Television Media in the Era of Al-Sisi." *Jadaliyya*, April 6, 2015, http://www.jadaliyya.com/pages/index/21305/we-completely-agree_egyptian-television-media-in-t, accessed July 14, 2015.

Elster, Jon, ed. *Deliberative Democracy*. Cambridge: Cambridge University Press, 1998.

Elster, Jon, Claus Offe, and Ulrich K. Preuss. *Institutional Design in Post-Communist Societies: Rebuilding the Ship at Sea*. Cambridge: Cambridge University Press, 1998.

Engelcke, Dörthe. "Processes of Family Law Reform: Legal and Societal Change and Continuity in Morocco and Jordan." PhD diss., St Antony's College, University of Oxford, 2014.

Esposito, John L. *Women in Muslim Family Law*. Syracuse: Syracuse University Press, 1982.

Fahmy, Ziad. *Ordinary Egyptians: Creating the Modern Nation through Popular Culture*. Palo Alto: Stanford University Press, 2011.

Faris, David. "(Amplified) Voices for the Voiceless." *Arab Media and Society* 11 (2010).

Farmanian, Roxane. "What is Private, What is Public, and Who Exercises Media Power in Tunisia? A Hybrid-Functional Perspective on Tunisia's Media Sector." *Journal of North African Studies* 19, 5 (2014): 656–678.

Farrell, Henry. "The Consequences of the Internet for Politics." *Annual Review of Political Science* 15 (2012): 35–52.

Fearon, James. "Domestic Political Audiences and the Escalation of International Disputes." *American Political Science Review* 88, 3 (1994): 577–592.

Ferree, Myra Marx, William A. Gamson, Jürgen Gerhards, and Dieter Rucht, "Four Models of the Public Sphere in Modern Democracies." *Theory and Society* 31 (2002): 289–324.

Feuer, Sarah J. "Religious Establishment and Regime Survival: The Politics of Religious Education in Morocco and Tunisia, 1956–2010.". PhD diss., Brandeis University Politics Department and Crown Center for Middle East Studies, 2014.

Fontana, Benedetto, Cary J. Nederman, and Gary Remer. *Talking Democracy: Historical Perspectives on Rhetoric and Democracy*. University Park: Penn State Press, 2004.

Frega, Roberto. "Equal Accessibility to All: Habermas, Pragmatism, and the Place of Religious Beliefs in a Post-Secular Society." *Constellations* 19, 2 (2012): 267–287.

Gaffney, Patrick D. *The Prophet's Pulpit: Islamic Preaching in Contemporary Egypt*. Berkeley: University of California Press, 1994.

Gallagher, Charles F. *Toward Constitutional Government in Morocco: A Referendum Endorses the Constitution*. Report, North Africa Series, Volume IX, No. 1 (Morocco). American Universities Field Staff: 1963.

Gamson, Joshua. "Taking the Talk Show Challenge: Television, Emotion, and Public Spheres." *Constellations* 6, 2 (1999): 190–205.

Garsten, Bryan. "The Rhetoric Revival in Political Theory." *Annual Review of Political Science* 14 (2011): 159–80.

Gerbaudo, Paolo. *Tweets and the Streets: Social Media and Contemporary Activism.* London: Pluto Press, 2012.

Gershoni, Israel. *Redefining the Egyptian Nation, 1930–1945.* Cambridge: Cambridge University Press, 2002.

Gräf, Bettin and Jakob Skovgaard-Petersen, eds. *Global Mufti: The Phenomenon of Yusuf al-Qaradawi.* New York: Columbia University Press, 2009.

Grehan, James. *Twilight of the Saints: Everyday Religion in Ottoman Syria and Palestine.* Oxford: Oxford University Press, 2014.

Grote, Rainer, and Tilmann Röder, eds. *Constitutionalism in Islamic Countries: Between Upheaval and Continuity.* Oxford: Oxford University Press, 2012.

Gutmann, Amy, and Dennis Thompson, *Why Deliberative Democracy?* Princeton: Princeton University Press, 2004.

Habermas, Jürgen. *Between Facts and Norms: Contributions to a Discourse Theory of Law and Democracy.* Cambridge: Cambridge University Press, 1996.

———. *Europe: The Faltering Project.* Cambridge: Polity Books, 2009.

———. *The Structural Transformation of the Public Sphere: An Inquiry into a Category of Bourgeois Society.* Cambridge: MIT Press, 1989.

Hallaq, Wael B. "From Fatwās to Furūʿ: Growth and Change in Islamic Substantive Law." *Islamic Law and Society* 1, 1 (1994): 29–65.

———. *The Impossible State: Islam, Politics, and Modernity's Moral Predicament.* New York: Columbia University Press, 2014.

———. *An Introduction to Islamic Law.* Cambridge: Cambridge University Press, 2009.

Hammon, Andrew. "Reading Lohaidan in Riyadh: Media and the Struggle for Judicial Power in Saudi Arabia." *Arab Media and Society* 7 (2009).

Hamoudi, Haider Ala. *Negotiating in Civil Conflict: Constitutional Construction and Imperfect Bargaining in Iraq.* Chicago: University of Chicago Press, 2013.

Hassner, Ran E. *War on Sacred Grounds.* Ithaca: Cornell University Press, 2009.

Hatina, Meir. *'Ulamaʾ, Politics, and the Public Sphere: An Egyptian Perspective.* Salt Lake City: University of Utah Press, 2010.

Hattox, Ralph. *Coffee and Coffeehouses: The Origins of a Social Beverage in the Medieval Near East.* Seattle: University of Washington Press, 1985.

Hefner, Robert, ed. *Shariʿa Politics: Islamic Law and Society in the Modern World.* Bloomington: Indiana University Press, 2011.

Hefner, Robert W., and Mohammad Qasim Zaman. *Schooling Islam: The Culture and Politics of Modern Muslim Education.* Princeton: Princeton University Press, 2007.

Hegel-Cantarella, Christine. "Kin-to-Be: Betrothal, Legal Documents, and Reconfiguring Relational Obligations in Egypt." *Law, Culture and the Humanities* 7, 3 (2011): 377–393.

Herrera, Linda Ann. "The Sanctity of the School: New Islamic Education and Modern Egypt." PhD diss., Columbia University, 2000.

Hill, Enid. *Mahkama! Studies in the Egyptian Legal System.* London: Ithaca Press, 1979.

Hirschkind, Charles. "Beyond Secular and Religious: An Intellectual Genealogy of Tahrir Square." *American Ethnologist* 39, 1 (2011): 49–53.

———. "Civic Virtue and Religious Reason: An Islamic Counterpublic." *Cultural Anthropology* 16, 1 (2001): 3–34.

———. "New Media and Political Dissent in Egypt." *Revista de Dialectologia y Tradiciones Populares* 65, 1 (2010): 137–153.

Hodgson, Marshall. *The Venture of Islam.* Vol. 1, *The Classical Age of Islam.* Chicago: University of Chicago Press, 1977.

Horowitz, Donald. *Constitutional Change and Democracy in Indonesia.* Cambridge: Cambridge University Press, 2013.

Howard, Philip N. *The Digital Origins of Dictatorship and Democracy: Information Technology and Political Islam.* Oxford: Oxford University Press, 2010.

Hroub, Khaled. *Religious Broadcasting in the Middle East.* New York: Columbia University Press, 2012.

Hudson, Leila. "Late Ottoman Damascus: Investments in Public Space and the Emergence of Popular Sovereignty." *Critique: Critical Middle Eastern Studies* 15, 2 (2006): 151–169.

Huntington, Samuel. *Political Order in Changing Societies.* New Haven: Yale University Press, 1968.

Husseini, Rana. *Murder in the Name of Honor: The True Story of One Woman's Fight against an Unbelievable Crime.* Oxford: One World, 2009.

Ismail, Salwa. "Islamism, Re-Islamization and the Fashioning of Muslim Selves: Refiguring the Public Sphere." *Muslim World Journal of Human Rights* 4, 1 (2007): 1–21.

———. *Rethinking Islamist Politics: Culture, the State and Islamism.* London: I. B. Tauris, 2006.

———. "Urban Subalterns in the Arab Revolutions: Cairo and Damascus in Comparative Perspective." *Comparative Studies in Society and History* 55, 4 (2013): 865–894.

Ivey, Kevin. "Social Media and Contentious Politics: Tunisia 2010–2013." Master's thesis, Elliott School of International Affairs, George Washington University, 2014.

Johansen, Baber. *Contingency in a Sacred Law: Legal and Ethical Norms in the Muslim Fiqh.* Leiden: Brill, 1998.

Jones, Linda G. *The Power of Oratory in the Medieval Muslim World.* Cambridge: Cambridge University Press, 2012.

Juergensmeyer, Mark. *Global Rebellion: Religious Challenges to the Secular State, from Christian Militias to Al Qaeda.* Berkeley: University of California Press, 2008.

Khadduri, Majid. "Constitutional Development in Syria." *Middle East Journal* 5, 2 (Spring 1951): 137–160.

Kuran, Timur. *Private Truths, Public Lies: The Social Consequences of Preference Falsification.* Cambridge: Harvard University Press, 1997.

Langohr, Vickie. "Too Much Civil Society, Too Little Politics: Egypt and Liberalizing Arab Regimes." *Comparative Politics* 36, 2 (2004): 181–204.

LeBas, Adrienne. "Polarization as Craft: Party Formation and State Violence in Zimbabwe." *Comparative Politics* 38, 4 (2006): 419–438.

Lombardi, Clark B. "Constitutional Provisions Making Sharia 'a' or 'the' Chief Source of Legislation: Where Did They Come From? What Do They Mean? Do They Matter?" *American University International Law Review* 28 (2013): 733–774.

———. *State Law as Islamic Law in Modern Egypt.* Leiden: Brill, 2006.

Long, Pietro. "Islamic Constitutionalism and Constitutional Politics in Post-Revolutionary Tunisia." WP 03/23 Working Paper Series. UNILU Center of Comparative Constitutional Law and Religion, 2013.

Lynch, Marc. "After Egypt: The Limits and Promise of Online Challenges to the Authoritarian Arab State." *Perspectives on Politics* 9, 2 (2011): 301–310.
———. *The Arab Uprising: The Unfinished Revolutions of the New Middle East.* New York: Public Affairs, 2012.
———. "The Rise and Fall of the New Arab Public Sphere." *Current History*, 114, 776 (December 2015): 331–336.
———. *State Interests and Public Spheres: The International Politics of Jordan's Identity.* New York: Columbia University Press, 1999.
———. "Taking Arabs Seriously." *Foreign Affairs* 82, 5 (2003): 81–94.
———. *Voices of the New Arab Public: Iraq, al-Jazeera, and Middle East Politics Today.* New York: Columbia University Press, 2006.
———. "Young Brothers in Cyberspace." *Middle East Report* 37 (2007): 26.
Lynch, Marc, ed. *The Arab Uprisings Explained: New Contentious Politics in the Middle East.* New York: Columbia University Press, 2014.
Macedo, Stephen, ed. *Deliberative Politics: Essays on Democracy and Disagreement.* New York: Oxford University Press, 1999.
Mah, Harold. "Phantasies of the Public Sphere: Rethinking the Habermas of Historians." *Journal of Modern History* 72, 1 (2000): 153–182.
Mahmood, Saba. *Politics of Piety: The Islamic Revival and the Feminist Subject.* Princeton: Princeton University Press, 2005.
Makiya, Kanan. *Republic of Fear: The Politics of Modern Iraq.* Berkeley: University of California Press, 1998.
Maktabi, Rania. "Female Citizenship in the Middle East: Comparing Family Law Reform in Morocco, Egypt, Syria and Lebanon." *Middle East Law and Governance* 5 (2013): 280–307.
Mansbridge, Jane, James Bohman, Simone Chambers, David Estlund, Andreas Føllesdal, Archon Fung, Cristina Lafont, Bernard Manin and José luis Martí. "The Place of Self-Interest and the Role of Power in Deliberative Democracy." *Journal of Political Philosophy* 18, 1 (2010): 64–100.
March, Andrew F. "Genealogies of Sovereignty in Islamic Political Theology." *Social Research* 80, 1 (2013): 293–320.
———. "Islamic Legal Theory, Secularism and Religious Pluralism: Is Modern Religious Freedom Sufficient for the Shari'a 'Purpose [Maqsid]' of 'Preserving Religion [Hifz Al-Din]?'" Islamic Law and Law of the Muslim World Research Paper Series Paper No. 09-78; Public Law Working Paper No. 208. Yale Law School, 2009.
———. "Rethinking Religious Reasons in Public Justification." *American Political Science Review* 107, 3 (August 2013): 523–539.
March, Andrew F. and Mara Revkin. "Caliphate of Law: ISIS' Ground Rules." *Foreign Affairs*, April 15, 2015, https://www.foreignaffairs.com/articles/syria/2015-04-15/caliphate-law, accessed July 16, 2016.
Marks, Monica L. "Convince, Coerce, or Compromise? Ennahda's Approach to Tunisia's Constitution." Paper Number 10. Brookings Doha Center Analysis, February 2014.
Masoud, Tarek. *Counting Islam: Religion, Class, and Elections in Egypt.* Cambridge: Cambridge University Press, 2014.
McGeehan, Nicholas. "Control, Halt, Delete: Gulf States Crack Down on Online Critics." *Al-Monitor*, August 8, 2013, http://www.al-monitor.com/pulse/originals/2013/08/gulf-states-online-critics-crackdown-cybercrime-social-media.html, accessed June 23, 2014.

McKee, Alan. *The Public Sphere: An Introduction.* Cambridge: Cambridge University Press, 2005.

Mellor, Noha. *The Making of Arab News.* Lanham, MD: Rowman & Littlefield, 2005.

Mendelberg, Tali, Christopher F. Karpowitz, and J. Baxter Oliphant. "The Deliberative Citizen: Theory and Evidence." *Political Decision Making, Deliberation and Participation* 6 (2002): 151–193.

———. "Gender Inequality in Deliberation: Unpacking the Black Box of Interaction." *Perspectives on Politics* 12, 1 (2014): 1–10.

Mestyan, Adam. "A Garden with Mellow Fruits of Refinement: Music Theaters and Cultural Politics in Cairo and Istanbul, 1867–1892." PhD diss., Department of History, Central European University, 2011.

"Minister Compares New Suez Canal to Prophet Mohamed's Battle Trench." Mada Masr, August 4, 2015, http://www.madamasr.com/news/minister-compares-new-suez-canal-prophet-mohameds-battle-trench, accessed December 30, 2015.

"[Ministry of] Education: Decisions are Issued to Organize Work in International Schools . . . and Saluting the Flag and the Anthem are 'Obligatory,'" al-Shuruq, September 15, 2014.

Moll, Yasmin. "Islamic Satellite Channels and the Ethics of Entertainment in Egypt" *al-Sada*, April 21, 2010.

———. "Islamic Televangelism: Religion, Media and Visuality in Contemporary Egypt." *Arab Media and Society* 10 (2010).

Myers, C. Daniel, and Tali Mendelberg. "Political Deliberation." In *Oxford Handbook of Political Psychology*, edited by Leonie Huddy, David Sears and Jack Levy. Oxford: Oxford University Press, 2012.

Nielsen, Marjatta, and Jakob Skovgaard-Petersen, eds. *Middle Eastern Cities 1900–1950: Public Spaces and Public Spheres.* Aarhus: Aarhus University Press, 2001.

O'Kane, Joseph P. "Islam in the New Egyptian Constitution: Some Discussions in al-Ahram." *Middle East Journal* 26, 2 (1972): 137–148.

Ober, Josiah. "Democracy's Wisdom: An Aristotelian Middle Way for Our Collective Judgment." *American Political Science Review* 107, 1 (2013): 104–122.

Opwis, Felicitas. "Maṣlaḥa in Contemporary Islamic Legal Theory." *Islamic Law and Society* 12, 2 (2005): 182–223.

———. *Maṣlaḥah and the Purpose of the Law: Islamic Discourse on Legal Change from the 4th/10th to 8th/14th Century.* Leiden: Brill, 2010.

Palestinian National Authority, Ministry of Education, *First Palestinian Curriculum Plan*, Ramallah: Ministry of Education, 1997.

Parkinson, John, and Jane Mansbridge. *Deliberative Systems.* Cambridge: Cambridge University Press, 2012.

Parolin, Gianluca. "(Re)Arrangement of State/Islam Relations in Egypt's Constitutional Transition." Public Law Research Paper No. 13-15, NYU School of Law, May 2013.

Petersen, Mark Allen. *Connected in Cairo: Growing up Cosmopolitan in the Modern Middle East.* Bloomington: Indiana University Press, 2011.

———. "Egypt's Media Ecology in a Time of Revolution." *Arab Media and Society* 14 (Summer 2011).

Przeworksi, Adam. "Deliberation and Ideological Domination." In *Deliberative Democracy*, edited by Jon Elster. Cambridge: Cambridge University Press, 1998, 140–160.

Rugh, William A. *Arab Mass Media: Newspapers, Radio, and Television in Arab Politics.* Westport: Praeger, 2004.

Said, Atef Shahat. "The Tahrir Effect: History, Space, and Protest in the Egyptian Revolution of 2011." PhD diss., University of Michigan, Department of Sociology, 2014.

Sakr, Naomi. *Satellite Realms: Transnational Television, Globalization and the Middle East.* (London: I. B. Tauris, 2001.

———. *Transformations in Egyptian Journalism: Media and the Arab Uprisings.* London: I. B. Tauris, 2013.

Salame, Zakiye. *Between Feminism and Islam: Human Rights and Sharia Law in Morocco.* Minneapolis: University of Minnesota Press, 2011.

Satti, Mohamed. "International Media and Local Programming: The Case of Kuwait." *Arab Media and Society* 18, 2013.

Sayed, Fatma. "The Contested Terrain of Educational Reform in Egypt." In *Education and the Arab 'World': Political Projects, Struggles, and Geometries of Power, World Yearbook of Education 2010,* edited by André E. Mazawi and Ronald G. Sultana. New York: Routledge, 2010, 77–92.

———. *Transforming Education in Egypt: Western Influence and Domestic Policy Reform.* Cairo: American University in Cairo Press, 2006.

Sayyid-Marsot, Afaf Lutfi. *Egypt in the Reign of Muhammad Ali.* Cambridge: Cambridge Universty Press, 1984.

Schielke, Samuel. *The Perils of Joy: Contesting Mulid Festivals in Contemporary Egypt.* Syracuse: Syracuse University Press, 2012.

Schwedler, Jillian, and Janine A. Clark. "Islamist-Leftist Cooperation in the Arab World." *ISIM Review* 18 (2006): 2.

Scott, James C. *Seeing Like a State.* New Haven: Yale University Press, 1998.

Selvik, Kjetil. "Elite Rivalry in a Semi-Democracy: The Kuwaiti Press Scene." *Middle Eastern Studies* 47, 3 (2011): 477–496.

Selvik, Kjetil, Jon Nordenson, and Tewodros Aragi Kebede. "Print Media Liberalization and Electoral Coverage Bias in Kuwait." *The Middle East Journal* 69, 2 (Spring 2015): 255–276.

Sezgin, Yuksel. *Human Rights under State-Enforced Religious Family Laws in Israel, Egypt and India.* Cambridge: Cambridge University Press, 2013.

Shaham, Ron. "Custom, Islamic Law, and Statutory Legislation: Marriage Registration and Minimum Age at Marriage in the Egyptian Shari'a Courts." *Islamic Law and Society* 2, 3 (1995): 258–281.

———. "Judicial Divorce at the Wife's Initiative." *Islamic Law and Society* 1, 2 (1994): 217–257.

———. "The Rhetoric of Legal Disputation: Neo-Ahl al-Ḥadīth vs. Yūsuf al-Qaraḍāwī." *Islamic Law and Society* 22, 1 (2015): 114–141.

Shapiro, Martin. "The Giving Reasons Requirement." *University of Chicago Legal Forum* 1 (1992): 179–220.

Sharafeldin, Marwa. "Islamic Law Meets Human Rights: Reformulating *Qiwamah* and *Wilayah* for Personal Status Law Reform Advocacy in Egypt," in *Men In Charge? Rethinking Authority in Muslim Legal Tradition,* edited by Ziba Mir-Hosseini, Mulki Al-Sharmaini, and Jana Rumminger. London: Oneworld, 2015.

Singer, Aaron Rock. "Prayer and the Islamic Revival: A Timely Challenge." *International Journal of Middle East Studies* 48, 2, 2016.

Singerman Diane. "Rewriting Divorce in Egypt: Reclaiming Islam, Legal Activism, and Coalition Politics." In *Remaking Muslim Politics: Pluralism, Contestation,*

Democratization, edited by Robert Hefner. Princeton: Princeton University Press, 2005, 161–188.

———, ed. *Cairo Contested: Governance, Urban Space, and Global Modernity.* Cairo: American University in Cairo Press, 2011.

Sirri, Mun'im, and A. Rashied Omar. "Muslim Prayer and Public Spheres: An Interpretation of the Qur'anic Verse 29:45." *Interpretation* 68, 1 (2014): 39–53.

Skovgaard-Petersen, Jakob. "A Typology of State Muftis." In *Islamic Law and the Challenges of Modernity*, edited by Yvonne Haddad and Barbara Stowasser, New York: Altamira Press, 2004, 81–98.

Smith, Sarah Cowles. "Crowdsourcing Shari'a: Digital Fiqh And Changing Discourses Of Textual Authority, Individual Reason, and Social Coercion." Masters thesis. Georgetown University, Arab Studies, April 2011.

Snyder, Jack, ed. *Religion and International Relations Theory.* New York: Columbia University Press, 2011.

Sonneveld, Nadia. "The Implementation of the 'Khul` Law' in Egyptian Courts: Some Preliminary Results." *Recht van de Islam* 21 (2004): 21–35.

———. *Khul` Divorce in Egypt: Public Debates, Judicial Practices, and Everyday Life.* Cairo: American University in Cairo Press, 2012.

Soudias, Dimitris. "Negotiating Space: The Evolution of the Egyptian Street, 2000–2011." *Cairo Papers in Social Science* 32, 4 (2014).

Starrett, Gregory. *Putting Islam to Work: Education, Politics, and Religious Transformation in Egypt.* Berkeley: University of California Press, 1998.

Stasavage, David. "Polarization and Publicity: Rethinking the Benefits of Deliberative Democracy." *Journal of Politics* 69, 1 (2007): 59–72.

Steiner, Jurg, Andre Bachtiger, Markus Sporndli, and Marco R. Steenberge. *Deliberative Politics in Action: Analysing Parliamentary Discourse.* Cambridge: Cambridge University Press, 2004.

Stephenson, Lindsey. "Women and the Malleability of the Kuwaiti Dīwāniyya." *Journal of Arabian Studies* 1, 2 (2011): 183–199.

Stilt, Kristen. "Constitutional Islam: Genealogies, Transmissions and Meanings." http://ontheground.qatar.northwestern.edu/uncategorized/chapter-10-constitutional-islam-genealogies-transmissions-and-meanings, accessed April 1, 2015.

Sunstein, Cass R. *Designing Democracy: What Constitutions Do.* New York: Oxford University Press, 2001.

Tétreault, Mary Ann. *Stories of Democracy: Politics and Society in Contemporary Kuwait.* New York: Columbia University Press, 2000.

Thompson, Elizabeth. *Justice Interrupted: The Struggle for Constitutional Government in the Middle East.* Cambridge: Harvard University Press, 2013.

Tobin, Sarah A. "Ramadan Blues: Debates in Popular Islam during Ramadan in Amman, Jordan." *Digest of Middle East Studies* 22 (2013): 292–316.

Toft, Monica Duffy, Daniel Philpott, and Timothy Samuel Shah. *God's Century: Resurgent Religion and Global Politics.* New York: W. W. Norton, 2011.

Tucker, Judith E. *In the House of the Law: Gender and Islamic Law in Ottoman Syria and Palestine.* Berkeley: University of California Press, 2000.

Turam, Berna. *Gaining Freedom: Claiming Space in Istanbul and Berlin.* Palo Alto: Stanford University Press, 2015.

Veg, Sebastian. "New Spaces, New Controls: China's Embryonic Public Sphere." *Current History* 114, 773 (September 2015): 203–209.

Wainscott, Ann Marie. "Defending Islamic Education: War on Terror Discourse and Religious Education in Twenty-First-Century Morocco." *Journal of North African Studies* 20, 4 (2015): 635–653.

Warren, David H. "The 'Ulamāʾ and the Arab Uprisings 2011–13: Considering Yusuf al-Qaradawi, the 'Global Mufti,' between the Muslim Brotherhood, the Islamic Legal Tradition, and Qatari Foreign Policy." *New Middle Eastern Studies* 4 (2014): 1–33.

Wedeen, Lisa. *Ambiguities of Domination: Politics, Rhetoric, and Symbols in Contemporary Syria*. Chicago: University of Chicago Press, 1999.

———. *Peripheral Visions: Publics, Power, and Performance in Yemen*. Chicago: University of Chicago Press, 2008.

Weiss, Bernard. *The Spirit of Islamic Law*. Athens: University of Georgia Press, 2006.

White, Jenny. *Muslim Nationalism and the New Turks*. Princeton: Princeton University Press, 2013.

Wickham, Carrie. *Mobilizing Islam*. New York: Columbia University Press, 2005.

Wolin, Sheldon. "Democracy: Electoral and Athenian." *PS: Political Science and Politics* 26, 3 (1993): 475–478.

Yousef, Mossab Hassan. *Son of Hamas*. Carol Stream, Il: Tyndale House, 2010.

Zaman, Muhammad Qasim. *The Ulama in Contemporary Islam: Custodians of Change*. Princeton: Princeton University Press, 2007.

Zollner, Barbara. *The Muslim Brotherhood: Hasan al-Hudaybi and Ideology*. Abington: Routledge, 2009.

Zuckerman, Ethan. "New Media, New Civics." *Policy and Internet*, 6 (2014): 151–168.

INDEX

Note: page numbers followed by n refer to notes, with note number.

argument in Arab political debate. *See also* religious argument in Arab cultures

anti-Islam/Shariʿa arguments, rejection of, 121

directing of toward already-convinced, 18, 115, 202, 203

flow across media and spheres, 18, 139

   as obstacle to government policing, 98

   and separation of argument and speaker's authority, 18, 43–44, 49–50, 85, 92, 94, 95, 98, 112–14, 182, 197, 201–2, 216, 242

   simplification of arguments during, 36, 56, 97, 216, 242

   social media and, 111–12

recent increase in, 241, 242

revival of Islamic context of, 248

vehemence of, as product of insufficient mechanisms for influencing public policy, 249

authoritarian regimes

constitution writing in, 176

control of public record, 51–52, 53

economic failures of, 249

mid-20th century development of, 54

multiplication of public spheres and, 248–49

ongoing relevance of, 14, 247

post 2011 Arab nations and, 247

suppression of links between public spheres in, 104–5

suppression of political debate in, 12–13, 248

turn to semiauthoritarianism

   and increased Islamist influence on constitution writing, 163–64

   and increased links between social spheres, 105–10

   as incremental process, 54–55, 107

   and opening of public sphere, 13, 53

   and retreat from strong ideological stance, 106

   and rise of republic of arguments, 53

   scholarship on, 107

authority

display of unity of, at Morsi rally, 119–20

impact of multiple public spheres on, 49–50, 92

influence of in democratic politics, 17

political, as increasingly contested, 121

al-Azhar

ʿAbd al-Galil TV program and, 184

consultation of by public, 58–59

and debates on personal status law, 212, 213

and democratization of shariʿa interpretation, 129

fatwa programs and, 100

as interpreter of Islamic law in constitution, 173, 174, 213

and legal application of shariʿa, 161

and links between spheres, 102

Morsi government and, 67, 119, 120

post-2011 environment and, 115

and public debates of shariʿa, 109

publications by, 75

schools run by, 232, 236, 237

as source of authoritative fatwas, 191

and wardrobe as message, 80

and *wasatiyya* (moderation/centrism) as principle, 136

Badiʿ, Muhammad, 171

Badran, Ibrahim, 225, 235

al-Bannaʾ, Rajab, 233

bar associations, and spread of debate, 102

bargaining, *vs.* deliberation, 35

Barnett, Michael, 119

bayt al- taʿa (house of obedience) decrees, 194, 195

Beissinger, Mark R., 44, 83–84

Bin Ladin, Usama, 132

Brand, Laurie, 223

broadcast media, 76–81. See also *fatwa* advice programs

and Arab public sphere, creation of, 78, 80

crossing of borders by, 77, 78, 79, 81

deliberation as inconsistent with, 80

general pattern of development, 76–77

government control of, 81, 98, 104

and political argumentation, 77

popular entertainment on, 77

private, development of, 77
public influence, growth of, 78–79
and "red lines," undermining of, 77
religious programming on,
    78–81, 188–89
satellite television, impact of,
    77–78, 98
segmentation of markets, 78
slackening government control
    over, 77
Browers, Michaelle, 39, 44, 204
Al-Buraq Center, 229, 230, 239n16
bureaucratization of Islam, and
    fragmenting of government
    ideology, 75
bureaucrats, isolation from public
    opinion, 144
Burhami, Yasir, 94, 171–72
Buskens, Léon, 198, 214

Cairo
    Maydan al-Tahrir square, 63–64
    Morsi rally in (2012), 119–20
    streets in, as historical
        accretion, 52–53
Cairo Book Fair, 61, 97
changing with the hand, 136–37,
    142n24
China, multiple political spheres in, 249
Christians
    Egyptian constitution of 2012 and,
        172, 177
    schools, 236
citizenship law, personal status law
    and, 200
civilizing force of hypocrisy, 35, 36–37
color revolutions in Eastern Europe, 82
common good, lack of generally accepted
    concept of, 40
communal nature of Islam
    implications for public debate, 242–43
    and state role in protecting
        values, 243–44
complex purposivism, March on, 142n22
constitutions
    and exclusion of demos as goal, 38
    global trend toward identity
        statements in, 161–62
    as markers of sovereignty, 144
    as public documents, 147–48

constitutions of Arab countries. See also
    specific countries
early
    colonial influence on, 150–51,
        152, 153
    few Islamic provisions in, 150,
        151, 153
    government officials as writers of,
        149–50, 151, 152–53, 176
    outward focus on establishing
        autonomy, 153
    practical procedural focus of,
        153, 158–59
on education, 223
and effort to define political
    community, 149
and executive dominance, move
    toward, 158–59, 162
guarantees for minority rights in, 152
Islamic provisions in
    as expressive identity statements,
        161, 176, 177–78, 246
    as intrusion of government into
        Islam, 158–59, 161, 166–67
    limited legal force of,
        157–58, 160–62
    move toward, 148, 149, 152–56,
        158–59, 160
    and shariʿa as basis of law, 156–58
    after uprisings of 2011,
        160, 163–64
turn to open and inclusive process
    for, 176
uprisings of 2011 and
    basis in previous constitutions, 165
    demands for reform of, 162
    focus on constitutional issues
        following, 163–64
    increased public input in, 148, 165
    and Islamic constitutional
        provisions, 160, 175
    Islamists' focus on political
        details rather than symbolic
        language, 165
    political conditions for, 165–66
writing of
    in authoritarian era, 176
    democratization of after uprisings
        of 2011, 148, 163–64, 165, 176
    by elected bodies, 160

constitutions of Arab countries (*Cont.*)
  as expressive statements of identity,
    161, 176, 177–78, 246
  history of, 149–56
  increased expectations for public
    participation in, 148, 152,
    154–55, 159–60, 175–76
  increased public interest in, 148
  as iterative process, 165
  and public participation as illusion,
    154–55, 157, 159–60
  and referendums, as ritualistic
    formality, 154–55, 160
courts, Islamic. *See also* judiciary
  government efforts to
    marginalize, 126
  and interpretation of shari'a, 131
  and Islam as way of ordering public
    life, 185
  in Jordan, and personal status law
    reform, 206–9
  limited overlap with fatwas and
    legislatures, 215–16
  traditional role in shari'a
    interpretation, 125
courts, personal status, 191–97
  in Egypt, and marriage and divorce
    laws, 193–95, 196
  family violence cases and, 195
  and fatwa advice programs, compared,
    192–93, 196–97
  and movement of argument *vs.*
    status, 197
  as public, in theory, 191–92
  as quasi-private, 192, 193
  skepticism of participants, 193
Crick, Bernard, 246
cultural pluralism, and collapse of public
    good concept, 40

Dar al-Ifta', 161
deliberation
  vs. bargaining or aggregation, 35
  by juries, 35–36
  nadwa (colloquiums/seminars) and, 60
  in public discourse
    argument as more realistic term for,
      33, 35, 37–39, 42, 242
    increasingly broad definition
      of, 34–35

as largely theoretical fiction, 34–37
  research on, focus on small groups, 36
democracy. *See also* liberal democratic
    thought
  characteristics of debate in, 17
  and minority rights, 28
  potential pernicious effects of, 28
  and public debate, assumed benefits of
    link between, 26, 27–30, 37–38
  public debate as corrective force in, 26
diwaniyya
  in Kuwait, 60, 61
  links between Kuwaiti parliament
    and, 92–94

education
  constitutional provisions for, 223
  and democratization of shari'a
    interpretation, 126–27
  government control of, 222, 235–38
  private schools, 232, 236, 237
  students' views on, 237
educational curriculum
  argument on, 221
    in Egypt, 231–34
    exclusion of public from, 224–25
    fierceness of, 221, 238
    in Jordan, 233–34
    limited impact of, 221–22, 225,
      231, 232–34, 235, 238
    in Palestine, 225, 226–31
  and critical thinking, underemphasis
    of, 224
  in elite schools, flexibility in, 235–36
  goals of, 223–24
  government control of,
    222–23, 224–25
  growing critique of among
    intellectuals, 225–26
  input of religious establishment
    to, 222–23
  in Jordan, 233–34
  and nationalism
    debate on in Egypt, 233
    debate on in Palestine, 227–28
  in Palestine, 223, 224, 225, 226–31
  progressive *vs.* traditionalist battles
    in, 228–30
  reform efforts, conservative resistance
    to, 225–26

and religion
  debate on in Egypt, 232–33
  debate on in Palestine, 227, 228
  dogmatic views on, 224, 226
  equation of with state, 224
  as mandatory subject, 222
  revival of Arab politics and, 225
  rigidity of as product of resource
    limitations, 226
educational establishments, Islamic
  government assertion of control over,
    126, 128–29, 158, 161
  traditional role in shari'a
    interpretation, 125
Egypt. *See also* Cairo; Muslim
    Brotherhood: in Egypt; *specific
    presidents*
  and bloggers as link to "the street," 43
  broadcast industry in, 79
  civil code, and Shari'a law, 108, 109
  constitution of 1923, 150–52,
    153, 154–55
  constitution of 1971, 154–55,
    157, 160
    and Islam as basis of legislation
      (Article 2), 109, 157, 159, 160–61,
      163, 172–73
    and state control over religion, 161
    on women's rights, 161
  constitution of 2012
    basis in previous constitution, 165
    debate on, and speakers' loss of
      control over words, 94
    democratization of drafting
      process, 163
    drafting process for, 170–73
    expressive identity statements
      in, 177–78
    and Islam as basis of legislation
      (Article 2), 169–70, 171
    Islamic provisions, debate on, 160,
      169–70, 171–72, 177
    Islamists' focus on political details
      over symbolism, 165
    Islamists' role in writing of, 164, 169
    non-Islamists and, 173
    as product of compromise, 173
    religious freedom as issue in, 172
    suspension of, 169, 173
    on women's rights, 165, 172

constitution of 2014
  complexity of negotiations for, 175
  drafting process for, 169, 173–75
  on education, 223
  and Islam as basis of legislation
    (Article 2), 174
  Islamic provisions in, 174–75
  Islamists and, 169
  non-Islamists and, 169, 170, 175
  public officials as drafters of, 174
  religious freedom in, 175
  similarity to earlier constitutions,
    169, 174, 176
  strengthening of presidency in, 175
  women's rights in, 175
constitution writing, open, inclusive
    process for, 176
constitutional committee of 1954, 159
contemporary, political repression
    in, 247–48
coup of 2013, 6, 65, 100,
    113–14, 173
  broadcast media and, 81
  failure to find compromise
    after, 144
  and ouster of Muslim Brotherhood,
    164, 169, 175
  and political resurgence of jihadist
    groups, 20
  press and, 74, 76
  salafis and, 65, 81
  violence in, 81
education in
  curriculum debates, 231–34
  education bureaucracy, 231–32
  education guarantees in
    constitution of 2014, 223
  private schools, 232, 236
  and rise of Islamist
    movements, 237
government control of mosques in,
    65–69, 109–10, 247–48
imams, deference among, 66
judiciary in, 101, 107
linking of social spheres in early 20th
    century, 102–3
local *vs.* government perspective on
    life in, 52–53
low impact of public debate on
    outcomes, 116

al-Ghazzali, Muhammad, 186, 218n23

governments, Arab. *See also*
      authoritarian regimes;
      semi-authoritarian regimes
   domination of public life, in early 20th
      century, 101
   efforts to control shariʻa
      interpretation, 126–27,
      128, 130–31
   as historical accretions, 53–54
   policing of media and speech by, 57,
      60, 61, 62, 70–72, 73, 74, 75,
      98, 108
   security apparatuses, 2011 uprisings
      and, 247
   and social welfare programs, retreat
      from, 13–14, 249
   varying degrees of control in, 51
graffiti and street art, marking of
      territory by, 64
Gulf war (1990–91), and broadcast
      media, 78
Gutmann, Amy, 30, 31

Habermas, Jürgen
   on corruption of public debate,
      6, 9, 246
   and democracy, public
      sphere in, 27
   on empirical dimensions of public
      discourse, 15, 26, 27
   focus of on normative public
      discourse, 26, 27
   influence on public sphere
      scholarship, 26–27
   on public sphere, 26, 33
      collapse of public good
         concept in, 40
      creation of, 40
      Islamic legal discourse as akin
         to, 41–42
      links between Arab public spheres
         and, 96
      vs. political sphere, 246
      recognition of empirical
         issues in, 15
   on rationality in public sphere, 35
   on religious discourse in public
      sphere, 31–32

Hamas
   and Palestinian educational
      curriculum, 230–31, 236,
      237, 239n16
   rise of after Palestinian election of
      2006, 110–11, 230
   and *wasatiyya* (moderation/centrism)
      as principle, 136
Herrera, Linda, 236
hierarchies of power and wealth
   influence in private discussions, 58
   influence in public debate, 17, 25,
      37–38, 42
Higazi, Safwat, 119
Hirschkind, Charles, 43, 68, 97, 107, 112
Hodgson, Marshall, 58, 130
honor killings, challenges to, 200
hudud (criminal penalties), debate on,
      98–99, 122
humanities, approach to political debate
      in, 15–16
Huntington, Samuel, 249
Husni, Mustafa, 188
Husseini, Rana, 205
hypocrisy, civilizing force of, 35, 36–37

intellectuals
   mid-20th century policing of, 105
   and religious sphere, 102
Internet. *See* social media and Internet
Iraq
   authoritarianism in, 105
   constitution of, 148, 150, 151, 152,
      153, 155, 163–64, 176
   Kurds in, and public debate, 37
   state collapse in, 20, 248
Islam
   broad spectrum of activities
      covered by, 5
   bureaucratization of, 75
   consensus on state's role in protecting
      values of, 135–36
   government efforts to marginalize,
      124–25, 140–41n10, 141n12
   influence of private arguments on
      public debate, 57
   as language of political debate, concern
      about, 4–6, 7, 16–17, 18, 21
   political behavior in, 55–56

Islam (*Cont.*)
  recent resurgence of religious
    authority, 124
  and social interaction, pervasive
    influence on, 120–21, 133
Al-islam wa-usul al-hukm (ʿAbd
    al-Raziq), 102
Islamic Action Front, 207
Islamic awakening, 107
Islamic counterpublic, creation of, 97,
    107, 112
Islamic institutions, trend toward
    government control over, 158
Islamic legal tradition. *See also* shariʿa
  opening of to influence of other
    spheres, 56
  and rationality, 32
  as specialist discourse, 56
Islamic public spheres
  creation of in religious practice, 56
  hybrid private/public spheres, 57
  maydans (public squares) as, 62–64
  media as, 69–85
  mosques as, 65–69
  police monitoring of, 57, 60, 61, 62
  small groups as, 57–62
  small-scale, development of, 64
  traditional, as private or
    specialist-based, 55–56
Islamic State (ISIS)
  democratization of shariʿa
    interpretation and, 127
  and political resurgence of jihadist
    groups, 20
  and *takfir* (charging apostasy), 137
  violent participation in public
    debate, 132
Islamist press
  in Egypt, 73
  in Jordan, 71
  in Kuwait, 71, 107
  and opening of Arab press, 75
  and turn to
    semi-authoritarianism, 107
Islamists. *See also* Muslim Brotherhood
  and constitution writing after 2011,
    163–64, 166–68
  and debate on personal status law, 202
  and democratization of shariʿa
    interpretation, 126–27

Egyptian civil code reform and,
    108, 109
  and Egyptian constitution, 164,
    165, 169
  and Egyptian education, 237
  and Egyptian personal status
    law, 210–13
  empowerment of by social and
    Internet media, 112
  focus on legislation over
    constitutional change, 164
  and Jordanian educational
    curriculum, 233–34
  and Jordanian personal status
    law, 206–9
  and links between social spheres,
    108, 109–10
  and Moroccan personal status law, 215
  and new media, loss of control over
    arguments in, 112–14
  and Palestinian educational
    curriculum, 229
  and shariʿa provisions in
    constitutions, 159
  as target of educational reformers, 226
Ismail, Salwa, 59, 115
Israel, control of mosques in, 67

Jarbawi, ʿAli, 227
al-Jazeera, 77–78, 79, 111
Jews, protections for in Egyptian
    constitution, 172
jihadist groups
  and Internet's penetration of multiple
    spheres, 85
  as marginal to public sphere
    debates, 19–20
  as outside broad consensus on
    shariʿa, 127–28
  and shariʿa interpretation, 132
  views on government-enforced
    shariʿa, 133
Johansen, Baber, 191
Jordan
  constitution of, 151, 159, 162
  debate on personal status law
    in, 204–9
  education in, 225, 233–34
  emergency legislative powers of
    cabinet, 206

mid-20th century
    authoritarianism, 105
monarchy, and reform efforts, 206, 209
press, history of, 70–71
public sphere in, 44, 64
turn to semiauthoritarianism, 105,
    106, 107
judiciary. *See also entries under* courts
in early 20th century, religious
    scholars in, 101
and turn to semiauthoritarianism, 107
Jum`a, `Ali, 114, 129, 186
juries, and deliberation, 35–36
jurisprudence of priorities (*fiqh
    al-awwaliyyat*), 134

Kayid, `Aziz, 239n16
Khalid, Amr, 79, 100
khul` divorce, 203
Egyptian debate on, 210–11
Jordanian debate on, 205–9
Kuran, Timur, 117–18n18
Kuwait
constitution of, 154, 155, 156,
    159, 160
diwaniyya in, 60, 61
mid-20th century
    authoritarianism, 105
Muslim Brotherhood in, 164
parliament in, 92–94
personal status courts in, 193
press in, 71–72, 76, 107
protection for domicile privacy in, 60
royal family, leaking of private
    information about, 71, 98
turn to semiauthoritarianism, 105,
    106, 107
uprisings of 2011 and, 4

labor unions, and spread of debate, 102
Langohr, Vickie, 44–45, 116
Lebanon, 151, 153, 222
liberal democratic thought
basic ethos of, 28
on democracy and public debate,
    26, 27–30
elitism of, 2, 29, 30
normative attraction of, 24
self-criticism in, 23
and standards of respectful debate, 2

Libya
constitution of, 148, 155
state collapse in, 20
uprisings of 2011 and, 4
Lynch, Marc, 2, 44, 71, 242

Mah, Harold, 30, 40
mahr (bride price), 194, 195
Mahshi, Khalil, 225
majlis, 60
Makram, `Umar, 63, 64, 101
Makruh actions, shari`a on, 122
Maktabi, Rania, 215
maqasid (goals) of shari`a
debate on, 134–35, 137,
    141–42n22
and loss of control over speech, 99
March, Andrew, 32, 141–42n22
marriage
bargaining and agreements in Egypt,
    194–96
troubled, multiple options for
    addressing, 197
marriage and divorce laws
debate on
    in Egypt, 209–13
    in Jordan, 204–9
    in Morocco, 214
in Egypt, 193–95, 196,
    209–13
and intimate importance of
    religion, 242
Masjid al-Nur, 109–10
maslaha (public interest)
in Arab world, multiplicity of, 30
increasing incorporation of into
    Islamic discourse, 32
as standard in shari`a interpretation,
    135, 137, 138–39
Masoud, Tarek, 144
al-Masri, Mahmud, 188
al-Masri al-Yawm (periodical), 73–74
Maydan al-Tahrir square
    (Cairo), 63–64
maydans (public squares)
government control of, 62, 64
as government-created space, 62–63
interplay of small-group public
    spheres with, 69
as Islamic public spheres, 62–64

media. *See also* broadcast media; press; social media
  government control of, 51–52, 53, 54, 104
  government policing of, 69, 70–72, 73, 74, 75, 98
  Habermas on, 26
  interaction with social media in 2011, 43, 96–97
  and loss of control over terms of publicity, 98
  political discussion in, 11, 12, 13
  as public sphere, 69
  relative freedom of in 19th and early 20th centuries, 54
  turn to semiauthoritarianism and, 107
  varying degrees of access to, 34
Mendelburg, Tali, 37–38
minority rights
  democracy and, 28
  public interest as term excluding, 30
Moll, Yasmin, 188
morality, consensus on state's role in protecting, 135–36
Morocco
  constitutions of, 155, 160, 176, 178n12
  educational reform in, 237
  personal status laws in, 198, 213–15
  turn to semiauthoritarianism, 105, 106
  uprisings of 2011 and, 4
Morsi, Muhammad
  clerical views on, 66, 67, 113–14, 115
  failure to find compromise after, 144
  Islamists and, 212
  overthrow of, 6, 65, 100, 113–14, 144, 173
  rally for (2012), 119–20
mosques
  donors of, 65, 68
  government control of, 62, 65–69, 158
  interplay of small-group public spheres with, 69
  as Islamic public spheres, 65–69
  possibility for oppositional discourse in, 66–68
Mubarak, Hosni
  overthrow of, 162, 169, 212
  public debate under, 116

muftis. See *fatwa* advice programs
al-Mujtama' (periodical), 76, 107
mulids (saints' birthdays)
  celebrations, 56, 64
Muslim Brotherhood
  and Arab press, 75, 76
  and democratization of shari'a interpretation, 126–27
  in Egypt (*see also* Morsi, Muhammad)
    constitutional reform agenda of, 162
    and debates on personal status law, 212
    educational policy and, 232–33
    ouster of, 164, 169, 175, 213
    repression of, 159
    and *sukuk* laws, 213
  and Egyptian constitution, 159, 162, 164, 169, 170, 171
  focus on political participation in, 103
  in Jordan, educational curriculum and, 233
  in Kuwait, 107
  and linking of social spheres, 102–3, 107, 109
  and personal status law debates, 204–5, 207, 208
  rise of, 107
  salafi views on, 131
  spread from Egypt, 103
  and Syrian constitution of 1950, 154
  and *takfir* (charging apostasy), 137
mustahabb actions, shari'a on, 122

nadwa (colloquiums/seminars), as Islamic public sphere, 59–60
Nagib, Fathi, 210–11
al-Nahda, and Tunisian constitution, 164, 166–68
Nasr, Muhammad ʿAbd Allah, 67–68
new preachers (*al- duʿa al- judad*), 183–91
New Yorker magazine, 85
nongovernmental organizations
  and democratization of shari'a interpretation, 131
  government welfare commitments and, 105–6

Obaydat, Ahmad, 206
Oman, 156
opposition parties, rise of, 106–7, 108

Ottoman empire
  constitution of 1876, 149, 150
  Islam under, 125, 126

Palestine
  control of mosques in, 67
  education in, 223, 224, 225,
    226–31, 236
  mid-20th century
    authoritarianism, 105
  rise of Hamas in, 110–11, 230
  turn to semiauthoritarianism, 106
  uprisings of 2011 and, 4
Palestinian National Authority (PNA),
    226–27, 230
parliaments. *See also* personal status law
    debates in parliaments
  and broadening of public
    sphere, 103–4
  coexistence of moral and state
    authority in, 198
  and education reform, conservative
    resistance to, 226
  governments as drivers of reform
    initiatives in, 216
  ineffectiveness of, 144
  in Jordan, educational curriculum
    and, 233–34
  limited overlap with fatwas and
    courts, 215–16
  meeting of public and political spheres
    in, 246
  mid-century authoritarianism
    and, 104
personal status law. *See also* courts,
    personal status
  argument about
    crossing of political boundaries by,
      18, 139
    in Egypt, 209–13
    government tolerance of, 201
    in Jordan, 204–9
    limited resolution of, 202, 203
    in Morocco, 213–15
    participants in, 201
    role of religious authorities in, 203
    separation of argument and
      speakers' authority in, 201–2
    stakes in, 184
    types of participants in, 201, 202

uprisings of 2011 and, 204,
    210, 211–12
  venues for, 184, 201–2
  for Christians in Egypt, 172, 177
  citizenship laws, 200
  connection to religious teaching, 183
  controversy provoked by, 139
  fatwa advice programs and, 182–91
  government assertion of control
    over, 126
  and international human rights norms
    vs. shariʻa, 202–3, 204, 208, 214
  Islamic, constitutional protections for,
    148, 152–53, 160
  Moroccan debate on, 198
  as nineteenth century
    development, 244
  public argument *vs.* private practice in,
    211, 212–13
  reform, in Egypt, 211
  reform, in Jordan, 206–9
  shariʻa-based
    applications of as disputed,
      200, 201
    as generally accepted by Muslims,
      199, 200, 201
    as political symbol of larger social
      values, 198
    rejection of apostasy in, 200
    as religious group-based system,
      199–200
    tenets *vs.* liberal frameworks,
      199–200
  spheres of specialist debate on, 200–1
  terminology, public familiarity
    with, 189
  as unquestioned, 199
personal status law debates in
    parliaments
  bypassing of, 206, 210
  difficulty of converting into public
    law, 198–99
  in Egypt, 210–13
  in Jordan, 207–9
  in Morocco, 214, 215
  role as ratifier of already-negotiated
    compromises, 216–17
Petersen, Mark Allen, 96, 112
piety trend groups, 58–59, 115, 129–30
"Piss Christ" (Serrano), 245

political debate in Arab countries.
See also Arab politics; argument
in Arab political debate; public
spheres, Arab; republic of
arguments
affective value of, 161, 176, 177–78, 246
benefits of analyzing, 6–7, 15, 16–17
focuses of this study, choice of, 17–18
greater authority of religious
figures in, 33
impact on perception of
government, 16, 19
impact on policy, 16
Islam as language of, concern about,
4–6, 7, 16–17, 18, 21
lack of in 1980s, 11, 12–13
as largely academic usage, 12
less-than-ideal use of public reason
in, 6, 14
micro-focused approach to, 15–16
mid-20th century suppression of, 104
vs. normative theories, 12, 14–15, 23,
24, 32–33
official control, loosening of, 12
overlapping institutions and
practices in, 12
and public sphere,
establishment of, 13
revival of, 2–3, 7, 12–14, 52
Western failure to note, 2–3, 13
ugliness of, 12
weak ties to instruments of political
action, 3, 7, 18, 21, 27, 39, 41,
44, 116, 143–44, 216–17, 221,
224–25, 242, 245–46, 249–50
political leaders, and civilizing force of
hypocrisy, 36–37
political parties
in early 20th century, 103
ineffectiveness of, 144
political structures in Arab world
construction of to shut out public
voices, 3, 7, 18, 21, 27, 39, 41,
44, 116, 143–44, 216–17, 221,
224–25, 242, 245–46, 249–50
decay of, as complicating factor, 20
politics (as discussion of public affairs).
See political debate in Arab
countries

politics (as struggle to control public
policy)
and Arab authoritarianism, 12–13
(see also authoritarian regimes)
coalitions and compromises needed
for, 143–44
as poorly linked to political debate,
3, 7, 18, 21, 27, 39, 41, 44, 116,
143–44, 216–17, 221, 224–25,
242, 245–46, 249–50
praetorianism, Huntington on, 249
prayer, communal, creation of public
spheres in, 56
preference falsification, 117–18n18
press in Arab nations
audience for in early 20th
century, 102
in Egypt, 72–74, 75, 76, 102, 103
fragmenting of government ideology
and, 75
general pattern of development,
70, 74–75
government policing of, 70–72, 73,
74, 75, 98
increasing openness to range of
religious opinions, 75–76
in Jordan, history of, 70–71
in Kuwait, 71–72, 76, 107
limited deliberation in, 74
nationalizations and privatizations of,
70–71, 73
private, development of, 70,
72, 73–74
as public sphere, 70–76
Samizdat publications, 75
as space for argument about
religion, 75–76
private sphere links to public sphere,
25–26, 42, 181–82
fatwa advice programs and, 182–91
professional associations
and spread of debate, 102
and turn to
semi-authoritarianism, 107
Przeworski, Adam, 34, 35
public(s)
multiplicity of in Arab world, 30, 242
unified, as assumption of public
sphere theory, 30

public debate. *See also* political debate in
    Arab countries
  argument *vs.* deliberation in, 33, 35,
    37–39, 42, 242
  definition of, 24
  differences from private discourse, 33
  history of excluding demos from, 38
  influence of power hierarchies on, 17,
    25, 37–38, 42
  issues more difficult to resolve in, 36
  liberal democratic standards for, 2
  medium and space for, 33
  mixed results of, 24, 26
  in nondemocratic settings, as
    under-studied, 44, 48n41
  prioritization of private
    interests in, 37
  private dimensions overlapping,
    25–26, 42
  restrictions on participants, 25, 36
public debate, normative theory
    on. *See also* scholarship on
    political debate
  assumed benefits of links to liberal
    democracy, 26, 27–30, 37–38
  assumption of single public in, 30
  elitism of, 2, 29, 30
  and exclusion of demos, 29–30,
    37–38, 42
  increasing recognition of empirical
    issues, 15, 45n4
  influence on public debaters, 39, 40
  positive effects of publicity claimed in,
    24–25, 26, 27, 37–39
  and public interest, assumed existence
    of, 26, 28, 30
  publicity as impetus toward rational
    debate in, 34–37
  and religious discourse, 31–32, 42
  and respect for people as ends in
    themselves, 28–29
public gatherings, restrictions on under
    authoritarian regimes, 54
public interest. See also *maslaha* (public
    interest)
  assumed existence of in public debate
    theory, 26, 28, 30
  as term excluding minority
    interests, 30

public opinion, meaning of in
    unified *vs.* fragmented public
    spheres, 48n40
public order
  Islamic regulation of, courts and, 185
  shari'a-based, broad consensus on
    need for, 133–39
public sphere(s). *See also* Habermas,
    Jürgen: on public sphere;
    public debate
  accessibility of as issue, 15, 34
  multiple
    difficulty of suppressing, 248–49
    Internet's ability to move
      information between, 85
    lack of accepted common good and, 40
    as modern conception, 40, 42
  necessity of for political discourse, 13
  unified
    ongoing influence of concept, 39, 40
    power of, 40
    power of claiming to speak for, 41
    uprisings of 2011 and, 43, 249
public spheres, Arab. *See also* republic of
    arguments
  access to, as issue, 15
  history of, 54
  interaction of in Arab republic of
    arguments, 49–50
  opening of, 2, 13–14, 52
  scholarship on, 17
  in semiauthoritarian systems, 44
  types focused on this study, 18
  variety of, 21
public spheres, Arab, links among
  aggravation of disputes by, 97, 98
  in Arab uprisings of 2011, 43
  in debates on personal status law, 202
  and democratization of religious
    authority, 95
  democratizing effect of, 97
  as dramatic change in Arab political
    argument, 92
  Habermas's public sphere and, 96
  history of concept, 96–97
  increase in, 91, 101
    and broader discussion of religion
      in public sphere, 110
    in current period, 110–15

public spheres, Arab, links among (*Cont.*)
and increased complexity of public
debate, 101
move to semiauthoritarianism
and, 105–10
and revival of Arab politics, 110
in Kuwaiti parliament and
diwaniyyas, 92–94
limited, in early 20th century, 101–4
and loss of control over terms of
publicity, 98
metaphors for, 96
policing of in semi-authoritarian
regimes, 108
political significance of, 97
rough political environment created
by, 95–96
social media and, 111–12
social movements and, 102–3
and speakers' loss of control over
words, 94–95, 96, 97–100
as subject of this study, 18
suppression of, in early 20th
century, 101–2
suppression of, in mid-20th
century, 104–5
theoretical importance of, 43–44
and Tunisian constitution of
2014, 167
as understudied, 16

Qadi al-Quda (Jordan), and personal
status law reform, 206–9
qanun al- dawla al- tunisiyya [Law of
the Tunisian State or Dynasty]
(1861), 149
al-Qaradawi, Yusuf, 79, 114, 134, 136
al-Qarani, ʿAyd, 188
Qatar
broadcast media in, 77–78
personal status courts in, 193
al-Quda, Muhammad Nuh, 184–85, 186,
187, 188, 190
Qutb, Jamal, 218n23
Qutb, Sayyid, 159

radio broadcasting in Arab countries
fatwa advice programs, 184–85
history of, 77
and regime rivalries, 77, 89n46

Rawls, John, 31, 32
"red lines" in semiauthoritarian regimes
broadcast media and, 77
probing limits of, 54–55
religious argument
claims of to represent unified public
sphere, 41–42
limited potential influence on liberal
opinion, 32–33
public debate theory's secular bias
and, 31–32
public-spirited elements in, 32
and rationality, 32
religious and political authority
in, 121
and resistance to compromise, as
issue, 4, 242
religious argument in Arab cultures.
See also argument in Arab
political debate
as accepted norm, 242, 243
authoritarianism and, 105
and communal nature of
Islam, 242–43
and competing sources of religious
authority, 242
focus on public conduct rather than
faith, 121
increase in, in turn to
semi-authoritarianism, 110
limited effectiveness of, 246
shariʿa as authority in, 122
religious authority
democratization of, 95
as increasingly contested, 121
shariʿa as, 122
religious freedom
in Egyptian constitution of
2014, 175
as issue in debate on Egyptian
constitution of 2012, 172
in shariʿa-based law, 199–200
religious groups
and democratization of shariʿa
interpretation, 125
provision of social services in
semiauthoritarian regimes, 106
religious people, views on normative
theories of secular public
sphere, 32

religious scholars, Muslim
changes in religious education and, 128–29
domination of public life in early 20th century, 101–2
and Islamic law tradition, 56, 125, 126
and public interest, speaking for, 42
religious unity, as political result, 119
republic of arguments. *See also* political debate in Arab countries
defined, 20, 49
distinctive characteristics of, 20–21
effect on constitutions, 221
effect on personal status law, 221
inequalities of status and class in, 115
interaction of multiple public spheres in, 49–50
loose connection to governing, 245
relation to private sphere, 181–82
religion in, 23
rise of, 53
and separation of political debate from speaker, 49–50
survival of 2011 uprisings by, 247
undemocratic, as real-world possibility, 27
variety of spaces and technologies in, 241
and violence and oppression, 241
republicanism
basic ethos of, 28
and benefits of public debate, 24, 27, 28
Rida, Rashid, 151

al-Sadat, Anwar, 73, 132, 157, 194
al-Sadat, Jihan, 210
salafis
and broadcast media, 80
concerns about *maqasid* misuse, 99
coup of 2013 and, 65, 81
critiques of extreme textualism of, 134–35
and Egyptian constitution, 159, 169, 170–72, 173, 174, 177
and Egyptian military coup of 2013, 169
and Egyptian school curriculum, 233
feeling of exclusion in, 95
increasing number of followers, 131
influence across public spheres, 43–44
and Jihad, 132
and loss of control of words across linked spheres, 94
move into political arena, 129, 131–32
on Muslim Brotherhood, 131
new media and, 113, 114
as outside current broad consensus on shari'a, 127
and rough politics of new linked public spheres, 95
and shari'a interpretation, 131, 132
and Tunisian constitution, 167, 168
views on government-enforced shari'a, 133
and *wasatiyya* (moderation/centrism) as principle, 136
Salama, Hafiz, 109
al-Sanhuri, 'Abd al-Razzaq, 233
Sasnal, Patrycja, 233
Saudi Arabia
Basic law of 1992, 155, 156–57
broadcast industry in, 79
regulation of mosques in, 66
turn to semiauthoritarianism, 105
Sayed, Fatma, 232
scholarship on political debate
on emergence of Arab public sphere, 17
macro focus on regime type in, 6, 14
misplaced concern about religion in, 4–5, 16–17
normative, *vs.* empirical reality, 12, 14–15, 23, 24, 32–33
secularism *vs.* religion, in public debate, 4–5
semi-authoritarian regimes
development of small-scale public spheres, 64
impact of public debate on political outcomes in
as deliberately limited, 116
as under-studied, 44, 48n41
links between public spheres in
increase in, 105–10
policing of, 108
as tentative and incomplete, 109–10
and opinions, reluctance to express, 117–18n18
privatizations of press in, 70
public sphere in, 44

semi-authoritarian regimes (*Cont.*)
  "red lines" in, as ill-defined, 54–55
  retreat from strong ideological stance, 106
  and small groups as developing public
    spheres, 57–62
  tolerance of opposition in, 53, 106–7, 108
Serrano, Andre, 245
Shaham, Ron, 114
Shahin, Mazhar, 64, 175, 213
al-Sha'ir, Nasir al-Din, 111, 230
Shapiro, Ian, 30
Shapiro, Martin, 35
Sha'rawi, Muhammad Mitwalli, 79
shari'a, 122–24. See also entries under
    fatwa; Islamic legal tradition
  application to public life, broad
    consensus on, 133–39
  as broad cultural form beyond
    challenge, 122, 130–31
  broadening of public discussion of, 17
  definitive binding rules in, 133–34
  fiqh as human interpretation of, 123
  flexible rules in, 134
  government entry into Islamic legal
    debate and, 56
  increased salience of, 133
  Islamic, Muslim contrast of to other
    shari'as, 122–23
  Islamic law as facet of, 122, 123
  Islamic scholarship on, 123
  as "Islamic way of doing things," 122
  and jurisprudence of priorities (*fiqh
    al-awwaliyyat*), 134
  piety trend groups and, 58
  revived emphasis on in public debate, 248
shari'a interpretation
  authority for, as issue, 123,
    124–32, 137–39
  broad consensus on, 133–39
    emergence of in late-20th
      century, 127
    ongoing conflict over details within,
      128, 137–39
  centrality to Arab political debate, 128
  democratization of, 123, 125, 126–32
    concerns about, 248
    conflict resulting from, 123, 127, 129
    and loss of doctrinal authority, 131
  governments' efforts to control, 126–27,
    128, 130–31

increasing politicization of, 128
individualist, Internet facilitation
  of, 84–85
institutions for, in traditional Islamic
  culture, 124, 125
local, as subject to question, 122
maslaha (public interest) as standard
  in, 135, 137, 138–39
necessity of, 123
salafis and, 131
specialized training in, debate on need
  for, 138
use of *maqasid* (goals) in, debate on,
  134–35, 137, 141–42n22
variation by time and place, 124
wasatiyya (moderation/centrism) as
  principle in, 136
Shi'a Islam, authority of religious figures
  in, 33, 140n6
al-Shuqayri, Ahmad, 186–87
al-Sisi, 'Abd al-Fattah, 66, 237
small groups
  diwaniyya, 60, 61
  efforts to formalize, 59–60, 61
  government tolerance of, 61
  interplay with larger public
    spheres, 69
  as Islamic public spheres, 57–62
  nadwa (colloquiums/
    seminars), 59–60
  piety trend groups, 58–59
  police monitoring of, 60, 61, 62
  private discussions among
    friends, 57–58
  and public-private line,
    contesting of, 61
  survival of under harsh
    repression, 61–62
  and uprisings of 2011, 61
Smith, Sarah Cowles, 84–85
social media and Internet
  analyst's focus on opposition groups
    and, 112
  and closed self-referential
    communities, 84–85
  differences in technology and, 82
  and difficulty of suppressing debate, 248
  factors affecting study of, 81–82
  fatwa advice and, 187
  government monitoring of, 84, 98

impact on public deliberation, as issue, 45–46n5
increased polarization created by, 112–13, 115
and individualist interpretations of shari'a, 84–85
and links between social spheres, 111–12
new preachers and, 186
as nondemocratic, 82, 83
poor quality of argument on, 82–83, 113–14
and power to overhear discourse of others, 85
primacy of drama over argument in, 113–14
as public sphere, 81–85
and rise of public sphere, 12, 13, 53
as tool for organizations and movements, 82, 83–84
in uprisings of 2011, 43, 81, 82, 96–97, 112, 167
and virtual civil societies, 83–84
social movements
and democratization of shari'a interpretation, 131
early 20th century, and linking of social spheres, 102–3, 104
emboldening of by early successes, 110–11, 117–18n18
mid-20th century suppression of, 104–5
social sciences
and Arab politics, importance of understanding, 19
micro approach to political debate, 15–16
social welfare programs, Arab state retreat from, 13–14, 249
Soviet Union, public sphere emergence in, 44
specialist discourse
claims of to represent unified public sphere, 41–42
defined, 92
Islamic law tradition and, 56, 125, 126
as ongoing practice, 96
Starrett, Gregory, 236–37
state muftis, 130, 244

state role in protecting Islamic values
communal focus of Islam and, 243–44
consensus on, 135–36, 139
details of, as issue, 138
Muslims' mixed feelings about, 181
nineteenth century rise of, 244
as ongoing practice, 96
scholars rejecting, 141n12
as space of argument, 92, 130
states, history of control over religion, 124
The Structural Transformation of the Public Sphere (Habermas), 26, 27
Sufi brotherhoods, mid-20th century authoritarianism and, 105
Sunni Islam
and constitution of 2012, 173
greater authority of religious figures in, 33
on interpretation of shari'a, 124
Sunstein, Cass, 35
Supreme Constitutional Court (Egypt)
and constitution of 2014, 174–75
and interpretation of Islamic legal principles, 172–73
on marriage law, 194
Muslim Brotherhood and, 171
and opening of public life, 107
and personal status law reform, 211
salafi views on, 173
and shari'a as basis of law, 109, 160
al-Suwaydan, Tariq, 187
Syria
constitutions, 151, 153, 154, 156, 159
Hama uprising and (1983), 61–62
ineffective government in, 248
mid-20th century authoritarianism, 105
political parties in, 103
turn to semiauthoritarianism, 105, 107
uprisings of 2011 and, 4
Syrian Arab Kingdom, constitution of, 150
Szerb, Antal, 51, 53

takfir (charging apostasy)
consensus on, 136–37
as means of regulating access to public sphere, 191